Tarot and Kabbalah

The Path of Initiation
in the Sacred Arcana

The Most Comprehensive and Authoratative Guide to the Esoteric Sciences Within All Religions

Samael Aun Weor

GLORIAN

2010

Tarot and Kabbalah
A Glorian Publishing Book
Fifth Edition (English)

Originally published in Spanish as "El Sendero Iniciatico a Traves
de los Arcanos de Tarot y Kabala" (1978).

This Edition © 2010 Glorian Publishing

ISBN 978-1-934206-37-9

Library of Congress Control Number: 2006908912

Glorian Publishing is a non-profit organization delivering to
humanity the teachings of Samael Aun Weor. All proceeds go to
further the distribution of these books. For more information,
visit our website.

glorian.info
gnosticbooks.org
gnosticteachings.org
gnosticradio.org

Tarot and Kabbalah

"And the Lord God caused to sprout
from the ground every tree pleasant to see
and good to eat, and the Tree of Life in
the midst of the garden, and the Tree of
Knowledge of good and evil." - Genesis 2:9

Contents

Third Part: The Kabbalah

Fourth Part: Numerology and Esoteric Mathematics

Arcanum (Latin; plural: arcana).
A secret, a mystery, known only
to the specially educated.

Introduction

Of his more than sixty books, it is in this one that Samael Aun Weor outlines the scientific foundations upon which all the world's religions depend. Although he exhaustively revealed the correspondances between religions throughout his other writings, it is here that we discover the actual blueprints from which all religions were constructed. The supreme profundity of this information and its corresponding difficulty may be why it was one of the last books that he wrote, being finished posthumously by his wife.

To reach understanding of this profound book requires intensive study and meditation. The reader should be prepared to comprehend that much of the knowledge presented herein is contrary to the popular or "official" teachings of many religions, traditions, and schools. We should have the courage and sincerity to ask ourselves, "With the knowledge I have learned so far, have I acheived profound realization of my Inner Self? Am I transcending my own karma and suffering?" We should be brave enough to recognize that if we have not acheived these conscious experiences, then we must revolutionize our concepts, ideas, attachments, and practices. We must seek to remove what holds us back, and the gravest limitations we are all bound by are precisely within our own minds and hearts. Thus, the study of this book—as well as any scripture—requires a continual revision of the concepts we have formed and inherited from others. Throughout the process of his development, Samael Aun Weor eagerly

sought to clarify and revise his own understanding of the science of awakening the consciousness, thus you find he corrected the mistakes he made in earlier writings; so, we must also perpetually question and revise our own understanding and practice.

Samael Aun Weor also corrects many mistakes and oversights made by Kabbalists and occultists. Many such corrections are made in this book but not explained. Primarily, it will be noted that many of the cards in the "popular" Tarot are improperly illustrated, interpreted, and numbered. This book provides a complete reference to the Tarot as it used and displayed by positively awakened beings in the Internal Worlds. For example, the Tarot is a set of cards arranged into two groups: the Twenty-two Major Arcana and the Fifty-six Minor Arcana. However, very few contemporary Tarot decks accurately reflect the true nature of these cards, especially in the Minor Arcana. These cards should be numbered and named in the same manner as the Major Arcana; for example, the Twenty-fourth Minor Arcanum is "The Weaver." So the author of this book will refer to these Minor Arcana not as Cups, Wands, etc. as is commonly practiced, but by their true name and number. There is a complete reference to the Minor Arcana in the Appendices of this book.

It is suggested that students who wish to consult the Tarot using the method given by Samael Aun Weor do so with a proper Tarot deck that contains the correct numbers and arrangement, else the answers given cannot be assured.

Interested persons may seek to purchase a Gnostic deck or may with some effort make their own deck based on the information provided in this text.

Students who seek to comprehend the full depth of the Tarot and the Kabbalah must seek such understanding in meditation. Moreover, students who seek to comprehend the full depth of this book must also seek such understanding in meditation. Make no mistake: **the true heart of this knowledge cannot be read from a page**. It is found between the lines, in the white space—the Emptiness—that can only be penetrated by the consciousness. Until we revolutionize our own minds and hearts and develop the capacity to retrieve such knowledge for ourselves, internally, directly, we will be "as a leaf tossed about by the wind." As we read in this book, "The intellectual loses the sense of a sentence only for the lack of a period or comma. The intuitive one knows how to read where the Master did not write, and to listen when the Master is not speaking."

May all beings be happy!

May all beings be joyful!

May all beings be in peace!

Prologue

The Kabbalah is lost within the night of time, within the womb of Maha Kundalini, the Great Mother, where the universe was engendered The Kabbalah is **the science of numbers**.

The author of the Tarot was the Angel Metraton. He is Lord of the Serpent Wisdom. The Bible refers to him as the Prophet Enoch.

The Angel Metraton, or Enoch, delivered the Tarot in which the entirety of divine wisdom is enclosed. The Tarot remains written in stone. He also left us the twenty-two letters of the Hebrew alphabet. This great Master lives in the Superior Worlds in the world of Atziluth, which is a world of indescribable happiness. According to the Kabbalah, this world is the region of Kether, a very high Sephirah.

All Kabbalists base themselves on the Tarot and it is necessary for them to comprehend the Tarot and study it deeply.

The universe was made with the Law of Numbers, Measurements, and Weight. Mathematics forms the universe and the numbers become living entities.

One who penetrates Chesed, the pure and ineffable world of the Spirit, can verify that in this region everything is reduced to numbers. This region is incredibly real. In this physical world, we do not see things as they are. We see merely the images of things. But when in Chesed, we can know the amount of atoms that form a table and the amount of Karma owed by the planet, as well as the amount of molecules that function in each body.

Chesed is a world of mathematics. It is a realistic world. In Chesed, one may believe that one is separated from the reality of the world; yet, one is actually in the reality. In a temple of Chesed, one can know the quantity of people who are Self-realized, and the quantity of those who are not. If one enters a kitchen, one knows the amount of atoms that are in the food that one is going to eat. This is an incredibly realistic world. In the world of Chesed, one knows who is truly a Human Being.

One night, when I was in the world of Chesed, I entered into a theatre where the Lords of Karma were shown passing by on the movie screen, which is actually the screen of creation. They were balancing the Karmas of the two strongest nations of the world upon a great scale. Each nation's Karma was placed on either side of the scale. The scale inclined towards the colossus of the North. This colossus holds a great deal of Karma. Its strength is weakening, and it will eventually fall fulminated. Unquestionably, any Karma that is owed must be paid.

The Theosophists speak of planes and sub-planes. These are the ten Sephiroth, the ten emanations of the Eternal Mother Space, the ten surges that serve as a foundation of the Great Mother.

The seven planets of the solar system are the seven Sephiroth. And the Thrice-spiritual Sun is the Sephirothic Crown. These Sephiroth live and palpitate within our consciousness and we must learn to manipulate and combine them in the marvellous laboratory of our interior universe. Thanks to the Sephiroth, one can transform oneself into a Human Being. There are feminine Sephiroth as well as masculine, just as we find positive ions and negative ions.

Our Inner Being needs the realization of these ten Sephiroth because they are within us, here and now. When these ten realized Sephiroth that resemble precious gems are encrusted into an individual, they convert the person into a Self-realized Human Being. This is something marvellous. The Sephirothic Crown is formed by Kether, Chokmah, and Binah. One has to comprehend the foundation of these three Sephiroth.

Christian	Gnostic	Hebrew	Attribute
The Father	First Logos	Kether	Wisdom
The Son	Second Logos	Chokmah	Love
The Holy Spirit	Third Logos	Binah	Power, Igneous Principle

Kether is the Elder of the Days, the Hidden of the Hidden, the Good of the Good. He has thirty-one curls in his hair, and thirteen ringlets in His beard. Thirteen symbolizes the Verb, the Word. Marvellous things have been spoken about Him. One can have a meeting with Him through Samadhi (ecstasy) in order to receive his commands. He is infinitely merciful. He is absolute wisdom.

Chokmah is the Christ, love. The Christ awaits the disciple that will work

in the Ninth Sphere, and He prepares him with infinite love.

The Instructor of the world is Love.

Binah is the Holy Spirit, the igneous power. The following is an example of Binah. A Hierophant was approached by a mentally ill woman, who wished to be healed. The Hierophant succeeded in curing her and asked the woman's relatives for payment for his service. Subsequently, he had a meeting with the Holy Spirit. The Holy Spirit took the form of a white dove. The Hierophant inquired if he was treading well on the path, and the Holy Spirit told him that he was not. "I am the one who heals," said the Holy Spirit. Because of this experience, the Hierophant decided to return the money. If one has the power to cure and collects payment, the individual commits a very grave crime.

Kabbalah is often spoken of in the Internal Worlds. One has to know how to add Kabbalistic numbers. If we ask a Master how long we are going to live, he will answer in numbers.

The objective of studying the Kabbalah is to be skilled for work in the Internal Worlds. For example, on one occasion, an initiate asked for the power of clairvoy-

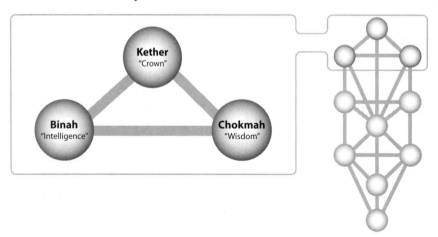

ance. Internally he received the answer, "It will be in eight days." One that does not understand will return to the physical body believing that within eight days he or she will be clairvoyant. For example, if the day is Wednesday, the person will believe he will be clairvoyant by the following Wednesday. In reality, eight is the number of Job. Thus, the answer was indicating that the initiate must have patience. One that does not comprehend remains confused in the Internal Worlds. Kabbalah is the basis in order to understand the language of these worlds.

It is obvious that the Kabbalistic studies must be combined with work on oneself. One must be conscious of these studies, for if they remain only in the intellect they will be lost when one dies. Yet, if one is conscious of them, the knowledge will manifest itself from childhood.

On a certain occasion, an initiate wanted to know how he was progressing in his esoteric studies. His Guru answered him Kabbalistically, saying: "You need fifty-eight minutes in order to complete the work, and you must bring thirty-six Bolivars, each one of them of thirty-two kilograms, and the initiations must be qualified."

Minutes: 58 (5 + 8) = 13 Death

Bolivars: 36 (3 + 6) = 9
The Ninth Sphere

Kilograms: 32 (3 + 2) = 5 The
Pentalpha, the Pentagram

If an initiate needs fifty-eight minutes, it means he has not even an hour in order to liberate himself, (5 + 8 = 13, Death). If minutes are spoken of it is because he has little time.

The thirty-six Bolivars, San Martines or Morelos (currency of South America)

are the liberators, (3 + 6 = 9, the Ninth Sphere), sex, the work with the spear. These are the thirty-six basic fundamental works.

The thirty-two kilograms are the thirty-two paths, the Pentalpha.

58 + 36 + 32 = 126

1 + 2 + 6 = 9

All of the work is in the Ninth Sphere. This is the Kabbalistic language that is used in the White Lodge. Do not forget that the additions themselves are Kabbalistic additions. One must be completely practical. When the meanings of the twenty-two arcana are known, then the practical part of predictions must be studied. This is in order to utilize the knowledge intelligently in cases of very important matters. The twenty-two arcana must be memorized. In order to be a complete Kabbalist, one has to study; one has to record the teachings in the memory.

Inverential peace,
Samael Aun Weor

First Part

Description and Study
of the Esoteric Tarot

"Howbeit we speak wisdom among them that are perfect; yet not the wisdom of this world, nor of the Princes of this world, that come to nought; But we speak the wisdom a mystery, even the occult wisdom, which God ordained before the world unto our glory, Which none of the Princes of this world knew, for had they known it, they would not have crucified the Lord of glory." - 1 Corinthians 2:6-9

Arcanum 1
The Magician

THE MAGICIAN

Description of the Plate

The eyes in the superior part of the card represent the eyes of the Father. Internally, they represent the infinite, the Holy Eight, the Caduceus of Mercury, the eight Kabirs that direct the planet. The Magician is in profile, showing his right side, meaning that the entire right side represents the Manifested One. The serpent is situated upon his forehead, indicating that he has risen and that he is a Self-realized Master. The left hand of the Magician holds the staff of power. This symbolizes the spinal medulla that points toward the infinite. His right hand points toward the earth, indicating that he dominates it with science and that one has to rise up from below. It is not possible to ascend without previously descending. One needs to descend to the Ninth Sphere, which has two representations. The first is sex, the Cubic Stone of Yesod. The second is the nine circles, the atomic Infernos where the initiate must descend. The right hand symbolizes the descent in order to ascend.

There is a triangle on his dress with a vortex pointing upwards, representing the three primary forces reunited in Kether, the One. By his side there stands a table which represents the four elements (earth, water, fire, and air), the physical plane.

Upon the table various objects rest in disorder: the sword of power, the lingam (sexual masculine organ); a chalice representing the physical brain, and also the yoni (feminine sexual organ); and a moon that must be converted into a sun. Beneath the table is the immortal Ibis, the Phoenix bird, the Kala Hamsa swan, the Holy Spirit that symbolizes love. It is beneath the table to indicate that one has to organize the disordered objects upon the table by means of the sacred fire of the Third Logos.

In the inferior part of the plate we find the Cubic Stone, the chiseled Philosophical Stone within the waters of life, indicating the work that we must perform. It is the

Cubic Stone of Yesod, sex, the stumbling stone, the rock of scandal.

Esoteric Significance of the Arcanum

The esoteric study of the Tarot is divided into two parts: the esoteric and the mathematic. The first has twenty-two arcana and is followed by the advancement of the second part through mathematics.

The First Arcanum is the Magician, that which begins, that which starts. It is the Unity, the Divine Spirit of each person, the Divine Monad, or immortal spark of every human being, of every creature. The number one is the Mother of all unities. The number one unfolds itself into the following arcanum, the Priestess.

With the First Arcanum we enter into the Sanctum Regnum of magic. The Holy Eight upon the head (illustrated by the two eyes) is the symbol of the infinite. It represents the eight Kabirs and is the symbol of life and death.

This sacred symbol of the infinite is found in the center of the earth, in the Ninth Sphere. All of the organisms rotate upon this symbol and also within the human body of anyone who wishes to Self-realize. There is always an internal struggle between the brain against sex, sex against the brain, and heart against heart. If sex commands the brain, the result is the fall, and the Pentagram (representing the Master) remains with the inferior points aiming upward and the superior point aiming downwards.

The Holy Eight is a very important and interesting symbol. It encloses, defines, and joins the magnetic currents that are established between the terrestrial and the spiritual man. This sign joins or separates all of the elements which are controlled by the atomic energy if it is traced with the middle finger, index finger and the thumb over the surface of the cardiac plexus.

Practice

Place the mind in quietude and silence and go to sleep imagining the figure of the Holy Eight (the infinite) and tracing the sign over the heart as previously mentioned. Let this figure submerge into your consciousness; clear your mind of all thoughts. After a certain time, you will awaken consciousness in the region known as the Astral World.

If we observe the spinal column we will see the Holy Eight, the Caduceus of Mercury, or Hermes. This represents the two ganglionic cords that entwine along the spinal medulla and that are known as Ida and Pingala, the Two Witnesses, the two olive branches, or, the two candlesticks which are before the throne of the God of the earth. They ascend towards the brain to the pineal gland, then ascend to the pituitary gland in the midbrow, and finally reach the heart through a fine thread called the Amrita-Nadi.

The solar atoms rise through the right cord, and the lunar atoms rise through the left cord. Our magical powers are lit when these atoms ascend along the dorsal spine.

The Holy Eight is, has been, and will always be the key of everything. A Magician cannot exist without the Holy Eight.

If we consider the tracing of this symbol, we see that it encloses a double circuit where the two forces cross. One closes and the other opens. This is the key to open all of the doors. It opens our interior temple. It is the sign that opens the Book of the Seven Seals. It is used for everything in the Sacred Order of Tibet, an Order that we have the honor of representing here in Mexico. It is the most powerful Order of all the Oriental traditions. This Order is formed by 201 members. The major rank is formed by seventy-two Brahmans. The great Regent of this order is the great Guruji Bhagavan Aklaiva. This Sacred Order of Tibet is the genuine owner of the real treasury of Aryavarta. This treasury is the Arcanum A.Z.F.

Exercise

Concentrate on the Sacred Order of Tibet and the Holy Eight. Moments before lying down, call upon the Master Bhagavan Aklaiva. With continued practice, he will help you to depart in your Astral Body. A given night, you will be called to assist the Tibetan Lodge and you will be submitted to seven ordeals in the Temple of the Himalayas. When you are called, the Masters pull your Astral Body from your feet so that you can present yourself standing.

We must be courageous because we will be submitted to many difficult ordeals. We will be decapitated and our heart will be pierced with a sword. One must be courageous. The one who has aspiration and consistency will succeed. This Sacred Order of Tibet is very strict. The true rulers of humanity are found there.

The fire of Phlegethon and the water of Acheron cross in the Ninth Sphere, sex, and form the sign of the infinite. It is necessary to work with water and fire, which is the origin of beasts, Human Beings and the Gods. One who wishes to ascend must have previously descended. This is the ultimate ordeal of which almost everyone fails. It is tremendous.

Everything in life has a price. Nothing is given as a gift. Life is the cost of the realization of the Self. One must be coura-

geous in order to be admitted into the Sacred Order of Tibet. Our organism is constituted just as the earth is constituted. We must work and descend into our own Infernal Worlds.

It is necessary to work with the sexual energy, which is the Cubic Stone of Yesod.

Arcanum 2
The High Priestess

THE HIGH PRIESTESS

DESCRIPTION OF THE PLATE

The two columns of the temple of
Isis appear within the waters of life,
the white column being Jachin, and the
black Boaz. Each column has four levels,
representing the four bodies of sin (the
physical, Vital, Astral, and Mental). Above
this, a Master appears seated between
two large columns. The two columns are
reversed because she is within the temple
facing towards us. The act of being seated
indicates her passive aspect. In the First
Arcanum, the Magician is standing, indicating an active aspect. She is in profile,
showing her left side, her negative aspect.

She holds upon her lap a partially
opened book that is slightly covered by her
mantle, indicating that she is wisdom. She
teaches the Kabbalah. She holds upon her
breast an Ankh cross, the symbol of life,
the foundation, Venus, the Tao cross. The
cross upon her naked breast signifies that
the milk which is the product of her breast
is the symbol of virtues.

The serpent upon her forehead indicates mastery, that she is risen.

Upon her head are the horns of the
sacred bull Apis, the spouse of the divine
cow.

Internally, the horns symbolize the
Father, and externally, they symbolize the
psychological ego, our defects. The attributes of the calf, or Kabir, are also found
in the horns. The circle is the serpent
that bites its tail, representing the Cosmic
Mother, the sacred cow. The veil that falls
before her face is the veil of Isis.

THE ESOTERIC SIGNIFICANCE OF THE ARCANUM

The Second Arcanum is the Priestess,
the occult science. In the area of the
Spirit, the number one is the Father who
is in secret. The number two is the Divine
Mother who is the unfoldment of the
Father.

The sacred book of the Mayans, the
Popol Vuh, states that God created man
from clay, and then from wood (the
Atlantean race). But that race forgot their
Fathers and their Mothers. They forgot

the "Heart of Heaven."
Then, came a great deluge
and everyone perished. They
entered into caves for shel-
ter, and the caves collapsed
(this is in reference to the
submergence of Atlantis).
Thus, every human being
has their own Divine Mother
and Father who are very
sacred. The two columns
Jachin and Boaz that sustain
the temple are seen in our
Father and in our Mother
Kundalini.

THE DUALITY OF THE SERPENT. SEE THE BOOK OF NUMBERS (CH. 21) IN THE BIBLE.

The Hebrew letter Beth
(ב) expresses the dualism
of the two columns of the
temple. The white, right
column, Jachin, represents
the man, the masculine principle, and the
black, left column, Boaz, represents the
woman, the feminine principle. The Great
Arcanum is between the two columns,
Jachin and Boaz. Actually, this is not
understood by many Masonic brothers.
The rustic Cubic Stone is placed between
the two columns and is later converted
into the chiselled Cubic Stone of Yesod.
This is nothing other than sex, the
Sephirah Yesod. It is necessary to know
the arcanum, the Maithuna, represented by
the chisel of intelligence and the hammer
of willpower.

The ineffable words of the Goddess
Neith have been sculpted on the resplendent walls of the temple of wisdom with
letters of gold. *"I am she that has been, is, and
will be, and no mortal has lifted my veil."*

The veil symbolizes that the secrets of
Mother Nature are hidden to the profane
and only the initiate achieves the unveiling
after incessant purification and medita-

tion. You must be courageous in order
to lift the veil of Isis. Our Gnostic motto
is **Thelema** (willpower). The number
one, the Father who is in secret, is the
Eternal Masculine Principle. He is within
Himself Brahma, who has no form, is
impersonal and ineffable, and who can be
symbolized by the sun. The number two
is the Divine Mother. She is the Eternal
Feminine Principle that can be symbolized
by the moon. Brahma has no form. He
is what He is. But, in Himself, He is the
governor of the universe. He is Ishvara, the
Eternal Masculine Principle, the Universal
Principle of life.

The Universal Principle of life
unfolds in the Eternal Feminine Universal
Principle, which is the great Pralaya of the
universe, of the cosmos, Her fertile bosom
where everything is born and where everything returns.

In the human being, the Cosmic
Mother assumes the form of the serpent.
There are two serpents: the tempting ser-

pent of Eden, which is the Goddess Kali, the abominable Kundabuffer organ; and there is the bronze serpent that healed the Israelites in the wilderness, the Kundalini Serpent. These are the two feminine principles of the universe, the virgin and the harlot, the Divine Mother or White Moon and Astaroth, Kali, or Black Moon, which refers to its tenebrous aspect.

The Second Arcanum is the Priestess. In occultism it is said that it is the dual manifestation of the unity. When the unity unfolds, it gives origin to the receptive and productive femininity in all of nature. It is obvious that the number two is within the human organism and the number one is related to it. **Willpower** is related to the number one, and **imagination** to the number two.

It is necessary to distinguish between intentional imagination and mechanical imagination. It is obvious that mechanical imagination is the same as fantasy. The key to power is found in the harmonious vibrating union of imagination and willpower.

There is a key in order to depart in the Astral Body which should be performed quickly in those moments of awakening from sleep. Upon awakening, you must close your eyes and, without movement, you must strongly imagine any given place. Do not imagine that you are imagining. It must be done factually. You must feel secure about being in the imagined place, uniting the will with the imagination. It is logical that one will triumph if this union is achieved. Place the imagination into motion and walk in the place which is being visualized with faith.

If this practice is performed without moving in bed, while working with imagination (which is feminine) and willpower (which is masculine), one can go to any place that one pleases. This is achieved through retaining the sleepy state, by imagining the place, and by walking with firmness through the use of willpower.

Once, I was in a jungle walking along a roadway, when someone spoke to me about a mountain. Due to the fact that this mountain's surroundings were so dangerous, I went to investigate it in the Astral Plane. I imagined the mountain. I saw fog, many steps, and a group of adepts. When entering the abode, they gave me a spoonful of honey, which is the food of the White Lodge, and the bread of wisdom. Then, they told me that I must purge myself with resinous oil in order to clean my stomach. The next day I left my physical body that was already cleansed in the stomach and I entered the Astral Plane. I then looked to the stars and performed the Rune **Man**. These adepts commanded me to descend into the Infernal Worlds. I entered a region of profound darkness, where terrible beasts attacked me. These were my egos. I had to pass through many doorways in which I could barely fit through, narrow ways that lead to a cemetery. Everything related to the ego is death and disgrace. The ego is Mephistopheles. It is necessary to work very hard.

Arcanum 3
The Empress

THE EMPRESS

DESCRIPTION OF THE PLATE

In the central part of the plate appears a woman crowned with twelve stars (1 + 2 = 3), which represents the twelve zodiacal signs, the twelve doors of the Holy City, the twelve keys of Basil Valentine, the twelve worlds of the solar system of Ors. On her head is a cup with a risen serpent symbolizing mastery, that she is risen. She holds the staff of power in her right hand, and with her left hand she tries to reach a dove, which represents the Holy Spirit. Her clothing is solar, which indicates that she is a Christified Soul, a product of the two previous arcana. She is seated on the perfectly chiselled Cubic Stone.

In the waters of life, the moon is under her feet, indicating that we must trample on the moon in order to convert it into a sun.

ESOTERIC SIGNIFICANCE OF THE ARCANUM

The number three is the Empress, the divine light. The light in itself is the Divine Mother. It corresponds to that part of Genesis that says, *"And God said let there be light and there was light"* (the first day of creation).

It is also the number of the Third Logos that dominates all forms of creation. It is the rhythm of the Creator.

The Celestial Mother in the material realm signifies material production. In the spiritual realm, She signifies spiritual production.

If this arcanum is analyzed more profoundly, a very interesting aspect is discovered. The number one is the Father who is in secret, or the Monad. From Him the Divine Mother Kundalini is born, thus forming the Duad. Then, this unfolds into the number three, which is the Father, Mother, and Son. The Son is the divine and immortal Spirit of every living being. The three—Osiris the Father, Isis the Mother, and Horus the Son—constitute what the sacred book of the Mayans, the *Popol Vuh*, called the "Heart of Heaven."

The Son also unfolds itself into the animated soul that everyone carries inside of themselves.

The Zohar, the most ancient Hebraic book which is the foundation of the Kabbalah and the Old Testament, insists upon the three principle elements that compound the world. These elements are:

ש SHIN: in Kabbalah, signifies **fire**.

מ MEM: in Kabbalah, signifies **water**.

א ALEPH: in Kabbalah, signifies **air**.

In these three principle elements dwells the perfect synthesis of everything that is from the four manifested elements.

The serpent or savior—who is the Logos—gives inspiration to human beings in order for them to recognize their own identity with the Logos. Thus, they can return into their own Essence, which is this Logos.

The powerful mantra **I.A.O.** summarizes the magical power of the triangle of the principle elements.

I: *Igneous,* fire

A: *Aqua,* water

O: *Origo,* Principle Spirit, air

This mantra should not be missing from the schools of mysteries.

Here we are seeing the esotericism of the Holy Three. **I.A.O.** is the fundamental mantra of the Maithuna. This mantra must be intonated in the Ninth Sphere. Those who want to raise the Soul of the world through their medullar canal must work with the Sulphur (fire), Mercury (water), and Salt (philosophical earth).

These are the three elements, the three principles, needed in order to work in the flaming forge of Vulcan.

The secret of the Great Work is found in the *Azoth,* a manuscript by Basil Valentine. The twelve secret keys of this manuscript are the sexual energy of the Logos only when the rose of the Spirit blossoms on the cross of our body.

The three principle elements are the three Hebrew letters that correspond with the three principle elements within the Great Work of Nature. Thus, we elaborate the living gold. One who does not make spiritual gold is not an esotericist.

One descends to the Ninth Sphere and creates the gold in the flaming forge of Vulcan. The Alchemist-Kabbalist must learn to utilize the Sulphur, Mercury, and Salt.

The larvae of the Astral Body, the Incubus and the Succubus which are formed by erotic imagination, are destroyed by utilizing sulphur inside our shoes. These larvae are transparent like the air and absorb the vitality of the Being. In movie theaters, dens of black magic where degenerate movies are shown, larvae adhere to those who frequent these places. One must carry sulphur in one's shoes in order to destroy them. The malignant forms of thought and the larvae enclosed within any room are disintegrated when one burns sulphur on a flaming charcoal. Mercury is used in order to prepare the radiant water. This is prepared for use by placing a mirror in the bottom of a copper container full of water (which must not be a cauldron) and then adding mercury. This helps to awaken clairvoyance. Nostradamus made his predictions with copper and mercury.

Salt has its virtues. When one needs to heal any ill person, one should light a fire in a container where salt and alcohol are mixed. This is done in order to invoke the

Masters of medicine Adonai, Hippocrates, Galen, and Paracelsus.

The ternary, the number three, is very important. It is the Word, plenitude, fecundity, nature, the generation of the three worlds.

The Third Arcanum of the Kabbalah is represented by a woman dressed with the sun, with the moon under her feet, and her head crowned with twelve stars. The symbol of the Queen of Heaven is the Empress of the Tarot. She is a mysterious, crowned woman seated with the scepter of command in her hand. The globe of the world is on top of the Scepter. She is Urania-Venus of the Greeks, the Christified Soul, the Celestial Mother.

The Divine Mother of the Third Arcanum is the particular Mother of each one of us. She is the Mother of our Being who must trample upon the moon, the lunar ego, in order for the twelve stars, the twelve faculties, to shine over Her head.

In order to create, we need the three primary forces that come from above, from the Father. They exist in all of creation:

Positive

Negative

Neutral

The man is the First Arcanum of the Tarot (the positive force), the woman is the Second Arcanum, (the negative force) and *the Christified Soul is the result of the sexual union of both.* The Arcanum A.Z.F is the secret that transforms the moon into a sun and represents the three aspects: positive, negative, and neutral.

Arcanum 4
The Emperor

DESCRIPTION OF THE PLATE

The serpent, which is a symbol of mastery, protrudes from the forehead of the Emperor. This crown, formed by an aspid, is the thermuthis which belongs to Isis, our particular Divine Mother Kundalini. Also on his head is a bonnet with four points, four angles, which represent the four elements, the four Gospels, the four Vedas, etc. On the bonnet there is also the still (the recipient, the sexual organs), the furnace (the Muladhara chakra, the spinal column), and the distillery (the brain).

He holds the staff of power in his right hand. He is seated on the perfectly chiselled Cubic Stone, product of the previous arcana. Within the stone is the cat, which is the fire. In the waters of life is the rod of command, which is the vertebral column.

ESOTERIC SIGNIFICANCE OF THE ARCANUM

The cross has four points. The cross of the initiation is phallic; the intersection of the vertical phallus in the feminine cteis forms the cross. It is the cross of initiation that we must carry upon our shoulders.

We must comprehend that the cross with its four points symbolizes the four cardinal points of the earth: north, south, east, and west; the four ages: gold, silver, copper and iron; the four seasons of the year; the four phases of the moon; the four ways of science, philosophy, art, and religion.

THE EMPEROR

When we speak about the four ways, we must comprehend that the four ways are really one way. This way is the narrow and straight way of the razor's edge, the path of the revolution of the consciousness.

The cross is a very ancient symbol that is continually utilized in all the religions of the world. One who considers it an exclusive emblem of a religious sect commits an error. When the Conquistadors of Spain arrived in the Holy Land of the Aztecs of

Mexico, they found crosses upon all the altars.

The sign of the cross, as in the sublime monogram of our Lord the Christ, the cross of Saint Andrew and the miraculous keys of Saint Peter are all marvellous replicas of equal Alchemical and Kabbalistic value. It is therefore the sign capable of securing the victory for the laborers of the Great Work.

THE MONOGRAM OF CHRIST, THE CROSS OF ST. ANDREW, AND THE CROSS OF ST. PETER.

The sexual cross, the living symbol of the crossing of the lingam-yoni, has the unmistakable and marvellous print of the three nails that were used to immolate the Christ-matter. These nails are the image of the Three Purifications of Iron and Fire. Our Lord could not achieve the Resurrection without them.

The cross is the ancient alchemical hieroglyph of the crucible (creuset), which in the past, in French, was called "cruzel," or "croiset." In Latin it was called "crucibulum," or "crisol," which had as its root "crux," "crucis," or "cross." It is evident that all of this invites us to reflect.

It is in the crucible that the raw matter of the Great Work suffers the passion of the Lord with infinite patience. In the erotic crucible of Sexual Alchemy, the ego dies and the Phoenix bird is reborn within its own ashes: **INRI**, *"In Necis Renascor Integer,"* which means, *"In death I am reborn intact and pure."*

The intersection of the vertical phallus within the horizontal uterus makes a cross. This is something that can be easily verified.

THE SERPENT THAT MOSES NAILED TO THE CROSS AS DEPICTED IN ALCHEMICAL ART. THIS ONE IS BY A. ELEAZAR, 1760.

If we reflect very seriously on that intimate relationship that exists between the "S" and the Tao Cross, or "T," we arrive at the logical conclusion that only through the crossing of the lingam-yoni, (phallus and uterus), with radical exclusion of the physiological orgasm, one can awaken the Kundalini, which is the igneous serpent of our magical powers.

In the Nahuatl and Mayan conception of the cross, the Nahuatl "Nahui-ollin," sacred symbol of the cosmic movement, is the sacred swastika of the great mysteries, which was always defined as the cross in movement.

The two possible orientations of the swastika clearly represent the masculine and feminine, positive and negative principles of nature. Two swastikas placed exactly over each other, in opposite directions, undoubtedly form the Potenzada cross, and represent the erotic conjunction of the sexes in this sense.

According to the Aztec legend, a couple, a man and a woman, were the ones that invented fire. This is only possible with the cross in movement, **INRI**, *"Ignis Natura Renovatur Integra,"* meaning, *"Fire Renews Nature Incessantly."*

The cross also reveals the quadrature of the circle which is the key of perpetual movement. That perpetual movement is only possible through the sexual force of the Third Logos. Perpetual movement will finish and the cosmic unhingement could happen if the energy of the Third Logos stopped flowing in the Universe. The Third Logos organizes the fundamental vortex of every rising universe and the infinitesimal vertex of the ulterior atom of any creation.

With the Fourth Arcanum of the Tarot, the Being carries the cross of initiation over his shoulder.

If we make the following Kabbalistic addition of the Fourth Arcanum (1 + 2 + 3 + 4 = 10) we find that 10 equals one (1 + 0 = 1), the Monad. Tetragrammaton is equal to the Monad.

THE HOLY TETRAGRAMMATON

Arcanum 5
The Hierarch

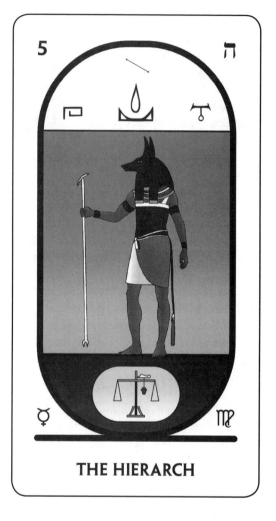

THE HIERARCH

DESCRIPTION OF THE PLATE

In this plate we find the Hierarch with his armor of war. He is holding in his right hand the staff of power. He utilizes the mask of a jackal only when he is officiating to do justice. This symbolizes the supreme pity and the supreme impiety of the law.

The scale of justice is in the waters of life indicating that the movements, actions and reactions of the physical body are based on energy.

ESOTERIC SIGNIFICANCE OF THE ARCANUM

The number five is grandiose, sublime, and is the number of severity and of the law. It is the number of Mars and of war.

The Fifth Arcanum of the Tarot shows us the teachings, Karma, and gives explanations. It symbolizes the fifth cycle, the fifth race, the fifth sun, the five tattvas, the five fingers, the five Gospels, the five senses, the five cells of the brain and ovaries, and the five aspects of the Divine Mother.

The fifth card of the Tarot is initiation, demonstration, teaching, karmic law, philosophy, science, and art. We live in the age of Samael, the fifth of the seven. The return towards the Great Light has been initiated. Life has started to flow from the outer towards the inner. We are faced with the dilemma of, *"To be or not to be."* We need to define ourselves as angels or demons, eagles or reptiles. We have to confront our own destiny.

The Fifth Arcanum is the Hierophant, the law, and severity. It is the flaming Pentagram, the flaming star, the sign of divine omnipotence. This is the symbol of the ineffable Verb made flesh, the powerful star of magicians.

The Pentagram represents man, the microcosmic human being, who with open arms and open legs is the star of five points.

The Pentagram with the two points aiming upwards represents Satan. It is utilized in black magic in order to invoke the

THE PENTAGRAM

tenebrous ones. The superior point aiming towards Heaven represents the internal Christ of every human being who comes into this world. It symbolizes the divine. It is utilized in white magic in order to call divine beings. When we place it at the foot of the door of our room with the two feet pointing towards the outside, tenebrous entities do not enter into our room. On the contrary, when the Pentagram is inverted with the two feet towards the inside, it permits the entrance of the tenebrous ones.

THE ESOTERIC PENTAGRAM

In the superior angle of the Pentagram, we find the eyes of the Spirit and the sign of Jupiter, sacred Father of all the Gods. In the arms is found the sign of Mars, symbol of strength. In the feet is found the sign of Saturn, which is the symbol of magic. In the center of the Pentagram is the symbol of occult philosophy, the Caduceus of Mercury, and the sign of Venus. The Caduceus of Mercury represents the dorsal spine. The two open wings represent the ascension of the sacred fire along the dorsal spine which opens the

seven churches (seven chakras) of the book of the Apocalypse (Revelation of St. John). This is done through scientific chastity. The chalice, symbol of the feminine yoni, also represents the Christified Mind. It contains the wine of light that seminizes the brain. The sword is the masculine phallus. We also find the key and the pentacle of Solomon. **Tetragrammaton** is a mantra of immense sacerdotal power.

According to transfinite mathematics, infinite plus infinite equals the Pentalpha.

$$\infty + \infty = 5$$

Students can elaborate an electrum in order to protect themselves against the tenebrous. In occultism, we call an electrum a Pentagram which has on it the seven metals of the seven planets.

1	☽	Moon	Silver
2	☿	Mercury	Mercury
3	♀	Venus	Copper
4	☉	Sun	Gold
5	♂	Mars	Iron
6	♃	Jupiter	Tin
7	♄	Saturn	Lead

The Pentagram is made and consecrated with the four elements fire, air, earth, and water. It should be smoked with the smoke of five perfumes: frankincense, myrrh, aloe, sulphur, and camphor. From these five substances that serve to consecrate the Pentagram, the first three are in order to invoke the white forces. Sulphur is used in order to reject tenebrous entities. Camphor is utilized in order to perfume and attract success. One has to learn how to handle these substances. We have to put the four letters of יהוה (Iod Hei Vav Hei) on the Pentagram and carry it around our neck. This gives us extraordinary protection.

In consecrating the Pentagram, the Pentagram must be blown on with the breath five times. This is in order for the real Christonic Being of the internal Master to be present in order to consecrate the Pentagram. The five Archangels Gabriel, Raphael, Samael, Anael, and Orifiel must also be invoked.

If we can elaborate a metallic Pentagram and consecrate it, we can also consecrate ourselves with the same rites and perfumes that we use to consecrate our metallic Pentagram. This is because the human being is a star of five points.

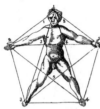

Those who feel that they are polluted with larvae, or are miserable, must incense themselves with the five perfumes in order to become clean. This must be performed in conjunction with treading on the path of perfect chastity. In the Lumisials, this custom of cleaning the brothers and sisters that are full of larvae should be established. Thus, they will receive the benefit in their Souls and in their bodies.

In the Egyptian *Book of the Dead*, the following is said:

> *Saith Nu, triumphant - I am the Jackal of Jackals, I am Shu and [I] draw air from the presence of the god of Light [Khu] to the bounds of Heaven and to the bounds of the earth, and to the bounds of the outer most limits of the flight of the Nebeh bird. May air be given unto these young divine beings.* - Chapter 55

The Hierarch of the Fifth Arcanum is the Jackal of the jackals. He is the lord of the Archons of Destiny. He is Anubis, the God with the head of a jackal.

The temple of Anubis is the temple of the Lords of Karma. Anubis carries the books of Karma in the underworld. Each human being has his own book of affairs.

Those who learn how to travel in their **Ka** (Astral Body) can visit this temple of the Jackal of jackals, in order to consult their book and to make their negotiations.

Credits can be requested from the Lords of Karma. Every credit must be paid for by working in the Great Work of the Father, or by suffering the unspeakable.

When the Logos of the solar system delivered unto me the tunic and the mantle of a Hierophant of Major Mysteries, He told me, "Here I pay unto you what I owe you for the practices you have been teaching."

One who wants light must give light in order to receive one's payment.

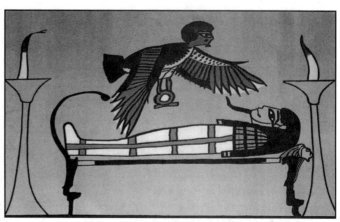

THE KA, THE ASTRAL BODY

The Human Soul of the Initiate (center) stands before Anubis, who weighs the heart (in the jar) against a feather (mind) to measure psychological equilibrium. This also weighs karma and dharma, bad and good actions. Behind the Initiate is his Ka, the Astral Body (bird with a human head). The Divine Father (Chesed) and Mother wait on the far left. Above are the forty-two judges of the Law. On the far right is Thoth, the Causal Logos of the Initiate, who records the judgment and waits to see if the Initiate is to be consumed by the demon Ammit with the face of a crocodile.

The Jackal of jackals conducts the light for all the limits of the firmament. He arrives to the frontiers of the bird Nebeh, the enormous serpent who is one of the forty-two Judges of Maat in the Judgement. This great Judge is the Logos of the solar system. The Jackal of jackals works under the orders of this great Judge. These young divine beings that work with Anubis are the Lords of Karma. The Alchemist must learn how to drive his Ka in order to visit the temple of the Jackal of jackals and to arrange his negotiations.

In our work with the blessed Stone, it is indispensable to learn how to consciously handle our own karmic negotiations. No one escapes from justice because in the depths of our consciousness exists the Kaom, the Karmic police, who take form each time that we register an action, be it positive or negative.

Arcanum 6
Indecision

DESCRIPTION OF THE PLATE

Standing in the waters of life is the disciple in front of a triangle that has its vertex pointing downwards. His left arm is placed on top of the right arm. All of this signifies that the disciple has fallen. That is why he feels more attracted towards the Medusa (the psychological "I") located to his left. At his right is a female Master.

This arcanum is called Indecision because the disciple does not know which path to choose.

In the superior part of the card, a Hierarch is seated in a triangle which is formed by the bow and has its vertex pointing upwards. He points his arrow at the head of Medusa in accordance with the axiom that one must decapitate Medusa.

Each female figure presents to the neophyte a different path: the path to the left and the path to the right. The arrow of justice points against the left path.

ESOTERIC SIGNIFICANCE OF THE ARCANUM

The Sixth Arcanum of the Tarot represents the Lover, which signifies realization. The Human Being is found between vice and virtue, the Virgin and the Whore, Urania-Venus and Medusa. One is found in the situation of having to choose between these two pathways.

The Sixth Arcanum is enchainment, equilibrium, an amorous union of man and woman, and the terrible struggle between love and desire.

INDECISION

Here we find the mysteries of the lingam-yoni. The Sixth Arcanum is interwinding.

In the Sixth Arcanum we find the struggle between the two ternaries.

It is the affirmation of the internal Christ and the supreme negation of Satan.

The Sixth Arcanum is the struggle between the Spirit and the animal beast. The number six represents the struggle between God and the devil. This arcanum is expressed by the Seal of Solomon. The superior triangle represents Kether,

The Sixth Arcanum as hidden in Christian teachings.
FROM THE SALZBURG MISSAL, CA. 1480.

Chokmah, and Binah, the resplendent
Dragon of Wisdom (Father, Son, and Holy
Spirit). The inferior triangle represents the
three traitors who become the antithesis of
the Divine Triad. They are the demons of
desire, of the mind, and the evil will, who
betray the internal Christ from moment
to moment. They are the basis of the ego:
Judas, Caiaphas, and Pilate. This inferior
triangle is the Black Dragon.

Arcanum 7
Triumph

DESCRIPTION OF THE PLATE

In the waters of life appear two sphinxes, a white and a black one, that are pulling the chariot. This symbolizes the masculine and feminine forces. A warrior, who represents the Inner Self, is standing in his chariot of war, which is the Cubic Stone (sex). He also stands between the four pillars that constitute science, art, philosophy, and religion, which he channels himself through. The four pillars also represent the four elements, indicating that he dominates them.

The flaming sword is in his right hand, and in his left is the staff of power. The armor represents the divine science that makes us powerful. The warrior must learn to use the staff and the sword in order to achieve the great victory.

On his head is a bonnet with three points that represent the three primary forces. Ra, the Cosmic Christ (the wings), appears in the superior part of the plate.

TRIUMPH

ZEUS BATTLING THE TITANS. GREEK.

ESOTERIC SIGNIFICANCE OF THE ARCANUM

The Seventh Arcanum represents the seven notes of the lyre of Orpheus, the seven musical notes, the seven colors of the solar prism, the seven planets, the seven vices that we must transform into the seven virtues, the seven sidereal genii, the seven bodies, the seven dimensions, the seven degrees of the power of fire, the seven secret words that were pronounced by the Solar Logos (on Golgotha), etc. The Seventh Arcanum is the chariot of war that the Monad has built in order to have the power to act in this world, and the power to work in this field of life. It is the already Self-realized Monad that is manifesting itself through the seven bodies. From another aspect, the number seven represents struggles, battles and difficulties. However, despite all these difficulties, there is always success in the end.

The Father who is in secret signifies the Divine Monad that is immortal and omniscient. But without realization of the Self, the Monad cannot dominate the physical. He does not have sovereignty over the elements. It is quite incredible that we, who are miserable slugs, have to make our Father powerful; it seems a blasphemy, but He has to realize Himself.

The Self-realized Monad is powerful. It has power over the fire, air, water, and earth. That is why in the Egyptian *Book of the Dead* the devotee directs himself towards Horus and says, "I fortify your legs and your arms." Likewise, the devotee asks Horus to fortify his three brains (intellectual, emotional and motor). This

is because Horus needs the devotee to have his three brains strong.

In Egyptian theogony, the Father (Father, Son, and Holy Spirit) is Osiris, or Ra. The Logos in its three aspects is Ra. When spoken of, the Monad is referred to as Osiris. He is the one that has to realize Himself. He has to unfold Himself into Father, Mother and Son. The Son unfolds himself into the Essence, and the Essence swallows us. Thus, the Monad remains Self-realized.

Essence → Son → Mother → Father

Our own particular Monad needs us and we need it. Once, while speaking with my Monad, my Monad told me, "I am self-realizing Thee; what I am doing, I am doing for Thee."

Otherwise, why are we living? The Monad wants to realize the Self and that is why we are here. This is our objective.

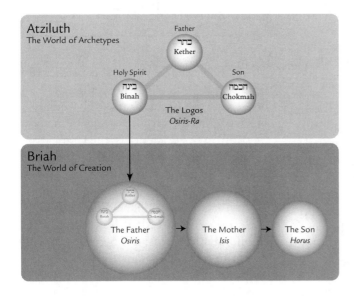

Arcanum 8
Justice

JUSTICE

DESCRIPTION OF THE PLATE

In the waters of life appears a serpent eating its tail, which forms the sign of the Cosmic Mother, the infinite, the number zero.

A woman kneels on a platform of three steps, representing the Arcanum A.Z.F. (water + fire = consciousness).

In her left hand, she holds the sword of power which is pointing upwards. With her right hand, she balances a scale, which points out that equilibrium should exist between the mind, the heart, and sex. In the superior part of the plate appears Ra (this is another symbol of Ra, other than the wings).

ESOTERIC SIGNIFICANCE OF THE ARCANUM

The Eighth Arcanum is Judgement. The number eight is the number of Job, of ordeals and of pain. In relation to esotericism, the number eight is represented by the sword.

The number eight is the number of the infinite. The vital forces of the fire of Phlegethon and the water of Acheron circulate in the form of an eight, intercrossing themselves in the Ninth Sphere, within the heart of the earth. In the dorsal spine, the symbol of the infinite is also formed. The sign of the infinite signifies work in the Ninth Sphere and this is sex.

The Eighth Arcanum of the Tarot is a woman with a sword in her hand before the scale of cosmic justice. Only she can deliver the sword to the Magician. Without woman, no initiate can receive the sword.

There exists the Eve-Venus, the instinctive woman; the Venus-Eve, the woman of home, and the Venus-Urania, the woman initiated into the great mysteries. Finally, we confirm the existence of the Urania-Venus, the female adept, the deeply realized woman.

The woman of the Eighth Arcanum of the Tarot has in one hand the scale and in the other the sword. It is necessary to equilibrate the forces; it is necessary and urgent to completely sanctify ourselves and to practice the Arcanum A.Z.F. The forces of man and woman are equilibrated in love and wisdom.

The miraculous ascension of the seminal energy towards the brain is made possible thanks to a certain pair of nervous cords that are unfolded in the form of an eight, from right to left, in the dorsal spine.

In Chinese philosophy, this pair of cords is known by the classical name of Yin and Yang. The Tao, the middle path, or the medullar canal is the secret path through which the serpent ascends.

It is obvious that the first of these two canals is of a lunar nature. It is clear that the second canal is of a solar nature.

When the lunar and solar atoms make contact within the triveni, close to the coccyx, the igneous serpent of our magical powers awakens.

The serpent that forms a circle with its figure while in the Gnostic trance of devouring its own tail is an extraordinary synthesis of the marvellous message of the Lord Quetzalcoatl. The serpent in a vertical position illustrates the Maya and Nahuatl idea, which is the divine viper devouring the Soul and Spirit of the man. Finally, the sexual flames consume the animal ego, annihilating it and reducing it to ashes.

Unquestionably, the serpent is the esoteric symbol of wisdom and occult knowledge. Since ancient times, the serpent has been related to the god of wisdom. The serpent is the sacred symbol of Thoth and all the holy Gods, like Hermes, Serapis, Jesus, Quetzalcoatl, Buddha, Tlaloc, Dante, Zoroaster, Bochica, etc.

Any Adept of the Universal White Fraternity can be correctly represented by the "Great Serpent," that within the symbols of the Gods occupies a very notorious place, as is shown in the Babylonian buildings where its form is carved in black stone.

Dupuis has said that Skulapius, Pluto, Esmund, Knepp, are all deities with the attributes of the serpent. All of them are healers and givers of spiritual and physical health and also of illumination.

The Brahmans obtained their cosmogony, science and art of culturalization from the famous Naga-Mayas, who were later known as Danavas.

The Nagas (serpents) and the Brahmans utilized the sacred symbol of the feathered serpent, an indisputably Mexican and Mayan emblem.

The Upanishads contain a treatise about the science of the serpents, or in other words, the science of occult knowledge.

NAGAS IN BUDDHIST ART

The Nagas of esoteric Buddhism are authentic perfect, Self-realized Human Beings. They are the protectors of the Buddha's law, because they correctly interpreted the metaphysical doctrines.

If the serpent was a symbol of evil, the great Kabir Jesus of Nazareth would never have advised his disciples to be wise like the serpent. It is good to remember that the Ophites, the Egyptian Gnostic wise men of the fraternity of the serpent, would never have worshipped a living serpent as an emblem of wisdom (Divine *Sophia*) in their ceremonies if this reptile was related with the potencies of evil.

The sacred serpent, or Savior Logos, sleeps nestled in the depth of the ark, mystically awaiting the moment of its awakening.

Kundalini, the igneous serpent of our magical powers, is entwined within the magnetic center of the coccyx (base of the dorsal spine). It is as luminous as lightning.

Those who study Nahuatl or Hindustani esoteric physiology emphasise the transcendental idea of a marvellous magnetic center located at the base of the vertebral column, which is located between the anus and the sexual organs.

In the center of the Muladhara chakra there is a yellow square invisible to the eyes of the flesh but perceptible to clairvoyance, or the sixth sense. According to the Hindus, this square represents the element earth.

It has been said to us that within the mentioned square a yoni, or uterus, exists, and that in the center of this yoni a lingam, or erotic phallus, exists in which the serpent, the mysterious psychic energy called Kundalini, is curled.

The esoteric structure of that magnetic center, as well as the exceptional position between the sexual organs and the anus, gives a solid and irrefutable foundation to the tantric schools of India and Tibet.

It is unquestionable that only through the Sahaja Maithuna, or Sexual Magic, can the serpent be awakened.

The crown formed by an aspid, the thermuthis, belongs to Isis, our particular and individual Divine Mother Kundalini. Each one of us has their own Divine Mother within.

The serpent as a feminine deity within each one of us is the spouse of the Holy Spirit. She is our Virgin Mother crying at the foot of the sexual cross with her heart pierced by seven daggers.

Undoubtedly the serpent of the great mysteries is the feminine aspect of the Logos, God-Mother, the wife of Shiva. She is Isis, Adonia, Tonantzin, Rhea, Mary, or, better if we say, Ram-Io, Cybele, Opis, Der, Flora, Paula, IO, Akka, the Great Mother in Sanskrit, the Goddess of the Lha, Lares, or spirits of here down, the anguished mother of Huitzilopochtli, the Ak or White Goddess in Turkish, the Chaldean Minerva of the initiatic mysteries, the Akabolzub of the Lunar temple of Chichen-Itza (Yucatan), etc.

A Hindu Symbol of Muladhara Chakra

Arcanum 9
The Hermit

THE HERMIT

DESCRIPTION OF THE PLATE

In this Arcanum, we find a rising moon in the waters of life. In the middle part of the plate is an old Hermit who is advancing forward, pointing out the path by holding in his left hand a lamp known as the lamp of Hermes, wisdom. With his right hand he holds on to the staff of the patriarchs, which represents the spinal column with its seven churches.

The prudent and wise Hermit is wrapped up in the protecting mantle of Apollonius, which symbolizes prudence. The palm of victory is behind him.

In the superior part of the plate is a sun that shines with three rays, indicating the three primary forces that descend to unite with the moon. The moon ascends and the sun descends, indicating that we need to transform the moon into the sun through transmutation. We need to convert the Lunar Bodies into Solar Bodies with the Arcanum A.Z.F.

Arcanum Nine clearly indicates the nine spheres of the atomic infernos of nature and the nine spheres of the nine Heavens. This arcanum also points out the nine planets represented in the nine spheres of the planet Earth.

The initiate must descend to the nine submerged spheres to later win the nine Heavens corresponding to each planet.

ESOTERIC SIGNIFICANCE OF THE ARCANUM

Arcanum Nine is the Hermit, solitude. This arcanum in its more elevated form is the Ninth Sphere, sex.

In the ancient temples, the descent into the Ninth Sphere was the maximum ordeal for the supreme dignity of the Hierophant. Hermes, Buddha, Jesus Christ, Zoroaster, Dante, and many other great initiates had to pass this maximum ordeal, the descent to the Ninth Sphere, in order to work with the fire and the water which originated the worlds, beasts, men and Gods. Every authentic White Initiation starts here.

In the Ninth Sphere, or ninth stratum of the Earth, in the center of the Earth, in the very heart of the Earth, the sign of the infinite is found resplendent. This sign has the form of an eight. The sign of the infinite is the Holy Eight. In this sign the heart, brain, and sex of the Genie of the earth are represented. The secret name of this Genie is Changam.

The Zohar emphatically warns us that in the depths of the abyss lives the Protoplasmic Adam, the differentiating principle of the souls. With that principle we have to execute a struggle to the death. This struggle is terrible: brain against sex, and sex against brain, and what is even more terrible and more painful, heart against heart.

It is obvious that in a human being all the forces are rotating over the base of the Holy Eight. One who wants to enter into the city of nine doors, mentioned in *The Bhagavad Gita*, must resolve to descend to the flaming forge of Vulcan.

In the human organism the Ninth Sphere is sex. One who wants to realize the Self has to descend to the Ninth Sphere to work with the water and the fire in order to achieve the Second Birth.

The flaming forge of Vulcan is found in the Ninth Sphere (sex). There, Mars descends in order to retemper his flaming sword and conquer the heart of Venus (the Venustic Initiation). Heracles descends in order to clean the stables of Augeas (our animal depths). Perseus descends in order to cut off the head of Medusa (the psychological "I," or terrestrial Adam) with his flaming sword; Medusa's head has many planted serpents which the esoteric

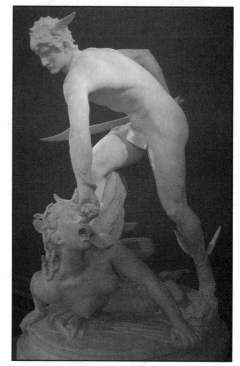

PERSEUS CONQUERS MEDUSA, BY LAURENT-HONORÉ MARQUESTE (1903)

student has to deliver to Minerva, the Goddess of Wisdom.

The fetus remains nine months within the maternal womb. In order for a planetary humanity to be born, nine ages are necessary in the womb of Rhea, Tonantzin, Cybele, or Mother Nature. As well, it is obvious that one has to descend into the Ninth Sphere in order to be gestated and to achieve the Second Birth.

Jesus said to Nicodemus, *"Verily, verily, I say unto thee, except a man be born again, he cannot see the Kingdom of God"* (John 3:1-15). This refers to the building of the Solar Bodies. No one can enter into the Kingdom if they are dressed with lunar rags.

One has to build the Solar Bodies and this is only achieved by transmuting the creative energy. In Egyptian theogony, these Solar Bodies are represented by the Egyptian Sahu. No one has the right to sit at the table of Angels if they are not dressed with the Solar Bodies. We have to build **To Soma Heliakon**, the body of gold of the solar human being.

It is written, *"Narrow is the way that leadeth unto light."* Whosoever wants to follow this path, *"let him deny himself and take up his cross and follow me"* (the three factors in the revolution of the consciousness: to **Die**, to be **Born**, and to **Sacrifice** [Mark 8:34]).

Those who want the realization of the Self must be ready to renounce everything: wealth, honor, peace, prestige, and must even give their own blood.

One must have a center of gravity, a permanent center of consciousness. Human beings are nothing but machines driven by the many "I's," (the pluralized ego). We are placed in a very disadvantageous situation, and this signifies that super efforts are required, as well as killing the "I." The ego is Mephistopheles. It is the root of all our suffering and pain. It lives in accordance to its own conditioning. We have to reduce it to cosmic dust in order to have our consciousness awake, in order to see the path.

By knowing, we understand what it is to see, hear, and touch the great realities. There is a necessity to understand what is signified by "the bottom of the abyss." When it is said that we must descend to the bottom of the abyss, that is a reality. When descending to the Ninth Sphere, we put ourselves in agreement with the planetary organism in which we live. This is by the law of concomitancies, or the law of relations. Those who work in the Ninth Sphere have descended to the bottom of their real aspect. If they have been working

in the Ninth Sphere, then when they die they will see that they really live in that region (the Ninth Sphere is the center of the earth). Of course, those who will notice this will be the ones that have awakened their consciousness. We must warn the neophyte that supreme pain exists within the Ninth Sphere, just as Dante explains in his *Divine Comedy*. Dante states that some of the condemned have tears coagulated in their eyes, and others have the water rising up to their creative organs. One needs to know how to understand. One needs to know how to learn to suffer, to be submissive. Those who are not are the ones that fail. It is impudent to want to find happiness in the Ninth Sphere. This is because the realization of the inner Self has a price. It costs the same life.

Was it not perhaps Hiram Abiff who was assassinated and sought by twenty-seven Masters? This makes the Kabbalistic addition of 2 + 7 = 9.

There are great pains in the Ninth Sphere, up to the moment that one reaches the Second Birth. When Jesus said to Nicodemus that he had to be born again, Nicodemus did not understand. Jesus knew the great mystery. Could someone ever depart from the Ninth Sphere? Yes, when one reaches the Second Birth.

After I created To Soma Heliakon in the forge of the Cyclops (sex), I had to pass a period of profound reflection. In the residence of love, in the Temple of the Twice-born, I found other brothers and sisters that had also worked intensely in the flaming forge of Vulcan (sex). All of them were shining gloriously within the divine, indescribable enchantments of Holy Friday. We were reunited in order to comment about our struggles and pains.

We had been victorious. But, all of this is the beginning of beginnings, the foundation of foundations. There is something more about this, and it is necessary for you to be informed about it.

If a Twice-born, or someone who has reached Adepthood, is intent to reach the Angelic state, this person has to *descend again* to the profound well of the Universe, to the Ninth Sphere. Then, when finished with that work, the Twice-born must rise up the ladder (Luciferic ladder), in order to reach the Angelic state. If this being wants to be an Archangel, Principate, Throne, or Cherubim, he or she must do the same: *descend in order to ascend.* We must understand and distinguish between what it means to **fall** and what it means to **descend**. One who is already decapitated cannot be recapitated. In the eve of entering the Absolute one has to descend to the Ninth Sphere.

If the Second Birth is achieved, the sexual act remains prohibited. The sexual act cannot be used at one's will, but only if the command of the White Brotherhood (the Sacred Order) or the command of the Father who is in secret is received, and that command is to descend to the well of the abyss. One needs to obey. This is not pleasure, but pain and sacrifice.

One must **descend** and one must suffer upon the Luciferic ladder. We need to transform ourselves into Masters, as much as with the superior forces, as the inferior forces. The Father who is in secret commands; He knows what must be done. Only by receiving His order can one descend.

Those who **fall** are the only ones that lose their initiatic degrees, never those who descend. By finishing the work, the commands are received and the sexual union

The Ladder of Lucifer as Seen by Jacob. Painting by William Blake.

is not performed in a capricious way. The Father is the owner of this act and the order has to come from the Father. The sexual union does not belong to us, but to the Father.

The law of the Leviathan is the law of the Mason that has already passed all of the works or esoteric degrees. Since he is already decapitated he cannot be recapitated. This Mason cannot receive damage, neither from above, nor from below. He lives in harmony with the law, the great law. This is the superior knowledge of esoteric Masonry.

In the beginning one does one's capricious will, then one does the will of the Father. When one does not have ego anymore the malignity will disappear and the individual will only know how to do the will of the Father. He is our own true Being; He is the Elder of the Days; He is beyond Atman. When He commands, His orders must be fulfilled.

One begins to gain liberation from the Ninth Sphere when one converts oneself into a Paramarthasattya (an inhabitant of the Absolute). Then, one submerges into the Abstract Joy. But before going there, a humiliation will occur. One needs to return to descend; otherwise one violates the law of Leviathan, the Seal of Solomon.

In the Apocalypse of the Holy Bible we also find the mysteries of the Ninth Sphere. *"And I heard the number of them which were sealed, and there were sealed a hundred and forty and four thousand of all the tribes of the children of Israel."* [Revelation 7:4] Kabbalistically adding the numbers together, we have the number nine (144,000 = 1 + 4 + 4 = 9). This is the Ninth Sphere, sex. Only those that have reached absolute chastity will be saved.

"And I looked and lo a lamb stood on the Mount Zion and with him an hundred and forty and four thousand having his Father's name written in their foreheads." [Revelation 14:1] Mount Zion is the Superior Worlds. These numbers are symbolic numbers. Kabbalistically, we make the additions as follows 1 + 4 + 4 = 9, the Ninth Sphere, Sex. Only with the Great Arcanum can we be saved and receive the name of the Father on our forehead. The people of Zion are the spiritual people of God. These people (people of chastity) are all those that practice Sexual Magic.

Related to the new Jerusalem, *"and he measured the wall thereof an hundred and forty and four thousand cubits according to the measure of a man, that is, of the Angel."* [Revelation 21:17] 1 + 4 + 4 = 9, sex. The number nine is the measurement of man, the one who is of the Angel. For nine months we remain within the maternal womb. The Son of

Man can only be born in the Ninth Sphere. There never was known an Angel that was not born in the Ninth Sphere.

Those who want to cut off the head of Medusa (the ego) must descend to the Ninth Sphere.

One who wants to incarnate the Christ must descend to the Ninth Sphere. One who wants to dissolve the "I" must descend to the Ninth Sphere. The Ninth Sphere is the *sanctum regnum* of the divine omnipotence of the Third Logos. In the Ninth Sphere we find the flaming forge of Vulcan.

Every fledgling that works in the Great Work must repose on their staff and must illuminate themselves with their own lamp and cover themselves with their sacred mantle. Every fledgling must be prudent. If you want to incarnate the Christ you must be like a lemon. Flee from lust and alcohol. Kill the most inner roots of desire.

There are abundant esoteric students who mistakenly affirm that there are numerous ways in order to reach God. But the divine, great Master Jesus said, *"Because straight is the gate, and narrow is the way, which leadeth unto life, and few there be that find it."* [Matthew 7:14] If the esoteric student searches patiently through all of the four Gospels, he will prove for himself that Jesus never said that there were many ways.

The adorable savior of the world only spoke of one narrow door and one straight and difficult way and that way is sex. There is no other way to reach God. Never was their known in all of eternity a prophet that had known any door other than sex.

Some mistaken and confused esoteric students wrongly object to these teachings and affirm that Pythagoras, Zoroaster, Jesus, and other initiates were celibate, never having been with a woman.

THE VESTAL VIRGINS OF THE TEMPLE

In all of the temples of the mysteries, sacred vestals existed. The materialists, the disrespectful ones, ones with evil intentions, arbitrarily pretended to call them "sacred prostitutes." Albeit, these vestals were initiated virgins, esoteric virgins, even when their bodies were not physiologically virginal.

The initiates of the temple, Pythagoras, Zoroaster, Jesus Christ, and all of the initiates from ancient times, without exception, indeed practiced the Arcanum A.Z.F. with the vestals of the temple. Only in the flaming forge of Vulcan could these great initiates retemper their weapons and conquer the heart of Venus.

Arcanum 10
Retribution

DESCRIPTION OF THE PLATE

In the waters of life, we find two serpents: the positive solar serpent that healed the Israelites in the wilderness, and the negative serpent, the tempting serpent of Eden which is related to the Lunar Bodies, the bodies of sin.

In the middle of the plate is the Wheel of Fortune, the Wheel of Samsara, or the wheel of death and birth. The evolving Hermanubis ascends on the right side, and on the left side, the devolving Typhon Baphomet descends. After 108 lives, the wheel makes one complete turn. As it rises, we pass through the process of evolution in the mineral, vegetable, animal, and human kingdoms. On descending, we

RETRIBUTION

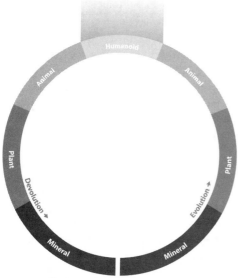

THE LAW OF EVOLUTION AND DEVOLUTION

Entrance into the superior kingdoms (angels, etc) is only possible from the humanoid kingdom.

fall through the same path. The Wheel of Samsara makes 3,000 turns, after which the Essence, after so many purifications and sufferings, returns to the Absolute. However, it returns without realization of the Self.

In the superior part of the plate is the Sphinx, which represents Mother Nature, balancing itself over the wheel. The Sphinx is the Elemental Intercessor of the blessed Mother Goddess of the world. We find the five elements represented in the Sphinx:

Water: the face of a man

Air: the wings of an eagle

Earth: the hoofs of an ox

Fire: the paws of a lion

Ether: the staff

Esoteric Significance of the Arcanum

In the Tenth Arcanum we find the wheel of destiny, the cosmogenic wheel of Ezekiel. On this wheel we find the struggle of the antithesis, Hermanubis at the right, Typhon at the left. This is the wheel of the centuries. It is the Wheel of Fortune, the wheel of reincarnation and karma, the terrible wheel of retribution. The mystery of the Sphinx is upon the wheel.

In the wheel of the antitheses, two serpents are fighting each other. In this wheel, the whole secret of the Tree of Knowledge is enclosed. The four rivers of Paradise emerge from this unique stream. One of the rivers runs through the dense jungle of the sun, watering the philosophical earth that is from the gold of light, and the other, tenebrous and disturbed, circulates within the kingdom of the abyss. Light and darkness, white magic and black magic, are mutually struggling. Eros and Anteros, Cain and Abel, live within ourselves in an intense struggle until the moment we discover the mystery of the Sphinx. Then we grasp the flaming sword, liberating ourselves from the wheel of the centuries.

The Tenth Arcanum is Kabbalistically called the kingdom or vital center. It is called the formed root of all of the laws of Nature and of the cosmos.

To form signifies to initially intellectually conceive, and then after, to build or draw. That is why the number ten is the formed principle of all things.

The circle with a point in the center is related with the mysteries of lingam-yoni. The circle is the Absolute, the eternal feminine principle. It is the yoni in which all the universes are born. The point is the lingam, the eternal masculine principle. The circle with a point in the center is the macrocosmos. These are the mysteries of the lingam-yoni with which universes can be created.

The circle is receptive, the point is projective. If the point is projected, it is lengthened and it becomes a line. It divides the circle into two. When the point is in movement, then we have the lingam-yoni, the two sexes, masculine and feminine.

$$⊙ \rightarrow ⊕ \rightarrow |O = 10 = IO$$

By taking the line out of the circle, we have the number ten, and the mantra of the Divine Mother. The entire universe is a product of the sexual energy. Without the power of the creative energy, the universe could not be formed. Without the sexual creative energy there is no universe. That is why the number ten is the formed principle of all of nature.

The circle with a point in the center can also be drawn as:

The number ten teaches many things. Let us remember the circle which is a symbol of the Divine Mother. We can say that the following symbols are essentially the same in their depth.

It is said that the number 10 is the base, the kingdom. The person that obeys the commandments of this arcanum sees the return of all things. If the student knows how to obey, he sees the return of all things. He elevates himself towards Illumination, and can see the flux and reflux of all things because he is an Illuminated One. The Kabbalah says that we see things in accordance to the way that we start obeying the number 10.

In this number 10 are the following principles:

Creation

Conservation

Renovation

Behold, here is the verb in its triple aspect.

The point within the circle that in movement makes itself into a line can be found in the following ways.

We have seen that the number ten comes from that symbol, as well as the **IO**, which is the mantra of the Divine Mother, that also gives place to the ten emanations of Prakriti, meaning the ten Sephiroth of the Kabbalah.

The ten Sephiroth are:

1. Kether: The Father

2. Chokmah: The Son

3. Binah: The Holy Spirit

One, two, and three are the three Logoi, the three-unity Sephirothic Crown. This is the first triangle.

After this Sephirothic Crown we find:

4. Chesed: Atman, the Innermost, our Divine Being

5. Geburah: The feminine Spiritual Soul, Buddhi. It is the superlative consciousness of the Being. It is the principle of justice, the law. Whenever

consciousness is spoken of, it is referring to Buddhi, the Elohim who say, *"Do battle for me in the name of Tetragrammaton."*

6. Tiphereth: Superior Manas, the Human Soul

Four, five, and six form the second triangle.

In the third triangle, we find seven, eight, and nine:

7. Netzach: The Solar Mind, the Christ Mind

8. Hod: The legitimate Astral Solar Body

9. Yesod - The Cubic Stone, sex

10. Malkuth - The physical body

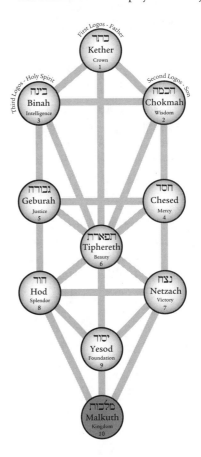

The ten Sephiroth are within each one of us. They subexist in all organic and inorganic matter. Every human being has them, but needs to incarnate them. When they are already Self-realized, the Sephiroth sparkle like precious gems within Atman. The Sephiroth form regions where the Archangels, Angels, Cherubim, Potencies, etc., live. The Sephiroth have their points of relation with the physical body.

Location of the Sephiroth within the physical body:

1. Kether: the crown, in the superior part of the head

2. Chokmah: right side of the brain

3. Binah: left side of the brain

4. Chesed: in the right arm

5. Geburah: in the left arm

6. Tiphereth: in the heart

7. Netzach: in the right leg

8. Hod: in the left leg

9. Yesod: in the sexual organs

10. Malkuth: in the feet

These are the points of contact of the Sephiroth with the human body. The Sephiroth are atomic. They are not atoms of carbon, oxygen, and nitrogen. They are atoms of a spiritual nature that belong to occult, esoteric, and spiritual chemistry.

The Sephiroth are masculine; however, there also exist feminine Sephiroth. Profound space constitutes the neutral zone, the magnetic field, etc. This is not found in books. One has to discover this for oneself. I have spoken to you from a direct, mystical point of view.

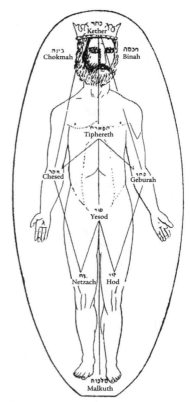

THE SEPHIROTH IN THE MICROCOSMIC PHYSICAL BODY. DRAWING FROM AN UNDATED JEWISH ENCYCLOPEDIA

Arcanum 11
Persuasion

DESCRIPTION OF THE PLATE

In the waters of life is found the Cubic Stone. Within the Stone is the bird and the long-legged creature; upon it is the dove of the Holy Spirit.

In the middle of the plate, a woman closes the jaws of a furious lion, indicating that she is superior to violence. On her head is a crown with a serpent projecting out from the forehead indicating her mastery.

The lion is the element fire and also represents gold. In ancient times, the chariot of the kings was pulled by lions. In esoteric symbolism, the chariot of war pulled by lions symbolizes the Solar Bodies.

ESOTERIC SIGNIFICANCE OF THE ARCANUM

The Eleventh Arcanum is known in Kabbalah as Persuasion. The hieroglyphic of this arcanum is a beautiful woman that with tranquillity and olympic serenity closes the jaws of a furious lion with her own hands.

The thrones of the divine kings were decorated with lions of massive gold. The gold signifies the sacred fire of Kundalini. This reminds us of Horus, the Gold.

We need to transmute the lead of personality into the gold of the Spirit. This work is only possible in the laboratory of the Alchemist. When the fledgling of Alchemy is crowned, he or she self-transforms into a God of Fire. Then, with bare hands, the terrible jaws of the furious lion can be opened. The potable gold

PERSUASION

of Alchemy is the sacred fire of the Holy Spirit.

The union of the Cross-Man in the Triangle-Spirit (Arcanum 12) would be impossible without the liquid gold.

The number eleven is thus Kabbalistically modified: 1 + 1 = 2.

> 1 = masculine
>
> 2 = feminine
>
> 1 man + 1 woman = 2, man-woman, the fire

The number eleven is formed by two unities that Heinrich Kunrath translated in these two words, "Coagula et solve." We need to accumulate the sacred fire and then learn to project it. The clue of this is in the connection of the *membrum virile* with the *genitalia murielis,* with quietude of the membrum virile and the genitalia murielis, and using a very soft movement once in a while. Thus, we transmute the animal instincts into willpower, sexual passion into love, lustful thoughts into comprehension, and vocalize the secret mantras.

Man is one unity; woman is the other. This is the number eleven of the Tarot. Therefore, only by working in the Great Work can the man with the woman incarnate the Child of Gold, Horus, the Verb, the great Word. Accordingly, the number eleven is the most multiplicable number.

Arcanum 12
The Apostolate

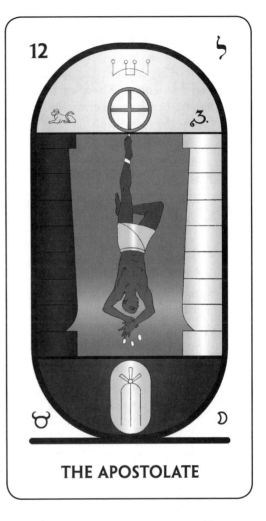

THE APOSTOLATE

Description of the Plate

In the waters of life is the pentacle of Solomon, a variant of the six pointed star.

The three upper points represent the three traitors of Hiram Abiff (the Internal Christ), Judas, Pilate, and Caiaphas (desire, mind and evil will).

In the middle of the plate are two columns that contain nine steps each, the Ninth Sphere (sex). Let us remember that there are nine Heavens (the white column) and nine infernal regions (the black column). In order to ascend one step, one must descend one step.

Between the two columns there is a man hanging from one foot with his hands tied. With his legs he forms a cross and with his arms he forms an inverted triangle.

Sex dominating reason

The first figure *(top)* signifies that sex dominates reason. It is necessary to invert this symbol.

The chemical symbol of sulphur

Esoteric Significance of the Arcanum

The Twelfth Arcanum represents the twelve zodiacal signs, the twelve Apostles, the twelve tribes of Israel, the twelve hours of cooking of the Alchemist, the twelve faculties, and the Hydrogen SI-12.

The Twelfth Arcanum of the Tarot is the Apostolate. The figure is of a hanged man forming a triangle with his arms with the vertex pointing downwards. With his legs, he forms a cross which is above the triangle. All of the Work has as its objective the acquiring of Soul, meaning the achieving of the union of the cross with the triangle. This is the Great Work.

The twelfth card of the Tarot is Sexual Alchemy. The Cross-Man must be united with the Triangle-Spirit through the sexual fire.

The Chinese tradition speaks of the ten trunks (Shikan) and the twelve branches, meaning the ten Sephiroth and the twelve faculties of the human being. It is necessary to know that the seven chakras plus the five senses are the twelve faculties.

Undoubtedly, the dorsal spine has seven magnetic centers. These are the seven chakras, or the seven churches of the book of Apocalypse of Saint John.

1. **Ephesus**: base of the dorsal spine; four petals

2. **Smyrna**: at the height of the prostate; six petals

3. **Pergamos**: at the height of the solar plexus; ten petals

4. **Thyatira**: in the heart; twelve petals

5. **Sardis**: in the creative larynx; sixteen petals

6. **Philadelphia**: in the mid brow; two petals

7. **Laodicea**: in the pineal gland; one thousand petals

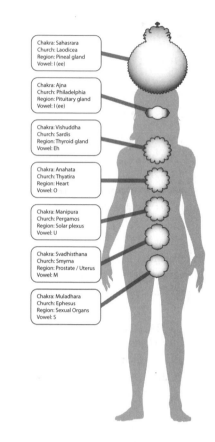

Chakra: Sahasrara
Church: Laodicea
Region: Pineal gland
Vowel: I (ee)

Chakra: Ajna
Church: Philadelphia
Region: Pituitary gland
Vowel: I (ee)

Chakra: Vishuddha
Church: Sardis
Region: Thyroid gland
Vowel: Eh

Chakra: Anahata
Church: Thyatira
Region: Heart
Vowel: O

Chakra: Manipura
Church: Pergamos
Region: Solar plexus
Vowel: U

Chakra: Svadhisthana
Church: Smyrna
Region: Prostate / Uterus
Vowel: M

Chakra: Muladhara
Church: Ephesus
Region: Sexual Organs
Vowel: S

These are the seven chakras, and with the addition of the five senses one is converted into an investigator of the Superior Worlds. These are the twelve faculties of every human creature.

The universe came out from the Chinese *Huel-Tum*, the Chaos. The ten trunks and the twelve branches also came out from the Chaos, that in Alchemy is the *"Ens Seminis"* in which all of the *"Ens Virtutis"* is contained, which is the raw matter of the Great Work. This is the entity of the Being in accordance to Paracelsus. This entity becomes the Philosophical Stone or *Lapis Philosophorum* for which the medieval Alchemists were fervently searching.

All of the misterium magnum is found enclosed in this summa matter (Latin terms in order to denominate the Arcanum

A.Z.F.). The Alchemist must extract from this mestrum universale (the Chaos) all of the potable gold or sacred fire, which has to rise through the spinal medulla and open all of the seven churches.

We can unite the cross with the triangle once we have extracted the potable gold, meaning the Cross-Man must be united with our immortal triad. We must incarnate the Spirit. Only thus can we convert ourselves into human beings. Before achieving this we are nothing but intellectual animals.

The Great Work or "Magnus Opus" is represented by the Twelfth Arcanum of the Tarot (it is called Magnus Opus in strict esoteric language). The arms of the figure form the triangle, his legs the cross, his head is the union of the triangle with the cross through the potable gold.

According to the Chinese, the God Fu Xi (the Adam-Christ) was born at midnight, the fourth day of the tenth moon, precisely during twelve years. The virgin Hoa Se, while walking along the shore of the river (the seminal liquid), conceived the Christ in her womb while putting her foot over the print of the Great Man.

All of these dates are very interesting.

The four days are the four elements.

In the number ten are all the secrets of the lingam-yoni, representing the ten Sephiroth.

The circle with the line cutting it in half is the mystery of sex.

The number twelve is the twelve faculties required to incarnate the Christ in the heart.

In the twelfth key of Basil Valentine, the Twelfth Arcanum is profoundly studied.

Thus, as the lion transforms the serpent into its own flesh when he devours it, so the power of Devi Kundalini, the sacred transmuted fire, eliminates all of its defects, its errors. What is important is the Great Work. We already know the key, the Maithuna. The Alchemists must work for twelve hours in order to achieve the fermentation of the gold. Behold the Twelfth Arcanum. We can have the joy of really **being** when we possess the fermented gold.

The Essence, or fraction of Incarnated Soul, is bottled up in the pluralized "I," or ego. This is within the animal mental body and the lunar body of desire, and manifests itself through the physical body. We are different from the animals only by the intellect, because the animals have mind but not intellect.

The authentic Human needs to eliminate ego and to build the Solar Bodies with the transmutation of the Hydrogen SI-12 (twelve laws). The manufacturing of the Solar Bodies is intimately related with music and the seven notes.

The Hydrogen SI-12 is made through initiating the process of digestion in the human organism.

DO: when the food is in the mouth.

RE: when it reaches the throat.

MI: when it reaches the lung area.

FA: when it reaches the stomach, splenic, hepatic.

SOL: when it reaches the solar plexus.

LA: when it reaches the colon, pancreas.

SI: when the Hydrogen SI-12 is made and here it can rise to another superior musical octave (after the note SI the note DO begins again, corresponding to other musical scales, to another superior octave).

THE TWELFTH KEY OF BASIL VALENTINE

The Hydrogen SI-12 has a second octave, giving origin to the Solar Astral Body when the sexual impulse and the ejaculation are refrained. The Hydrogen will pass to a third octave that will give origin to the Solar Mental Body while this one is having a third shock. A fourth octave gives birth to the body of Conscious Will. All of this work is with the Maithuna. Our Divine Being will enter through the pineal gland when we are in possession of the four vehicles. Then, we will achieve the Second Birth, and we will convert ourselves into true Human Beings. While we have the animal Lunar Bodies, we are intellectual animals. We are a chrysalis that can be transformed into a celestial butterfly. This is achieved with super efforts.

The food of the physical body is the Hydrogen 48 (48 laws). If we save this Hydrogen, it can be transformed into Hydrogen 24 (24 laws that serve as food to the Solar Astral Body). This Hydrogen 24 is wasted through excessive work, worthless efforts, desires, emotions, anger. The Hydrogen 12 is the food of the Solar Mental Body. It is wasted through intellectual efforts. If we save the Hydrogen 12, we will obtain the Hydrogen 6 in order to nourish the body of Conscious Will.

One who has the Superior Existential Bodies of the Being has the right to incarnate their Divine Triad Atman-Buddhi-Manas.

Then it is stated a new Son of Man, a Master, a Mahatma, is born.

Everything which is written in the book of the Apocalypse is for the times of the end. We have to inform humanity that the times of the end have already arrived. All of this poor humanity is divided into twelve tribes. All of humanity is unfolded and developed within the zodiacal womb.

The zodiac is a uterus in which humanity is gestated. The twelve tribes can only receive the seal of God on their foreheads by practising with the Arcanum A.Z.F., *"And I heard the number of them which were sealed."* [Revelation 7:4] *"Of the tribe of Judas were sealed twelve thousand, of the tribe of Reuben were sealed twelve thousand."* [Revelation 7:5-8]

There are only twelve thousand sealed of each of the twelve zodiacal tribes. Behold here the Twelfth Arcanum of the Tarot. Behold here the union of the cross with the triangle. Behold here the Sexual Magic. Behold here the Realized Work, the living Human Being that does not touch the earth, but only with thought.

Only twelve thousand sealed of each of the twelve tribes of Israel will be saved from the great cataclysm (this quantity is symbolic). Only those that have achieved the union of the Cross-Man with the Triangle-Spirit will be saved.

Related with the new Jerusalem we find the following, *"And had a wall great and high, and had twelve gates* (the twelve zodiacal gates in the universe and in the human being) *and at the gates were twelve Angels* (from the zodiac) *and names written thereon, which are the names of the children of Israel* (the twelve types of humanities in accordance with the influence of the twelve zodiacal signs). [Revelation 21:12]

"As above so below." The human being has twelve faculties controlled by twelve atomic Angels. Twelve zodiacal signs exist in the starry space and in the human being. It is necessary to transmute the sexual energy and to make it pass through the twelve zodiacal gates of the human organism. The prophet continues speaking about the twelve zodiacal gates as follows, *"On the east three gates; on the north three gates;*

on the south three gates; and on the west three gates." [Revelation 21:13]

"And the wall of the city had twelve foundations and in them the names of the twelve apostles of the Lamb." [Revelation 21:14] The twelve zodiacal signs and the twelve energetic spheres penetrate and co-penetrate without confusion. The solar humanity is completely realized in the twelve planes.

The Twelfth Arcanum is the foundation of the celestial Jerusalem. The Twelfth Arcanum is the symbol of Sexual Alchemy. This is the sacrifice and the Realized Work.

One has to work with the gold and silver. One has to work with the Moon and the Sun in order to edify the celestial Jerusalem within each person. Gold and silver, the sun and the moon, are the sexual forces of the man and woman.

All of the signs and philosophy of the Great Work are found enclosed within the Twelfth Arcanum. The secret, living and philosophical fire is hidden within the Christonic semen. The mysticism of Sexual Alchemy is the mysticism of all the ancient initiates.

The philosophy of Sexual Alchemy has its principles in the school of the Essenes, in the school of Alexandria, in the teachings of Pythagoras, in the mysteries of Egypt, Troy, Rome, Cartago, Eleusis, in the wisdom of the Aztecs and of the Mayans, etc.

The science of Sexual Alchemy and its procedures must be learned from the books of Paracelsus, Nicholas Flammel, and Raymond Lully. Also, we find the procedures hidden within the veil of all the symbols in the geriatric figures of the old Hieroglyphics of many ancient temples in the Greek myths, Egyptian myths, etc.

You who are searching for initiation, you who read immensely, you who live fluttering from school to school always searching, always longing, always sighing, tell me with sincerity... Did you awaken your Kundalini? Did you open the seven churches of your spinal medulla? Did you incarnate the Lamb? Answer me beloved reader, be sincere with your own self. Put your hand on your heart and answer me with sincerity, are you Self-realized? Are you sure that with your theories you will convert yourself into a God? What have you achieved? What have you received with all your theories?

One who wants to realize the Self needs the revolution of the consciousness: to die, to be born, and to sacrifice oneself. There exists a revolution of the consciousness when we decapitate the ego, the "I." There exists a revolution of the consciousness when we build the Solar Bodies. There exists a revolution of the consciousness when we incarnate the Being. Until that moment, we do not have a real existence.

Arcanum 13
Immortality

IMMORTALITY

Description of the Plate

In this arcanum, the sheaves of wheat and the flowers represent rebirth. The flowers symbolize the beginning of life; the wheat symbolizes the end.

A Hierarch of the law cuts some stalks of wheat that have large and small grains, which are called **Bobbin-Kandelnosts.** They represent the values, the capital, that each human being carries in the three brains (intellectual, motor, emotional).

Whosoever carries small grains lives little, dying within a few days, months, or within the first year of life. One lives by thirds and dies by thirds. Whosoever squanders their intellectual capital falls into insanity, schizophrenia, etc. Whosoever squanders their motor center, or center of movement, ends up paralyzed, deformed, etc. Whosoever squanders their emotional center suffers from illness of the heart.

This arcanum has a physical and internal representation. It is the arcanum of Judas Iscariot, which represents the death of the ego.

The scythe is the funeral symbol of the Angels of Death.

Esoteric Significance of the Arcanum

Indeed, death is the return to the womb. Life and death are two phenomena from the same source.

Death is a subtraction of common fractions. After this mathematical operation, only the values of the consciousness remain. The values of the personality are subtracted; there is no tomorrow for the personality of the dead; it has a beginning and an end. The values of the consciousness are found bottled up within the ego, which when seen clairvoyantly resemble legions of phantoms. This is what continues.

In actuality, the Soul does not return because the individual has not incarnated their Soul yet. Only the values return.

The returning values of the consciousness belong to the mechanics of nature.

The Angel of Death who is in charge of cutting the thread of existence approaches the bed of the one who is in agony when the hour of death arrives. The Angel of Death takes the individual out of the physical body and with the scythe cuts the silver cord (a certain mysterious silver thread that connects the internal bodies with the physical body.) This is done in the precise instant when the last breath is exhaled.

That magnetic cord can contract or extend itself to the infinite. In the moment of awakening from the world of dreams, we can return again to the physical body thanks to that thread.

Those that are in agony see the Angel of Death. When the Angels of Death are at work, they dress themselves with funeral robes and assume a skeletal, spectral appearance as they grasp the scythe with which they cut the silver cord. This gloomy appearance is assumed only when they work. When they are not on duty, they adopt very beautiful features, such as children, women, or as venerable elders. The Angels of Death are never evil or perverse. They always work in accordance with the Great Law. Everyone is born in their hour and dies exactly at their time.

The Angels of Death are very wise and develop and unfold themselves under the ray of Saturn. They not only know everything related with the common and current death of the physical body, but these Ministers of Death are profoundly wise in all that is related with the death of the pluralized "I."

Proserpine, the Queen of Hell, is also Hecate, the blessed Goddess Mother Death, under whose direction the Angels of Death work. The Mother Space converted into the Mother Death loves her sons and daughters in a very odd way, for she takes them away.

The blessed Goddess Mother Death has the power to punish us when we violate the Law, and she has the power to cut our life. It is indubitable that she is a magnificent aspect of our mystical Duad, a splendid form of our own Being. The Angel of Death would not dare to cut the thread of life, the silver cord, the Antakarana, without her consent.

Three human forms go to the grave:

1. The physical corpse

2. The vital body or lingam Sarira

3. The personality

The physical body disintegrates within the sepulchral grave in a gradual process.

The vital body floats before the sepulcher like a fluorescent phantom which is sometimes visible to very psychic people. This vital body slowly disintegrates together with the physical body.

The personality is energetic. The personality takes form during the first seven years of childhood and is strengthened with time and experiences. The personality is created at a particular time. It is born in its time. There is no tomorrow for the personality of the dead. After the death of the physical body, the personality remains within the sepulcher. However, it comes out when someone brings it flowers, when some mourner visits it. The personality goes about the cemetery and returns to its sepulcher. The personality disintegrates slowly in the cemetery.

That which continues, that which is not going to the sepulcher, is the ego, the "itself," the "myself," the "I," a certain collection of devil "I's" that personify our psychological defects.

Therefore, that which continues after death is not something beautiful. That which is not destroyed with the physical body is nothing but a bunch of devils, psychological aggregates, a bunch of defects. The Essence, the psyche, the Buddhata, is the only decent thing that exists in the depth of all of those hellish entities that constitute the ego.

Normally such psychological aggregates are processed in the Astral or Mental Worlds. Rare are the Essences that achieve the emancipation from within such subjective elements in order to enjoy a vacation in the Causal World before returning to this valley of tears. This is only possible with the dissolution of the ego.

Normally, the egos submerge themselves within the mineral kingdom in the Infernal Worlds, or they return, either in an immediate or gradual way, into a new organism.

The ego continues in the seed of our descendants. We incessantly return in order to continuously repeat the same dramas, the same tragedies. We have to emphasize the following statement that not all of the psychic aggregates achieve human return. In reality, many devil "I's" are lost due to the fact that some either submerge themselves into the mineral kingdom, continue reincorporating themselves into animal organisms, or obstinately fasten themselves, adhering to certain places.

Arcanum 14
Temperance

Description of the Plate

In the waters of life we find three flowers. A serpent is climbing the middle one. These three flowers represent:

1. **Sat**, the Innermost, Atman
2. **Chit**, Buddhi, the Spiritual Soul
3. **Ananda**, Superior Manas, the Human Soul

The three flowers also represent:

1. The sacred fire
2. The raw matter
3. The mixture

In the middle of the plate, an Angel shows the triad and the quaternary (the four bodies of sin) on her vesture. On her forehead shines a sun with fourteen rays; seven visible rays and seven invisible rays. The visible rays represent the seven planets and the invisible ones represent the seven chakras.

The Angel has two cups, or jars, with which she mixes two elixirs. One cup is of gold and contains the red elixir. The other is of silver containing the white elixir. Combined they produce the Elixir of Longevity.

Many Masters such as Babaji, Sanat Kumara, Paracelsus, etc., have achieved immortality.

Esoteric Significance of the Arcanum

In the Fourteenth Arcanum appears an Angel with the Sun on her forehead, with a cup in each hand, performing the mixing of the red elixir with the white elixir. The Elixir of Longevity is a result of the mixture of these two. Undoubtedly, this is the elixir that was sought after by so many medieval alchemists. The white elixir is the woman and the red elixir is the man. It is impossible to create the Elixir of Longevity without these two. The woman's elixir emanates from the Moon and the man's elixir from the Sun. This is the significance of the colors of the two elixirs.

When the septenary man is sexually united with the septenary woman, the addition is made that gives us the

Fourteenth Arcanum of the Tarot. Furthermore, it is important to state that both the man and the woman have seven principles. The most important and the fastest center of the human being is the sexual center.

The process of creating a new being is performed within the laws of the musical octaves. The seven notes of the musical scale are the foundation of all creation. If we transmute the creative energy, we initiate a new octave in the Ethereal World. The result is the creation of a vehicle with which we can consciously penetrate all of the departments of the kingdom.

A third octave will permit us to engender the true Astral Body, the Christ Astral. When reaching these heights, the old lunar Astral Body, the phantom, is left reduced to an empty shell which, little by little, will be disintegrated.

A fourth octave permits us to engender a Christ Mind. This vehicle gives us true wisdom and unity of thought. Only one who engenders the Christ Mind has the right to say, "I have a Mental Body." The common current Mental Body is only a phantom shape. This Mental Body really converts itself into an empty shell when the true mind is born. Then, the old one is disintegrated and is reduced to cosmic dust.

In the fifth musical octave, the true Causal Body is engendered. When reaching this height, we incarnate the Soul.

Thus, we can have a real existence. Before this moment, we do not have real existence.

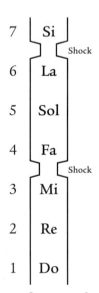

THE LAW OF THE OCTAVE AND THE SOLAR BODIES

The creation of each Solar Body
is one complete octave.

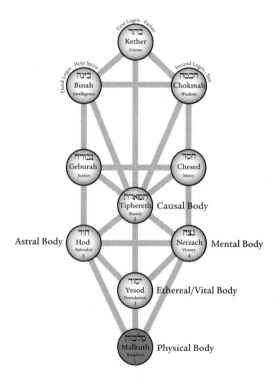

Arcanum 15
Passion

DESCRIPTION OF THE PLATE

In the waters of life (the lower third) is found the representation of Geburah (the law). In the middle of the plate appears Typhon Baphomet, holding in his left hand the staff of command and in his right hand an ascending serpent. His right hand is masculine and his left is feminine. His breasts indicate that he is androgynous. He covers wisdom with his apron and from the same apron a tail results.

His face is deformed due to errors and sins. The Baphomet represents the brass that humanity has actually blackened due to degeneration. We should whiten the brass. We should whiten the devil, who is the psychological trainer and guardian of the doors of the sanctuary, so that only the chosen, those that have passed all the tests imposed by the devil, can enter.

ESOTERIC SIGNIFICANCE OF THE ARCANUM

The Fifteenth Arcanum of the Tarot represents the male goat of Mendes, Lucifer, Typhon Baphomet, the devil.

The Alchemist must steal the fire from the devil. When we work with the Arcanum A.Z.F. we steal fire from the devil and we convert ourselves into Gods. Thus, the five pointed star shines.

The horns end in six points. The Sixth Arcanum is sex, indicating that in sex is either liberation through chastity, or slavery of man through passion.

A difference exists with the First Arcanum. The right hand is above, and the left is towards the earth. The mystery

PASSION

THE BAPHOMET OF MENDES,
DRAWN BY ELIPHAS LEVI

THE SABBATIC GOAT

of Baphomet is Sexual Alchemy, a mystery based on the comprehension of the transmutation of the creative energies. The Baphomet of the Templars must be read backwards, "Tem-o-h-p-ab," which is the symbol of the Latin words, *"Templi ommun hominun pacis abbas."* The meaning of this is, "The Father of the temple of universal peace for men."

The Fifteenth Arcanum appears after the Thirteenth, which is the death of the ego, the "I," the "myself," and after the Fourteenth, which is the card of temperance or chastity that occurs after the death of the ego. The Fifteenth Arcanum is then the Divine Androgyny that once again shines. It is the whitewashed brass.

We know that the interior Divine Logoi is beyond the body, the feelings, and the mind. Unquestionably, that which is the ineffable, that which is the Reality, projects its own reflection, its particular shadow within each one of us, here and now. Obviously, that shadow, that Logoic reflection, is the psychological trainer, Lucifer the tempter. Each one of us has our own particular Lucifer.

In the time of the Pharaohs, in Egypt, the Sun of the middle day, the sacred Absolute Sun, was always symbolised by Osiris, while its shadow, its reflection, its Lucifer, was symbolised by Typhon.

When the neophyte was ready to suffer the ordeals of initiation in the sacred temples of the ancient Egypt of the Pharaohs, the Master approached the novice and murmured this mysterious phrase, *"Remember that Osiris is a black God."*

Evidently, this is the specific color of darkness, of shadows, and of the devil to whom black roses were always offered. Also, it is the color of the primitive Chaos where all the elements and germs of life

Faust confronting his Lucifer, Mephistopheles. From Goethe's *Faust*

are totally mixed and confounded. It is the symbol of the element earth, of the night and of the radical death of all of those psychological aggregates, that in their conjunction constitute the "myself."

We need to whitewash the devil with maximum expedited urgency. This is only possible through fighting against our own selves, by dissolving all those conjunctions of psychological aggregates that constitute the "I," the "myself," the "itself." Only by dying in ourselves can we whitewash the brass and contemplate the Sun of Midnight (the Father). This signifies that we must defeat all temptations and eliminate all of the inhuman elements that we carry within (anger, greed, lust, envy, pride, laziness, gluttony, etc.). A trainer in the psychological gymnasium of human existence is always required. The divine Daimon, quoted many times by Socrates, is the very shadow of our own individual Spirit. He is the most extraordinary psychological trainer that each one of us carries within. He delivers us into temptation with the purpose of training us, teaching us. Only in this way is it possible for the precious gems of virtue to sprout from our psyche.

Now I question myself and I question you. Where is the evil of Lucifer? The results speak for themselves. If there are no temptations there are no virtues. Virtues are more grandiose when temptations are stronger. What is important is not to fall into temptation. That is why we have to pray to our Father, saying, *"Lead us not into temptation."*

Only through the struggle, the contrast, the temptation, and rigorous esoteric discipline, can the flowers of virtue sprout from us.

Lucifer as Ayo, teacher, mentor, certainly is exceptional, unusual, and extraordinary. There exists in the Luciferic temptation an unparalleled didactic, a portentous pedagogy, an astonished attraction, an unmistakable incentive, an occult instigation with secret divine propositions, seduction, fascination... Lucifer-Prometheus is one with the Platonic Logos. He is the minister of the creative Demiurge and the resplendent lord of Sabbath, the seven mansions of Hades (Infernos), and of the manifested world. Lucifer is he who bears the sword and the scale of cosmic justice, because to him is undoubtedly committed the norm of the weight and measure and number. He is Horus, Brahma, Ahura-Mazda, etc., always ineffable.

Lucifer (*luci* = light, *fer* = fire) is the Guardian of the Door, who alone is entrusted with the keys of the lumisial that no one enter therein, save the anointed ones having the secret of Hermes...

Those that dare to curse Lucifer pronounce themselves against the cosmic reflection of the Logos. They anathematize the living manifested God in matter and abhor the ever-incomprehensible wisdom when rebelling against the contraries of light and darkness, against countenance, resemblance, similitude, sun and shadow, day and night, the law of the contraries...

The devil, the reflection of our interior Logoi, was the most sublime creature before we fell into animal generation. All of the Masters of the Hermetic art repeat unto us, *"Whitewash the brass and burn your books."*

One who whitewashes the devil, turning it into its resplendent and primogenitary state, one who dies in oneself, here and now, liberates the chained Prometheus. Thus, Prometheus pays the individual with abundance because he is a colossus with power over the Heavens, the Earth, and the Infernos.

Lucifer-Prometheus, radically integrated with all of the parts of our Being, makes of us something distinct, a different and exotic creature, an Archangel, a terrific and divine power.

Arcanum 16
Fragility

FRAGILITY

DESCRIPTION OF THE PLATE

In the waters of life is the staff of power, the staff of command, and the flail (whip) which represents fragility. The two serpents, the positive and the negative, are on both sides of these symbols.

From the superior part descends the ray of cosmic justice destroying the tower that the Kabbalists call the Tower of Babel. Two personages are precipitated to the bottom of the abyss, one to the right and the other to the left. They fall forming the sign of the inverted flaming star, with their arms, legs and heads hastening downwards, symbolizing the fall of the Bodhisattvas. The fall is the outcome of sex, the outcome of spilling the glass of Hermes.

One must distinguish between a **fall** and a **descent**. The initiate descends to the Ninth Sphere during the work in the Forge to destroy his defects in the inferior regions to then ascend to the Heavens. One wins a Heaven after having worked through a hell. The initiate falls when the semen is spilled.

ESOTERIC SIGNIFICANCE OF THE ARCANUM

The Sixteenth Arcanum is the arcanum of the Fulminated Tower. This is the Tower of Babel.

Many are the initiates that let themselves fall. Many are the fulminated towers. Every initiate that spills the glass of Hermes inevitably falls.

The legend of the fallen angels has been, and will be, eternally repeated.

Actually, there are many fallen Gods living in the world. These Gods are now disguised with human bodies.

It is necessary to awaken the consciousness in order not to fall into the abyss of perdition. Actually, many chiefs of esoteric groups have their consciousness profoundly asleep (blind guides of blind men will all fall into the abyss). This is the law. All human beings live absolutely asleep. It is necessary to awaken conscious-

THE TOWER OF BABEL

ness in order to not walk blindly. The blind can fall into the abyss. The Sixteenth Arcanum is very dangerous.

All of those students that practice esoteric exercises without working in the Arcanum A.Z.F. are similar to the man who is foolish enough to build his house on sand. His house will fall with a great crash to the abyss. We must build upon the living rock. This rock is sex. Those who develop the chakras, having their lunar internal bodies, will fall into the abyss. Their temples will be the fulminated tower. Those who engender the Christic bodies with the Arcanum A.Z.F. and work in the development of the chakras will be converted into living Christs.

Arcanum 17
Hope

HOPE

DESCRIPTION OF THE PLATE

In the waters of life are two triangles, the positive and the negative. In the middle of the plate is a woman sprinkling the earth with two elixirs (masculine and feminine). On her head is the lotus flower, indicating her developed chakras.

In the superior part shines the star of Venus with its eight rays, symbolizing that the Initiations of Light come after the Initiations of Fire.

ESOTERIC SIGNIFICANCE OF THE ARCANUM

The hieroglyph of the Seventeenth Arcanum is a radiant star and eternal youth. In this arcanum a naked woman appears who sprinkles over the earth the sap of universal life, a sap which comes from the two glasses, a glass of gold and the other of silver.

If we carefully study the esoteric content of this arcanum, we discover perfect Alchemy. We need to work with the gold and with the silver, with the sun and with the moon, in order to incarnate the star of eight points, the star of dawn.

Really, the star of eight points is Venus. One who reaches the Venustic Initiation has the joy of incarnating the Dragon of Wisdom (the internal Christ).

One has to work with the fire and the water in order to receive the Venustic Initiation. The star crucified on the cross is the Christ of the Abraxas, the Son of Man, the incarnated Verb.

Venus, the star of dawn, is documented in the Apocalypse of Saint John, *"And he that overcometh... I will give him the morning star."* [Revelation 2:26-28] *"I Jesus have sent mine Angel to testify unto you these things in the churches. I am the root and the offspring of David, and the bright and morning star."* [Revelation 22:16]

Christ is the star of dawn. Christ enters into the Soul when one receives the Venustic Initiation.

When we decapitate and dissolve the "I," the "myself," then we receive the Venustic Initiation. One who receives it incarnates the star.

The star is the Son of Man, the Truth. No one can search for the Truth. The Truth cannot be known by the "I." No one can search for that which one does not know. Satan, the "I," the ego that we carry within, cannot know the Truth. The Truth cannot be studied, read, or known by the mind. The Truth is absolutely distinct to all of that which can be read, studied, or known by the mind. The Truth comes unto us when we have decapitated and dissolved the "I."

The distinct truths of the people are nothing but projections of the mind. You should decapitate your own "I," dissolve it with rigorous purifications. Thus, you will reach the Venustic Initiation. Then, you will incarnate the Truth. The Verb will make flesh in you. You will incarnate the Son of Man and you will receive the star of dawn.

Everyone that wants to incarnate the Star has to work with the sap of life contained in the two sacred glasses that the naked woman in the Seventeenth Arcanum has within her hands.

The star that guides us internally is the Father Star. What is important for us is to incarnate that Father Star. Behold here the mystery of the Seventeenth Arcanum. The sap contained in the glasses of gold and silver, when combined and transmuted wisely, permit us to reach the incarnation of the star. The crucified star on the cross is the Christ.

The final plate of the wordless alchemical treatise "Mutus Liber" (Mute Book) representing the goal of alchemy: reunion with the Divine Spirit. Heracles (the prone figure at bottom) incarnates in the initiate who enters the Straight Path and subsequently receives the Venustic Initiation. The Christ inside the Human Soul must labor and sacrifice. Here he is psychologically dead after completing his work. The result is the Perfected Stone, the square formed by the union of the man and woman and the Father above. The man and woman have achieved equilibrium (the Sun and Moon have switched places between them). From their mouths come the words Oculatis Abis: "Thou departest seeing." The work is finished: the ladder to Heaven (in the back) is set aside. The Father receives His Glory in Heaven as He crowned by the Cherubim and is illuminated by the light of the Christ (the Sun), with whom He is now One. On either side of the image are the two olive branches tied to the wings of the spirit, a variation on the Caduceus of Mercury. MUTUS LIBER, 1677.

Arcanum 18
Twilight

TWILIGHT

DESCRIPTION OF THE PLATE

A scorpion within an inverted triangle is in the waters of life. It signifies that we kill the Divine Mother like a scorpion when we spill the glass of Hermes.

In the middle of the plate are two pyramids, one white and the other black, symbolizing the positive and the negative forces. Two dogs, or wolves, one white and the other black, bark at the moon. The white is positive and symbolizes friendship, the black is negative and symbolizes the psychological "I." They represent the terrible struggle that occurs between the tenebrous forces. The moon by itself represents sex. We should work with the moon to convert it into a sun. The dog also represents the sexual instinct. That is why it is the dog that takes us through the very doors of the Absolute.

ESOTERIC SIGNIFICANCE OF THE ARCANUM

It is necessary to study, to analyze, and to reflect profoundly on the esoteric content of this arcanum.

The Eighteenth Arcanum is light and darkness, white magic and black magic. This is found represented in the white dog and the black dog, the white pyramid and the black pyramid.

By Kabbalistically adding the Eighteenth Arcanum, we find 1 + 8 = 9, the Ninth Sphere, sex. We have already stated that within our planetary organism there are nine interior layers. These are the nine cellars of occult Masonry.

The ninth cellar corresponds to the nucleus of the planetary organism. There, we find the sepulcher of Hiram Abiff or Chiram Osiris, who is the Intimate Christ of each one of us, of every person that comes to this world. It is an error to believe, or to suppose, that the Christ is only Jeshua ben Pandira, which is the name of Jesus the Christ. We do not deny that he is the living incarnation of the Verb, the Logos.

All of us need to resurrect this intimate Christ, and in order to achieve this, it is obvious that we have to descend to the Ninth Sphere, sex. That is why Hiram Abiff is in the ninth circle in the ninth cellar.

All of us are children of sex. That is why in *The Divine Comedy* the condemned ones are seen in the ninth circle with the water reaching their creative organs. They cry and their tears freeze in their eyes because it is a valley of tears and afflictions. The fact that the waters reach up to the creative organs is due to the fact that these are the spermatic waters. We are born crying and we die crying.

If we add 9 + 9 = 18, we then find that in the Eighteenth Arcanum the number nine is found twice. Within these two nines there is a balance. One nine is the positive aspect and the other is the negative aspect. But the number eighteen results negatively and fatally within itself, representing the secret enemies that are in the Arcanum of Twilight. This is because in the work of the Ninth Sphere, one has to fight immensely, because one has to learn how to sublimate the sexual energy. The clue or key to all of the empires is here.

In the Eighteenth Arcanum, the Ninth Sphere is repeated twice. We already know that the number one is positive and the number two is negative. Thus, if we repeat the Ninth Sphere for the first time and then for the second time, we will have sex in its two aspects, positive and negative. Now you can comprehend why the Eighteenth Arcanum is light and darkness, white magic and black magic. In the Eighteenth Arcanum we find the secret enemies of initiation.

Now we are going to study the symbolism of the dog. The dog participates in magic. It is a generous animal that in the ancient times was always consecrated to the God Mercury. The dog of Mercury is strictly symbolic because it clearly allegorizes the sexual power. Therefore, the high honor that the Hierophants of ancient Egypt granted to the dog is obvious.

The sexual fire, the dog, the erotic instinct, is that extraordinary and marvellous agent that can radically transform us.

The dog Cerberus is in the Infernal Worlds, and we must take him out from there. We have to steal him from the Infernos. This signifies the liberation of the sexual force.

To take Cerberus from the abode of Pluto is urgent. Cerberus, the wondrous terror, with his bark and with his three enormous flat-muzzled heads (which have necks surrounded by serpents), happily lives there. He barks at all of the dead and fills them with fear.

The dog and the swan that fly upon the waters of life are the same as the dog and the Egyptian ibis, the force of the Holy Spirit, the sexual force. All of this is the glass of Hermes that must be elevated very high.

In the archaic doctrine, in occult wisdom, the guide dog is spoken of. It is a dog that conduces the initiates to the sanctum regnum.

There are occasions when the initiates forget their dog and believe that without it they can continue on the path, but this is not so. Sooner or later, when they feel themselves stagnant, they have nothing more to do but to grasp onto the dog. When we are stagnant, the dog is the one that teaches us the path. One has to take it out from the abyss. We must not forget that the Cerberus-Tricipite pulls the cart of its owner, taking the owner along on the craggy path that leads to the Final Liberation.

Heracles took the dog out of the abyss in order for it to serve him as a guide. We have to do the same thing when we achieve chastity. Then, by working in the forge of the Cyclops by practising Sexual Magic, by transmuting our creative energies, we advance on the path of the razor's edge until we reach Liberation.

Woe to the initiates that abandon their dog. They will go astray from the path and will fall into the abyss of perdition. Unfortunately, the intellectual animal that is incorrectly called a human being, has not achieved chastity, meaning Cerberus has not been taken out of the infernal dominions.

Now you will understand for yourselves why the dead suffer in the Plutonian abysses when they listen to the bark of Cerberus, the dog of the three hungry jaws.

Let us never forget that Cerberus, the guardian dog of the Infernos, caressed those that entered, and without pity, devoured those that tried to leave.

It is obvious that the lost ones suffer with the insatiable thirst of lust in the frightful Tartarus.

We have to win very bloody battles against the tenebrous ones in the Eighteenth Arcanum. Heaven is taken by force; the courageous one has taken it. In the Internal Worlds the tenebrous ones of the Eighteenth Arcanum violently assault the student.

This path is full of dangers from within and from without. Many are those who begin, few are those who arrive at the end. The majority shift direction towards the

The Twelfth Labor of Heracles is the capture of the three-headed dog Cerberus.

black path. In the Eighteenth Arcanum, there exist very subtle dangers that the student ignores.

The number nine is simultaneously positive and negative. This is the mystery of the Eighteenth Arcanum. In this disturbing arcanum we find all of the potions and witchcraft of Thessalia. The books of the grimoires are full of tenebrous recipes which are very proper to the Eighteenth Arcanum, such as erotic magical ceremonies, rites in order to be loved, dangerous potions, etc... All of this is the Eighteenth Arcanum. We must warn the Gnostic students that **the most dangerous potion that the tenebrous ones use in order to take the student out of the path of the razor's edge is the intellect.** They use it in order to invite us to ejaculate the seminal liquid, or in order to shift the direction of our path by showing us other schools, theories, sex, etc., etc...

We have to remember that mislead men worshipped the great Beast saying, *Who is like unto the Beast? Who is able to make war with him?* - Revelation 13:4

> *Here is wisdom. Let him that hath understanding count the numbers of the Beast for it is the number of a man; and his number is six hundred and three score and six.* - Revelation 13:18

The mark of the Beast is the pair of horns on the forehead. Millions and millions of "human beings" already have the mark of the Beast on their foreheads and on their hands.

Almost all of the "human" population of this valley of tears have the mark of the Beast already on their foreheads and on their hands. All of these Souls are lost. Since 1950, they have been entering into the abyss. The human population has totally failed.

The number of the great Beast is 666. This is the number of man because this number is Kabbalistically decomposed as follows 6 + 6 + 6 = 18. By adding this total together, the result is 1 + 8 = 9, sex. Nine is man because man is the son of sex.

Finally, in the 666, the Eighteenth and Ninth Arcanum are contained. The Eighteenth Arcanum is the abyss, darkness, and sexual temptations which the initiate has to fight against. The Ninth Arcanum is the Ninth Sphere, initiation.

The Gods judged the Great Harlot whose number is 666. The sentence of the Gods was:

To the abyss!
To the abyss!
To the abyss!

Arcanum 19
Inspiration

INSPIRATION

DESCRIPTION OF THE PLATE

The three flowers in the waters of life represent the three primary forces.

In the middle is a couple holding hands forming the key of Tao.

In the superior part, a radiant sun with seven rays is over their heads which reminds us of the seven degrees of power of the Fire.

This arcanum teaches us that we attain the Final Liberation through transmutation.

ESOTERIC SIGNIFICANCE OF THE ARCANUM

The Nineteenth Arcanum is the arcanum of the Alliance and represents the creative fire, the Philosophical Stone.

In order to perform the Great Work we need to work with the Philosophical Stone.

The ancients worshipped the sun under the symbolic figure of a black stone. This is the Heliogabalus stone. This is the stone that we must put in the foundation of our temple. This stone is sex, which is represented by the Philosophical Stone, by the Heliogabalus Stone.

The Elixir of Longevity cannot be attained without this Stone. The two columns of the temple, Jachin and Boaz, are the Alliance of man and woman in order to work with the Philosophical Stone. One who finds the Philosophical Stone transforms into a God.

Those that build upon the Living Stone will incarnate the Verb. Those that build upon the sand will fail and their buildings will crumble into the abyss. The sand is the theories, the dead religions, etc...

The Nineteenth Arcanum of the Tarot is the arcanum of the work of the sun. The man and the woman are holding hands and the sun is shining upon them. This indicates to us that this arcanum is related to the mystery of the Fire. The sexual aspect of this arcanum is found in the Kabbalistic addition of 1 + 9 = 10. The number ten is a profoundly sexual number. Here are the circle and the line, the mysteries of lingam-yoni. Only by sexual transmutation is it possible to reach realization of the Self. This is the sacred Alliance between man and woman in order to perform the Magnus Opus.

When meditating on the Saints of the medieval epoch I can prove to myself that these Saints, even when they were celibate, had been working in the Ninth Sphere in other lives. They had developed the sacred fire through the Sahaja Maithuna.

By analyzing the life of Saint Philip, we find that while feeling love for the divine he fell to the floor. When he rose up from the floor, he touched his thorax with his hand and discovered a bulge had formed there. He was examined and it was verified that a bulge had formed over his heart. He had felt that the sacred fire of the Holy Spirit was consuming him. After his death, it was discovered that the artery that goes from the heart to the lungs had a great thickness. However, he lived until an elderly age and could even predict the hour that he was going to die. There is no doubt that he had the sacred fire within because of the practice of the Maithuna in previous lives.

Catalina of Bourbon was an extraordinary mystic. She manifested this extraordinary mysticism when she was alive. When she died, they buried her without a box, and when people passed close by her tomb they noticed that a very delightful fragrance or perfume was coming from it. Many sick people were healed by this perfume. Then the priests decided to take her out in order to give her a proper burial. After many months, her body was undecayed and had a very delightful fragrance. She was placed on exhibition with the corpse having only had a short bleeding haemorrhage through the nose. She was sweating and exhaling perfume. She was seated on a chair in a chapel in Italy when she opened her eyes and remained with her body undecomposed.

The Tao says that one of the tests in order to prove that somebody has reached intimate realization of the Self, of the Being, is when one can preserve the physical body without decay and have it exhale perfume.

When the Akash, the *causa causorum* of the ether and basic principle of the Tattvas, is concentrated in the sexual organs, then this becomes the psychic foundation of the blood, and the pure Akash becomes the food of mystic persons. They take such substances into the blood and can live without eating. There are initiates that can live naked in the snow without eating. In order to reach this, we need very extraordinary concentration.

Catalina from Sena felt herself in the Christ, feeding herself from his blood. The relationship of the Akash with the blood and the blood with the Akash is tremendous.

The mystics were concentrated in the blood of Christ and they attracted all of the pure Akash. In order to do this, tremendous concentration is needed, as well as the transformation of the energies.

In the gallant epoch of the Renaissance, a time of wigs, crinolines, purple cassocks, beautiful dances, and beautiful wagons, men knew how to appreciate a woman and sacrificed themselves for her. A man was capable of any sacrifice for his lady. He knew how to appreciate her and did not even hesitate to deliver his own life for her. There is no doubt that sometimes these customs were abused, but in this epoch, the man knew how to see all of his ideals in the woman.

In the twentieth century, man has forgotten the sexual mysteries. The male has lost the sense of moral value. Humanity is in decay.

The animated Essence is spread within all of the entities of the ego. When the ego is dissolved, the Seminal Pearl is formed. When the ego is destroyed, the Auric Embryo is formed; then the immortal principles enter into the initiate; however, the whole matter is sexual. Premonitions about what the creative energy is, was greatly felt in other times.

Actually, the human being is nothing but a legion of devils, full of inner contradictions. The unique value that we have within is the Essence which is spread within the "I's."

Arcanum 20
Resurrection

RESURRECTION

DESCRIPTION OF THE PLATE

In the waters of life is a column which is a symbol of edification. The foundation of the column is the Cubic Stone. From the two columns, the white and the black, only the white, which is the symbol of purification, has remained.

In the middle of the plate is a mummy. From it escapes a sparrow hawk with a human head which flies toward the world of the Spirit. It represents the Soul. It is indubitable that upon awakening the consciousness we transform ourselves into sparrow hawks with human heads, being able to fly freely throughout the starry space. On top of the heads of the sparrow hawk and the mummy is a symbol which represents the pineal gland, a sign of illumination.

The Soul of any Egyptian Hierophant has four bodies:

1. The mummy
2. The **Ka** (Astral Body)
3. The **Ba** (Mental Body)
4. The **Ku** (Causal Body)

Woe unto those who, after having attained the Second Birth, continue with the ego alive.

They shall in fact convert themselves into **Hanasmussen** (abortions of the Divine Mother Kundalini) with a double center of gravity.

ESOTERIC SIGNIFICANCE OF THE ARCANUM

The Twentieth Arcanum is the Resurrection. In order for

Resurrection to be achieved, death needs to be previously achieved. Without death, there is no Resurrection.

How beautiful it is to die from instant to instant! The new comes only with death.

If it is true that we want individualization for ourselves, then we need to die from moment to moment. The pluralized "I" excludes any individualization. There cannot be any individualization of any type when the multiple entities (I's) exist.

These "I's" fight amongst themselves and originate a variety of psychological contradictions within us.

When Seth (the ego) dies in an integral way, only the Being remains within us. The Being is that which gives us authentic individuality.

When Seth is disintegrated in a total form, then the consciousness, the Soul, is liberated; it awakens radically, and the interior illumination comes.

Indeed, the resurrection of the Soul is only possible through the cosmic initiation. Human beings are dead and can only resurrect through the initiation. Let us remember the words of Jesus the great Kabir, *"Let the dead bury their dead."* [Matthew 8:22] *"God is not the God of the dead, but of the living."* [Matthew 22:32]

In the same way that three basic types of energies exist (masculine, feminine, and neutral), three types of resurrection exist as well:

1. Spiritual resurrection
2. Resurrection with the body of liberation
3. Resurrection with the physical body

No one can pass the second or third type of resurrection without having first passed the spiritual resurrection.

1. **Spiritual Resurrection:** This is achieved through initiation. First, we must spiritually resurrect in the Fire, and then in the Light; meaning first we must raise up the Seven Serpents of Fire and then the Seven Serpents of Light, reaching the Venustic Initiation and Spiritual Resurrection.

2. **Resurrection with the Body of Liberation:** This is performed in the Superior Worlds. This body is organized with the best atoms of the physical body. It is a body of flesh that does not come from Adam. It is a body of indescribable beauty. With this body of Paradise, Adepts can enter into the physical world and work in it by making themselves visible and tangible at will.

3. **Resurrection with the physical body:** The initiate comes with the Astral Body, on the third day after the death of his physical body. In front of his holy sepulcher, accompanied by the divine hierarchies, the initiate invokes his physical body. With the help of the divine hierarchies, the physical body rises up, penetrating into hyperspace.

This is how an initiate escapes from the grave. In the suprasensible worlds, in hyperspace, holy women treat the body of the initiate with perfumes and aromatic ointments. Then, by obeying superior orders, the physical body penetrates within the Astral Body through the top of the head. This is how the Master once again possesses his physical body. This is the gift of Cupid. After the resurrection, the Master does not die again. He is eternal. With this immortal body, he can appear and disappear instantaneously. Masters can make themselves visible in the physical world at will.

Jesus the Christ is a Resurrected Master who for three days had his physical body in the Holy sepulcher. After the resurrection, Jesus appeared before the disciples who were on their way to the village of Emmaus and dined with them. After this, he was before the unbelieving Thomas, who only believed when he put his fingers in the wounds of the holy body of the great Master.

Hermes, Cagliostro, Paracelsus, Nicholas Flamel, Quetzalcoatl, St. Germain, Babaji, etc. preserved their physical body thousands and even millions of years ago without death harming them. They are Resurrected Masters.

Only with the Arcanum A.Z.F. can the Elixir of Longevity be elaborated.

Resurrection is impossible without the Elixir of Longevity.

Arcanum 21
Transmutation

DESCRIPTION OF THE PLATE

In the superior part we find the black moon and the white moon, the antitheses.

In the middle of the plate is a magician with the staff of the patriarchs in one hand and the Ankh cross, or Tao cross, in the other hand. He is standing on a crocodile that is waiting to devour him with its open jaws.

The crocodile is Seth, Satan, the psychological "I," the "myself," who is always waiting for those who let themselves fall in order to devour them. The magician courageously holds the Tao cross (the Arcanum A.Z.F.) to defend himself.

The magician is covered with a tiger's skin. Undoubtedly, the dog and the tiger are esoterically associated with the same work of mystical death.

The dog is the sexual fire, the erotic instinct, found in the very root of our seminal system. The tiger is different, and this is known by "the Knights of the Tiger," those jaguars that struggle against the ego, who like authentic felines of revolutionary psychology, have launched themselves against their own selves, against their own psychological defects.

The sagaciousness and fearlessness of the tiger are really necessary to kill the human personality and to cause the Dragon of Wisdom of the Seven Serpents (symbols of the decapitated) to shine in him.

TRANSMUTATION

AZTEC JAGUAR WARRIOR CONQUERING THE EGO. FROM THE *CODEX MENDOZA*.

Esoteric Significance of the Arcanum

The Twenty-first Arcanum has been confused with the Twenty-second Arcanum, which is the Crown of Life. The Twenty-first Arcanum is the Fool of the Tarot, or Transmutation. The Kabbalistic addition of twenty-one gives us 2 + 1 = 3. In this Twenty-first Arcanum, the initiate has to fight against the three traitors of Hiram Abiff: the demon of desire, the demon of the mind and the demon of evil will.

The danger of being a demon is never so close as when one is very close to being an Angel.

Any initiate that lets himself fall is really the Fool of the Tarot. When the Alchemist spills the glass of Hermes, he converts himself into the Fool of the Tarot, "foolishness."

It is necessary to annihilate desire if we want to avoid the danger of falling.

One who wants to annihilate desire must discover the causes of it. The causes of desire are found in sensations. We live in a world of sensations, and we need to comprehend them. There are five types of sensations:

1. Visual sensations
2. Hearing sensations
3. Olfactory sensations
4. Taste sensations
5. Tactile sensations

The five special types of sensations transform themselves into desire. We must not condemn the sensations; we must not justify them. We need to profoundly comprehend them.

Only by comprehending sensations do we kill desire. Only through annihilating desire is the mind liberated, a mind that is normally found bottled up within the bottle of desire. The awakening of the consciousness occurs when the mind is liberated. If we want to exterminate the causes of desire, we need to live in a state of constant awareness. It is urgent to live in the state of alert perception and alert novelty. The ego is a big book, a book of many volumes. We can study this book only through the technique of internal meditation.

Arcanum 22
The Return

THE RETURN

DESCRIPTION OF THE PLATE

In the waters of life is the swastika cross symbolizing the Muladhara chakra of four petals.

A woman, who represents the truth, plays a harp, plucking the sexual lyre of nine chords until she finds the key note. In the superior part of the plate are the four Gods of Death—Mestha, Hapi, Duamutef, and Kebhsennuf—who represent the four elements—earth, fire, water, and air—and the four mysterious animals of Sexual Alchemy.

Above the four Gods of Death we find the sacred serpent that illuminates the sphere of Ra, the serpent that was granted to the Osirian adept, the Son of the Light.

ESOTERIC SIGNIFICANCE OF THE ARCANUM

The Twenty-second Arcanum is the Crown of Life, the return to the light, the incarnation of the truth in us.

Beloved disciples, you need to develop each of the twenty-two major arcana of the Tarot within yourselves. You are **imitatus**, or rather, one who others have put on the path of the razor's edge. Exert yourself to become **Adeptus**, one who is the product of one's own deeds, the one that conquers science on their own, the child of one's own work.

One must conquer the degree of Adeptus by departing from the animal state and by acquiring consciousness.

Gnosis teaches three steps through which every one who works in the flaming forge of Vulcan has to pass. These are:

1. Purification
2. Illumination
3. Perfection

It happens that curious people who enter into our Gnostic studies want immediate illumination, astral projection, clairvoyance, practical magic, etc., and when they do not achieve this, they leave immediately.

No one can achieve illumination without having been previously purified. Only those that have achieved purification and sanctity can enter into the hall of illumination. There are also many students that enter into our studies just for pure curiosity. They want to be wise immediately. Paul of Tarsus said, *"We speak wisdom among them that are perfect."* [1 Corinthians 2:6] Only those who achieve the third step are perfect. Only among them can divine wisdom be spoken of.

In the ancient Egypt of the Pharaohs, among the occult Masons, the three steps of the path were:

1. Apprentice

2. Companion

3. Master

The candidate would remain in the degree of Apprentice for seven years and sometimes even more. Only when the Hierophants were completely sure of the purification and sanctity of the candidate could he or she then pass to the second step.

Really, only after seven years of being an Apprentice does illumination commence.

The Crown of Life is our resplendent Dragon of Wisdom, our internal Christ.

The Holy Trinity emanates from the Ain Soph, the interior Atomic Star that always smiles upon us.

1 (Monad) + 3 (Trinity) = 4 (Tetragrammaton)

The Twenty-second Arcanum when added Kabbalistically gives us:

2 + 2 = 4 (Tetragrammaton)

The result is the Holy Four, the mysterious Tetragrammaton; יהוה Iod Hei Vav Hei; man, woman, fire, and water; man, woman, phallus, and uterus. Now we comprehend why the Twenty-second Arcanum is the Crown of Life.

The Apocalypse says, *"Fear not of those things which thou shalt suffer. Behold the devil shall cast some of you into prison, that ye shall have tribulation ten days. Be thou faithful unto death and I will give thee a Crown of Life."* [Revelation 2:10]

The prison that is mentioned is the prison of pain. The ten days are the tribulations that occur while one is submitted to the wheel of return and karma.

One who receives the Crown of Life is liberated from the wheel of return, recurrence, and karma.

The Crown of Life is the three-unity. It has three aspects:

1. The Elder of the Days

2. The Adorable Son

3. The very wise Holy Spirit

The Crown of Life is the Sun-Man, the Sun-King, so worshipped by the emperor Julian. The Crown of Life is our incessant eternal Breath, profoundly unknowable to Himself, the particular ray of each human being, the Christ. The Crown of Life is

Kether, Chokmah, Binah (Father, Son, and Holy Spirit).

The one who is faithful until death will receive the Crown of Life.

In the banquet of the Lamb, the faces of all of the Holy Ones that have incarnated Him shine as suns of love. The immaculate white tablecloth is dyed with the royal blood of the immolated Lamb. *He that hath an ear let him hear what the Spirit saith unto the churches. He that overcometh shall not be hurt of the Second Death.* [Revelation 2:11]

The one who will not overcome shall divorce from the Beloved One and will sink into the abyss. Those who will enter into the abyss will pass through the Second Death. The demons of the abyss are being disintegrated slowly through many eternities. Those Souls are lost. One who overcomes will not receive harm from the Second Death.

When we receive the Crown of Life, the Verb is made flesh within each one of us.

Every Saint that reaches the Venustic Initiation receives the Crown of Life.

Our very beloved savior Jesus Christ reached the Venustic Initiation in the river Jordan.

And the Word was made flesh, and dwelt among us, (and we beheld his glory, the glory as of the only begotten of the Father) full of grace and truth. - John 1:14

And the light came into the darkness and the darkness comprehended it not. - John 3:19

He is the savior because he brought unto us the Crown of Life and he gave his blood for us. We need to reach the supreme annihilation of the "I" in order to receive the Crown of Life.

We need to resurrect the Lamb within ourselves.

We need the Easter Resurrection.

Second Part

Initiation Through the Arcana of the Tarot

"If the Logos surged from within the Unknowable Divine, the Devil gave Him liberty to do it." - Samael Aun Weor

Pater Noster
The Lord's Prayer

Our Father, who art in Heaven,
hallowed be thy name.

Thy Kingdom come, Thy will be done,
on earth as it is in Heaven.

Give us this day our daily bread.

And forgive our trespasses,
as we forgive those who trespass against us.

And lead us not into temptation,
but deliver us from evil.

For thine is the Kingdom,
and the Power,
and the Glory,
Forever and ever.

Amen.

Chapter XXIII
Arcanum 1

The First Arcanum is the Magician of the Kabbalah. It is obvious that this arcanum represents that which begins. In practical life, anything that begins is the First Arcanum. It is the unity.

It is easy to comprehend that there is difficulty in everything that begins, which is why it is necessary to work very hard in the beginning. In order to harvest, we need to plant. This is why in the First Arcanum we find the unity of the original principle. The origin of every unity comes from the First Arcanum because it is clear that everything begins with the number one.

The unity becomes the origin of duality, or of the binary (1 + 1 = 2). Subsequently, in this unity is found the performing synthesis of the ternary. The unity, the number one, is the divine Monad, the First Logos. It is the Father who is in secret. Each one of us has our own individual Monad. Madame Blavatsky stated that "there are as many Fathers in heaven as there are human beings on earth."

The Father in his turn or by his own will unfolds into the Divine Mother; thus, He and She become Brahma because She becomes the feminine aspect of Him. Therefore, here we can see how the unity is the root of the binary, because the latter cannot exist without the unity. The Divine Mother would not exist if the Monad did not exist. So, the Monad is the root of the duality. There are as many Mothers in heaven as there are human beings on earth. Each one of us has his own interior God or her own particular heavenly Father

and Mother. By clarifying this it becomes clearer why the unity is the performing synthesis of the ternary, and also why and how this is performed.

When Jesus prayed, he prayed to the Father who is in secret, and he left us The Lord's Prayer, an absolutely magical prayer. It takes a couple of hours to properly pray The Lord's Prayer because each supplication that one makes to the Father is absolutely magical. People make the mistake of praying The Lord's Prayer in a mechanical way which brings no results. One must disassemble this prayer and analyze it; thus, in order to perform this, the relaxation of the body is indispensable, not a single muscle should have any tension. Afterwards, one concentrates in order to combine prayer with meditation.

People imagine that our Father who is in Heaven is a Lord who is seated there. Yet, if we profoundly reflect on this, we discover the Monad, the number one, the origin of all of the other unities or Monads. It is clear that the Monad needs something in life in order to Self-realize. What is it that the Monad needs? We find the answer in the light of Sanskrit. It needs "Vajrasattva," which means "a Diamond Soul." This is a Soul that has no "I," that has eliminated all of the subjective elements of perception; these subjective elements are the "I's" and the three traitors of Hiram Abiff, or in other words, Judas, the demon of desire, who is mistakenly confused with the Astral Body; Pilate, the demon of the mind, who is confused with the Mental Body; and Caiaphas, the demon of Evil Will. Why is it that pseudo-esoteric schools ignore all of this?

The subjective elements of perception are the aggregates, the distinct compounds of the human being, or the distinct red demons that constitute the "I's."

In psychology, the subjective elements of perception are defined as all of the psychological processes of the human entity. These are defined as psychological processes of the unconsciousness, subconsciousness, preconsciousness, infraconsciousness, and everything which is of a metaphysical type.

What do modern psychologists understand as "objective?" They understand it to be that which is external to the mind: the physical, the tangible, the material.

Yet, they are totally mistaken, because when analysing the term "subjective," we see that it signifies "sub, under," that which is below the range of our perceptions. What is below our perceptions? Is it not perhaps the Infernal Worlds? Is it not perhaps subjective that which is in the physical or beneath the physical? So, what is truly subjective is what is below the limits of our perceptions.

Psychologists do not know how to use these terms correctly.

Objective: the light, the resplendence; it is that which contains the truth, clarity, lucidity.

Subjective: the darkness, the tenebrous. The subjective elements of perception are the outcome of seeing, hearing, touching, smelling, and tasting. All of these are perceptions of what we see in the third dimension. For example, in one cube we see only length, width, and height. We do not see the fourth dimension because we are bottled up within the ego. The

OSIRIS, HORUS, AND ISIS

subjective elements of perception are constituted by the ego with all of its "I's."

The unity, the Father, unfolds himself into the Mother. The Mother in her turn unfolds herself by giving origin to the Son that she carries in her womb.

Osiris: The Father

Isis: The Mother

Horus: The Divine Spirit, the Innermost of each Being

The unity is the performing synthesis of the ternary.

In the Egyptian *Book of the Dead* it is stated that Ra delivered Horus (the child that the Divine Mother carries in her arms) unto the region of "Buto." This is the region of pure Spirit, meaning the region of Atman-Buddhi-Manas.

Seth transformed himself into a black boar that hurt the "Eye of Horus." Horus complained before Ra. "I will heal you," said Ra unto Him, and in order to console Him, Ra gave unto Horus the region of Buto. This is clarified in the following way: one has to kill the black boar. Only thus is the "Eye of Horus" restored, meaning clairvoyance is restored.

Horus can exterminate the black boar but He cannot do it alone; He has to ask the Divine Mother for help. Horus triumphs by eliminating the black boar, and the Essence that was bottled up is now liberated, fusing itself with Horus, with the Diamond Soul; thus, the latter is united with its Father and Mother, and they are three flames that come to form one single flame: a Self-realized flame. The Essence is an unfoldment of Horus. Therefore, it is necessary to ask Horus to fortify our three brains. Horus is being fortified while the ego is dying. That is why it is necessary to ask him to fortify our three brains.

When Horus swallows the Essence, he then needs the Solar Bodies, so a germinal atom of each one of the bodies remains.

Solar Physical Body

Astral Solar Body: Complete Consciousness

Mental Solar Body: Complete Knowledge

Body of the Conscious Will

The more small and microscopic one feels the better, because the human being is nothing but a human being. We as human beings must realize that we are ants. God is God because the one that has the power is the Divinity. We are nobody. We are wretched devils, and even the Human Being, being a complete human being, is an ant in comparison to God.

A Master once told me, "Venerable Master Samael Aun Weor, true happiness is to have God within, because even when one is in the Absolute, or in Nirvana, if one does not have God within, one is not happy, although the Beings that dwell there have God already incarnated."

These words made a tremendous impact on me. So, I went to consult the great sage Saturn. I performed before him various esoteric salutations and he answered all of them, but he said, "There is no greater salutation than the one of the seal of the heart."

There was no necessity to speak. He answered unto me everything in silence. When God is not within oneself, one is not even happy within the Absolute. This answer satisfied me. These consultations cost money, and I paid with the capital of good actions, which are metallic coins that represent Dharma.

SYNTHESIS

- This arcanum, the Magician, represents the Man. It is the masculine principle.

- The number one signifies that which starts, that which begins.

- All of the psychological processes of the work are developed and contained within the Tarot.

- The unity is the performing synthesis of the ternary.

- We cannot know anything about the Soul and Spirit when we do not know ourselves.

- The four conditions that are needed to be a magician are the following:

  To know how to suffer.

  To know how to be silent.

  To know how to abstain.

  To know how to die.

Chapter XXIV

Arcanum 2

The number two is negative. In ancient times there were always both a priest and priestess within the temples. There were both a male and female Master in primordial Masonry. The Count Cagliostro intended to establish Egyptian Masonry in England, but he had many enemies and in the end he established **two thrones**. Giovanni Papini met Count Cagliostro on a ship. They became friends, and the Count told him who he was. Cagliostro tried to stop the Second World War and because no one paid attention to him, he went again to Tibet saying that he was going to return sixty years later.

In ancient times, Egyptian Masonry was grandiose. At that time, sacred hermaphrodites existed and the numbers one and two were fused. Humanity was androgynous in the first Protoplasmatic Root Race, during the Polar Epoch. Back then, sexual reproduction was performed during specific times of the year. To reproduce, they divided their human organism into two, and the number two was the son.

A ritual was performed during that epoch when someone was born. These human beings were capable of elongating themselves or shrinking themselves to the size of an atom. When a Master wanted to speak in a sweet way he would bring his feminine principle to the surface, and when he wanted to show his severity, the masculine principle was presented. This is how the Elohim are.

The Latin tradition tells us that Aeneas was present in the sanctuary of Apollo (*The Aeneid*, Book VI, by Virgil) when he

had an interview with a Pythoness who prophesied unto him his forthcoming fate. Aeneas requested to see his dead father. He petitioned to enter into the Infernos. The terrible Sibyl, guardian of the forest of Hecate Proserpine (third aspect of the Divine Mother), the forest of Avernus, answered unto him:

> The gates of hell are open night and day;
> Smooth the descent, and easy is the way:
> But to return, and view the cheerful skies,
> In this the task and mighty labor lies.
> To few great Jupiter imparts this grace,
> And those of shining worth and heav'nly race.

She asked him to obtain a bundle of leaves and branches of gold consecrated to Proserpine, the Divine Mother in her infernal aspect. Aeneas sacrificed some black sheep, and then he saw **two** flying doves. The hero recognized that those birds were the birds of his Divine Mother (symbol of the Holy Spirit). He intelligently interpreted this message, and the two birds directed him to the forest of Proserpine where he found the bundle that would permit him to enter into the Infernos. Aeneas sacrificed four black cows and the Sibyl guided him through the Avernus till he reached the place where his dead father was.

The masculine and feminine principles are conjugated in the holy and mysterious **Tetragrammaton**, an esoteric name that should not be pronounced in vain and which in Hebrew is related with the letters of the name of the Eternal.

HEBREW IS READ FROM RIGHT TO LEFT: ← Hei Vav Hei Iod

י **Iod:** eternal masculine principle

ה **Hei:** eternal feminine principle

ו **Vav:** phallic masculine principle; the lingam

ה **Hei:** feminine principle; the uterus, the yoni

יהוה Iod Hei Vav Hei is reduced to *Sssssssssssssssssssssssssssssss*. These four letters are in themselves of tremendous sacerdotal power. They must be pronounced as if imitating the howling of a tornado that is within the hills, or as if imitating the wind. When one wants to heal an ill person or to invoke a deity, it must be pronounced softly. They also serve for meditation. In those four letters, the two feminine and masculine principles of the macrocosm and microcosm are represented: the reed, masculine principle, and the cup, feminine principle. The principle of the Eternal One is in these four letters that must not be pronounced in vain.

The number two is vital. In the temples of the mysteries, two altars were never absent. One cannot pass into the temple without passing through the two columns where two guardians are always present.

What would life be like if the number two did not exist? The Matripadma (womb of nature) receives the masculine Fohat ray, the Holy Spirit, spouse of the Divine Mother, who becomes fecundated and the universe appears. What would be of life without the other principle?

Before the dawn of the Mahamanvantara, the Cosmic Day, nothing existed. The Gods were living within That which has no name, no form, no sound, no silence, nor ears in order to perceive it.

When life dawned, when the dawn of creation commenced, the First Logos called the Third Logos and He said unto Him, "Go and fecundate your spouse in order for existence to begin." He then started to work with the Seven Spirits before the Throne, and the Army of the Voice. Then the Masonic rituals were performed and the chaotic matter became fecundated; the Matripadma was fecundated and the universe came into existence. Each one of the seven Cosmocreators emanated from itself the two souls: Buddhi, the feminine soul,

LAKSHMI, THE LOTUS GODDESS, MATRIPADMA, SOURCE OF ALL ABUNDANCE, AS DEPICTED IN HINDUISM

and the Causal masculine soul; this pair of souls are symbolized by the constellation of Pisces.

These two souls, husband and wife, practiced a transcendental maithuna. She separated the superior waters from the inferior waters in order for the waters to be fecundated by the fire; they projected these waters by means of the Verb. Then, the germs of the Matripadma proliferated; the Matripadma swelled like a lotus flower, and thus fructified, a cosmos was born.

The eternal positive and the eternal negative are in electricity.

In India, the masculine principle is represented by a bull, and the feminine principle by the sacred white cow which represents the Divine Mother and that has as its antithesis the black cow.

We need to christify ourselves. No human being can return to the Father without being devoured by the serpent. No one can be devoured by the serpent without having worked in the flaming forge of Vulcan (sex). The key of christification is in the Arcanum A.Z.F. The mantra of the Great Arcanum is **I.A.O.**

    I: *ignis*, fire

    A: *aqua*, water

    O: *origo*, principle, Spirit

Mars descends into the flaming forge of Vulcan in order to retemper his sword and to conquer the heart of Venus. Heracles descends in order to clean the stables of Augeas with the sacred fire, and Perseus descends in order to cut off Medusa's head.

Remember, beloved disciples, that our Divine Mother is Nut and her word is "56." By Kabbalistically adding the numbers together we have: $5 + 6 = 11$, then $1 + 1 =$

2. One is the Father; two is Her, Nut, the Divine Mother Kundalini.

Behold, here the wonder of the number two.

Synthesis

- Woman is the Athanor of Sexual Alchemy. The human being departed from paradise through the doors of Eden, and Eden is precisely sex.

- The door of paradise is sex. Woman is the door.

- The Kundalini is the sacred fire of the Holy Spirit. It is the Pentecostal fire. It is the igneous serpent of our magical powers.

- Kundalini is enclosed in the Muladhara chakra situated in the coccyx.

- The secret in order to awaken Kundalini is the following: *introduce the virile member into the vagina of the woman and withdraw it without spilling the semen.* This practice must be performed slowly.

- The Arcanum A.Z.F., Sexual Magic, or Maithuna, must only be practiced between man and woman, between legitimate husband and wife of lawfully constituted homes.

- The practice of the arcanum must only be performed once a day. If it is practiced twice a day, one falls into negativity by violating the magnetic recuperative pause.

Chapter XXV

Arcanum 3

In Kabbalah, everything is numbers and mathematics. The number is holy and infinite. In the universe everything is measurement and weight. For the Gnostics, God is a geometrist. Mathematics are sacred. No one was admitted into the school of Pythagoras if they were not knowledgeable about mathematics, music, etc. Numbers are sacred.

All of the splendors of the world and the extraordinary interplay of the Sephiroth on the thirty-two paths of wisdom within God and within the human being are described in a marvellous way in the *Sepher Yetzirah*, a very ancient sacred Hebraic book of the Rabbis.

All the science of the Sephiroth is hidden within the mystery of the sexes. The secret key of the *Sepher Yetzirah* is within the science of numbers. Anyone can think in thirty-two ways, but in reality, the thirty-two paths of wisdom are equal to 3 + 2 = 5, equal to the star of five points, the Pentalpha, meaning equal to the human being, which signifies that the paths are within the human being. Everything is within oneself. It is written in a very symbolic way; that is why it refers to thirty-two paths.

The Kabbalists state that in reality the Soul has three aspects.

1. **Nephesh**: The Animal Soul
2. **Ruach**: The Thinking Soul
3. **Neshamah**: The Spiritual Soul

The Sephiroth are the substratum of these three aspects of the soul. The Sephiroth are atomic.

Nephesh

One must distinguish the difference between the Astral Body and the Lunar Bodies. The Lunar Bodies are active during the night and after death. Conventionally, these bodies have been called the Astral Body, but they are not the legitimate Astral Body. Whosoever wants to have the luxury of having the legitimate Astral Body must perform the work of the Maithuna where the Hydrogen SI-12 is built (H = Hydrogen, SI = musical note, 12 = 12 laws). The Hydrogen SI-12 vibrates in our organism with the musical scale and crystallizes in the Astral Solar Body if the practice is intense.

The initiate must descend into the Infernal Worlds for forty days and has to recapitulate all of the evil deeds and frightful dramas of his past incarnations; little by little, the initiate departs from these tenebrous regions. Before departing, the three souls Nephesh, Ruach, and Neshamah are submitted to ordeals. How interesting it is to see the Animal Soul submitted to ordeals, as well as the Thinking Soul and the Essence, which are also submitted to ordeals.

The Bible states, *"Nephesh, nephesh, blood is paid with blood."* Within these Hebrew words wisdom is hidden.

Ruach

This is the thinking emotional soul that is inserted within the Lunar Bodies of desire.

Neshamah

That fraction of soul that is trapped within the previously mentioned principles is submitted to very difficult ordeals. After triumphing, the initiate ascends to the Causal World to have a meeting with Sanat Kumara, a venerable Elder mentioned in very ancient religions. He is one of the Four Thrones of which the Bible speaks. Three are gone and only he remains. He grasps the rod of Aaron, the scepter of the kings. He is ineffable and is related with Sattva, Rajas, and Tamas, the three Gunas that are in equilibrium. Sanat Kumara gives the esoteric initiation of the Astral Solar Body.

Synthesis

- Our disciples must learn how to depart in the Astral Body in order to visit all of the White Lodges of the world, where they can personally converse with Christ and with all of the Masters of the White Lodge.

- The atoms of laziness are a grave obstacle for the progress towards the Superior Worlds.

- The Great Law is the return of life towards the Superior Worlds.

- Pray and meditate intensely. The Divine Mother teaches her children. Prayer must be performed by combining meditation with the sleepy state. Then, as in a vision of a dream, illumination emerges. The Divine Mother comes to the devotee in order to instruct them in the great mysteries.

Chapter XXVI

Arcanum 4

The Fourth Arcanum is very interesting. It refers to the cross of four points, the cubic stone which is the foundation of the Great Work. It is a stone that must be chiselled.

When referring to the schools of the Fourth Way, we find that Gurdjieff, Ouspensky, and Nicoll had written what they knew, but their expositions suffer from many mistakes. For example, Gurdjieff committed the error of mistaking the Kundalini with the abominable Kundabuffer organ, and Ouspensky committed the same error. We cannot desist recognizing the existence of that blind fohatic force that has people hypnotized; yet this one has nothing to do with the Kundalini, but with the Kundabuffer that is the lunar fire. The Bible refers to the forty-four fires, but only two great fires can be spoken of: Kundalini and Kundabuffer.

The Kundalini is the Pentecostal fire, the lightning of Vulcan ascending through the dorsal spine, the positive fire that crystallizes in worlds and suns. Its antithesis is the Kundabuffer, the negative fire that crystallizes in those psychological aggregates, those quarrelling and screaming "I's" that we carry within and which are negative crystallizations that have people immersed into unconsciousness.

Gurdjieff also committed the error of not speaking about the Lunar Bodies that everyone has. He only says that we must transform the Being and that we must build the Solar Bodies. Ouspensky speaks about the Second Birth, but his teachings are incomplete. To begin with, the Solar Bodies have to be built in the Ninth Sphere, thus reaching the Second Birth. But neither Gurdjieff nor Ouspensky give the clue.

The school of the Fourth Way is very ancient; it comes from the archaic lands. It is the foundation of the great mysteries and is found alive in Gnosticism, and in the religions of the Egyptians, Lemurians, Atlanteans, Phoenicians, etc.

One has to tread the path by that Fourth Way. We need to march with equilibrium in science, philosophy, art, and religion.

In the staged arts of long ago, the individual would receive information in his three brains: motor, emotional, and intellectual. In the schools of today however, only the intellectual brain receives information. Neurosis and the sick states of the mind are due to this. Mental disequilibrium is avoided by balancing the three brains.

Science itself is contained within all of the cosmos; science exists even when the study of sciences does not exist.

The Fourth Arcanum of the Tarot is the holy and mysterious Tetragrammaton. The sacred name of the Eternal One has four letters: יהוה (Iod, Hei, Vav, Hei).

י	Iod	Man	Man
ה	Hei	Woman	Woman
ו	Vav	Phallus	Fire
ה	Hei	Uterus	Water

These are four letters which take us into the Ninth Sphere, the forge of the Cyclops, the famous flaming forge of Vulcan, sex, in order to raise the sacred serpent of our magical powers, and to take this serpent into our heart. Thus, we receive the sacred cross of the initiation in the temple of the Divine Mother.

The number four also represents the four physical elements, and the four elements of Alchemy:

Earth	⊕	Salt	⊖
Fire	△	Sulphur	⇧
Water	▽	Mercury	☿
Air	△	Azoth	

The ancient Alchemists stated that the sulphur must fecundate the mercury of the secret philosophy in order for the salt to be regenerated. In other words, the fire must fecundate the water in order for the human being to be regenerated and Self-realized.

In the Fourth Arcanum we also find the secret of the Sphinx, and this arcanum reminds us of the four sacred animals of Sexual Alchemy.

> **Lion:** Hides the enigma of the Fire; claws of a lion
>
> **Man:** Water; the face of a man; Intelligence
>
> **Eagle:** Air; the wings of the Sphinx; Spirit
>
> **Bull:** Earth; the back hooves; Tenacity

These are the values representative of the Sphinx, the four elements of Solar Alchemy. We need the tenacity of the bull and the wings of the Spirit.

The Sphinx speaks to us about the Great Work that must be performed with the four elements. During a certain occasion I had an interview with the elemental of the Sphinx; this is a marvellous elemental. The elemental came with its feet covered with mud. The elemental blessed me and I said unto it, "I understand why you come with your feet covered with mud. It is because of this age of Kali Yuga."

The entrance into the old, archaic temples was commonly a hidden hole in some mysterious spot of the dense jungle. We departed from Eden through the door of sex, and only through that door can we return to Eden. Eden is the same sex. It is the narrow, straight and difficult door that leads us into the light.

In the solitude of these mysterious sanctuaries, the neophytes were submitted to the four initiatic ordeals. The ordeals of fire, air, water, and earth always defined the diverse purifications of the neophytes.

The neophytes are submitted to the four initiatic ordeals which are verified in the Internal Worlds. The human being still is not a king or queen of nature, but the human being is called to be a king in accordance to Melchizedeck.

Disciples must be tested by the four elements in order to examine them. They are submitted to ordeals in the forty-nine regions of thought. These ordeals are for everyone, man and woman. One can help oneself by having pure thoughts, but this is not enough: meditation is necessary.

All students of Kabbalah must be familiar with all of the elemental creatures:

> **Air:** Sylphs
>
> **Water:** Undines and Nereides (Mermaids)
>
> **Fire:** Salamanders
>
> **Earth:** Gnomes

These elements are utilized in order to work on the transmutation of lead into gold upon the central mountain range (the dorsal spine).

In the words Iod-Hei-Vav-Hei, we find the mystery of the Tetragrammaton (the Holy Four), the four words, the four elements. More profoundly, we find our Being, our most complete Divinity.

From the Ain Soph, which is a Super-Divine Atom of each one of us, the three Primary Forces (the Father, the Son, and the Holy Spirit) emanate and give their final synthesis: 3 + 1 = 4.

Tetragrammaton is: יהוה. This is the sacred summation of the number four.

Synthesis

- The Master is formed by Atman-Buddhi.

- Atman is the Innermost.

- Buddhi is the Divine Soul, meaning the Divine Consciousness of the Innermost.

- When a Logos wants to redeem a world, it emanates from itself a celestial proto-type formed by Atman-Buddhi.

- The Logos is the Sephirothic Crown, the individual Ray from which the Innermost Himself emanated. This Ray is Triune; it is the Holy Trinity within each one of us.

- Thus, every Logos is Triune.

- The Father is Kether, the Elder of Days.

- The Son is the Cosmic Christ in us.

- The Holy Spirit is the Divine Mother in us.

- The Mother carries a lamp in her hand. That lamp is the Innermost who burns within our heart.

Chapter XXVII

Arcanum 5

The Fifth Arcanum of the Tarot is the flaming Pentagram, the blazing star. The Pentagram represents the microcosmic human being. We can see from an esoteric point of view that there is a struggle between the brain and sex. If sex overcomes the brain, then the star of five points (the human being) falls into the abyss with the feet pointing upwards and the head pointing downwards. Then, the human being transforms himself into an entity of darkness. This is the inverted star, the male goat of Mendes.

The male goat represents black magic. A human figure with the head aiming downwards and the feet aiming upwards naturally represents a demon.

All magical power is found within the star of five points. The whole science of Gnosis is found summarized in the flaming star. Many Bodhisattvas (Human Souls of Masters) have fallen inverted, like the five pointed star, with the superior ray aiming downwards and the two inferior rays aiming upwards.

We must have complete cognizance of what a Bodhisattva is. The superior triad of every immortal Spirit of every human being is formed by Atman, Buddhi, and Manas.

1. **Atman:** the Being, the divine immortal spark, has two Souls that in esotericism are called Buddhi and Manas.

2. **Buddhi:** the basic principle, the feminine Spiritual Soul,

the superlative consciousness of the Being.

3. **Manas:** the masculine Human Soul.

The Master in himself is Atman (the Being), Buddhi, and Manas. When a Master comes into the world, he needs to take a human body. Then, Atman sends Manas, his human soul, and Manas appears living in the physical world. This is what is called "the Bodhisattva," who performs what has to be performed. Moreover, that which is called Buddhi can penetrate within Manas in order to do what has to be done.

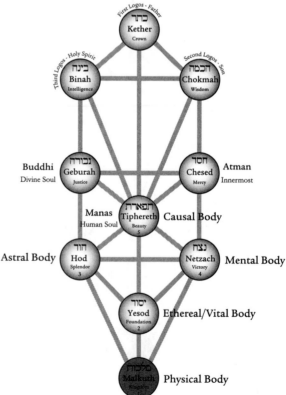

Thus, we have the case of the Master Jehovah that sent his Bodhisattva to Chile. At the present time (1970), he is a young boy who is living foolishly. So, this Master is only waiting for the Bodhisattva to mature in order to penetrate within him. Jehovah is the Regent of the ancient Moon. He is a great Master that has been intentionally confused with Javhe, who is the chief of the Black Lodge. Javhe tempted Jesus by offering him all of the world's treasures. Jesus answered, *"Thou shalt not tempt the Lord, thy God."* [Matthew 4:7] Javhe can be represented by a star of five points with the feet aiming upwards.

A Bodhisattva that allows himself to fall is converted into a black magician. If he does not raise himself up he will enter into a very difficult and more bitter incarnation, suffering frightfully. If he does not rise up at the end of many incarnations, each time more difficult, he will be sent to the Infernal Worlds, being accused of three crimes:

1. To have assassinated the Buddha.

2. To have dishonoured the Gods.

3. To have performed diverse crimes of minor value.

Madame Blavatsky explains very well what a Bodhisattva is, but her followers do not understand her.

In this present epoch, the majority of the Bodhisattvas are fallen; they wander from life to life. We need to be humble in order to acquire wisdom, and after acquiring it, we need to be even more humble. The Bodhisattvas fall because of sex, and they also rise up because of sex.

The sex is the Philosophical Stone. The decapitation of Medusa (the Satan that we carry within) would be impossible without the precious treasury of the Philosophical Stone. Remember that Medusa is the maiden of evil (the psychological "I"), whose head is covered with hissing vipers. In occult science, it is stated that the union of the sophic mercury with the sophic sulphur results in the Holy Philosophical Stone. The Ens Seminis is the mercury; the sulphur is the sacred fire of love.

Apollo and Diana, man and woman, must work in the Great Work, decapitating Medusa, defeating the tempting serpent, killing the lion of Nemea, taking the infernal dog Cerberus from within the Tartarus. We must work in this Great Work through performing the Twelve Labors of Heracles.

Heracles (the Cosmic Christ), the son of Jupiter (IO Peter) and Alcmene, performed the **Twelve Labors**:

1. Capture and death of the lion of Nemea (the strength of the uncontrollable instincts and passion that devastates and devours everything).

2. Destruction of the hydra of Lerna (the psychological defects of the subconsciousness).

3. Capturing the stag of Cerynitia and the boar of Mount Erymanthus (the lower animal passions).

THE HYDRA OF THE SECOND LABOR

4. The cleaning of the Augean stables (the submerged depths of the subconsciousness).

5. Killing the birds of the lake of Stymphalian (witch-like psychic aggregates from the depths of the unconsciousness) with arrows.

6. The capturing of the bull of Crete (passionate, thoughtless sexual impulses, infrahuman elements).

7. Capturing the mares of King Diomedes (passionate, infrahuman elements that are profoundly submerged in our own unconscious abysses).

8. He eliminated the giant thief Cacus (the evil thief that squanders the sexual center in order to satisfy his animal passions).

9. The conquest of the girdle of Hippolyta (the feminine psychic aspect of our own interior nature).

10. The conquest of the cattle of Geryon (related to detachment).

11. The stealing of the golden apples from the garden of Hesperides.

12. The taking of the dog Tricipite (Cerberus) from its Plutonian dominions (the guide dog, the sexual instinct).

Heracles, the instructor of the world, has to perform the Twelve Labors, a complete work of pacification, each time that he comes. The Cosmic Christ practices what he preaches. When he is little, the tenebrous serpents of evil come to attack him, Herod persecutes him, etc.

The Cosmic Christ demands the same as what he practices. He is the Master of Masters. He performs his works of purification and dissolution of the "I," of the ego.

In mythology, the efforts of the blowers [puffers] are often spoken of, those who try to take the stone to the summit, and after such efforts, the stone falls again. This indicates the efforts of those students that spill the Ens Seminis.

The number five is the law. This arcanum represents the Karma of the initiate. We must know that Karma in its final synthesis serves in order to live out all the drama of the passion of our Lord Jesus Christ in the body of flesh and bone.

It is necessary for people to understand what the Sanskrit word **Karma** means.

My friends, a law which is called Karma exists. It is not irrelevant to assert that this word signifies the law of action and consequence. Obviously, a cause cannot exist without its effect; neither can an effect without a cause.

The law of the scale, the terrible law of Karma, governs everything created. Every cause converts itself into an effect, and every effect transforms itself into a cause.

You must comprehend what the law of compensation is. Everything that is done must be paid for, for a cause without an effect does not exist, neither an effect without a cause.

Liberty and free will have been granted unto us and we can do as we wish; however, it is clear that we must answer for all our deeds before God. Any action of our life, good or evil, has its consequences.

The law of action and consequence governs the course of our varied existences, and each life is the result of the previous one.

To integrally comprehend the basis and "modus operandi" of the law of Karma is indispensable in order to orient the ship of our life in a very positive and edifying manner throughout all of the diverse levels of life.

Karma is the law of compensation, not of vengeance. There are some who confuse this cosmic law with detriment and even with fatality, believing that everything that happens to the human being in life is inexorably determined beforehand. It is true that the acts of the human being are determined by inheritance, education, and the environment. Yet, it is also true that the human being has free will and can modify his actions to educate his character, to form superior habits, to fight against weaknesses, to fertilize virtues, etc..

Karma is a medicine that is applied unto us for our own good. Disgracefully, instead of bowing with reverence before the internal living God, people protest, blaspheme, they justify themselves, they stubbornly excuse themselves and wash their hands like Pilate. Karma is not modified with such protests; on the contrary, it becomes harder and more severe.

When one comes into this world, one carries his own destiny. Some are born on down-filled mattresses and others are born in disgrace. If we murdered in our previous existence, now we will be murdered. If we previously had hurt someone, now we will be hurt. If we stole, now we will be robbed, and *"with the same measurement that we measure others, we will be measured."*

We demand loyalty from our spouse while in this life and in previous lives we have been adulterers. We ask for love when we have previously been pitiless and cruel. We ask for comprehension when we never previously comprehended anyone, when we never learned the point of view of another.

We long for immense joy when we have always been the origin of many disgraces. We would like to have been born in a very beautiful home and with many comforts when in other existences we did not know how to give to our children a good home and beauty.

We protest against the insulters when we were always insulting those that surrounded us. We want our children to obey us when we never knew how to obey our parents. Slander bothers us terribly while we were always slandering others, and the world was filled with pain because of it. Gossiping disgusts us, we do not want anyone to murmur against us, meanwhile, we always have been engaged in gossiping and rumors, speaking evil of our neighbors and mortifying the life of others. In other words, we always demand what we have never given. We have always been saved in other lives, and we deserve the worst, but we suppose that the best should be granted to us.

Fortunately, my dear friends, justice and mercy are the two main columns of the universal White Fraternity.

Justice without mercy is tyranny. Mercy without justice is tolerance and complacence with guilt. Karma is negotiable and this is something that can greatly surprise the henchmen of the diverse orthodox schools.

Certainly, many pseudo-esotericists and pseudo-occultists have become great pessimists in regards to the law of action and consequence. They mistakenly assume that this law unfolds itself in a mechanical, automatic, and cruel way. These erudites believe that it is not possible to alter this law. I sincerely regret to have to disagree with this way of thinking.

If the law of action and consequence, the nemesis of existence, is not negotiable, then where would divine mercy be? Frankly, I cannot accept cruelty within

Divinity. The Reality, that which is perfection, that which has diverse names, such as Tao, Aum, INRI, Sein, Allah, Brahma, God, or, better if called Gods, etc., in no way could be without mercy. It is not cruel, or with tyranny, etc. As a result of this, I repeat in an emphatic way that Karma is negotiable.

To modify our own destiny is possible because, *"when an inferior law is transcended by a superior law, the superior law washes away the inferior law."*

By modifying the cause, the effect is modified. *"The lion of the law is fought with the scale."* If we put our good deeds on one plate of a scale, and in the other we put our evil deeds, both plates must weigh the same, or some disequilibrium will exist. If the plate with evil actions weighs more, then we must put good deeds on the plate with the good actions, with the purpose of inclining the scale towards our favor; thus, in this way, we will cancel Karma. Perform good deeds in order to pay your debts. Remember that payment does not only have to be with pain, but can also be paid with the performing of good deeds.

Now you will comprehend my good friends how marvellous it is to perform good deeds. There is no doubt that right thoughts, right feelings, and right actions are the best of the negotiations.

We must never protest against Karma; what is important is to know how to negotiate it. Disgracefully, when people are found in great despair, the only thing that occurs unto them is to wash their hands like Pilate, saying that they did not do anything bad, that they are not guilty, that they are just souls, etc., etc., etc.

To those who are in misery, I say to them that they should examine their own conduct; that they must judge themselves; that they should sit on the bench of the accused at least for a moment. Thus, after strictly analyzing themselves, they must modify their conduct. If those who are found without a job would become chaste, infinitely charitable, peaceful, and one-hundred percent helpful, they obviously would radically alter the cause of their disgrace, consequently modifying the effect in itself.

To alter an effect is not possible if the previous cause that created it has not been radically modified. As we have already stated, there is no effect without a cause, neither a cause without an effect.

We must always work without expecting any rewards, always with infinite love towards humanity. Thus, we alter those evil causes that originated evil effects.

There is no doubt that misery has its cause in alcoholism, filthy lust, violence, adultery, squandering, avarice, etc.

Do you want to be healed? Then, heal others. Are some of your relatives in jail? Then, exert yourself for the freedom of others. Are you hungry? Then, share your bread with those who are in a worse position than you, etc.

Many people who suffer only remember their bitterness and wish to find a remedy. But, they do not remember the suffering of others; neither do they remotely think of remedying the needs of their neighbors. Their existence in this egotistical state is worthless; so, the only thing that they achieve is the aggravation of their suffering.

If those people would think of others, serve their neighbors, feed the hungry, give a drink to the thirsty, dress the naked, teach those who are ignorant, etc., then it would be clear, they would be putting good deeds on the plate of the cosmic scale. The scale will then incline towards their favor. Thus, they would alter their destiny, and good luck would come in their favor. In other words, all of their necessities would be remedied. But people are very selfish; this is the reason for their suffering. No one remembers God nor their fellowman except when they are in desperation. This is something that the whole world has proven for themselves; thus, this is the state of our humanity.

Disgracefully, my dear friends, this ego that each one of us carries within does exactly the contrary that we have stated here. Because of such reasons, the reduction of the "myself" to cosmic dust is considered urgent, unpostponable and undelayable.

Let us think for a moment of the humanoid multitudes that populate the face of the earth. They suffer the unspeakable. They are victims of their own errors. If they did not have ego they would not have those errors, nor would they suffer the consequences of such errors.

The unique thing required in order to have the right to true happiness is, before all, to not have this ego. Certainly, when psychic aggregates, the inhuman elements that make us so horrible and evil, do not exist within us, then the payment of Karma is non-existent. Thus, the result is happiness.

It is important to know that when we have radically eliminated the ego, the possibility of delinquency remains annihilated. As a consequence, Karma can be forgiven.

The law of Karma, this law of the cosmic scale, is not a blind law. A credit can also be solicited from the Masters of Karma. This is something that many ignore, although it is urgent to know that every credit must be paid with good deeds. If it is not paid in such a way, then the law collects it with supreme pain.

We need to make ourselves conscious of our own Karma. This is only possible through the state of alert novelty. Every effect in life, every event, has its cause in a previous life; but we need to become cognizant of this.

Every moment of happiness or pain must be continued into meditation with a quiet mind and in profound silence. Then the result is the experience of the same event in a previous life. Therefore, we become conscious of the cause of that event, whether it is pleasant or unpleasant.

The one who awakens consciousness can travel with his internal bodies out of the physical body with complete conscious will. Thus, one can study his own book of destiny in the temple of Anubis and his forty-two judges.

The chief priest of the Tribunal of Karma is the great Master Anubis. The temple of Anubis, the supreme regent of Karma, is in the Molecular World. This world is called the Astral World by many people. Only the terror of love and justice reign in this tribunal. In this temple, a book of debits and expenditures exists for each human being in which is written daily, in detail, good and evil actions. The good actions are represented by rare coins that the Masters accumulate on behalf of the men and women that perform these good deeds. Defense lawyers are also found in this tribunal. Yet, everything must be paid. Nothing is granted as a gift. The one that has good deeds pays and does well in his affairs. The granted credits are paid with unrewarded good deeds and inspired love towards those that suffer.

The Masters of Karma are conscious judges that live in the Jinn state. We constantly have to perform good deeds in order to have currency to pay our debts of this life and our previous lives. All the actions of the human being are controlled by laws; some laws are superior, others are inferior. All of the superior laws are summarized within love. An action of love cancels past actions that were inspired by inferior laws. This is why upon speaking of love the Master Paul stated:

> Love suffereth long, and is kind; love envieth not, love vaunteth not itself, is not puffed up, doth not behave itself unseemly, seeketh not her own, is not easily provoked, thinketh no evil; rejoiceth not in iniquity, but rejoiceth in the truth; beareth all things, believeth all things, hopeth all things, endureth all things. - 1 Corinthians 13:4-7

The Masters of Karma use a sacred mask in the form of a jackals head or a plumed wolf when they are officiating as judges. With this mask they present themselves to the initiates in the internal worlds. This is the cruelty of the law of love.

To negotiate with the lords of the law is possible through meditation. Pray, meditate, and concentrate yourself on Anubis, the most exalted regent of the good law.

All of the doors are closed for the unworthy except for the door of repentance. *Ask and it will be granted unto you; knock and it shall be opened unto you.*

SYNTHESIS

- Karma is paid not only for the evil that is done, but also for the good that could be done, yet is left undone.

- Each evil action is a bill of exchange that we sign in order to pay in the next life.

- When an inferior law is transcended by a superior law, the superior law washes away the inferior law.

- *Let no one cheat himself. Whatever a human being sows he will later reap, and his actions will follow him.* - Galatians 6:7

- The lords of Karma in the tribunals of objective justice judge souls for their deeds, for the concrete, clear, and definitive facts, and never for their good intentions.

- Results always speak for themselves. Good intentions are worthless if the facts are disastrous.

- During the esoteric initiatic processes of the fire, I had to comprehend in a complete way the following statements:

The lion of the law is fought with the scale.

Whosoever has capital with which to pay, pays and does well in their negotiations.

Whosoever does not have capital to pay with must pay with pain.

Perform good deeds so that your debts can be paid.

Chapter XXVIII

Arcanum 6

The Sixth Arcanum is expressed by the Seal of Solomon. The Star of Bethlehem is the Seal of Solomon. The six points of the star are masculine. The six outer obtuse angles that exist between point and point are feminine. (In synthesis, this star has twelve rays: six masculine and six feminine). In them, the mysteries of the Arcanum A.Z.F. (Sexual Magic) are summarized and synthesized.

The Seal of Solomon

masculine point

feminine indentation

The Seal of Solomon, the star of Nativity, is the perfect symbol of the Central Sun (the Cosmic Christ, the perfect multiple unity). The God Child can never be born within the heart of the human being without the resplendence and life of the brilliant star of nativity. One must work with the Arcanum A.Z.F. in order to incarnate Him.

All of the zodiacal measurements are found summarized within the Seal of Solomon. The twelve rays of the brilliant star crystallize by means of Alchemy in the twelve zodiacal constellations. All of the inner relations that exist between the zodiac and the invincible Central Sun are found written in the Seal of Solomon. The sexual genesis of the zodiac is represented in the Seal of Solomon. The venerable

Master of the light Hilarion IX, when speaking of the brilliant star, said:

It is the basic form of all crystallizations and the schematic model of all flourishments. Its two triangles that join or separate love are the two shuttles with which the ineffable mystery of eternal life is woven or unwoven. Above is the most Holy Eternity that acts as the Father, the Son and the Holy Spirit, below is its counterpart, with the power that governs, the power that liberates, and the power that executes.

John, the well-beloved of Christ, exclaimed when receiving the Venustic Initiation from Christ's very hands, *"I am the bright and morning star."* Revelation 22:16

Thus, each time that the Eternal Geometrist fixes His attention on one point of space, from that point emerges the Glorious Star (of Nativity), announcing the birth of a new state of consciousness, the archetype of a being, a globe, a star, a sun. Fourth Message of Aryavarta Ashrama

The eternal, immortal triad is represented in the superior triangle of the Seal of Solomon.

Yet, the inferior triangle represents the three traitors that are within ourselves:

1. Demon of desire

2. Demon of the mind

3. Demon of the evil will

These three traitors are the three evil friends of Job. These are the three assassins of Hiram Abiff:

Judas, Pilate, Caiaphas: Christian Symbology

"And the LORD said unto Moses, Make thee a fiery serpent, and set it upon a pole: and it shall come to pass, that every one that is bitten, when he looketh upon it, shall live." - Numbers 21

Apopi, Hai, Nebt: Egyptian Symbology

Sebal, Orteluk, Stokin: Masonic Symbology

These three traitors live within the mind. They are within ourselves. Let us remember that Dante represents Lucifer in the center of the earth with three mouths, and in each one of his mouths there is a traitor.

The Bible cites these three traitors in the book of the Revelation of Saint John, *"And I saw three unclean spirits like frogs come out of the mouth of the dragon, and out of the mouth of the beast, and out of the mouth of the false prophet."* - Revelation 16:13

These three unclean spirits like frogs are the three traitors that betray the internal Christ from moment to moment and constitute the foundation of the rein- carnating ego, the psychological "I," the

Satan which must be dissolved in order to incarnate the internal Christ.

Sacred Phallic Symbols

In the center of the triangles of the Seal of Solomon, the Tau cross or the sign of the infinite is found. Both signs are phallic (sexual). The soul is found between the two triangles and has to decide between two ways, the way of light or the way of darkness; this dilemma is absolutely sexual.

The clue to these symbols is found in the sacred serpent and the rooster that represent the I.A.O., the Verb, the Word. The tempting serpent of Eden exists, which is the serpent of darkness that forms the horrible tale of Satan. There also exists the bronze serpent of Moses which is inter-winding in the Tau, meaning the sexual lingam, the one that healed the Israelites in the wilderness. The serpent is dormant, coiled three and a half times within the church of Ephesus; the serpent must depart from this church in the Muladhara chakra and ascend into the medullar canal in order to convert ourselves into Angels. If the serpent descends downward to the atomic infernos of the human being, then we convert ourselves into demons. Now you can comprehend why in the Caduceus of Mercury there are always two serpents.

When the students spill the semen during the practices with the Arcanum A.Z.F. they commit the crime of the Nicolaitans (Revelations 2:6) who work with the Maithuna in the Ninth Sphere but spill the semen. They use that system in order to make the serpent descend and to be precipitated downwards, towards the atomic infernos, thus forming the tail of Satan. This is how the human being is converted into a demon.

I remember Krumm-Heller who taught White Tantra, but his son taught Black Tantra, which is the practice of Maithuna with the spilling and loss of the seminal liquor. Krumm-Heller's son allowed himself to become fascinated with Black Tantra's doctrine and was converted into a demon with a tail and horns on his forehead. There were many students who were diverted by the son of Krumm-Heller. He was a sincerely mistaken one that departed from here (Mexico) and justified himself by saying that the great law threw him out.

The Alchemical Weddings signify the perfect marriage. The Alchemist must not only kill desire but even the very shadow of the horrible tree of desire. It would be worthless to renounce sex without having previously worked and built the Solar Bodies, reaching the Second Birth. Only then is this renunciation worthy. In the beginning, one has to work with the Third Logos, in the terrific forge of the Cyclops, then afterwards to work with the Second Logos, Heracles, and subsequently with the First Logos. The error of monks and nuns is to renounce sex without having previously built the Solar Bodies. Thus, monks and nuns are found in Limbo dressed with rags; they need to dress in wedding attire in order to enter into the kingdom of Heaven.

In the mysteries of Eleusis, couples danced in order to mutually magnetize themselves. It is necessary to imitate nature in everything; in other words, it is necessary to transmute the energy.

In the temple of the Sphinx, the book of the laws of nature is studied, after which the ordeal named "Ordeal of the Sanctuary" comes. Upon passing this ordeal, a ring with the Seal of Solomon is granted unto the student. (This ring should not be touched with the left hand). It shines with great force in the Internal Worlds.

In the works of High Magic, it is necessary to trace a magical circle. It must be closed with the Seal of Solomon.

We can manufacture with the seven metals medallions and rings of the Seal of Solomon. The Seal of Solomon must be utilized in all of the works of invocations and in the practices with elementals. The elementals of nature tremble before the Seal of the Living God. The Angel of the Sixth Seal of the Apocalypse has reincarnated at this time into a feminine body (this Angel is a specialist in the sacred Jinn science). The Bible states in the book of Apocalypse:

> *And I saw another Angel ascending from the east, having the seal of the living God:* (the Seal of Solomon) *and he cried with a loud voice to the four Angels* (the four karmic archivists that control the four points of the earth with the Law) *to whom it was given to hurt the earth and the sea, saying, Hurt not the earth, neither the sea, nor the trees, till we have sealed the servants of our God in their foreheads.* - Revelation 7:2-3

Time was needed in order for the people to study the doctrine of the Christ and to define themselves for Christ or for Javhe, for the White Lodge or for the Black Lodge.

The servants of God were already sealed on their foreheads. As well, the servants of Satan were already sealed on their foreheads (the mark of the beast).

The times of the end are at hand, and we are in them. The ten days (the wheel of the centuries, the Tenth Arcanum) are already past due.

Humanity remains classified with the Seal of the Living God. The majority have already received the mark of the beast on their foreheads and on their hands. A few have received the sign of the Lamb on their foreheads.

SYNTHESIS

- We have entered into the world of will-power and love.

- It is necessary to steal the fire from the devil in order to enter into the amphitheatre of cosmic science.

- The lover must steal the light from the darkness.

- The man must intensely practice Sexual Magic with the woman.

- It is necessary to reconquer the flaming sword of Eden.

Chapter XXIX

Arcanum 7

The Seventh Arcanum represents magical power in all its strength. The Holy Seven is the sanctum regnum of *magia sacra*, of high esoteric magic of Kabbalah, the Chariot of War.

The number seven is the Innermost, our real Being, assisted by all of the elemental forces of nature. Nature is a great living organism. In the final synthesis, this great machine is directed by elemental forces.

From the physical point of view, the sacred fire is produced by combustion, although from the point of view as Essence, the elemental fire can exist in itself; this is the fire of the wise, and it is within this elemental fire where the salamanders live. The salamanders are described in Franz Hartmann's book, *The Elementals*. Esotericists know that elementals and the elemental Gods of fire exist. If we look at the angelology of the Mayans, Aztecs, etc., we will find the Gods of fire there. The elemental fire of the wise exists in all of nature.

In its final synthesis, air is elemental. The Vayu tattva is the elemental principle of air; this is animated by the elemental creatures, or the sylphs of which the Kabbalists speak. In reality, this elemental air of the wise is ether in movement. Physicists state that the wind is air in movement. But occultists see that within this moving air exist forces that propel the air. These are the sylphs.

Water has an elemental principle. The Apas tattva is this elemental principle. We find the Undines, Nereides, and Nymphs

within this principle, this base, this substance. Whosoever has studied the Latin or ancient classical works will find references to the elementals of water within these works.

The element earth is controlled by certain elemental creatures which are the Gnomes and Pygmies of Kabbalah who dwell within the elemental principle of the earth, the tattva Prithvi.

The fire is transformed into air, the air into water, and the water into earth. The tattvas help us to transmute the lead into gold through the Caduceus of Mercury.

Tattva	Element
1. Akash	Principle of Ether
2. Vayu	Principle of Air
3. Tejas	Principle of Fire
4. Prithvi	Principle of Earth
5. Apas	Principle of Water

The former written order is in accordance with Rama Prasad. The true order is:

1. **Akash**	Principle of Ether
2. **Tejas**	Principle of Fire
3. **Vayu**	Principle of Air
4. **Apas**	Principle of Water
5. **Prithvi**	Principle of Earth

The first thing that exists within creation is the infinite space that is a Great Soul. Fire emerges from it and is transformed into air, the air into water, and the water into earth; thus the planets appear. This is the true order of the elements. The Innermost is the Divine Spirit. He is the chief of all of the elemental forces.

Every one who works with the Arcanum A.Z.F. receives the flaming sword.

This sword corresponds to the Seventh Arcanum of the Kabbalah.

The guardians of the ancient temples of mysteries use the flaming sword. The one who has awakened the Kundalini receives this flaming sword. In occult Masonry the sword is utilized; it is received with the Advent of the Fire. From the point of view of occult Masonry, the flaming sword is the result of incessant transmutations.

The Elohim, or Prajapatis, carry the flaming sword. These Elohim are divine. An Elohim without the sword would be inconceivable. We know that the sexual organs constitute the legitimate *sanctum laboratorium* of the Third Logos. These are the organs that create the flaming sword.

In the depth of the matter, the twenty-two arcana belong to the Ninth Sphere. The *anfiteatrum* of the *sapiencia eterna* is in the creative organs because from here all life emerges.

In the alchemical garden of pleasures, we find the word **VITRIOL**, which is also found in treatises of Alchemy and ancient treatises of the Kabbalah. This word (Vitriol) is an acrostic, derived from the phrase *"Visitam Interiore Terras Rectificatur Invenias Ocultum Lapidum"* (Visit the interior of our earth, which by rectifying you will find the occult stone).

We must search within the interior of our philosophical earth (the human organism), which by rectifying and working with the Arcanum A.Z.F., the Maithuna, we will find the Philosophical Stone.

The Sun (phallus), masculine principle, is the father of the Stone. The Moon (uterus), feminine principle, is the mother of the Philosophical Stone. The wind (seminal steam) bears the sun in its womb, and the earth nourishes it. This is related

VITRIOL. Engraving by D. Stolcius V. Stolcenberg, Viridium chymicum, 1624.

"The Father of that one only thing is the Sun, its Mother is the Moon; the Wind carries it in its belly, but its nurse is a spiritous Earth." - Hermes Trismegistus, *The Emerald Tablet*.
Engravings by Michael Maier, 1618

The seven planets around the Caduceus of Mercury, which is in the chalice that rests upon the stone.
PAINTING FROM FIGUARUM AEGYPTIORUM SECRETARUM, 18TH CENTURY

with the four elements, which are living manifestations of the Akash.

The masculine and feminine principles, the Sun and the Moon, are combined within the chalice (the brain) which is supported by the Caduceus of Mercury with the two cords Ida and Pingala; these two influences, one of masculine character and the other of feminine character, act over the Brute Stone. We need to give this stone a perfect cubic form.

The human being has seven bodies. Each body has its spinal medulla and its sacred serpent. The seven bodies of the human being are:

1. Physical Body

2. Vital Body

3. Astral Body or Body of Desire

4. Mental Body

5. Causal Body or Body of Will

6. Body of the Consciousness

7. Body of the Innermost

We have seven serpents: two groups of three, with the sublime coronation of the seventh tongue of fire that unites us with the One, with the Law, with the Father.

The whole work is performed with the Great Arcanum. The star of seven points is the vital and inseparable part of the Vitriol, which is that work with the Maithuna. The seven serpents of Alchemy are related with the seven planets, the seven great cosmic realizations, and the seven degrees of the power of the fire. The acrostic Vitriol, with its seven letters and its seven words, symbolizes all of the Great Work and the Seven Secret Words pronounced by the Solar Logos on Golgotha. The mysteries of the Seventh Arcanum are terribly divine.

In the National Museum of Anthropology in the capitol of Mexico, there is an Aztec sculpture in the form of a decapitated man. Instead of a head, he has seven serpents that represent the seven degrees of the power of the fire. The seven vipers (his phallus) are related with the

seven planets, the seven basic fundamental dimensions, the seven vowels **I.E.O.U.A.M.S.** that resound in Nature with the seven words of the Vitriol; all of this is related with the Law of Heptaparaparshinokh. This is the eternal Law of Seven, the ineffable cosmic law.

A powerful talisman and an esoteric Kabbalistic symbol is the star of seven points surrounded by a double circle and with the signs of the seven planets. The two circles represent the eternal masculine and feminine principles.

Those students of occultism who think they can attain realization of the Self without the Arcanum A.Z.F. are absolutely mistaken. Madame Blavatsky, after having written the six volumes of *The Secret Doctrine,* stated that those who want to know the mysteries of Chiram must search among the ancient Alchemists. She was in Agarthi. She renounced Nirvana in order to achieve the Venustic Initiation. She is already a Twice-born because she possesses the Solar Bodies and lives in the sacred monasteries. She is going to return into this world which is more bitter than bile. She is preparing to take a physical body in the United States, in New York. The great Master Blavatsky was a true Yogini, a disciple of Kout Humi, although after becoming a widow of the Count Blavatsky she married Colonel Olcott in order to work with the arcanum of Sexual Magic. Only in this way did she achieve in-depth realization.

The great Yogi-Avatar Sri Lahiri Mahasaya was called to initiation by the immortal Babaji when he already had a spouse. Thus, this is how the Yogi-Avatar was Self-realized. In Hindustan, Sexual Magic is known by the Sanskrit term Urdhvarata [Oordhvarata].

Authentic Yogis practice Sexual Magic with their spouse. There are two types of **Bramacharya** (sexual abstinence): solar and lunar. The solar type is for those that have performed the Second Birth. The lunar type is that absurd sexual abstinence that serves only to produce filthy, nocturnal sexual pollutions with all of its fatal consequences.

There are seven vices that we must transmute:

Vice		Virtue
Solar Pride	into	Faith, Humbleness
Lunar Avarice	into	Altruism
Venusian Lust	into	Chastity
Martian Anger	into	Love
Mercurian Laziness	into	Diligence
Saturnian Gluttony	into	Temperance
Jupiterian Envy	into	Philanthropy, Happiness for Others

We can disintegrate our defects and dissolve the psychological "I" only by means of this science of transmutations. We can modify our errors, transmute the vile metals into pure gold and command only by means of the science of transmuta-

HELENA PETROVNA BLAVATSKY AND HUSBAND COLONEL OLCOTT IN 1888

LAHIRI MAHASAYA

tions. Work with the Arcanum A.Z.F. so that you can receive the sword.

The Seventh Arcanum, "Triumph," is achieved through many struggles and bitterness. This is seen in the seven capital sins that we must transmute into the seven virtues, the transmutation of the seven inferior metals into pure gold.

The Governors of the seven planets are:

Governor	Planet	Symbol
Gabriel	Moon	☽
Raphael	Mercury	☿
Uriel	Venus	♀
Michael	Sun	☉
Samael	Mars	♂
Zachariel	Jupiter	♃
Orifiel	Saturn	♄

The seven Kabbalistic signs of the planets are:

Moon: A globe divided by two half moons.

Mercury: A Caduceus and the cynocephalus.

Venus: A sexual lingam.

Sun: A serpent with the head of a lion.

Mars: A dragon biting a sword's flyleaf.

Jupiter: A pentagram or an eagle's beak.

Saturn: A limping elder or a rock entwined by a serpent.

The seven talismans have the power of attracting the seven planetary forces. Perfect talismans can be prepared with the proper stones and metals.

SYNTHESIS

- The Pater Noster (Lord's Prayer) is the most perfect prayer. Among the magical prayers is found the Lord's Prayer with its seven esoteric petitions. One has to meditate on each petition. [SEE PAGE 74].

- Whosoever wants to be a magician has to acquire the sword.

- The sword is the Kundalini. The sword is the fire of the Holy Spirit.

- It is necessary to work with the Arcanum A.Z.F. in order to acquire the sword. The struggle is terrible. The warrior can liberate himself from the four bodies of sin only by way of the Arcanum A.Z.F.

- We gain nothing by filling our head with theories.

- It is better to love a good spouse with whom one can practice Sexual Magic everyday, rather than wasting time with polemics, theories, and intellectualism.

- Thus we acquire the sword of the Kundalini and we awaken all of our magical powers in order to enter through the doors of the triumphant city.

Chapter XXX

Arcanum 8

We find the Eighth Key of Basil Valentine in the Eighth Arcanum. There is no doubt that he was a great Gnostic. The gospel of Valentine is admirable. The processes of life and death in the Philosophical Stone, which is chiselled with the hammer of intelligence and the chisel of willpower, are referred to in the Eighth Key.

The Eighth Key is a perfect and clear alchemical allegory of the processes of death and resurrection that inevitably are occurring in the esoteric preparation of the Philosophical Stone, which is between the two columns of Jachin and Boaz. One has to polish the brute stone in order to make it cubic.

The stone is Peter and it refers to the blessed waters of Amrita. We see the human being that worked with Amrita in the sharp edges and perfect angles of the Stone. The brute stone and the chiselled stone are situated at the entrance of the temple, behind the columns. The chiselled stone is on the right-hand side; its particularity is that it has nine angles that form four crosses. Those who build the temple upon the sand fail. One must build it upon the living boulder, upon the stone. All

human material employed in this work dies, decays, corrupts, and blackens in the Philosopher's Egg; then, it is marvellously whitened.

Meaning, the blackened material dies within us; then the whitened material appears, which is what makes us Masters. Let us remember for an instant the work in the Ninth Sphere, the dissolution of the "I." Let us remember the work in the Purgatorial region. There, the initiates resemble putrefactive corpses, because all of the larvae which are inside each one of us flourish, giving the bodies of the initiate the appearance of a decomposed corpse.

The Eighth Key, an illustration of the *Viridarium Chymicum*, shows death represented as a corpse, putrefaction represented by the crows, the sowing as a humble agriculturalist, the growth as a wheat stalk, and the resurrection by a deceased person who rises from the grave

THE EIGHTH KEY OF BASIL VALENTINE

and by an Angel that plays the trumpet of the Final Judgment.

All of this represents that the "ego," the "myself," must die within us until we remain whitened, pure, clean, and perfect. The putrefaction is when one is within the Purgatorial region which is represented by the crows. There, a putrefying corpse appears with repulsive animal forms which resemble reptiles, spiders, filthy slugs, and horrible larvae. These animal forms are reduced to cosmic dust with the help of the Divine Mother Kundalini.

After having incinerated the seeds of the "ego" through the purification of our corruption in Purgatory, the initiate then bathes in the rivers Lethe and Eunoe. Thus, the bodies shine marvellously. Afterwards the initiate must have the confirmation of the Sex-Light; then the Initiatic Resurrection comes, which is represented by an Angel who plays the trumpet. Jesus instructed his disciples during the many years after his Resurrection.

It is important to notice that all of this putrefaction happens within the Philosopher's Egg (sex). One is confirmed by the Light in the Eighth Key of Basil Valentine. The sexual act remains prohibited after achieving the Second Birth and the Master is warned, "You cannot return to work in the Ninth Sphere because then the "I" will resurrect, and you have remained free from it. Your esoteric ordeals have been fulfilled and sex remains prohibited to you for all of eternity." Sex is the lowest part of the initiation. If we want to reach illumination, realization of the Self, we must lift the veil of Isis, which is the Adamic Sexual Veil.

The whole Great Work is found contained in the Philosopher's Egg (sex), that represents the germ of all life. The mas-

THE PHILOSOPHICAL EGG.
ENGRAVING BY G. STENGELIUS, OVA PASCHALIA SACRO EMBLEMATA, 1672.

culine and feminine sexual principles are found contained in the egg. As the fledgling emerges from the egg, as the universe emerges from the Golden Egg of Brahma, so as well from the Philosopher's Egg the Master emerges. Thus, it is stated that the Masters are Children of the Stones, and for this reason there is the surrendering of worship to the stones.

We the Gnostics know that the corpse, death in the Eighth Key, represents the Two Witnesses of the Apocalypse (Revelation 11:3-6) that are now dead. By means of alchemical putrefaction, by means of the works of Alchemy, represented by the crows, the Two Witnesses resurrect. This whole power is found enclosed within the wheat stalk. The sacred Angel that we carry within plays his trumpet, and the Two Witnesses rise from the grave.

The Two Witnesses are a pair of sympathetic cords, semi-ethereal, semi-physical, that are entwined along the spinal medulla forming the Caduceus of Mercury, the sacred eight, the sign of the infinite. They are known in the Orient as Ida and Pingala.

Eight is the number of Job, the man of holy patience. This number represents the life and sacrifice of Job, which is the path that takes the initiate to the Second Birth. The ordeals are very difficult, and we need the patience of Saint Job. Without patience, it is impossible for the work to be performed. A very grave sickness afflicted Job (Book of Job 2:9). Lazarus' sores were rotten (Luke 16:19-31). The friends of Job—Eliphaz, Bildad, and Zophar (the three traitors of the internal Christ)—told him that if he is a friend of God, why doesn't he complain? Job answered, *"The Lord has given, and the Lord has taken away."* Job 1:21 The number of Job is patience and meekness. Behold the way in order to "rot" ourselves. This is testified by the original Bible that included the books of *The Aeneid, The Odyssey,* and *The Macabeus.* Examples of such a Bible are found in the Museum of London, in the Vatican, and in the Museum of Washington. The modern Bible is a corpse. The Bible is an arcanum. In the Book of Psalms, chapter XIX, the Tarot is discussed.

In the Eighth Arcanum, the initiatic ordeals are enclosed. Each initiation, each degree, has its ordeals. These initiatic ordeals are each time more strict, in accordance with the initiatic degree. The number eight is the degree of Job. This sign, this number, signifies ordeals and pain. The initiatic ordeals are performed in the Superior Worlds and in the physical world. The ordeals of initiation are very terrible. A great deal of patience is needed in order not to fall into the abyss. We are tested many times.

JOB AND HIS THREE TRAITORS

SYNTHESIS

- When our disciples want to ask for help from the Lords of Karma, they need to trace a six-pointed star on the ground. They then open their arms in the form of a scale, which they move from above to below, while concentrating their minds on Anubis.

- Then we can mentally ask the Lords of Karma for the desired service. Whilst moving the arms in the form of a scale, we must vocalize the syllables: *Ni, Ne, No, Nu, Na.*

- This is how we can ask for help from the Lords of Karma in moments of necessity and danger. But remember, every credit must be paid.

Chapter XXXI
Arcanum 9

The Ninth Arcanum is the arcanum of the Hermit. It is represented by an Elder who carries a lamp in his right hand. This lamp must be raised up in order to give light on the path; it must be raised aloft in order to illuminate.

The number nine when multiplied by any number always results in nine. For example:

$$2 \times 9 = 18 \quad \text{then} \quad 1 + 8 = 9$$
$$4 \times 9 = 36 \quad \text{then} \quad 3 + 6 = 9$$
$$5 \times 9 = 45 \quad \text{then} \quad 4 + 5 = 9$$

This becomes more interesting because there are nine inferior circles within the interior of the Earth. It can be stated that there are nine infernal parallel universes, from the epidermis of the Earth into the interior. These universes extend until reaching the very heart of the Earth, with the ninth circle in the center of the Earth. These nine circles are the nine demonic or diabolical regions.

There also exist nine superior circles that in occultism are called the nine Heavens. These nine Heavens are represented by the nine planets.

For example, when we refer to the Moon, we must not think about the Moon as the physical satellite. The sub-lunar diabolical regions must not be searched for in the Moon but in the interior of the Earth.

Let us consider now the lunar Heaven. These Heavens do not mean precisely that they are related to the physical Moon, but to the superior regions, those molecular regions which are lunar. They are governed by the Moon. It is a molecular lunar world which is found here in our world.

This first Heaven of the Moon has its science; here we find the souls that deserve to rise into that region because not all of the dead achieve the arrival into that Heaven. The majority of the dead return from the threshold in order to enter into the region of the dead; then they penetrate into a new womb. Others enter into the submerged involution of the nine infernal spheres.

The first Heaven of the Moon is entered as a resting place. The Moon is related with chastity, with sex. Here, one can remember the distinct errors committed with sex.

A grave problem exists because the Moon tends towards materiality. The whole terrestrial mechanism is controlled by the Moon. The whole life of the Earth, the whole terrestrial mechanism, is controlled by the Moon. This whole mechanical life in which we live in is of a lunar type.

The Moon, like the weight of a great clock, makes the terrestrial machinery move. The sprouting of vegetables, the animals, ovulation in women, the flux and reflux of the ocean, high and low tides, etc., all depend on the Moon. Since life is so mechanical, if triumphing is what is really required, then the Moon must be taken advantage of. The crescent moon as well as the full moon is for our activities.

Planet	Symbol
Moon	☽
Mercury	☿
Venus	♀
Sun	☉
Mars	♂
Jupiter	♃
Saturn	♄
Uranus	♅
Neptune	♆

However, if the waning moon is utilized, we fail. The new moon is very difficult as well; it does not have strength. If we want to triumph in any activity, or in business, inevitably we will have to take advantage of the crescent moon and the full moon. Never start a business during the waning moon or new moon.

It is necessary to have the perfumes of the rose and violet plants accessible in order to control the lunar materiality. These perfumes must be used in order to control materiality, because the Moon exercises a materialistic influence over the human mind. Moreover, to our disgrace, the subjective elements which we carry within are controlled by the Moon.

The soul of every living being emanates from an atom. This atom is the Ain Soph. Each person has his own Ain Soph. This is a star that shines in infinite space beyond the nine Heavens. Souls must return to their Star, to their own Ain Soph. This return towards their Star, the Ain Soph, is a divine event. The day when the soul is Self-realized will be when it has the luxury of returning to its star. This was commented on by Plato in his *Timeus*. Each three-brained biped being needs to create the butterfly in order to return to that star.

The nine Heavens are intimately concordant with the nine infernal circles; they are compaginated. In total we have:

9 Heavens + 9 Infernal Circles = 18

1+ 8 = 9; this is the number of the Master, of the initiate.

We need to Self-realize within the eighteen circles. An individual that does not Self-realize within the eighteen circles is not a Master. In synthesis, in order to be a Master, to be the perfect nine, is to be able to act with assurance in any of the eighteen circles.

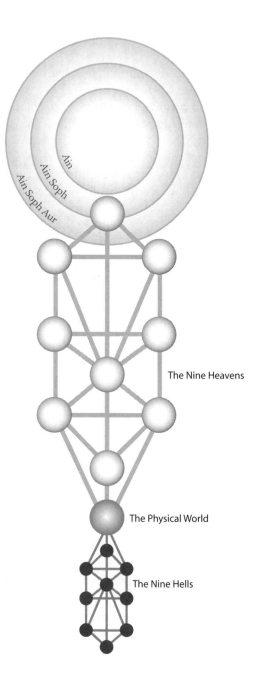

Ain

Ain Soph

Ain Soph Aur

The Nine Heavens

The Physical World

The Nine Hells

Atman is the Divine Spirit (an emanation from the Logos). He has two souls, Buddhi and Manas. It is vital to comprehend this. In the Middle Ages, when the medieval knight departed in order to fight for his lady, it was nothing more than the Human Soul struggling for the conquest of his Spiritual Soul.

I achieved the comprehension of this when my real Being took me into the Causal World, which is a world of an intense electric blue color. The King, Atman, the Lord, was seated at a table with a beautiful lady who was his Spiritual Soul, his Beatrice, his Valkyrie. They were seated forming a triangle with the Human Soul. Atman began to speak and said, "I have two Souls: the Spiritual Soul and the Human Soul. While the Human Soul works, the Spiritual Soul plays and lives happily. This is my doctrine. Thus, we three are one."

We—Atman, Buddhi, and Manas—were reunited in the Causal World, in that region of causes. So without such experience I could not explain this in a clear form.

Atman unfolds into Buddhi and Buddhi into Manas, just as when we look at ourselves in a mirror. Thus, the Trinity is created. The Essence is an enfoldment of the Superior Manas. This Essence in its turn is bottled up within the "ego." The awakening of this Essence is the awakening of consciousness; it is to make oneself cognizant of the mysteries of life and death. Many want to awaken the consciousness but they abandon the work at any moment. This is why the Maithuna was not communicated to anyone if previously this person did not have an awakened consciousness. *The Christmas Message of 1968-69* [*The Gnostic Magic of the Runes*] is a book that explains the Runes for the awakening of the consciousness.

To incarnate the Being, the Divine Triad, is something that is very difficult; to accomplish this, the building of the Solar Bodies is necessary. Without having the Solar Bodies built, if the Being was incarnated, this would produce an electric shock that could not be tolerated and one would die.

The building of the Solar Bodies is vital. One must work in the Ninth Sphere; one must descend into the forge of the Cyclops in order to work with the water and the fire. The creative energy is the Holy Spirit, Vulcan, who is the Third Logos, the sexual force; He is Shiva.

The sacred fire is "She," the igneous serpent that rises through the medullar

VENUS, THE GODDESS OF LOVE, REQUESTING HEPHAISTOS (VULCAN), THE GOD OF FIRE AND CREATIVITY, TO MAKE WEAPONS AND ARMOR (THE SOLAR BODIES) FOR THE HERO AENEAS.

canal. She is the Mother Kundalini. She marries her husband in the pineal gland. The Third Logos, the Holy Spirit, the eternal spouse, begets the Divine Mother Kundalini, the root of the Monad, the Mother Space.

The cosmic seed plot—the Matripadma—is the Devamatri, the chaotic matter, the substance mater, the raw matter of the Great Work. She is Mother Space. The Holy Spirit is the Third Logos who fecundates her, who is latent within the Matripadma. Without him, she remains quiet, and with him, she ignites herself; she reverberates; she swells.

The Father is the First Logos, the Second Logos is the Son, and the Third Logos is the Holy Spirit. These three aspects are behind Atman, Buddhi, and Manas. From the Ain Soph emerges the Father, from the Father emerges the Son, and from the Son emerges the Holy Spirit. These Three Logoi are the Tao, Brahatma, and the universal Spirit of life; beyond this is the Absolute. These Three Logoi emerge from this Universal Ocean of Life; a tide that rises could be Ishvara, a Purusha that instructs. Once he instructs he returns into the ocean of the Spirit. He fuses himself with the Ocean of the Spirit.

The Absolute in itself has three aspects: the Ain, the Ain Soph, and the Ain Soph Aur. To talk about the Ain is difficult, for it is the unmanifested Absolute. No form, no figure, no number, nor weight exists within the Absolute. When a universe is dissolved, only the memory of it remains in the consciousness of the Gods. With those memories, the universe of Pleroma is formed. If something wants to be taken out of this place, it does not exist because it is only a memory.

Synthesis

- It is understood that a Self-realized Being is someone who has built the Solar Bodies and who has finished with the ego.
- The descent into the abyss is only under the command of the Elder of Days, and this will be in order to ascend.
- Initiation is your own life.
- The one who receives initiations is the Innermost.
- Thus, initiation has nothing to do with those fantastic tales which are so abundant in certain books.
- Thus, nothing is given to us for free. Everything has its price. Whosoever has not earned anything cannot collect anything.
- Initiations are payments that the Logos gives to human beings when the disciples have sacrificed themselves for humanity.
- Those who only preoccupy themselves with their own spiritual progress and do not work for others achieve absolutely nothing. Whosoever wants to progress must sacrifice the self for others.
- Initiation is this same life intentionally lived with rectitude and love.

Chapter XXXII

Arcanum 10

The Tenth Arcanum of the Tarot is the wheel of fortune; it is the same wheel of samsara, the tragic wheel that symbolizes the ancient law of return. We must differentiate between return, reincarnation, and transmigration, which are all completely different.

Return

The worlds, the heavens, the stars, the four seasons return to their original point of life. The ego returns through all of the 108 lives of each human being, in accordance with the 108 beads of the Buddha's necklace. Disincarnated egos penetrate into the Infernal Worlds and others return into a new womb when death arrives. The ego is a compound of many entities; some of those entities return into animals or plant-organisms, and some of them return into human wombs. This is how the ego returns into a new organism. The Buddhata (Essence) which is our divine and substantial part, returns bottled up within the ego. Undoubtedly, many parts of ourselves live within animal organisms.

The same events are repeated when we return into this valley of tears by law of recurrence. Everything returns and occurs as it was in other lives. The law of return is intimately united and associated with the law of recurrence. In other words, everything occurs as it occurred before, with its good or evil consequences; the same dramas are repeated. This is called Karma.

The Wheel of Destiny

Reincarnation

This is the descent of divinity into a human being. The incarnation of Vishnu into a human being is what is called an Avatar. Properly, Vishnu is the Christ, the Solar Logos. This is why in India they say that reincarnation is performed by Vishnu. Krishna spoke about this by saying, *"Only the Devas reincarnate."*

Transmigration

This starts when the Being becomes part of the mineral kingdom, then evolves into the plant kingdom; after a lot of time, subsequently through eternities, the Being rises into the evolution of the animal kingdom in order to rise up to the human state where 108 lives are assigned to us. If at the end of the 108 lifetimes, the Self has not reached realization, then the devolving process commences in the submerged kingdoms of the planet Earth, where the Essence or Buddhata recapitulates its previous states as an animal, plant, and mineral. The Essence or Buddhata is purified in the profoundness of the abyss, in the atomic infernos of nature. This Essence is purified, is liberated from within the ego through the disintegration of the ego. Thus the Essence, free after eternities, comes back to rise again, beginning a new evolution from the mineral kingdom, then the plant, the animal, until finally claiming the human state which was previously lost. This is the law of the transmigration of souls.

Only through awakening the consciousness is it possible to know if we have already devolved and started again. Everything related with return and transmigration is of a **lunar** type. Only reincarnation is **solar**.

The solar forces are separated from the law of return and the law of recurrence. All of this is part of the Tenth Arcanum. While we do not disintegrate the ego we have to return.

To die is necessary in order to be liberated. The death of the ego is indispensable. Only thus will return cease.

If the Egyptian *Book of the Dead* is studied, it will be noticed that Isis is the one who is called in order to kill the ego. The death of the ego is impossible without the Divine Mother. The Essence is liberated with the death of the ego and is lost within

OSIRIS

Osiris, the Divine Christ. The Essence resurrects within the heart of Osiris. Thus, the affections, the attachments to things, our desires, all of this will cease to exist.

We must die in order to liberate ourselves from the tragic wheel. The seeds of the ego must be burned in order for them not to resurrect, and then we bathe ourselves in the waters of Lethe and Eunoe, thus confirming ourselves in the Light. We must kill Cain, which is the lunar mind. This mind is worthless and it must be eliminated. It must be killed because it is animalistic.

For this reason, the ancients saw the figure of Cain in the Moon. The mind is called Cain. The mind is a hunter. The mind is hunting for fortunes, social positions, fame. This mind is utilized by the know-it-all-scoundrels in order to triumph; they feel they are wise and powerful with that animal lunar mind that is well-cultivated.

WINGED VICTORY OF
SAMOTHRACE. GREEK.

A sculpture exists of a figure of a decapitated angel, the Angel of Samothrace. This sculpture signifies that after the ego has been dissolved, after having burned the seeds of it, after having bathed ourselves and having been confirmed in the Light, etc., the initiate has to pass through the decapitation. This is because the death of the lunar body and the lunar mind is missing. These two bodies that form Cain are the two subjective elements which must be decapitated. After all this, only Osiris remains, and the Essence that remains within the heart of Osiris; thus, the right to carry the asp (the serpent) on the forehead is granted. As the *Book of the Dead* states: he can sit down as the great Osirises who are chiefs of their abodes are seated, he then can carry the serpent on his forehead, he already has the Verb, he has triumphed, and he does not utilize powers in an egotistical way.

Osiris is a Cosmic Christ. An Osirified Human Being is one who has the Cosmic Christ, one who does not have subjective elements, one who has been liberated from this tragic wheel of life and death where the cause of pain resides.

The most violent struggle that we go through in order to achieve the elimination of the ego is that struggle against the terrible tempting serpent which is the abominable Kundabuffer organ, the tail of Satan. This serpent is the horrible python that Apollo hurt with his darts. This serpent is the antithesis of the Divine Mother. This is a dense and frightful matter that fights against us.

While we are not within the "boat of Isis" we are worthless.

According to Egyptian wisdom, Thoth is Hermes, and Hermes is Mercury, the great Hierophant, the Minister, the Ambassador of the Solar Logos, the great Instructor, the one who raises us from initiation to initiation. However, who is he within us? He is the **Ens Seminis**.

We can escape from the great wheel and from the pain of this world, which is totally transitory and painful, only by means of the Great Death. To go beyond the affections, beyond our most beloved beings, is necessary, and this is a very difficult exertion.

This world is terribly painful. The only thing that is worth living for is the realization of the Being, because all else is vanity.

SYNTHESIS

- We liberate ourselves from the wheel of Samsara only by means of the Arcanum A.Z.F.

- The body of Adam-Kadmon is formed by the Sephiroth.

- The human being enters into the kingdom of Adam-Kadmon when he attains in-depth realization of the Self.

- The kingdom of Adam-Kadmon is finally absorbed into the Absolute, where life, free in its movement, shines.

Chapter XXXIII
Arcanum 11

The Eleventh Arcanum in Kabbalah is known as the arcanum of Persuasion. Persuasion in itself is a force of a subtle spiritual order. Occult wisdom states, *"Vivify the flame of the Spirit with the force of Love."*

Love in itself is a powerful omnipotent force. The force of love keeps the worlds around their centers of cosmic gravity. Those centers of cosmic gravity are the suns. This is why Hermes Trismegistus stated, *"I give thee love, within which the whole Summum of Wisdom is contained."*

A soft word pacifies anger. Persuasion has more power than violence. If a violent person wishes to attack us, then a gentle phrase should be sent unto this person; thus, his violence will be pacified. This is why in the Eleventh Arcanum a woman who is opening the mouth of a lion appears, representing the living force of Persuasion.

If we delve more profoundly, we find the lion with a double head which represents the two earths: the visible and the invisible. The lion as an animal is very important and very interesting. Lions served as hauling animals in Atlantis. They hauled wagons; they were meek. After the submergence of Atlantis, they became furious. The lion is a living symbol of fire.

Observe the Sphinx for yourselves; you will notice that it has lion's claws, representing fire. In the Aztec Calendar, or Solar Stone, we find the lion's claws.

These claws have a very grandiose significance. If we Kabbalistically add the number eleven, we get: 1 + 1 = 2.

The Divine Mother Kundalini as Durga, riding upon her lion and slaying the demon-ego

The Second Arcanum is the arcanum of the Priestess, occult science, the Divine Mother. She in herself is living fire. This is why She is known in the east as Devi Kundalini in Her individual aspect, and Maha-Kundalini in Her macrocosmic aspect. To learn how to work with this fire is vital; this is why the number 2 is Kabbalistically deconstructed as 1 man + 1 woman, and these are the two who must work with the fire in the Magisterium of Fire.

The chariot hauled by the lions is a very esoteric allegory originating from very archaic times. The chariot represents the human being, the lion represents the fire. This is nothing but a living symbol of the solar man, the Sun Man. When the chariot is spoken of it is alluding to the internal bodies of the human being: the physical, Vital, Astral, and Mental bodies. In this chariot the real Being must ride. *The Zohar* portrays the Elder of Days as travelling in his chariot through the infinite. There is no doubt that the real Being has to always travel in his chariot in order to work in the worlds.

The lions of fire are the synthesis of this Kabbalistic number, because eleven is deconstructed as $1 + 1 = 2$. The number two is deconstructed in the two unities, man and woman, the two columns of the temple, Jachin and Boaz; between these two columns is the arcanum. By analyzing this arcanum we get the magisterium of the fire as a conclusion. This sacred fire cannot be awakened with Pranayama or respiratory exercises in combination with meditation. With these exercises only small fractions

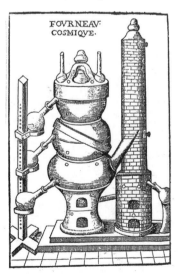

An ancient alchemical "cosmic oven" that clearly represents the lingam-yoni of all the ancient mystery schools.

or sparks are enflamed for the awakening of the chakras. Those sparks are elevated towards the centers, but this does not signify that the serpent Kundalini has risen.

Agni, the God of Fire, helps to awaken the fire, but only through working in the Ninth Sphere. Single people can help themselves with Pranayama in order to cause sparks to rise, but this does not signify that they raise the serpent.

We have a furnace, which is the coccyx, or Muladhara chakra, where according to the Alchemists, we must place the receptacle. Within this receptacle the Mercury of sacred philosophy is found, or the Ens Seminis. Within the **Ens Seminis** the **Ens Virtutis** is found. One must close the receptacle in order to impede the raw matter (the semen) to be totally lost, in order for it not to be totally lost.

The laboratory has a chimney through which all of the steam must rise; this chimney is the spinal medullar canal. It also has a distillery within the brain, to be used for the distillation of the pure gold. This is the laboratory of those medieval Alchemists who were transmuting lead into gold.

Many despise the elementals. We must not do this.

Salamanders keep the fire; Undines are within the raw matter, which is enclosed within its receptacle. The Undines can help us if we dominate them; if we do not, then they do what they want because they are very whimsical. The sylphs make the steam that escapes from the raw matter to rise. The Gnomes are in charge of the distillation of the raw matter, in order for it to be converted into gold within the brain.

I have known true Devas of fire; I have been in contact with them. They live in the Causal World, or the world of conscious will. They told me that beyond clairvoyance is **intuition**, which is superior because it belongs to the pure Spirit. With clairvoyance, the molecular world and the superior and inferior regions can be investigated; yet in the world of pure Spirit only intuition functions directly. This is why intuition is superior. Intuition has its roots in the pineal gland, the chakra Sahasrara or lotus of one thousand petals. This faculty is related with Shiva, or the flaming fire. This is the reason that this center gives us access to the world of the pure Spirit.

Forty-nine fires can exist within a human being. The seven chakras or churches multiplied by seven levels gives as a result forty-nine fires.

$$7 \times 7 = 49$$

There are many types of fire: the fire of lightning; the fire that is concentrated within plants; the fire that burns in the interior of the mountains and that is vomited by the volcanoes of the earth; the fire that is utilized in order to cook; the fire that is in each world. But in synthesis, we will speak about two fires: the Solar and Lunar fire. The Solar Fire is Christic, sublime; it is Devi Kundalini. The Lunar Fire is Luciferic, negative, fatal.

The Solar Fire crystallizes in worlds, suns, and universes. The Lunar Fire crystallizes in all of those entities that constitute the animal ego.

A human being has to develop the forty-nine fires in his chakras.

SYNTHESIS

- The Eleventh Arcanum is the work with the fire, with the force of love, in order to convert ourselves into living flames.
- The Undines work in the Ens Seminis.
- The Salamanders keep the fire lit.
- The Sylphs raise the steam.
- The Gnomes distil the Ens Seminis in the brain.
- The creatures of the water are commanded while holding a cup.
- The creatures of the air are commanded while holding a bird's feather.
- The creatures of the earth are conjured while holding a rod or staff.
- The creatures of the fire are conjured while holding a sword.

Chapter XXXIV

Arcanum 12

Arcanum number twelve implies sacrifice. It is the card of the Apostolate, of sufferings. Nevertheless, this number is a very complete number. It is the famous dodecahedron upon which are supported all of the universal creations of the solar system, which have twelve foundations, twelve planets.

Esoteric science teaches that seven principle planets exist:

1. Moon

2. Mercury

3. Venus

4. Sun

5. Mars

6. Jupiter

7. Saturn

With Uranus, Neptune, and Pluto, there would be a total of ten planets. Yet, esoteric science sustains that there are two more planets beyond Pluto. Twelve savior planets have always been spoken of. The Master Jesus had twelve disciples. In *The Pistis Sophia,* which is from the Gnostic texts, twelve saviors are referred to.

The Twelfth Arcanum brings a lot of suffering and many struggles. This arcanum has a very pleasant synthesis, because 1 + 2 = 3, which signifies material and spiritual production.

Let us remember the marvellous union of the cross with the triangle. In the Twelfth Arcanum, we see a man who hangs from one foot and is aiming downwards; this indicates the fertile work in the Ninth Sphere, without which the union of the cross with the triangle cannot be achieved.

The Philosophical Gold cannot be achieved without this union.

Sex was abhorred and hated during the Age of Pisces, which had a regressive, retarded asceticism. In the Caucasus, vestiges still exist of a sect that mortally hates sex. Whosoever entered into that sect had to castrate themselves with an iron stick that was heated until red. The minor lips of the vulva were taken off of the women; this was the first step. In the second step, the men had to amputate the phallus from themselves, and to the women, one breast was cut off during a religious ceremony. They drank the blood and ate the flesh. Afterwards, each woman lay down in a bed of flowers. This is monstrous, abominable. See for yourselves into where the horror towards sex reaches. This belongs to the sphere of Lilith.

Kabbalistic tradition states that Adam had two wives: Lilith, who is the mother of abortions, homosexuality, and hatred towards sex, and in contrast, Nahemah, who is the mother of malignant beauty, mother of passion, adultery, lust, and everything that is related to the abuse of sexuality. The Caucasian sect belongs to Lilith. They abhor the Third Logos, the Holy Spirit.

See for yourselves how hatred towards sex discards the Philosophical Stone. This is absurd; nonetheless, they believed that they were doing very well. The authorities intervened in another sect, where each year a man was crucified until death, in order to remember the great Master Jesus. These are types of barbarism that belonged to the Age of Pisces.

The Age of Aquarius is governed by Uranus which is the planet and regent of the sexual glands. We must learn how to utilize sex. "Sexual arousal" must be intelligently combined with "enthusiasm." From this wise mixture results the intelligent and revolutionary erotica of the Age of Aquarius.

The Age of Pisces was conservative, regressive, and retarded. To depart from vulgar copulation is necessary in order to pass into male/female polarization. When a man and woman are united, something is created; the "*genius lucis* of sex" was created in the ancient mysteries. Sexual Magic was practiced in those times. Collective copulation was performed in those times. Those were very different times because the degree of degeneration that we find today had not yet arrived. During this ancient time, people pronounced the name of the divinity in the moment of *genius lucis*.

The lance of Longinus is the extraordinary emblem of the *genius lucis*; that is the Odic or magnetic force with which the animal ego is converted into cosmic dust.

LONGINUS AND HIS LANCE

We must learn how to utilize the *genius lucis* in order to eliminate the "I." The *genius lucis* of man and woman can eliminate all of those entities that form the "I," the "myself," because it is the weapon used in order to destroy the ego.

Krishnamurti taught this humanity to dissolve the ego. But, his doctrine is incipient because he believed that only on the basis of comprehension is anger, jealousy, etc., eliminated. This is not possible. A power capable of eliminating the ego is necessary. This is the serpentine fire, Devi Kundalini, She who has the power to eliminate all of our psychological defects. Comprehension and elimination must act in unison. Devi Kundalini can grasp the lance, and She does it during the Sahaja Maithuna. She knows how to utilize the Genius Lucis.

To pray on the bridal bed of the garden of delights, on the nuptial bed of erotic marvels, to beg in the moment of enjoyment, in the unforgettable instant of coitus, to ask unto our divine and adorable Mother Kundalini to grasp with splendor the magical lance, in those instants of kisses and tenderness, in order to eliminate that defect which we have comprehended in all of the departments of the mind, and then to withdraw ourselves without spilling of the sacred wine, the Ens Seminis, signifies death, rapture, delight, pleasure...

This death signifies something transcendental and is performed by degrees. The transformation of the initiates is astonishing when absolute death within their minds is achieved; that death implies a radical death. This death cannot be achieved unless performed in the region of Mercury; the element that can help us is that *genius lucis* of man and woman, who is Isis, Cybele, Insoberta, or Kundalini Shakti.

She is the only one who can take us in depth into that intellectual transformation.

This death is performed in the spheres of diverse planets. The Angels work in the Astral World, and they are governed by the Moon.

The Archangels are developed under the regency of Mercury and their work is performed in the world of the mind. They handle or drive the substance or essence of the Mental World. They have achieved this power in the Ninth Sphere from moment to moment.

In Venus, we find a different work that we need to perform. This world corresponds to the Causal World, the kingdom of the Principalities.

The Virtues correspond to the Intuitive World, Buddhi, which corresponds to the sphere of the Sun.

The Potencies correspond to Atman, the sphere of Mars.

Then, Jupiter corresponds to Dominions.

Continuing with Saturn, which is the most elevated among the seven planets; it is the most divine, the most exalted. The Paranirvanic world relates to Saturn.

Beyond is the Empireum; the most elevated beings are the Seraphim. The whole solar system is within each one of us.

Initiatic Degree	Region	Planet
Angels	Astral World	Moon
Archangels	Mental World	Mercury
Principalities	Causal World	Venus
Virtues	Intuitive Buddhic	Sun
Potencies	Atmic World	Mars
Dominions	Nirvanic World	Jupiter
Thrones	Paranirvanic World	Saturn
Cherubim	Mahaparanirvanic World	Uranus
Seraphim	The Empireum	Neptune

We have to perform specific works in each one of these planets. How can we have our willpower under the service of our Father if we have not worked in the sphere of Venus?

Firstly, we have to liberate ourselves from the planet Earth. We have to achieve the Second Birth. Then, we must liberate ourselves from the Moon by performing the work related with the Moon. One is free from evil will in Venus. This is something grandiose.

Firstly, one must be liberated from the solar system (Deuterocosmos), and then from the galaxy (Macrocosmos). Then by means of transcendental works we enter into the Protocosmos; this is within the Absolute. Nonetheless, we must liberate ourselves from the Protocosmos. The path is sexual. There is no other path.

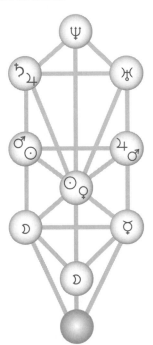

The Age of Aquarius is an age of knowing; everything is revolutionary.

Uranus = the Lord of the sexual glands

Uranas = Fire and Water

Every school that does not teach the Sahaja Maithuna is not Aquarian. Aquarius does not reject sex; rather, sex is investigated. A *mutant* is a Human Being in the broadest sense of the word. Taboos are finished in the Age of Aquarius.

The psychology of the Age of Aquarius with its famous five "M's" (the Pancatattva Ritual) is revolutionary.

The one that hates sex is as absurd as the one that abuses it. The one that gets drunk is as absurd as the one that cannot drink a small amount. The middle path must be tread upon in order not to fall into extremes.

SYNTHESIS

- The Alchemist needs an Athanor (furnace) in order to work in the Great Work. This Athanor is the woman.

- The man who wants to be converted into an ineffable God has to adore the woman.

- Realization of the Self is impossible without a spouse.

- To be an Alchemist is impossible if one is not working with the Philosophical Stone. This blessed Stone has four names: Azoth, Inri, Adam, Eve.

- The Sun King is begotten within each one of us by practicing Sexual Magic intensely with our spouse.

- Women convert men into ineffable Gods, and vice versa.

AQUARIUS, THE BRINGER OF KNOWLEDGE

Chapter XXXV

Arcanum 13

In the Thirteenth Arcanum, death embraces two aspects. The first aspect is the death of all human beings, and the second aspect is from the esoteric point of view.

In the first aspect, all of the texts of occultism, pseudo-occultism, pseudo-Rosicrucianism, and Theosophy affirm that one is born at a certain hour and dies on a determined day, hour, and second in accordance with the law of destiny. This concept is not precise because the Lords of Karma deposit determined "cosmic values" into human beings. One can preserve that "capital" and life can be prolonged for a long time. Life can be shortened by squandering those values.

Life is prolonged by accumulating cosmic capital. If there are no good deeds, the Lords of Karma may prolong life but only in determined cases.

The Lords of Karma deposit a determined quantity of vital values into each one of our three brains:

First: Thinking or Intellectual Brain; in the head.

Second: Motor Brain; situated in the upper part of the vertebral column.

Third: Emotional Brain; situated in the solar plexus and nervous sympathetic centers.

If one exhausts the vital values of the thinking brain by abusing the intellect, then it is clear that the death of this brain is provoked or a nervous type of sickness is contracted, such as neurasthenia, imbecility, or schizophrenia. Madness or manias are produced in people who have exhausted the values of the intellectual center.

If one exhausts the vital values of the emotional center, then psychic and nervous sicknesses related with the heart are provoked, as well as sicknesses related with emotional or emotive aspects. Many artists exhaust the emotional brain resulting in certain psychopathic, emotive, and or cardiac states.

Those who exhaust the vital values of the motor brain end up with paralysis or with sicknesses related with the muscles, knees, joints or with paralysis or damage to the dorsal spine, etc.

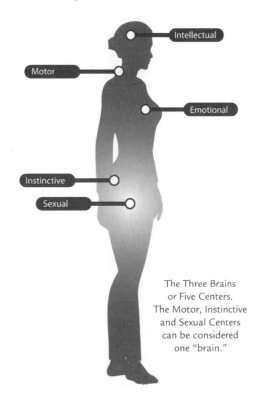

The Three Brains
or Five Centers.
The Motor, Instinctive
and Sexual Centers
can be considered
one "brain."

In general, all sicknesses are the outcome of the wrong use of the three brains. In other words, one dies by thirds, little by little. For example, football players, runners, and boxers are people who abuse the motor brain. These people end up ill. Their death is a result of the wrong use of the motor brain.

If one learns how to use the three brains in an equilibrated way, then the vital values that the Lords of Karma have deposited are conserved and life is prolonged. In Asia, there exist monasteries where the monks live until the age of 300 or even more. This is because they drive the three brains harmoniously; they preserve the vital values of the three brains in an equilibrated way. Then, what about the statement regarding the hour and exact date of life or death?

If one exhausts their vital values, one dies soon. If one preserves them, one prolongs life. It is clear that some have more capital than others. This capital depends upon the debits and expenditures of each one of us. When one believes that one has abused the thinking brain then one has to put the motor brain in activity.

In order to prolong life when one is in these esoteric studies, one has to negotiate with the Lords of Karma. One has to pay with the performance of good deeds.

Every human being who incarnates the Soul can ask for the Elixir of Longevity. This is a gas of immaculate whiteness. This gas is deposited in the vital depth of the human organism. After Resurrection, the Master does not ever die again. The Master is eternal.

We have the case of the Master Paracelsus; he did not die; he lives in Europe with the same body. He is one of those who "swallowed soil." He remains as a vagabond and passes himself off as different persons.

The initiate Nicholas Flamel lives in India with his spouse Perenelle. He also swallowed soil along with his spouse. The Count of Saint Germain—who directs the ray of worldly politics—was working in Europe in the XVI and XVII centuries; Giovanni Papini found him a little while ago. The Yogi Christ of India, the immortal Babaji, and his immortal sister Mataji have lived with their physical bodies ever since millions of years ago. The immortals can instantaneously appear and disappear; they make themselves visible in the physical world at will. Cagliostro, Saint Germain, Quetzalcoatl, and many other immortals have made great works in the world.

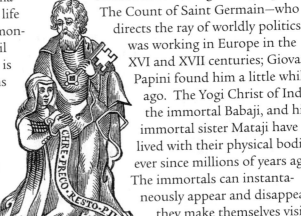

Nicolas Flamel and Perenelle, his wife, from a painting executed at the end of the 15th century, under the vaults of the Cemetery of the Innocents, in Paris, France

Death is the crown in the path of life. This path is formed by the hooves of the horse of death.

The Egyptian *Book of the Dead* is for those that are alive, yet are dead. It is necessary to know how to understand this book. It is related to the deceased initiates who already are dead, yet still are alive. They have already penetrated into the region of the dead, and they go out in sunlight in order to give their teachings.

The first thing that we must do in order to die is to dissolve the "I." This "I" is a conjunction of demons, which the

Egyptians refer to as the "red demons of Seth." We must dissolve the "I" in order to awaken consciousness, in order to receive direct knowledge. The red demons of Seth are all of the demons that we have within. They are Satan. They must be killed. Horus must defeat those demons.

Seth has two aspects. His negative aspect is Satan and in his positive aspect he corresponds to the dorsal spine. This tenebrous and satanic Seth must be killed. This is the lunar ego which is constituted by thousands of demons and which Horus must defeat with the help of Isis, the Divine Mother. These demons must die.

Those "I's" must be reduced to dust; their seeds must be scorched and then one must be bathed in the waters of Lethe in order to forget, and in Eunoe in order to fortify virtues, to then ascend to Heaven. In order to ascend to each of the Heavens one has to first descend into the Infernos. That is not all. Tremendous battles come.

All of this must be studied at the foot of *The Pistis Sophia*.

The initiate must be converted into a "crocodile." For this, one must destroy the body of desires, which is lunar, to then ascend into the lunar Heavens. In order to destroy the body of desires, one must submerge himself; this signifies a frightful descent through enormous sacrifices. Thus, this is how the lunar body is discarded, which is disintegrated little by little. When the initiate has already discarded the body of desires, the initiate then emerges with the Solar Astral Body.

Then one must pass into Mercury for decapitation in order to discard the lunar mind. Thus, the initiate cries out asking for his head, the head of Osiris. Nonetheless, the initiate has to pass through many killings. We must fight

SETH AND HORUS AS ONE.

against the demons. In the same way that eight Kabirs exist, also eight Anti-Kabirs exist, two in each cardinal point who are the antithesis. The initiate must fight against the eight black Kabirs. One cannot ascend without descending.

One cannot enter into the Absolute "until passing through the Great Death" and submerging the Essence into the Being.

One must descend when one is on the path towards the Absolute. Here is where one is converted into a dead crocodile; then one has to ascend. That ascension is very difficult. When one has been submerged within the Being, one can say, "I am Horus." One can talk in the language of the Gods; one can be a living God before the sight of the red demons that constitute the ego.

SEBEK-RA

The thirteenth card contains the Gospel of Judas. Judas represents the death of the ego. The death of the ego is his Gospel. The script that he performed was commanded by the great Master Jesus. Judas is now working with the demons in the Infernal Worlds in order to redeem them. He has succeeded with a few. When he finishes his work, he will depart with Jesus into the Absolute because he will have greatly earned it.

SYNTHESIS

- One must convert oneself into the sacred crocodile Sebek through enormous ordeals and great sacrifices.

- Efforts are not enough for this, only **super efforts**.

- We must give form to ourselves. This requires super efforts through constant and intensive daily work.

- We must work in order to terminate anger.

- The dead live in the sphere of Yetzirah; the dead live in the world of Nogah (Astral World).

- The deceased that were fornicators are cold and tenebrous. They live in the world of Assiah and are full of coldness and darkness.

- The disciples that have been chaste and have awakened the Kundalini are full of youth and fire after death.

- The thirteenth hour is intimately related with death. Resurrection cannot be achieved if there is no death. The Liberation is the thirteenth hour of Apollonius.

- The twelve doors of mercy are the twelve zodiacal signs, the twelve worlds or twelve supra-sensible planes. Liberation is the Thirteenth Door in order for one to escape into the Absolute.

- One dies to the Cosmos when one is born for the Absolute.

- One must die in order to live. One must die and resurrect.

Chapter XXXVI
Arcanum 14

The profound wisdom of the Fourteenth Arcanum is classically divided into three parts:

1. Transmutation of the creative energy
2. Transformation
3. Transubstantiation

We are going to study each one of these parts separately.

Transmutation

The mixture of the elixirs of man and woman, the red and the white, results in the origin of the "Elixir of Longevity." We have the concrete case of Nicholas Flamel and his spouse Perenelle, who at the present time live physically in India. They have the "Elixir of Longevity." Paracelsus, at the present time, lives on a mountain in Bohemia, within a temple which is in the Jinn State. Those who posses the "Elixir of Longevity" know how to live as vagabonds.

The great Master Sanat Kumara, founder of the College of Initiates of the White Lodge, lives in an oasis in the Gobi desert; his body is not from the planet Earth. He is from the planet Venus. He came during the time of Lemuria in a cosmic ship. He is one of the four Shaddai, one of the four Thrones, one of the four Kumaras. He is working by helping all of those who are on the path. He helps intensely. He lives together with a Lemurian Guru. He is mentioned in very ancient scriptures where they called him the Great Immolated One. Today he is immortal.

This "Elixir of Longevity" is a metaphysical and electric substance. When somebody receives it, it remains deposited in the vital body. Whosoever receives this "Elixir of Longevity" has the right to live for one thousand years, although the initiate can prolong this amount of time. Thus, Sanat Kumara has already lived for three million years. To acquire the "Elixir of Longevity," the transmutation of the sacred fire is necessary.

Transformation

The second part of the Fourteenth Arcanum refers to the transformation of the energies. One type of energy can be transformed into another, for example, hatred into love.

Many forms of energetic transformations exist. It is known in esoteric wisdom that the initiate must be transformed into a bird, into a sparrow hawk with a human head. When the "I" is dissolved, the consciousness is free, thus, transformed into birds, we penetrate into the World of the Dead who are living. Thus, we can fly over the seas and go across the mountains.

We need to be transformed into serpents of wisdom or "Nagas." We need to be transformed into crocodiles. If we want to ascend, we must first *"submerge ourselves into the depth of the abyss."* This is the law. The Twice-born must be transformed into true, dead, esoteric Adepts of mystical death. This is something transcendental. One can be an Adept, but previously one has to have descended and destroyed the ego. Otherwise one is transformed into a Hanasmuss with a double center of gravity.

A Hanasmuss is someone who has built the Solar Bodies but who has not passed through the philosophical death of the Masters, and so in this way the Hanasmuss polarizes as an individual with a double center of gravity. Thus, the Hanasmuss has two personalities: one Angelic personality and the other a demonic personality. This type of being is called an abortion of the Cosmic Mother, a false project.

The Adept must pass through the Ascension after having lived all of the drama of the Crucifixion. The Adept must live this Ascension as the Master Jesus lived it, and this Ascension must be performed through all of the Nine Heavens:

1. Moon
2. Mercury
3. Venus
4. Sun
5. Mars
6. Jupiter
7. Saturn
8. Uranus
9. Neptune

The initiate has to pass through these planets after having lived the drama of the dissolution of the ego. The initiate is transformed into the crocodile Sebek, for the purification and elimination of the different egos. This is because in order to ascend up to the respective Heavens of each planet, one has to descend into their respective atomic Infernos. The two last planets do not have Infernos.

WITH HER POISONED CUP, CIRCE TRANSFORMED MEN INTO SWINE. FROM *THE ODYSSEY* BY HOMER.

The initiate leaves the body of desires, the Astral Lunar Body, in the Infernos of the Moon. In the Infernos of Mercury the initiate leaves Cain, the mind, to then ascend to the Mercurian Heavens. Thus, likewise, the initiate has to be converted into a crocodile seven times by descending seven times, in order to ascend seven times up to the Heavens.

All of this process is in order to be liberated from the laws of the solar system; after this, the initiate has to be liberated from the laws of the galaxy. Posteriorly, the Adept must be liberated from the laws of the universes and be transformed into the most pure lotus flower, thus converting the Self into a Cosmocreator, meaning a Lord Creator of Universes. Posteriorly, the Adept is submerged and absorbed within the bosom of the Absolute.

Transformations of inferior orders exist. Circe transformed men into pigs. The legend states that Apuleius transformed himself into an ass. If one puts the physical body into the fourth dimension by utilizing the "Jinn State," the physical body can assume any given figure. The physical body can be transformed into a bird, a fish, or whatever is desired. Within the fourth dimension, the physical body is elastic and can be transformed into an animal. The Latin mantras for the transformation are the following: **EST SIT, ESTO, FIAT**. We can be physically transformed only in the Jinn State.

THE HOLY GNOSTIC UNCTION AT THE LAST SUPPER

Transubstantiation

The Last Supper of the adorable Savior of the world comes from archaic epochs. The great Lord of Atlantis also practiced this ceremony as Jesus did.

This is a blood ceremony, a blood pact. Each one of the Apostles put their blood into a cup and then they mixed their blood with the royal blood of the Adorable One within the chalice of the Last Supper (the Holy Grail). Thus, the Astral Bodies of the Apostles are united with the Astral Body of Christ, by means of the blood pact. The Apostles drank the blood contained within the chalice and Jesus likewise drank from it.

The Holy Gnostic Unction is united to the Last Supper through the blood pact. When the Christic atoms descend into the bread and the wine, they are actually converted into the flesh and blood of Christ. This is the mystery of the transubstantiation.

The bread and the wine, the seed of wheat and the fruit of the grapevine, must be royally transformed into the flesh and blood of the intimate Christ.

The Solar Logos with its powerful life makes the seed of wheat germinate in order for the stalks to grow from millimeter to millimeter. The Solar Logos then becomes enclosed within the dark hardness of this grain which is like a precious coffer. The enchanted germ of the sacred stalk has its intimate exponent in the human seed.

The solar rays which penetrate into the stump of life are developed and unfolded in concealment until ripened in the sacred and holy fruit of the grapevine. This is an emblem of life that manifests itself with all of its splendor in the substance.

The Gnostic Priest perceives this cosmic substance of the Sun-Christ which is enclosed in the bread and wine when he is in the state of ecstasy. The Priest unbinds this substance from its physical elements in order for the Christic atoms to victoriously penetrate within the human organisms.

When Jesus established the Gnostic school he cut the bread and said unto everyone, *"Take, eat this is my body,"* and he gave the wine and said, *"Drink ye all of it, for this is my blood."* [Matthew 26:26-28] *"He that eateth my flesh, and drinketh my blood, dwelleth in me, and I in him."* [John 6:56]

During the Gnostic ritual, we put ourselves in communication with the world of the Solar Logos, with the Egyptian "Ra," with **Tum**. This last word is very important; it has three aspects which represent the three primary forces:

T: The Father

U: The Son

M: The Holy Spirit

This is a powerful mantra. When pronouncing it, the forces of the Logos are attracted towards us. In the instant when the consecration of the bread and wine is performed the Christic atoms descend and are actually transformed into the flesh and blood of Christ. This is achieved by means of a channel which is open and directly communicates with the Logos through the mantra.

When we are in a state of ecstasy during the transubstantiation, Christic atoms of high voltage descend and give us light within the darkness. These Christic atoms help us in the battle against the red demons of Seth. Thus, we make light within the darkness.

We are profound darkness. It is written, *"The light emerges from the darkness."* The Gods emerged from the abyss and then they lost themselves in the Absolute. Therefore, the abyss is indispensable in order for the Gods to exist.

The Gods have to know good and evil. The abyss is the cosmic amphitheater where the Gods are made. For this reason we need to descend in order to ascend.

The Solar Christic atoms, these igneous lights, these secret agents of the Adorable One, work silently within the heart temple in order to invite us over and over again to tread the path that must conduct us into Nirvana. The mysterious help of the Christic atoms stands out at twilight with complete meridian clarity.

And the light shineth within the darkness, and the twelve loaves of hallowed bread of the proposition appeared upon the altar. This manifestation alludes to the twelve zodiacal signs or distinct modalities of cosmic substance. This reminds us of the Twelfth Arcanum, the Magnus Opus, that is, the union of the cross with the triangle.

Regarding the wine, which is derived from the ripe fruit of the grapevine, it is the symbol of the fire, of the blood of life which has manifested in this substance.

It is unquestionable that even though the words *vino, vida, vid* (wine, life, grapevine) have distinct origins, nonetheless they do not deny having certain symbolic affinities. By no means can the relationship of *vino* (wine), *vis* (strength), *virtus* (moral strength) and *virgo* (virgin), who is the igneous serpent of our magical powers, be omitted.

The Sahaja Maithuna (Sexual Magic) between male and female, Adam-Eve, on the delicious bed of authentic love, keeps truly sublime rhythmic concordances with the mystical agape of the great Kabir, Jesus.

Transforming the bread (seed) into solar flesh, and the exquisite wine into the Christic blood and holy fire, is the most extraordinary miracle of sexual yoga. The Golden Body of the Solar Man, the famous "To Soma Heliakon" (the complete synthesis of the Christic vehicles), is the flesh, blood, and life of the Creator Logos or Demiurge.

The living secret crystallization of sexual energy into the resplendent form

"Transforming the bread (seed) into solar flesh, and the exquisite wine into the Christic blood and holy fire, is the most extraordinary miracle of sexual yoga."
ENGRAVING BY MICHAEL MAIER, 1618

of that glorious body is only possible with amorous magic.

Einstein, one of the great luminaries of the intellect, wrote a wise statement that states literally: "Matter transforms into energy; energy transforms into matter."

It is clear that through the Sahaja Maithuna, we can and we must transform the Ens Seminis into energy. To transform the bread into flesh and the wine into royal blood or philosophical and living fire is really the miracle of transubstantiation.

One has to sublimate the sexual energy towards the heart. The communion of bread and wine has the power of sublimating the sexual energy to the heart. We can put a piece of bread and a cup of wine (grape juice) next to our bed, praying and blessing the bread and wine after having worked with the Arcanum A.Z.F. We then eat the bread and drink the wine. The Fourteenth Arcanum transforms the bread

and the wine into the blood of Christ. This arcanum charges the bread and wine with Christic atoms which descend from the Central Sun.

SYNTHESIS

- The Master who renounces Nirvana for the love of humanity is honored three times.

- The Master who renounces Nirvana in order to remain in the physical plane must ask for the Elixir of Longevity.

Chapter XXXVII

Arcanum 15

The Fifteenth Arcanum corresponds to that which the Bible points to as Satan, and it also corresponds to that which the Egyptians call Seth in his negative aspect.

If Kabbalistically we add the numbers of the number 15, we have 1 + 5 = 6; we already know that the number six corresponds to sex. This signifies that within sex is a major force that can liberate the human being, but also a major force that can enslave the human being.

Let us remember the Egyptian "constellation of Orion." It is evident that this constellation is governed by twelve great Masters. Esoterically speaking, it is stated that these twelve Masters hold hands, but the sixth Master is missing; meaning that in order to reach realization of the Self, "we need to lift the Veil of Isis," in other words, the Adamic Sexual Veil.

One can reach the Final Liberation only by absolutely liberating oneself from sex. Many schools preach that we have to liberate ourselves from sex; nonetheless, they ignore that before this we need to create the Solar Bodies. What is wrong with this is that it is like saying, "I want to saddle the horse before having it."

Firstly, the Solar Bodies must be created, then afterwards sex must be renounced. It is a matter of entitlement, and the things that we are entitled to. In the Work, first comes that which is animal and afterwards that which is spiritual.

The constellation of Orion has a marked influence over the Atomic Star that guides our inner Self. This is the Ain Soph Paranishpanna, our intimate Star. A Master once said: "I raise my eyes towards the stars that will come to my rescue; nevertheless, I always guide myself with my Star, which I carry within my inner Self."

The Fifteenth Arcanum of the Tarot is the "pluralized I." Esoterically speaking, it is named Satan.

The sign of the infinite [∞] is very important. Eight Kabirs correspond to this sign who govern all creation, all of nature. They are the rectors of the universal life which governs our planet Earth. They have their antitheses who are the eight hierarchs of the Black Lodge, meaning the eight anti-Kabirs: two towards the East, two towards the West, two towards the North, two towards the South. We mention them because they belong to the Fifteenth Arcanum; they belong to Typhon Baphomet, to Satan. The esotericist must know how to defend himself from those eight Kabirs. We have the conjurations and all of the esotericism of High Magic for this objective.

Those who work with High Magic need to protect themselves with the magical circle. They must know how to utilize the sacred viper that makes the tenebrous flee. The ancient Egyptians knew how to project this viper through the heart. One must know how to invoke Ra in order to defend oneself from the eight anti-Kabirs of the Black Lodge, because in the same way that there are Adepts who are crystallizations of the White Lodge, likewise there are Adepts who are crystallizations of the Black Lodge.

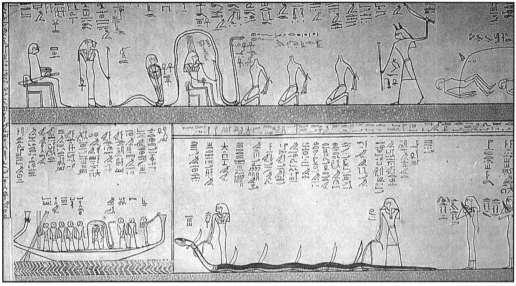

The duality of the serpent force as seen in the seventh hour of the Sun God's journey through the underworld. In the top portion, the God Osiris, protected by an arisen serpent, watches the decapitation of his enemies (egos) by a god with cat ears (Seth-Lucifer in his positive aspect). Below, the Solar Boat prepares to face the serpent that opposes the journey of the Sun, the Christ, but this serpent has been bound by a man and woman and secured with five swords.
EGYPTIAN PAINTING

They are adepts of the left-hand path, and they are filled with power.

Tenebrous adepts of this type crystallize through Black Tantra. There exists in Black Tantra the same connection of the lingam-yoni, but with the spilling of the Ens Seminis. The eight anti-Kabirs are the eight types of negative and fatal crystallizations of the Hydrogen SI-12 which is in the Ens Seminis.

It is said that when an adept wins the battle, the Adept is sheltered in the Eye of Horus and covered by a triple veil. The Adept remains protected with this veil from the red demons of Seth. These demons can no longer harm the Adept. The Adept becomes invisible to the red demons. These red demons are nothing but the "pluralized I" of each one of us, which are legions of demons. There is no doubt that all of these devils are living personifications of our errors and psychological defects.

It is good to know that the most difficult demon to defeat among all of these demons is the demon of lust. This is the main defect represented in the Fifteenth Arcanum of the Tarot as sexual passion or lust.

The Fifteenth Arcanum represents "Passion," because this passion is based on the modus operandis of the Luciferic fire. Passion constitutes the functionalism of that fire.

In synthesis, two great fires exist: the sacred fire of Kundalini that ascends through the dorsal spine, and the Kundabuffer that descends, precipitating downwards towards the infernos.

Kundalini is the serpent of bronze that healed the Israelites in the wilderness, the serpent which Moses rose upon the staff. The Kundabuffer fire is the tempting serpent of Eden, which descends downwards towards the Atomic Infernos of the human being. In Egyptian wisdom, this tempting serpent receives the name of **Apep**. In the rituals of ancient Egypt, Apep was portrayed in wax and with its head aiming downwards. Thus, they exorcised it and conjured it.

The initiate must fight against this tempting serpent of sexual passion, against this horrible Apep. The initiate must fight to the death.

This negative fire of Apep is the negative aspect of Prakriti, in other words Kali. Kali assumes the aspect of a horrible viper which is writhing in the mud (see the life of Krishna). If we want to defeat this viper in the cosmos, we must first defeat it within ourselves.

The living foundation of animal passion is within this Luciferic fire or the serpent Apep. The crystallization of this negative Luciferic fohat (fire) is personified in those red demons, in that pluralized "I." The red demons of Seth exist within this sexual Luciferic fire.

If we want to dissolve the "I," we must start by terminating lust. If the water is taken away from the fish of the sea they will die. If the Luciferic fire is taken away from our "I's," these psychological "I's" will die. We must stop the nourishment from which they live.

The Atomic Infernos of the human being are a reality. Wars are won in the battlefields; we must win those battles against the red demons. The Fifteenth Arcanum signifies the work with the demon which is performed by means of the phallus/Osiris and the uterus/Isis. The phallus and uterus are in possession of Satan or Seth. The phallus of the Gods is of pure gold.

It is necessary to eradicate all of that which has a taste of animal passion.

In the ancient mysteries among the illuminated Gnostic-Rosicrucians, a ceremony of initiation existed in which the blindfolded neophyte, when being submitted to certain ordeals, was guided to a certain place. The most interesting point during this ordeal was when the veil was removed from him and suddenly he was in an illuminated room. All the initiates were in the center of the room around a male goat. The Pentalpha was shining between the huge horns of this male goat. The neophyte was then commanded to go and kiss the devil's behind, in

THE DUALITY OF THE SERPENT AS DEPICTED IN THE BOOK OF EXODUS

other words the tail. When going around to the animal's back, he would suddenly find a beautiful lady who would welcome him. She would hug him and kiss him on the forehead. He was then triumphant. However if he was opposed to this act then he would fail, and he would be taken out of the precinct without the neophyte ever knowing the secret.

The lady who would kiss him represented Isis, the Divine Mother. She kissed him on the forehead, like saying unto him: *The hour of working with the sacred serpent has arrived.* One must steal the fire from the devil, from the male goat, by means of the transmutation of the vile metals into gold in order to convert ourselves into Gods. This is the mystery of Alchemy. This male goat has to be eliminated. Each defect must be transformed, must be killed, in order for a virtue to be born. Behold here the reason for the phrase, *"Solve et Coagula."* The Gods emerge from the abyss and they become lost in the Absolute.

The magician carries the power in the sexual organs because within these the Laboratorium Oratorium of the Third Logos resides.

SYNTHESIS

- Millions of Black Lodges exist in the world of Assiah.

- The most dangerous black magicians of the universe exist within the Mental World.

- Every occultist who recommends the seminal ejaculation is a black magician.

- Every fornicator is a black magician. Every association of fornicators forms Black Lodges.

- Our disciples must learn to conjure the tenebrous in order to make them flee with fear. The Conjurations of the Four and Seven must be utilized [see the Appendices].

- The tenebrous must be conjured with the sword.

EMBLEMA XXV FROM ATALANTA FUGIENS BY MICHAEL MAIER, 1618.

Chapter XXXVIII

Arcanum 16

The Sixteenth Arcanum is the Fulminated Tower, which in Kabbalah is known as the Tower of Babel. The Bible refers to this Tower of Babel. The falling of the initiated from this Tower, where the initiate forms the inverted pentagram in his downfall, is observed.

The sacred sign of the infinite represents the brain, the heart, and sex. If sex dominates the brain, then the downfall occurs—the Fulminated Tower, the inverted star of five points, the upside-down pentagram; then the human being with the head aiming downwards and with the two legs aiming upwards is precipitated to the bottom of the abyss. Let us remember the sacred statement, *"The infinite is equal to the pentalpha."*

If we carefully analyze the Sixteenth Arcanum, it invites us to reflect: who are the ones that fall? They are those who spill the Glass of Hermes. This is why Krumm-Heller stated: "One must carefully raise the cup aloft." He was referring to the "sacred wine."

In archaic epochs, in ancient Lemuria, I attained the Elixir of Longevity. This Elixir is based on the primordial substance that can grow new life, fresh and green again. It is the "nectar of the Gods." Paracelsus named this substance "Ens Seminis" within which the "Ens Virtutis" is enclosed.

In the continent "Mu," or Lemuria, which was situated in the gigantic Pacific Ocean, the White Brotherhood granted unto me this "marvellous Elixir," the "gift of Cupid" with which one can preserve the physical body for millions of years. I preserved my physical body for thousands of years in Atlantis; I was an immortal. But, the same thing that happened to the Count Zanoni happened unto me when starting the first Aryan subrace. The Count Zanoni fell in love with a chorus girl in Naples and his immortal body was taken from him because of this.

This is how I was left reincarnating myself in distinct bodies until this present time, when I have risen again.

One must attain a transformation by means of Nu, the Divine Mother; with her help we can eliminate the whole of that conjunction of tenebrous entities, Satan... Nu can radically and in a definitive way transform us.

It is necessary to perform a complete transformation. Let our head and our countenance be from Ra, and our body, our hands, and our legs be from Tum.

Ra is the Father.

Tum is the body of the Father.

Tum is a terribly divine mantra and must never be pronounced in vain or played with, because our Father who is in secret descends immediately from where ever He might be.

We must convert ourselves into workers of the Great Work of the Father. Ra is the Christ, is life; Ra is the Second Logos. Tum is the Father, the First Logos.

Fire acts and descends when pronouncing **TUM**. This is a mantra of immense magical sacerdotal power.

We can incarnate the Father only when we have developed the seven degrees of the power of the fire. It is clear that the initiate falls if he violates his vows of chastity.

If we Kabbalistically add the numbers of the Sixteenth Arcanum: 1 + 6 = 7, we find the seven degrees of the power of fire, the seven ladders of the mind. If the initiate falls, then the initiate is fulminated by the Sixteenth Arcanum and rolls downward on those stepladders of the mind. In occult science, it is stated that the initiate is left without INRI (Ignis Natura Renovatur Integra), meaning the initiate is a failure. This is then the Fulminated Tower.

Woe unto those who remain without INRI; they are falling downwards from the Tower. The victorious ones, those who achieve the Second Birth, enter into the Order of Melchizedeck, into the Order of Keb, the Genie of the Earth.

In order for the Lunar Bodies to remain within the Amenti, one must die, die, and die. The new comes only through death.

The true defunct initiates are those who really have killed the "I" and have taken possession of the Two Earths. They can enter into Amenti or here at will. This is why it is said that the initiate is made King and Priest of the Earth in accordance with the Order of Melchizedeck. It is clear that if the initiate lets himself fall, then he looses the scepter of command and is precipitated downwards from the Tower.

Every one of us must fight on the esoteric path, even the Twice-born. There are initiates whose throats are stagnant; thus the battle is strong. The more exalted the initiate is, the more terrible and deep is the downfall.

We must be careful of the nourishment that the mind receives, careful with newspapers, television, and movies. We must verbally and mentally transmute the seed with sepulchral offerings. In other words, we must not nourish ourselves with refuse, because this is worthless. Bad literature, bad movies, bad television, bad words, are rotten for the mind. We must not forget that we have a very terrible legion of devils, which is "Kali," the abominable Kundabuffer Organ, the frightful "Apopi" serpent. People are victims of Kali, the tempting serpent of which the Hindus speak.

The initiate who allows himself to fall loses his crown and sword. The pineal gland, the Sahasrara chakra, is the crown. The sword is the flaming sword which we must place at the feet of Osiris.

The four secret occult pillars are granted unto the triumphant and victorious one. These four secret occult pillars grant power to the initiate over the four regions of the cosmos:

1. Life
2. Submerged Mineral Region
3. Molecular Region
4. Electronic or Spiritual World

By delving more profoundly into esotericism, we will find that the midbrow, the third eye, the center of clairvoyance, is the Eye of Horus. Horus is in himself the Innermost, our Divine Being, who is within the arms of our Divine Mother.

HORUS AS FALCON WITH A SOLAR DISC. EGYPTIAN

SYNTHESIS

- When the Astral Light is coagulated in a flower, we fall in love with the flower. If the Astral Light is accumulated within a woman, then men fall in love with this woman.

- The man who lives bewitched by many women does not stop being a weak little bird fulminated by the bewitching eyes of she, the tempter of the Astral Light.

- The sorcerers of the Astral Light are dangerous.

- "Woe unto the Samson of the Kabbalah if he permits himself to be put asleep by Delilah! The Heracles of science who exchanges his royal sceptre for the distaff of Omphale will soon experience the vengeance of Dejanira, and nothing will be left for him but the pyre of Mount Oeta in order to escape the devouring folds of the coat of Nessus." - Eliphas Levi

The falcon is the symbol of Horus. The Falcon of Gold strengthens Horus (pronounced "Aurus") with the complete death of ourselves. This Falcon of Gold is related with the sunrise. We must be in contact with the Spiritual Sun.

We need to strengthen Horus so that we may have the right to ask unto him to strengthen our three brains:

· Intellectual

· Emotional

· Motor

We need to strengthen our three brains for the battle.

Chapter XXXIX
Arcanum 17

The star of eight points of the Seventeenth Arcanum represents Venus, the Star of Dawn. The work with gold and with silver, the work with the Sun and the Moon, is found represented in this arcanum. The ancient Alchemists stated that the transformation of the Moon into the Sun must be performed. To understand this is necessary. What they meant was, "We must abandon the Lunar Path and enter into the Solar Path."

All people are lunar. The Moon brings them into existence and the Moon takes them away. Let us analyze this in detail: the first seven years of childhood are lunar, so the Moon brings them. The second septenary from seven to fourteen is Mercurian. The child moves from one place to another, the child goes to school, the child needs to move.

The third septenary is from fourteen to twenty-one years; it is Venusian. People feel flutters in their heart and they start falling in love. It is obvious that at the age of fourteen the sexual glands enter into action and their influence is manifested in the human being.

From twenty-one to forty-two there are three septenaries (4th, 5th, 6th) or three solar stages. This is the epoch for the fight in order to conquer our place in life. This epoch (21-42) manifests itself as it must be.

The seventh septenary is from forty-two to forty-nine years; this is Martian.

Stage	Planet	Age
1	☽	0 - 7
2	☿	7 - 14
3	♀	14 - 21
4	☉	21 - 28
5	☉	28 - 35
6	☉	35 - 42
7	♂	42 - 49
8	♃	49 - 56
9	♄	56 - 63
10	♄ + ☽	63 - 70
11	♄ + ☿	70 - 77

There are struggles in this epoch; this is a decisive epoch for everyone.

The eighth septenary is from ages forty-nine to fifty-six. This is the epoch in which Jupiter influences the human being. Those who have good Karma thrive economically during this epoch; those who do not, suffer.

The ninth septenary from fifty-six to sixty-three brings old Saturn. Then the elderly stage enters into the human being. This is a Saturnine epoch governed by the elder of the Heavens. The person can boast about anything that he wants. After sixty-three years of age, we enter into the elderly stage. Then the lunar influence returns again. So then, the Moon brings them and the Moon takes them away.

If the life of a human being is examined, it will be verified that everything is ruled by the Moon. When one enters into the Internal Worlds, one enters through the doors of the Moon. What is important is to transform the Moon into the Sun. In order to perform this, one must work with gold and with silver. This arcanum would be impossible to understand without Alchemy. The most important matter is to transmute the lead into gold. This work must be performed in the forge of the Cyclops.

The vital point of the Seventeenth Arcanum is the **Venustic Initiation**, which is the higher part of this arcanum. This is represented by the star of eight points, by Venus. If we carefully examine the symbol of Venus, we find:

THE CIRCLE IS THE SPIRIT

THE CROSS IS SEX

SEX UNDER THE CONTROL OF THE SPIRIT

The inverted symbol represents that the Spirit is dominated by sex.

This is what has happened on the Earth: sex has dominated the Spirit.

Venus, the Star of Dawn, is very great in its positive aspect. It is marvellous; it is the Venustic Initiation. But in its negative aspect, we find the Luciferic aspect.

The ideal hour for astral travel is the hour of dawn, the hour of Venus, but if one is not in a pure state, the Luciferic currents pull them. Let us remember Venus-Lucifer, which has two aspects. Thus, as the sacred ascending fire of Kundalini exists, the descending fire of Kundabuffer also exists.

The whole work with Alchemy is in order to attain the Venustic Initiation. Indeed, this is very difficult. We have the case of Madame Blavatsky who married the Count Blavatsky, and precisely two months later, she separated from him without having had a sexual relationship. Then she travelled through India, and was in Shangri-La. Her mission was grandiose; she wrote *The Secret Doctrine.* In the sixth volume of *The Secret Doctrine,* she ends by inviting those who have read it to practice Alchemy. Without Alchemy, the attainment of the realization of the Self is impossible. Madame Blavatsky married Colonel Olcott when she was already elderly; she married him not because of passion. The answer about her marriage is found in the Internal Worlds: she built the Solar Bodies.

Madame Blavatsky is a great Adept who accomplished a great work. Nevertheless, she did not reach the Venustic Initiation, because she sought to have a male body for it; thus, this unique incarnation of Christ will be in her new male body. So, she is preparing herself in order to reincarnate with a male body. She is going to be born in the U.S.A. Courage has been given to her in order that she not dismay, because to renounce the great Nirvana and to have to come back into this world is not pleasant.

Sex is needed in order to attain the Venustic Initiation. Sex is needed because there are seven serpents of fire which correspond to the seven bodies: Physical, Vital, Astral, Mental, Causal, Buddhic, and Atmic, or Innermost bodies. One serpent corresponds to each one of them. There are seven serpents in total, two groups of three with the sublime coronation of the seventh one which unites us with the Father, with the Law.

Whosoever wants to reach the Venustic Initiation has to raise the seven Serpents of Light. The serpent which belongs to the physical body must first be raised in order to receive the first Venustic Initiation. Afterwards, the serpent which belongs to the vital body must be raised in order to receive the second Venustic Initiation and likewise successively.

The incarnation of the Christ starts with the Venustic Initiation, and it is lived in two forms: firstly, in a symbolic way; afterwards, it is necessary to live it by developing all of that which was granted in the initiations. This must be lived, this is the crude reality; we must practice what we preach. This is an arduous work.

Christ is the Master of Masters. To believe that Jesus is the only Christ is a mistake people make. Hermes, Quetzalcoatl, Fu Xi, Krishna, etc. also incarnated the Christ. The incarnated Christ has to perform what He preaches, and this is what He practices. He, being God, becomes a human being, and has to fight against His own passions, against everything. Gold is always tested in fire, and He always emerges victorious. He incarnates and becomes a human being at any time that He considers it to be necessary. He does it with the objective of changing the world. He is the Being of our Being. All of us are One within Him. He, He, He submerges within the Father, and likewise the Father within Him.

Whosoever incarnates the Christ passes the test. Then, this one goes far beyond Nirvana, into worlds of super-happiness and joy.

Only courageous ones enter onto this path. If one does not know how to grasp onto our Father and Mother with soul, life, and heart, one does not arrive, one fails.

One must grasp oneself onto our Father and Mother by developing love. How is one going to take refuge in our Father and Mother if one does not have love?

At this present time there is not a Rosicrucian school in this physical world. The only and unique Rosicrucian Order is in the Internal Worlds. In this Rosicrucian monastery, I was submitted to one ordeal, the ordeal of patience. The ordeal of patience is intentionally imposed upon ourselves.

SYNTHESIS

- The highest objective is to reach the Venustic Initiation. This initiation relates to the First Arcanum, the incarnation of Christ.

- Christ has no individuality, personality, or "I." He is the true instructor, the "Supreme Great Master," the Master of Masters.

- Christ is the Lamb of God who washes the sins of the world, but for this one must work.

- He is the True Instructor of the world.

- Christ was Osiris in ancient Egypt. Whosoever incarnated Him was another Osirified one. This one had to sacrifice the self for humanity.

- We have to know how to be patient.

- We have to know how to be serene.

Chapter XL

Arcanum 18

When we Kabbalistically add the Eighteenth Arcanum, we have 1 + 8 = 9, the Ninth Sphere, sex. Esoteric traditions affirm that the Earth has nine strata or subterranean regions. It is clear that what is called the planetary nucleus is found in the ninth stratum. This nucleus is of an extraordinary density. The Kabbalists state that in the center of the Earth, the sign of the infinite is found. It is obvious that within the heart of the Earth its vital energies circulate.

This is the reason why Kabbalists affirm that in the center of the Earth the brain, heart, and sex of the Genie of the Earth, or Planetary Genie, is found. Upon this model all of the organizations of creatures are built, in other words, built within ourselves. The struggle is terrible: brain against sex, sex against brain, and the worst is heart against heart.

The Pentagram with the vertex aiming upwards represents the human being. If sex wins the battle, then the Pentagram is inverted with the vertex aiming downwards and thus originates the downfall of the Fulminated Tower of the Sixteenth Arcanum.

The major force that can liberate or enslave the human being is in sex. In ancient times, the descent into the Ninth Sphere was the maximum ordeal for the supreme dignity of the Hierophant. All of the treatises refer to the descent of Aeneas into the Ninth Sphere, the Greek Tartarus (*The Aeneid*, part VI). The Sibyl of Cumae warned him what the descent into the Avernus signifies:

Offspring of Gods by blood, Trojan Anchises' son, the way downward is easy from Avernus. Black Dis's door stands open night and day. But to retrace your steps to heaven's air, there is the trouble, there is the toil. A few whom benign Jupiter has loved or whom fiery heroism has borne to heaven, sons of Gods, could do it.

Kabbalists speak about the Adam Protoplastos, who converts himself into something distinct, different, by means of the transmutation of the creative energies. Kabbalistic traditions tell us that Adam had two wives: Lilith and Nahemah. It is stated that Lilith is the mother of abortion, homosexuality, mother of sexual degeneration, and Nahemah is the mother of adultery, fornication, etc.

Lilith and Nahemah are the two aspects of infrasexuality. These two women correspond to two submerged spheres within the very interior of the Earth, the infradimensional and the mineral. However, the Greek Tartarus and the Avernus are symbols of the submerged mineral kingdom. There is life everywhere; we live in the element air, and such an element is invisible to us. Thus, likewise, the fish cannot see the water. Similarly, I can assure you that there is life in stone. There are living beings in the stone and such an element is invisible for them. They are not beings of flesh and bones, of course; they are subtle. They are lost and degenerated germs, which are in a devolving process.

Aeneas found his father and the beautiful Helen in the Tartarus, and likewise

Dante found multitudes of beings there, as *The Divine Comedy* tells us. The nine circles of Dante's *Divine Comedy* are related with the nine spheres in the submerged mineral element.

It is necessary to descend into our own atomic Infernos in order to work with the fire and water that originated the worlds, beasts, and human beings. In all of the pseudo-occult schools, the Ascension, the rising up towards the Superior Worlds, is spoken of. But the descent is not spoken of, and the serious aspect of this matter is that a humiliation preceeds any exaltation.

In the submerged sphere of Lilith, we find the women who choose to have abortions and likewise people who like to use contraceptive pills in order not to have children; thus, the consequences are obvious. In the sphere of Nahemah we find those who fascinate themselves with sex. Terribly fornicating men and women who deliver themselves to adultery, pride, vanity, women who like divorce in order to get married again. Kabbalistic traditions say that when a man abandons his spouse in order to marry another woman, he remains with the mark of Luciferic fire on his forehead. The Kabbalists affirm that when a woman marries a man who does not correspond to her, then the day of the wedding she appears "bald." She unconsciously covers too much of her head.

No one can realize the Self without transmutation.

The Ninth Sphere is repeated twice in the Eighteenth Arcanum. This leaves much material for reflection: the first nine is positive and the second nine is negative. Then, the Eighteenth Arcanum manifests the fatal or negative aspect of the Ninth Sphere. Such a negative aspect is found in the two spheres of Lilith and Nahemah.

Lilith, supported by Animal Instinct, is flanked by her attendant Barn Owls, symbols of witchcraft, and flaunts her naked body in order to entice the desire-filled mind. SUMERIAN

It is obvious that the Infernal Worlds are infrasexual. It is evident that infrasexuality reigns with sovereignty within humanity. Humanity is divided; some are in the sphere of Lilith and others in the sphere of Nahemah.

When one intends to work in the Ninth Sphere, immediately one is attacked by the red demons. These demons fight in order to swerve us from the main path of the razor's edge. It is clear that many dangers from within and without exist in the Magisterium of Fire.

When the igneous serpent or Kundalini ascends through the dorsal spine, it advances slowly. This is performed slowly from vertebra to vertebra. Each vertebra represents the determined virtues which correspond to an esoteric degree. The ascension to a certain vertebra can never be attained without previously having acquired the conditions of sanctity which are required for the vertebra to which we are aspiring. The 33 vertebrae correspond to the 33 degrees of occult magic, the 33 degrees of the Masonic Master, and the 33 years of the life of Jesus. Many ordeals correspond to each vertebra, and the ascension is performed in accordance to the merits of the heart. Those that believe that the Kundalini, once awakened, instantaneously rises towards the head leaving us in complete illumination, are really ignorant people.

The sacred fire has seven degrees of power. These seven degrees of power must be developed in order for us to realize the Self.

In this present reincarnation, when I was struggling with the fourth degree of the power of the fire and still had not dissolved the ego, I saw on the movie screen of a theater a couple performing an erotic scene. Then at night, in the World of the Mind, I was submitted to an ordeal in which the same couple from the screen were performing the same scene. Such

a scene was reproduced by my mind. It appeared in movement and was alive. I passed the ordeal. When I left the World of the Mind and entered into the Astral World, I was strongly reprimanded and was warned that if I should return to those places (the movie theaters) I would lose the sword. They told me that it would be better to study my past lives in the Akashic records.

The atmosphere of movie theaters is tenebrous. There are millions of larvae created by the minds of the spectators. For this reason, these people have nocturnal pollutions in the night. This is the Eighteenth Arcanum. It is the darkness.

In *The Divine Comedy*, the dog Cerberus (sex), which we must take out of the Tartarus and into the sunlight, is spoken of. This refers to the ascension of the sexual forces in us, sexual forces that must be raised; we must also eliminate the "I." This is the basis for the intimate realization of the Being. This is the struggle between light and darkness in the Eighteenth Arcanum.

This terrible struggle is affirmed in the three Tantric schools that are dedicated to sex.

The Divine Mother Kundalini (Athena) observes Heracles as he trains Cerberus to serve him.
Greek vase painting

1. **White Tantra:** Connection of the lingam-yoni without the ejaculation of the Ens Seminis (without reaching orgasm). This Tantra takes us to the ascension of the Kundalini and to realization of the Self.

2. **Black Tantra:** Ejaculation of the Ens Seminis during the Maithuna exists in order to develop the Kundabuffer organ.

3. **Grey Tantra:** They sometimes work with ejaculation and sometimes without ejaculation. They work solely for the enjoyment of sexual pleasure but with the immanent danger of falling into Black Tantra.

Indeed, when reaching the Eighteenth Arcanum, we find ourselves before the dilemma of *To be or not to be.*

No one can attain realization of the Self without the practice of Maithuna. One has to awaken consciousness. Without the consciousness awake, the path is abandoned, because there is no seriousness.

In ancient times, the secret of the Arcanum A.Z.F. was not granted unto anyone that did not previously have the consciousness awakened. This was in order for individuals not to abandon the path.

SYNTHESIS

- Whosoever defeats Satan in sex defeats Satan in all of his aspects.

- To extract the dog Cerberus signifies the liberation of the sexual energy, the utilization of it in a transcendental form.

- The eyes are the windows of the Soul. The man that allows himself to be driven by the eyes of all women and vice versa must resign to live in the abyss.

- There are women who practice sorcery against men and vice versa. These victims must incessantly defend themselves with the Conjuration of the Four and Seven.

- We can defend ourselves against witchcraft by invoking our own Elemental Advocate. This Elemental must be invoked with all of our heart while we go to bed.

Chapter XLI

Arcanum 19

The Nineteenth Arcanum is the arcanum of the alliance and of victory. We spoke in previous chapters about the Salt of Alchemy, symbol of the physical body; the Mercury, symbol of the Ens Seminis, within which the Ens Virtutis is enclosed; and the Sulphur, symbol of Fire, the Fohat, the Kundalini. The Mercury must be transmuted into Sulphur, which is the serpentine fire, the outcome of Transmutation. These three elements are the passive instruments of the Great Work.

We have to search for the positive principle, the Interior Magnes of Paracelsus, the Magical Principle. The three elements Salt, Mercury, and Sulphur are negative elements when they are not working in the Magnus Work; yet they become positive by working in the Magnus Work. This is the Magical Principle or Interior Magnes.

It is obvious that in the Nineteenth Arcanum a great Alliance is established between man and woman, a great Alliance in order to perform the Great Work.

This great Alliance has many aspects. The Gospel speaks of the necessity of having the Wedding Garment. Let us remember the wedding in which a man did not bring the wedding garment. This one was bound, and the Lord ordered to cast him into outer darkness *"where only weeping and the gnashing of teeth are heard"* [Matthew 22:1-14]. This famous garment is the Egyptian Sahu or the Greek "To Soma Heliakon," in other words, the Body of Gold of the Solar Man. This is the Wedding Garment required in order to attend the banquet of the Pascal Lamb. It is necessary and

essential to understand that in order to have the Body of Gold of the Solar Man, the great Alliance is necessary, that is, the work in the Ninth Sphere between man and woman.

Thus, as the great Alliance is necessary down here in order to attain illumination, another great Alliance up there is needed.

The two Souls must be fused; the masculine Human Soul with the feminine Spiritual Soul. This is not achieved without having previously eliminated the "I," and having eliminated the Body of Desires. The two Souls must be one.

This is the great Alliance between the knight and the medieval lady. This is found in the books of chivalry, *The Romancer,* in the ballads of Count Roldan, in the minstrel songs of the Troubadours. The knight who fights for his lady is the Human Soul. The lady is the Spiritual Soul. The knight has to fight for his lady; otherwise he is left without her.

In order to attain total illumination, the knight and his lady must be completely integrated. The knight must fight for her at every moment until developing the lotus of one thousand petals. Buddhi gives the illumination in the great matrimony or Alchemical Wedding of Manas-Buddhi. Without Buddhi, the complete development of the one thousand petalled chakra Sahasrara cannot be achieved.

With this matrimony a spark is produced; thus, the illumination comes as a result of this great Alliance. That divine spark upon the pineal gland gives illuminated intuition along with polyvoyance. This is the total triumph.

Intuitive illumination is better than clairvoyance. What counts is the Spiritual Sun. The Sun of Midnight guides us and orients us. *"We must expect everything from the west; do not expect anything from the east."* The Sun Sirius is the Central Sun, the gravitational point of the Milky Way.

The goal of our studies is to enter into the Absolute. In order to perform this, we must emancipate ourselves from all of the laws of the seven cosmos that control us.

With the Alliance, we liberate ourselves from:

> The 96 laws of the abyss (Tritocosmos)
>
> The 48 laws of the human being (Microcosmos)
>
> The 24 laws of the Earth (Mesocosmos)
>
> The 12 laws of the solar system (Deuterocosmos)
>
> The 6 laws of the galaxy (Macrocosmos)
>
> The 3 laws of the Firmament (Ayocosmos)
>
> The 1 law of the Solar Absolute (Protocosmos)

Then, we enter into the Absolute.

The arrival into the Absolute is sowed with renunciation and death. One has to renounce Omnipotence and even Omniscience in order to enter into the Absolute.

Synthesis

- The Philosophical Stone is the semen.

- Whosoever practices Sexual Magic everyday is working with the Philosophical Stone.

- The only thing that is needed in order to work with the Philosophical Stone is a good spouse.

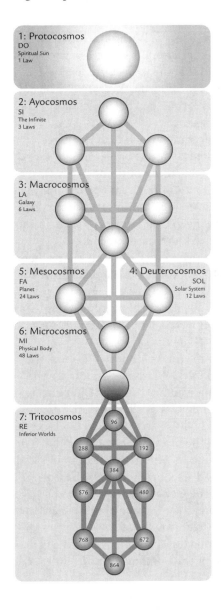

1: Protocosmos
DO
Spiritual Sun
1 Law

2: Ayocosmos
SI
The Infinite
3 Laws

3: Macrocosmos
LA
Galaxy
6 Laws

5: Mesocosmos
FA
Planet
24 Laws

4: Deuterocosmos
SOL
Solar System
12 Laws

6: Microcosmos
MI
Physical Body
48 Laws

7: Tritocosmos
RE
Inferior Worlds

96
288   192
384
576   480
768   672
864

Chapter XLII

Arcanum 20

The hieroglyphic of the Twentieth Arcanum is the resurrection of the dead. It is necessary that we concentrate well on this topic of resurrection, which has many aspects. First of all, in order for resurrection to happen, it is necessary for death to happen. Without death, there is no resurrection. It is necessary to comprehend that life is the outcome of death. Death is the crown of everyone. The path of life is formed by the hoofprints of the horse of death.

Everything which exists in life is submitted to death. Something of mortality and something of immortality exists within everything. I want to tell unto you that mortality and immortality are very relative. Even God Himself, who is immortal, in the long run is mortal.

It is necessary to analyze that which is understood as God. God is "the Army of the Voice," God is "the Great Word." Certainly, the Gospel of John states, *"In the beginning was the Word, the Word was with God, and the Word was God."* [John 1:1]

God is the Voice of the Elohim, the Chorus of the Masters who initiate the Mahamanvantara (Cosmic Day); this is what God is. When the night of Pralaya (Cosmic Night) arrives, these Gods cease to exist in the universe and they are born in the Absolute. This is why it can be stated that God also dies. Yet, after the Cosmic Night, the Gods re-emerge from the Absolute; they are reborn in the new aurora of the Cosmic Day.

Let us now concentrate on the constitution of the human being. In order to be a human being in the most complete sense of the word, first of all it is necessary to have or possess Solar Bodies. We have been talking a lot about the Egyptian Sahu, which is the same Wedding Garment from that parable in which one man came to be seated at the table of the Lord without the Wedding Garment. Then the Master commanded that he be cast into the darkness. So then, without a Wedding Garment or Solar Bodies we also cannot enter into the Kingdom of the Heavens. It is logical that whosoever does not possess the Solar Bodies is dressed with the Lunar Bodies, which are cold, spectral, diabolic, and tenebrous bodies.

An *anima* (Latin for "soul") dressed with Lunar Bodies is not a Human Being, but is an intellectual animal, which is a superior animal (anima). The mistake of humanity is to believe that they are already Human Beings, but they are not. Let us remember the story of Diogenes and his lantern; he was looking for a **Man** (Human Being) and he did not find one. Only Kout Humi, the Master Morya, Saint Germain, etc. are Human Beings; what we have abundantly in this present time are intellectual animals.

The first body which must be built in the forge of the Cyclops is the Astral Body. Thus, we become immortals in the world of 24 laws. Afterwards, we need to build the Mental Body, which is ruled by 12 laws. Whosoever builds the Mental Body is Immortal in the world of 12 laws. Afterwards, one must build the Body of

Conscious Will, and become immortal in the world of 6 laws.

Whosoever builds the Solar Bodies has to pass through many deaths. We need the Solar Adam, the Abel to which the Bible refers, to be born within ourselves. In order to become immortal, the possession of the Solar Bodies is necessary.

If we want to emancipate ourselves or enter onto the path of the razor's edge, the path of the revolution for the consciousness, we must descend into the Ninth Sphere of Nature. To descend into the Ninth Sphere is to enter into a revolution, a revolution against ourselves, against

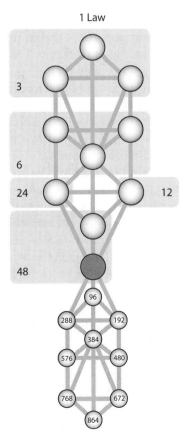

1 Law

3

6

24 12

48

96
288 192
384
576 480
768 672
864

THE NUMBER OF LAWS IN EACH LEVEL OF EXISTENCE

Nature, against everything. Thus, we build the Solar Bodies and we incarnate the real Being and convert ourselves into a Twice-born.

> *Verily, verily, I say unto thee, except a man be born again, he cannot see the kingdom of God.* - John 3:3

The Celestial Adam, who dresses with the Solar Bodies, has to pass through many deaths. This Adam must kill the "I."

We carry from the past this multiplicity of "I's." There is no true individuality within the human being, and those "I's" personify laziness, gluttony, lust, anger, etc., etc. That ego which is dressed with the Lunar Bodies is the Lunar Adam, the Sinful Adam. We need the birth of the Solar Adam within each one of us.

The Twice-born is found between two paths: the path of the right, and the path of the left. Whosoever decides to dissolve the ego takes the path of the right in order to be converted into an ineffable being. Those who do not decide to dissolve the ego take the path of the left, and they convert themselves into diabolical beings (a Hanasmuss is an abortion of the Cosmic Mother). Yet, this is not all: one must destroy the seeds of these "I's," be bathed within the waters of Lethe in order to forget all of the malignities of the ego, and afterwards be bathed in the waters of Eunoe in order to fortify the virtues and to be confirmed in the Light.

Up until this point, all of the work corresponds to the planet Earth; innocence has been attained here. But the shells of the Lunar Bodies remain, and these must be destroyed within the lunar Infernos. One must destroy the demon **Apopi** or "Body of Desires," which retains the sexual desire, and desires of any type. This Apopi is a terribly perverse demon and is destroyed within the Lunar Infernos before one rises into the Lunar Heavens.

Later on, the work is continued in the planet Mercury, where the animal mind, or demon **Hai**, which is the diabolic and animal mind, must be destroyed. Such a vehicle is nothing but a demon, and one has to go and destroy it in the Atomic Infernos of Mercury.

The death of the demon Apopi, the terrible monster of desires, signifies tremendous super-efforts, super-works. Only like this can the destruction of the demon Apopi and demon Hai be achieved.

The sinful Adam must die. It is necessary that all we have that is terrestrial or animal dies in order to resurrect in the heart of Osiris. Whosoever builds the Solar Bodies no longer needs to carry these bodies of desires and cravings. One has to kill these bodies through tremendous purifications.

Osiris signifies that which is beyond all profundities, beyond all desires and the mind. When we return to the Father Osiris, the Mother Isis, and the Son Horus, the triad becomes complete, perfect. The triad becomes Self-realized. This is the resurrection of the dead, because in this way, we have death and resurrection.

I was reincarnated in the sacred land of the Pharaohs, during Pharaoh Kephren's dynasty. I knew the ancient mysteries of secret Egypt in depth, and truly I tell you I could not have forgotten them.

There are two types of **mummies**: one of these mummies corresponds to the deceased whose corpse was submitted to the processes of mummification. The other type corresponds to the deceased who are in a state of "catalepsy."

There was a very special secret concerning mummification: the brain, heart, and visceras had to be taken out. These organs were preserved in sacred vessels, and the sacred cow of gold and the attributes of Athor were placed in the hollow cavity where the heart was. The bodies were preserved thanks to the fact that the Egyptians also knew how to preserve the Ethereal Body (Vital Body). They utilized very wise bandages over the palm of the hands and on the curvature of the feet. The honey of the bee helped to preserve the mummy, and on top of all this an Elemental Genii was placed there to guard the mummy. These Elementals were placed under the protection of Keb, the Genie of the Earth.

Even though my words might appear enigmatic and strange, truly I tell you that my physical body did not die; nonetheless, I went into the sepulcher. This is another type of mummy, a mummy of catalepsy. My case was certainly not an exception; many other Hierophants passed into their sepulchers into this cataleptic state.

The fact that this type of mummy can continue alive and without any nourishment, with all of its' natural faculties in suspension, is something that in no way must surprise us. You must remember that toads during winter, while buried in the mud, remain like corpses without any nourishment. Nonetheless, in spring they become alive again. Did

The preparation of a mummy.
EGYPTIAN

you ever hear about hibernation? Egyptian catalepsy goes much further, and likewise, this catalepsy is wisely combined with magic and occult chemistry.

It is obvious that my soul escaped from my body. It is unquestionable that this type of mummification was not an obstacle in order to continue with my cycle of reincarnations.

After the death of my present physical body, my Soul could definitely reincorporate within that mummy if Tum (the Father) wanted it. Then, that body would definitely come out of the state of catalepsy, and my Soul dressed with that flesh could live travelling from country to country, just as any person. This mummy could live, eat, drink, etc., under the sunlight again. Such a mummy could definitely be taken out from within its sepulcher through the fourth dimension.

Aztec and Egyptian wisdom was Atlantean and likewise Lemurian. The Lemurians and Atlanteans were giants. They built the great pyramids of Egypt and those of San Juan in Teotihuacan.

SYNTHESIS

- The Potable Gold is the same fire of Kundalini. The universal medicine is within the Potable Gold.

- We must end all types of human weakness.

- The serpents of the abyss are intent on stealing the Potable Gold from the disciple.

- The disciple that allows himself to fall has to fight a lot in order to recuperate what he has lost.

Chapter XLIII

Arcanum 21

The Twenty-first Arcanum is the "Fool of the Tarot" or "Transmutation." It has been confused with the Twenty-second Arcanum which is "The Crown of Life."

The Twenty-first Arcanum can be represented with the inverted pentagonal star, which represents black magic.

It is emphatically established within esoteric schools that we have a luminous Astral Body. This is very arguable, because the Astral Body must be built in the Ninth Sphere by means of the transmutation of the Hydrogen SI-12. What the current and common people possess is the body of desires [kama rupa], which is confused with the Astral Body. So, to assert that we have an Astral Body is a severe error, a tremendous mistake, because the body of desires is not the Astral Body.

In the Egyptian mysteries, this body of desires is known as **Apopi**, which is the Demon of Desire. Such a demon is frightfully malignant. Woe unto us, because everybody has this demon! All of the people in this world are malignant, and in order to stop being demons, efforts and super-efforts on this path are required in order to achieve this.

Mr. Leadbeater describes the Mental Body as a marvellous yellow body with a resplendent aura. Everybody mentions the Mental Body and says it is sublime, but when it is studied it is discovered that it is not the authentic Mental Body. The authentic Mental Body must be built with the transmutations of the Hydrogen SI-12. The real Mental Body is a precious body that does not come from Adam. Thus, the Mental Body that the people have is another demon, which is known in the Egyptian mysteries as the demon **Hai**. This demon is terribly perverse and must be killed with the Egyptian mysteries and decapitated in the sphere of Mercury.

Theosophy speaks to us about the Causal Body; however, people do not have the Causal Body, but the Demon of Evil Will. Within the Egyptian mysteries, this Demon of Evil Will is known as **Nebt**.

The Demon of Desire, the Demon of the Mind, and the Demon of Evil-Will are the **Three Furies** to which classical mythology refers. These three demons are

AFTER KILLING HIS MOTHER, ORESTES IS PURSUED BY THE ERINYES, THE THREE FURIES.

the three assassins of Hiram Abiff, the three traitors who crucified the Christ: Judas, Pilate, and Caiaphas. They are the same three traitors that Dante found in the Ninth Circle: Judas, Brutus, and Cassius.

In order to incarnate the Real Being, one must build the Solar Bodies by means of the transmutation of the Hydrogen SI-12. Thus we convert ourselves into true Human Beings. However, when reaching this state, one must dissolve the ego in order to not be converted into a Hanasmuss with a double center of gravity, like for example, Andrameleck.

A Hanasmuss is a Master of the Black Lodge *and* of the White Lodge. In the East, some sects give the name of Marut to these beings, and some Mohammedan sects worship them. Hanasmussen did work in the forge of the Cyclops, but they did not dissolve the ego. They are abortions of the Cosmic Mother.

The Twenty-first Arcanum is the Failure, or Fool of the Tarot, and also Transmutation, indicating that we have to transmute. Whosoever works for realization of the Self risks commiting insanities; therefore, one must work with the **Three Factors** for the revolution of the consciousness:

1. To die.

2. To be born.

3. To sacrifice for humanity.

The dissolution of the ego is necessary because the ego is nothing but an addition of tenebrous entities. We have arrived at the conclusion that every human being must dissolve the ego, burn the seeds of the ego, and be bathed in the waters of Lethe in order to be finished with the memories of the past. Then after the Confirmation in the Light, one is wel-

comed into the White Brotherhood; there one signs papers and is warned that one must be careful. From this instant, one must tear the Veil of Isis, which is in sex.

If the wife disagrees with the Maithuna, let her not work with it; then while in copulation the husband must work in silence, and vice-versa. If the husband disagrees to work with the Maithuna, let the wife work with it in silence.

The destruction of the Lunar Bodies is most difficult. Whosoever dissolves the ego has a very fertilized field. So the man or the woman who are already old must take advantage of their time by dissolving their ego to awaken consciousness, to acquire illumination. But the young man and woman who are married must work in the Ninth Sphere.

One is not alone; one is assisted by the Father-Mother. The Mother assists as the mother who cares for her child and the Father as well. If one violates the oath of chastity, then the downfall is produced and one is abandoned by the Mother; one is then submitted to pain and bitterness.

In the Twenty-first Arcanum the danger is precisely indicated by the crocodile. It is madness and a mistake to go astray from the path.

SYNTHESIS

1. Our single disciples of both sexes can practice the transmutation of their sexual energy with the practice of the **Rune Olin**: while standing with a rigid position, the disciple will make various rhythmic inhalations and exhalations.

2. While air is inhaled, disciples must unite their **imagination** and **willpower** in vibrating harmony in order to make the sexual energy rise up through the two ganglionic cords of the medulla into the

brain, midbrow, neck, and heart. This is done in a successive order.

3. Afterwards, the disciples exhale the air by firmly imagining that the sexual energy is established within their hearts.

4. While exhaling the air, disciples will vocalize the mantra **Thorn**, as follows: *Thooooooooorrrrrrrrnnnnnnnn.*

5. We must perform various movements of the arms while working with the Rune Olin.

6. To begin, the disciples must place both hands on their waist as in the Rune Dorn or Thorn and profoundly and rhythmically inhaling.

7. Secondly, the disciples will extend both hands downward towards their left side, the left hand a little bit more elevated than the right. The arms must be straight and must form an acute angle with the trunk. In the same way that the Rune Fa has its two arms upwards, the second diagram of the

Rune Olin has them downwards, and this is profoundly significant. When performing the second movement, exhale the air by firmly imagining that the sexual energy is established within your heart. While exhaling the air vocalize the mantra Thorn, as follows: *Thooooooooorrrrrrrrnnnnnnnn.*

8. Place both hands on the waist and repeat the exercise. Observe very carefully the two diagrams of the Rune Olin in order to understand the correct postures.

- This is how our single disciples of both sexes can transmute their sexual energy.

- The sexual energies can also be transmuted with the aesthetic sense, with love towards classical music, towards sculpture, and with long walks, etc.

- Single disciples who do not want to have any sexual problems must be absolutely pure in thoughts, words, and actions.

RUNE DORN

RUNE OLIN

Chapter XLIV

Arcanum 22

The Twenty-second Arcanum is the Crown of Life, the return into Light, the incarnation of truth in us.

The Apocalypse states, *"Be thou faithful unto death, and I will give thee a crown of life."* [Revelation 2:10] Undoubtedly, this deserves to be profoundly studied. Let us remember the crown of the saints. In the pineal gland exists the church of Laodicea. During the time of the Hyperboreans, a virgin with the name of **Laodicea** existed. She carried offerings to Delos, or Delphi, of ancient Greece.

THE VIRGIN MOTHER RECEIVES THE CROWN OF LIFE FROM THE THREE LOGOI.

This arcanum represents a crown that has many radiations. This is the chakra Sahasrara, situated in the pineal gland. When the sacred fire of Kundalini reaches the pineal gland, the lotus of a thousand petals is put into motion. Delving with more profundity, we must know that the Mother Kundalini has to be betrothed with the Holy Spirit in the pineal gland. The Holy Spirit is the Third Logos or Vulcan of Greek mythology. He is the Tibetan Maha-Chohan. Kundalini develops, evolves and progresses within the aura of the Maha-Chohan. Therefore, in the pineal gland is where the sacred tattva of Shiva-Shakti—in other words the Divine Mother Kundalini and the Third Logos—intensely vibrates (the tattva is a vibration of the ether).

Absolute sanctity cannot be achieved until the three traitors that assassinated Hiram Abiff, the Master Constructor of the temple of Solomon, are completely terminated.

Sebal: Demon of Desire (Apopi, Judas)

Ortelut: Demon of the Mind (Hai, Pilate)

Stokin: Demon of the Evil Will (Nebt, Caiaphas)

To stop being demons is the objective of our studies.

1. **Judas** is the Demon of Desire. He is a terribly perverse demon. Everybody possesses him, therefore all of us are demons and only the initiatic mysteries can show us how we can stop being demons. We have to start recognizing that we are demons.

2. **Pilate** is the Demon of the Mind. This demon always washes his hands and will always do it.

3. **Caiaphas** is the Demon of Evil Will. The initiate who does not do the will of the Father is disobedient. One must perform the will of the Father here and in the Internal Worlds.

Those who are asleep must do the will of the Father. The will of the Father must be done if there is:

> **Upright Thought**
> **Upright Feeling**
> **Upright Action**

If we do something wrong, it is not the will of the Father.

In conclusion, we have to totally eliminate all subjective elements. None must remain within, and one must remain with pure Spirit like Gautama the Buddha. This is why he is called the Great Illuminated One. In order to reach this state, one has to pay, and the price of this is our own life.

The vanities of the world must be forgotten, and we must dedicate ourselves to the Great Work, to work, to work, to work, until it is attained.

This is not a matter of evolution or devolution, which are merely two cosmic laws of Nature. One must build the Solar Bodies and dissolve the ego. I have spoken to you from my direct experiences, not from theories. I know the Egyptian mysteries, the Tibetan mysteries, the mysteries of the Hyperboreans, and the mysteries of Lemuria, for I was reincarnated in the continent Mu. If the path is explained, it is in order for it to be followed. The teachings can be given only with proficiency.

SYNTHESIS

- Samael Aun Weor, the authentic and legitimate avatar of the new era of Aquarius, declares that all of the sciences of the universe are reduced to Kabbalah and Alchemy.

- Whosoever wants to be a magician must be an alchemist and a kabbalist.

- There are black magicians who teach their disciples negative Sexual Magic in which they ejaculate the seminal liquor.

- These phallic cults were practiced by the perverse black magicians from Cananea, the sorcerers from Cartago, Tyre, and Sidon. These phallic cults were practiced by the Lemurian-Atlantean black magicians in order to ingratiate themselves with the demons.

- Those cities were reduced to dust and all of these perverse ones entered the abyss.

- When a man spills the semen, he collects from the Internal Worlds millions of demonic atoms that infect his Brahmanic cord and this sinks him within his own atomic infernos (the same happens to a woman who reaches the orgasm).

- The three breaths of pure Akasha are reinforced with Sexual Magic.

- Nonetheless, if a person ejaculates the semen (reaches the orgasm), these three breaths will make the Kundalini descend downwards towards the atomic infernos of the human being. This is the tail of Satan.

- The disciple must not even spill a single drop of semen.

- Here I deliver unto humanity the key to all the empires of Heaven and Earth, because I do not want to see this anthill-like humanity suffer anymore.

Chapter XLV

Now Certain Combinations of the Arcana Will Be Studied

Arcana 13, 2, 3, and 14

מ   ב   נ

13 (Mem)   2 (Beth)   14 (Nun)

13 + 2 + 3 = 18

1 + 8 = 9, The Ninth Sphere

In Kabbalah, we have to constantly look at the Hebrew letters. The above capital letters refer to the Word of the Master Mason, a Word that because of an oath cannot be revealed. The three capital letters can be spoken about separately.

In the first place it refers to that Word which corresponds to the death and resurrection of Hiram Abiff, meaning that the Spirit separates itself from matter. It also signifies that the flesh separates itself from the bones. That is why it is said that one must die in order to resurrect; if one does not die, one is not born.

In the second place it refers to the construction that follows destruction. Thus, as we are constituted, we must be destroyed. All of us are demons, because we have the terrible demon Apopi of the Egyptian Mysteries inside. This demon is the body of desires wrongly mistaken for the Astral Body. This Astral Body must be built in the forge of the Cyclops, sex, because it does not exist.

Then we have the animal Mental Body which is much worse. It is the demon Hai of the Egyptian mysteries. This demon must be destroyed and decapitated. See for yourselves that there is no peace over the face of the Earth; we live constantly in wars, fornication, adulteries, vengeance. This Mental Body has nothing angelic.

We do not have the Causal Body; this must be built in the forge of the Cyclops. Instead of this body, we have the Demon of Evil Will. Evil will is the demon who says, "That person makes me sick."

These three demons are never absent in any of the gospels.

In the gospel of Buddha they appear as the Three Furies, the three daughters of the famous Mara. We must understand that we are demons and start from ground zero, to put ourselves in the place where we belong. We need the great destruction of ourselves, the death of the "I," the destruction of the seeds of the "I," and the Lunar Bodies.

"That which has been born from the Father is in the state of putrefaction." This signifies that Christ is dead, that He is in the state of putrefaction. That is why it is said that each person is a living sepulcher. It is said that He is dead because He does not live within any one of us.

The Son must be born in us, and then He must be liberated. He must live the whole drama, to then ascend towards the

Father. What is born from the Father lives in the Son; it is born from the Ens Seminis and lives within Christ.

The pure waters of life are the basic element of regeneration. When Buddha was meditating, fighting against the Three Furies, Mara unleashed a tempest. Buddha was going to be drowned by the waters. Suddenly a serpent appeared and by slithering underneath the seated Buddha, it coiled itself three times and a half, and while the waters were rising, the serpent rose. So the Buddha did not drown. The serpent represents the Divine Mother.

Regeneration is impossible without the waters of life. The Son of Man emerges from within these waters of life.

It is good to proceed with a deep understanding of the esotericism in these sacred things, but truly understanding them. Let us remember the fish, which is life; it is born and it dies within the waters. Let us remember the case of the Fish Dari of the Chaldeans, which represents the same. It represents the Christ emerging from within the waters, the Son of Man who is being born from within the waters.

BUDDHA IS UNAFFECTED BY THE TEMPTING DAUGHTERS OF MARA.

The first letter is: **Faith** (מ Mem).

The second letter is: **Hope** (ב Beth).

The third letter is: **Charity** (נ Nun).

The first letter is death and regeneration. See for yourselves what an intimate relationship exists between death and water. The Thirteenth Arcanum, which is death, is related with the waters. To attain the Second Birth is impossible without the transmutation (Fourteenth Arcanum) of the waters.

To die is necessary, and the foundation of death is a sexual topic. Death is within sex, and likewise, life is within sex. Sex must be eliminated after having reached the Second Birth. Let us remember the expression: *"Lead me from the Darkness into the Light."* Death is a guide into immortality. Death guides from unreality into reality.

All of these must be performed by the Master, and He does it when He finds the Lost Word. This is the Word that accomplished the resurrection of Hiram Abiff. This Word is the Verb, the Word of the Light, or the superior doctrine that the initiate receives, and by means of it, attains the magisterium. It is clear that the modus operandis of this is the Arcanum A.Z.F., and likewise for the destruction of the ego.

Therefore, the Thirteenth Arcanum signifies death and resurrection and is related with Tantra (Fourteenth Arcanum).

The second letter is the Second Arcanum which is the house of the Spirit; it is related with the *sanctum sanctorum*, which signifies the consciousness, the Philosophical Stone without which transmutation cannot be achieved. It is necessary to build the Solar Bodies. It is not possible to put new wine (the intimate Christ) into an old flask (the Lunar Bodies). It is necessary to build the Solar Bodies in order to accommodate this sacred wine.

RESURRECTION COMES AFTER DEATH.

The Philosophical Stone is in the Second Arcanum, with which all of the transmutations must be performed. This stone must be chiselled, because without it, the sexual transmutation cannot be attained. This signifies that one has to work very hard. This is pointed out by the Fourteenth Arcanum, which is transmutation.

Therefore, in the resurrection, or in the elevation towards magisterium, the following is needed:

1. To deny oneself: death.
2. To take the cross: elevation of oneself towards the magisterium.
3. To follow the Christ.

The sacred N (Nun - נ) is found in the Fourteenth Arcanum. It is the fish of life that is born and dies within the waters, thus reaching the Light; let us remember the multiplication of the fish. We cannot be elevated towards the magisterium if we do not descend to destroy the ego, even if we have already reached the Second Birth.

It is necessary to descend in order to ascend. Victory exists in the Third Arcanum, whether it is material or spiritual victory.

The Third Arcanum is the Divine Mother, the Kundalini. She is the Goddess of the Verb; She is Hadit, the Winged Goddess. The Third Arcanum is the "Lost Word," it is the universal language which is mentioned in the Bible in the famous banquet of Nebuchadnezzar.

Chapter XLVI

Arcana 7, 8, and 9

The Seventh, Eighth, and Ninth Arcana are "the Three Degrees of the Master." These are the tools required for the labor in the Great Work.

In the Seventh Arcanum we find the Chariot, the emblem of Triumph. The Eighth Arcanum is Justice, the emblem of equilibrated strength in all directions. The Ninth Arcanum is the Hermit, the emblem of the occult cross and of its quest. All aspirants are looking for this cross, but we know in depth that this cross is the Ninth Sphere, sex.

The Seventh Arcanum is the qualities and capacities that are indispensable for the magisterium by means of self-dominion. One has to, or must learn how, to dominate oneself, to control oneself, in order to someday reach Mastery, the magisterium of fire. If we carefully examine the Seventh Arcanum, we see that the chariot is pulled by two sphinxes, one white and the other black; this is the necessary yoking of the inferior nature symbolized by the two sphinxes that pull the chariot. *To yoke* signifies to dominate, to control the passions, to yoke the beast. The chariot is our life. The two sphinxes signify the pair of opposites: hatred and love, light and darkness.

The Eighth Arcanum, when considered in detail, signifies vigilance, justice. The sword aiming upwards signifies rightness. We need to be righteous in our thoughts, in our words, and in our deeds. The left hand of the woman holds the scale of equilibrium. Equilibrium and precision are represented in the scale of justice.

Thus, as the Seventh Arcanum, Triumph, is achieved through self-dominion of the chariot of life, by the dominion of oneself, by knowing how to drive our own life—in other words, intelligently directing the chariot of life—likewise the Eighth Arcanum represents righteousness, justice, firmness, equilibrium. Firmness is the sword, and equilibrium the scale. This firmness must be converted into the axis of life, into the central point of gravity of life, and of our existence.

In regard to the Ninth Arcanum, it is the Occult Light that manifests itself in initiation, thus vivifying the powers. In order to see this Light, one must be converted into a Master; and it is clear that any aspirant must reach the magisterium.

The Seventh, Eighth, and Ninth Arcana are the tools of the work. The Seventh Arcanum teaches us how to control ourselves. The Eighth Arcanum teaches us justice and righteousness in our thoughts, words, and actions. The human being must live with righteousness. The Ninth Arcanum tells us of the Hermit who holds in his right hand the rod and in his left the lamp. What is important is to elevate this lamp aloft; it is vital to raise it in order to illuminate the path of others.

The Ninth Arcanum is fundamental. It is the arcanum of authentic Mastery. The Ninth Arcanum is in the whole cosmos. Observe for yourselves the construction of the universe, and you will see the Ninth Arcanum everywhere. We find the nine above and the nine below.

$$9 + 9 = 18 \qquad 1 + 8 = 9$$

Chapter XLVII

Arcana 11 and 12

It is clear and evident that the trunks or tablets of the law where the Prophet Moses wisely wrote the Ten Commandments by command of Jehovah are indeed none other than a double Runic lance, whose phallic significance is widely documented.

It is not irrelevant to emphasize the transcendental idea that two more commandments exist in Mosaic esotericism. I want to refer to the Eleventh and Twelfth Commandments, which are intimately related with the Eleventh and Twelfth Arcana of Kabbalah.

The Eleventh Commandment has its classical expression in the Sanskrit *Dharmam Chara:* **Do thy duty.** Remember, dear reader, that you have the upright duty of searching for the straight, narrow, and difficult path that leads to the Light.

The Eleventh Arcanum of the Tarot illuminates that upright duty. The marvellous force that can dominate and hold the lions of adversity is essentially spiritual. That is why this force is represented by a beautiful woman who, without any apparent effort, opens with her delicate hands the terrible mouth of Leo, the frightful cougar, the furious lion.

The Eleventh Commandment is related to and joined with the Twelfth Commandment of the Law of God, illustrated by the Twelfth Arcanum: **Make thy light shine!**

In order for the Light, which constitutes the Essence that is bottled up within the ego, to really shine and glow, the Essence must be liberated. This is only

EXODUS CHAP. XXXI.
Moyses receiveth the two Tables.

EXODUS 31. Verse 18.
The Lord gave unto Moses, when he had made an end of communing with him upon mount Sinai two tables of testimony &c.

possible through the Buddhist annihilation, by dissolving the ego.

We need to die from moment to moment, from instant to instant. Only with the death of the ego comes the new.

Thus, as life represents a process of gradual and always more complete exteriorization, or extroversion, likewise the death of the ego is but a process of gradual introversion, in which the individual consciousness or Essence is slowly divested of its worthless vestments, such as Ishtar, who in her symbolic descent remained completely naked before the great Reality of life which is free in its movements.

The lance, sex, the phallus, are also included in many great plays, in numerous Oriental legends, as marvellous instruments of liberation and salvation, that when wisely wielded by the eager soul it permits the reduction of all those cavernicolus entities, which in their sinful conjunction constitute "the myself," into cosmic dust.

The sexual energy is highly explosive and marvellous. Verily I say onto you that whosoever knows how to use the weapon of Eros (the lance, sex) can reduce to cosmic dust the pluralized "I."

To pray is to converse with God, and one must learn to pray during coitus. In those instances of supreme enjoyment, *ask and it will be granted unto you, knock and it will be opened unto you.*

Whosoever puts their heart into the prayer and begs their Divine Mother Kundalini in order for her to grasp the weapon of Eros, they will obtain the best results because the Divine Mother will then help by destroying their ego.

A previous condition to every elimination is the integral comprehension of the defect that one wants to eliminate.

Chapter XLVIII

Arcana 6, 9, 12, 13, 14, 15, 16, 17, and 20

The Twentieth Arcanum is Resurrection; this is very important: it is stated in occult esotericism that Hiram Abiff or Chiram Osiris is dead in the Ninth Sphere, in the heart of the Earth. It is said that in order to reach the sepulcher, we must pass through the nine underground cellars, the nine strata of the interior of our planetary organism. This Ninth Sphere is in our human organism; it is the sex. Yes, the intimate Christ is dead in the sex, and the resurrection of Him is only possible in the sex.

The subject matter about the resurrection is something grandiose. Jonah was in the belly of the whale for "three days" and Jesus resurrected on the "third day." This is symbolic; the great whale of Jonah is the same Earth, our very planetary organism. The three days are symbolic because these are "three periods of esoteric work" before reaching the resurrection of the intimate Christ within ourselves:

First Day: the Second Birth.

Second Day: the killing of the three traitors.

Third Day: the resurrection of the Lord.

WORK-TABLE FOR THE THIRD DEGREE (MASTER) MASON. ENGLAND, c. 1780.

Here we find the Three Factors of the revolution of the consciousness:

1. To die
2. To be born
3. To sacrifice for humanity

Lobsang Rampa stated that he was as if dead for three days inside of a sarcophagus. This is symbolic; there is no school that does not talk about these three days. Various pseudo-esoteric schools emphasize the fact that three days must be endured in a sepulcher in order to attain realization of the Self. Lobsang Rampa said that in that interval of time of three days, his body lay as if it were dead in the grave, and that he learned many things in the Superior Worlds. This is a symbolic initiatic ceremony that delivers to us a teaching. However, we must make a differentiation between the symbolic teaching and the teaching that is lived.

Jesus was in the sepulcher and He resurrected after three days; then He remained for eleven years teaching and instructing (*The Pistis Sophia* refers to this). It was well known in the archaic times about these three days in the sepulcher. In the traditions of the Samothracians and among the Mayans, the Egyptians, and the Aztecs, the sepulcher and the three days are found. The aspirants to adepthood were taken to volcanoes, chambers, or closed sepulchers which had the form of a fish. Let us remember that the coffin of Osiris, in the ancient Egypt of the Pharaohs in the sunny land of Kem, had the form of a fish.

This reminds us of Oannes who remained for three days within his sepulcher, a tradition which has been lost in the profound night.

It is stated by ancient traditions that are lost within the frightful night of all times, that during this interval, while the body of the initiate was laid down as a cadaver within the coffin, the Soul which was absent from the dense human form experienced directly in the superior worlds the ritual of life and death. Masonry has not forgotten its coffin.

There is something which shows that Tuesday Lobsang Rampa and other authors do not possess an integral knowledge; this is due to the fact that they mistake the funeral symbol of three days with the crude reality hidden within the depth of it. It is as if we get confused with the flag, which is a symbol, or confused with the two columns Jachin and Boaz which are an esoteric symbol representing the man and the woman. Likewise, the funeral coffin is a symbol. In ancient times there was the custom of leaving the initiate three days within the sepulcher, but everything has its limits, and beyond that limit we have to develop all of the knowledge. It is necessary to go deep in the reality.

What is signified by Jesus rising out of the sepulcher? What is signified by Jonah being vomited out from the belly of the whale after being three days within it?

An evil and adulterous generation seeketh after a sign; and there shall no sign be given to it, but the sign of the prophet Jonah:

For as Jonah was three days and three nights in the whale's belly; so shall the Son of Man be three days and three nights in the heart of the earth. - Matthew 12:39-40

This is symbolic; Jonah states that he was submerged within the waters and into the bottom of the mountains. The earth with her bars was about him forever, but he cried from within the profundities of the earth unto Jehovah. The abyss that closed around him is very significant. By going into this more profoundly, let us remember the "Leviathan," that marvellous fish that lives beneath the waters of the sea. [Isaiah 27:1; Job 41:1; Psalms 74:14, 104:26]

This is the **First Day**, when we submerge within ourselves. It is that day when all of us must descend into the subterranean worlds in order to build the Bodies which will grant unto us the Second Birth. The First Day is when we have to descend into the bottom of the Tartarus, thus, as the Law of Leviathan.

In the **Second Day**, it is necessary to return to the bottom of the abyss in order to remain there until the creations that we made with our evil actions are destroyed.

It is indubitable that superlative transformation is only possible with the resurrection of the intimate Christ in the heart of the Human Being. This is the culminating step of the **Third Day**, the instant in which the Earth, or the glowing constellation of the whale, vomits out the Prophet Jonah in order for him then to go and teach at Niniveh in order for him to return unto the Father. Jonah was converted into a Resurrected Master after being vomited from the whale. He then was sent to teach. For that reason he has a right to the Ascension. Every exaltation is preceded by a humiliation. The humiliation is the descent into the Infernal Worlds.

These three days will give us an answer related with something more profound; whosoever has understanding let this person understand. It is necessary to comprehend and meditate that the Leviathan, that one who is moving through the waters, is the true Master that has been decapitated and decapitated again. Who is capable of decapitating the Leviathan? Who is capable of hurting the one who has already received all harms and become resurrected? Let us be converted into Resurrected Masters.

The cross as symbol is one thing, but the work that we have to perform in the Ninth Sphere is another. The symbol and the work are correlated.

All of the progress in these studies is based on the Kabbalah.

The Thirteenth and Fourteenth Arcana have not been well understood; this is why it is necessary to be more profound in these studies. In the ancient Egypt of the Pharaohs, when Typhon had the form of a fish, he cut the body of Osiris into pieces. When Isis—the Divine Mother, spouse, and sister of Osiris—intended to resurrect him, she only found "thirteen" pieces; the fourteenth piece, which was the phallus, was not found. Thirteen is death; it is obvious that Osiris must pass three days in the sepulcher, and those three days are equivalent to the three steps of the decapitation of the ego. Isis found thirteen pieces, and She did not find the fourteenth, the "phallus," because every lustful element was already dead in Him. He attained a complete

death. Only like this can Osiris present himself victorious in the Temple of Maat (the Truth). Only like this can He utter the Negative Confession, because He no longer has ego; He has a pure Spirit.

The subject matter about Osiris in the sepulcher is very important. He is completely dead, and only on the Third Day is He resurrected.

1. Generation

2. Degeneration

3. Regeneration

The extraordinary and marvellous form of the old coffin of Osiris, because of its likeness and significance, naturally brings into the memory another fish which is magnificently represented in the Semitic alphabet by the letter ס Samech, which is a letter that occupies the Fifteenth Kabbalistic place, which in the beginning undoubtedly symbolized the famous constellation of the whale, a constellation under which we have to perform all of the works in the Ninth Sphere. This constellation is related with the event of Jonah and also related with the measurements of the coffin of Osiris which has the form of a fish. This is why Osiris had to descend into the black and terrifying precipice in order to pass through the three days in the belly of the whale.

This is intimately related with the Thirteenth Arcanum, in other words **three descents** into the Infernal Worlds. Each descent takes a period of time and gives three days in the Holy Sepulcher. Jonah worked three days, three periods, with sex, and at the end of the three days, the whale vomited him, and afterwards he went to preach.

The whale corresponds to the Fifteenth Kabbalistic Arcanum, and this invites us to reflect. The Fifteenth Arcanum is Typhon Baphomet, the Devil, the animal passion. This invites us to comprehend what the work in the Ninth Sphere (sex) is.

If one fails in the Thirteenth, Fourteenth, and Fifteenth Arcana, if one is not capable to work within the whale, then it is obvious that one goes downward, towards the precipice with the Sixteenth Arcanum, which is the Fulminated Tower. The initiate who spills the Glass of Hermes will be fulminated by the Sixteenth Arcanum of the constellation of Aries. The initiate, straightened by the lightning of cosmic justice, will fall from the tower with the head aiming downwards and the legs aiming upwards as the inverted pentalpha.

The Seventeenth Arcanum, the Star of Hope, is for the individual who has never been fulminated, to the one who is capable of reaching the Venustic Initiation. If we add this arcanum in itself we have: $1 + 7 = 8$, which is the number of Job, related with patience, ordeals, and sufferings.

If we Kabbalistically add the numbers of the Fifteenth Arcanum of the constellation of the whale, we will have the following result: $1 + 5 = 6$. The number six in the Tarot is the arcanum of the Lover. It is the arcanum of the Human Soul who is between virtue and passion. You must be wisely polarized with the Sixth Arcanum, in order to defeat the frightful Fifteenth Arcanum of the constellation of the whale.

Remember dear reader, that in the center of your chest you have a very special magnetic point which captures the waves of light and glory that come from your Human Soul. The Human Soul is

Tiphereth, the Sixth Arcanum of the Tarot. Listen and obey the orders which emanate from your Human Soul, act in accordance with those intimate impulses. Work in the forge of the Cyclops when your Soul requires it from you. If you learn to obey you will not perish in the belly of the whale.

Behold! You have turned into a fish who works within the chaotic waters of the first instant. Now you will comprehend why the coffin of Osiris has the form of a fish.

It is unquestionable that the seven days or periods in the book of Genesis of Moses are synthesized in these three days and three nights of Jonah within the belly of the whale. This is an initiatic ceremony that was repeated by the great Kabir Jesus in the holy sepulcher.

The Prophet Jonah, working under the regency of the constellation of the whale, being inside of the well of the universe, in the Ninth Sphere (sex), performed his work in three days or three more or less long periods:

First Day: He descends into the Infernal Worlds in order to build the Solar Bodies, the Wedding Garment of the Soul, and to establish within himself a permanent center of consciousness. To descend into the Infernos of Nature is necessary; this is a period of elimination until destroying Seth, until achieving the Second Birth.

Second Day: He descends into the abyss in order to confront frightful sacrifices; he utilizes the creative energy for the destruction of the subjective elements of the ego. This work is performed in the Lunar Infernal Worlds, within the sub-lunar regions to which the esoteric books refer. Then, the three traitors of the intimate Christ—Judas, Pilate, and Caiaphas—are radically eliminated, as well as the atoms of the Secret Enemy. Also the Dragon of Darkness, the Red Dragon, must be disintegrated. Then the work is continued by eliminating the submerged secondary beasts within which the consciousness is bottled up.

Third Day: One must return to the bottom of the abyss in order to finish with innumerable deeds from previous lives. One continues dying in the spheres of Mercury, Venus, Sun, Mars, Jupiter, Saturn, etc. On the Third Day, the black waters are transformed into resplendent Light, and the destruction of ancient atoms culminate with the mystical resurrection.

Each one of the three days culminates with the following:

A) The first period of time concludes with the Second Birth, of which the great Kabir Jesus spoke unto the Rabbi Nicodemus.

B) The second period finishes when the consciousness is liberated, with a marvellous wedding resulting. The wedding of the Human Soul with the Valkyrie or Guinevere, the Queen of the Jinns, who is the Spiritual and feminine Soul, Buddhi, within which the flame of the Spirit is always burning, the flame of Brahma. Unto the women we say that they then get married with the Eternal Beloved One.

C) The third period magisterially concludes with the resurrection of the intimate Christ within our own heart. The Ascension into the Superior Worlds comes as a logical consequence.

Now we are just receiving information, but one must live and experience this information directly. Do not stray, but keep firm.

You must study the prayer of Jonah; it is precious. Magnificent esoteric arcana are enclosed in it.

You must study the book of Jonah in the Old Testament; investigate all of the archaic information concerning these three days. They must be comprehended very deeply because many people are ignorant about the work in the subterranean world.

Indeed, this subject matter is related with the Twelfth card of the Tarot, because 1 + 2 = 3 (three days). In this card a man is hanged from his foot and forms a cross with his legs; his arms form a triangle with his head aiming downwards. All this indicates to us that he descends into the well of the abyss. This is the Apostolate.

There are twenty-two arcana because Twenty-two is the Truth, the Tetragrammaton, the Iod Hei Vav Hei, and there must be twenty-two arcana in order to clarify it.

Third Part

The Kabbalah

"There are two types of Kabbalists: Intellectual Kabbalists and Intuitive Kabbalists. The Intellectual Kabbalists are black magicians, whilst the Intuitive Kabbalists are White Magicians."

- Samael Aun Weor

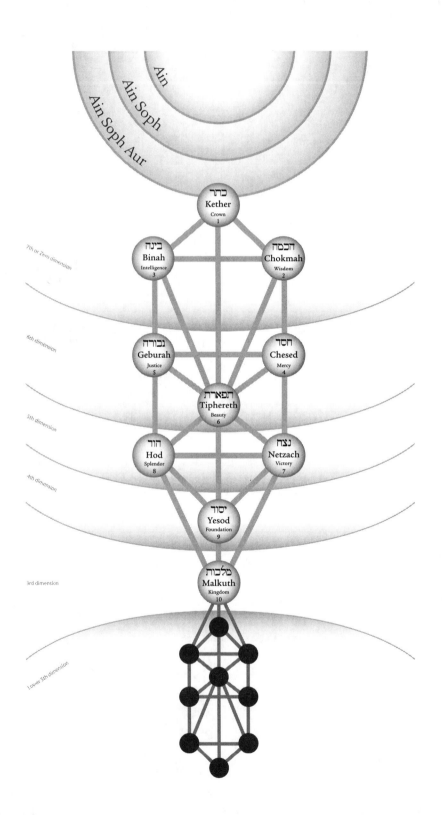

Ain

Ain Soph

Ain Soph Aur

כתר
Kether
Crown
1

בינה
Binah
Intelligence
3

חכמה
Chokmah
Wisdom
2

גבורה
Geburah
Justice
5

חסד
Chesed
Mercy
4

תפארת
Tiphereth
Beauty
6

הוד
Hod
Splendor
8

נצח
Netzach
Victory
7

יסוד
Yesod
Foundation
9

מלכות
Malkuth
Kingdom
10

7th or Zero dimension

6th dimension

5th dimension

4th dimension

3rd dimension

Lower 5th dimension

Chapter XLIX

The Absolute

The substantial content of this work is for a more advanced humanity, because the people of this barbarian epoch are not capable of understanding these things.
- Samael Aun Weor

The Absolute is the Being of all Beings. The Absolute is that which is, which always has been, and which always will be. The Absolute is expressed as absolute abstract movement and repose. The Absolute is the cause of Spirit and of matter, but it is neither Spirit nor matter. The Absolute is beyond the mind; the mind cannot understand It. Therefore, we have to intuitively understand its nature.

The Absolute is beyond conditioned life. It is beyond that which is relative. It is the real Being; It is Non-being because it does not keep any concordance with our concepts, but the Absolute is the "real Being." This is why we do not intellectually comprehend it, because for us the Absolute is like Non-being; nonetheless, it is the real Being of the Being.

To be is better than *to exist*, and the reason for the Being to be is to be the Being itself. Our legitimate existence is within the Absolute, which is a non-being, a non-existence to human reasoning.

The Absolute is not a God, neither a divine nor human individual. It would be absurd to give form to that which has no form; it would be nonsense to try to anthropomorphize space.

Indeed, the Absolute is the unconditional and eternal abstract space, far beyond Gods and human beings. The Absolute is the Uncreated Light which does not project a shadow in any place during the profound night of the Great Pralaya.

The Absolute is beyond time, number, measurement, and weight; beyond causality, form, fire, light and darkness. Nonetheless, the Absolute is the Fire and the Uncreated Light.

The Absolute has three aspects:

Ain is the same as **Sat** in Sanskrit—in other words, the Unmanifested Absolute.

Ain Soph is the second aspect; it is where a certain manifestation already exists. It is the place where all creatures abide when the Great Pralaya (Cosmic Night) arrives, because they do not have the right to enter into the **Ain**, into the Unmanifested Absolute, which is beyond thought, word, atom, sound, beyond all of that which has form, number, weight, etc.

Ain Soph Aur is the third aspect in accordance with the Hebrew Kabbalah. Here we find the first cosmos, the purely spiritual Protocosmos. It is the Solar Absolute, which is formed by multiple Spiritual Suns.

Practice

Meditate on the Absolute and on the Pralaya by placing the mind in quietude and in silence.

Chapter L

The Ain

Abstract space is the *causa causorum* of everything which is, has been, and will be.

The profound and joyous space is certainly the incomprehensible "Seity" that is the ineffable mystic root of the seven cosmoses. It is the mysterious origin of all of that which we know as Spirit, matter, universes, suns, worlds, etc.

"That," the Divine, the space of happiness, is a tremendous reality beyond the universe and the Gods. "That" does not have any dimension, and truly It is what always will be and has been. It is the life which intensely palpitates within each atom and within each sun.

Let us now talk about the "Ocean of the Spirit." How can It be defined?

Certainly, the Ocean of the Spirit is Brahma, which is the first difference or modification of "That," before which Gods and human beings tremble.

Is "That" Spirit? Truly I tell you that It is not. Is "That" matter? Certainly I tell you that It is not.

"That" is the root of Spirit and of matter, but It is neither Spirit nor matter.

"That" overcomes the laws of number, measurement, and weight, side by side, quantity, quality, front, back, above, below, etc.

"That" is the immutable in profound divine abstraction. Light which has never been created by any God, neither by any human being. "That" has no name.

Brahma is Spirit, but "That" is not Spirit. **Ain** the Unmanifested is Uncreated Light.

The Absolute is life free in its motion; it is the supreme reality, the abstract space that only expresses itself as absolute abstract motion, happiness without limits, complete omniscience. The Absolute is Uncreated Light and perfect plenitude, absolute happiness, life free in its motion, life without conditions, without limits.

Within the Absolute we pass beyond Karma and the Gods, far beyond the Law, beyond the mind, and the individual consciousness which only serves for mortifying our life. Within the Absolute we have neither an individual mind nor individual consciousness. "There," we are the free and absolutely happy unconditioned Being.

The Absolute is life free in its motion, without conditions, without limitations, without a mortifying fear towards the Law. It is life beyond the Spirit and matter, beyond Karma and pain.

The Absolute is absolute abstract space, absolute abstract motion, absolute liberty without conditions, without reserves, absolute omniscience, and absolute happiness.

We have to terminate the process of the "I" in order to enter into the Absolute. The human "I" must enter into the house of the dead, must go to the common grave of the astral rubbish. The "I" must be disintegrated in the abyss in order for the Being, full of majesty and power, to be born.

Only impersonal life and the Being can give us the legitimate happiness of the Great Life free in its motion.

To struggle, to fight, to suffer, and to be free in the end, in order to get lost as a drop within the ocean of Uncreated Light, is certainly the best longing.

One needs to be prepared within the region of Atala before entering into the Absolute. In Atala, the Beings are uncolored. A certain man who could not enter into the Absolute lives there, due to the fact that he invented the two words "good" and "evil" instead of using the words **evolutionary** and **devolutionary**. This man created a type of Karma because humanity has been damaged with the two words "good" and "evil." In everything, we say, "this is good," or "this is evil," so humanity is stagnant in all of that which attracts them to the studies of internal values. This is why this holy man is waiting.

We have to help people in order for them to exchange the two words "good" and "evil" for evolutionary and devolutionary.

Within the bosom of the Absolute exists the Paramarthasattyas in great exaltation; they become exalted little by little until they pass beyond all possible comprehension.

ENGRAVING BY GUSTAVE DORÉ FROM *THE DIVINE COMEDY*

Chapter LI
The Ain Soph

All of creation emanates from the **Ain Soph**, but creation, in essence and in potency, is not equal to the Ain Soph.

The Ain Soph irradiates intelligence, a power by means of its divine Uncreated Light; an intelligence, a power that, if it originally participates in the perfection and infinitude of its (Ain Soph) own creed, it has a finite aspect because it is being derived from the Ain Soph. Unto this first spiritual emanation of the Ain Soph the Kabbalah gives the name the ineffable **Ancient of Days** who is the Being of our Being, the Father/Mother within us.

The Ain Soph, not being able to express Itself in the limited physical plane, does it through Its "ten Sephiroth."

A strange evolution that not even the Gods or the human beings know about exists within the Ain Soph. Much beyond the Innermost we find the Logos or the Christ. Much beyond the ineffable Ancient of Days is the Ain Soph or the Absolute, whose exhalation is called Cosmic Day (Mahamanvantara), and whose inhalation is called Cosmic Night (Mahapralaya).

During the Cosmic Night, the universe is disintegrated within the Ain Soph; then the universe only exists in the mind of the Ain Soph and in the mind of its Gods. The universe that exists in the mind of It and in the mind of Them is only objective within the abstract absolute space.

After the Great Pralaya, before the beginning of the intensive palpitation of the flaming heart of this solar system called Ors in which we live, move, and have our Being, time did not exist; time was lying asleep within the profound bosom of the abstract absolute space.

If at the end of the Mahamanvantara the seven basic dimensions of the Universe remain reduced to a simple mathematical point which is lost as a drop of water within the Great Ocean, then it is evident that time ceases to exist.

The worlds, human beings, animals, and plants, are born, grow, age, and die. Everything that exists under the Sun has a defined time.

Ancient wisdom states that Brahma, the Father, the universal Spirit of life, is submerged within the abstract absolute space for seven eternities, when the Great Night (that which the Hindustanis named Pralaya, or dissolution of the universe) arrives.

The seven eternities signify "evos," or totally defined, clear, and precise periods of time.

It has been said unto us, that a Mahakalpa—a Great Age or Cosmic Day—has the totality of 311,040,000,000,000 years. It is obvious that a Mahapralaya, a Cosmic Night, is equivalent to the same quantity of time.

When the profound night for the creators of this solar system arrives, they will be absorbed within the bosom of the Absolute, and only a group of moons will remain, and the planets, the Sun, the Earth, and life with all its virginal sparks will disappear. A virginal spark corresponds to each one of us; a virginal spark corresponds to each living creature, and these sparks are absorbed within the Absolute for seven eternities.

If we observe Selene (our Moon), we will see that it is a cadaver, but that it had plenty of life, oceans, and volcanoes. There are other moons that rotate around Mars, Saturn, etc., which had plenty of life in the previous Cosmic Day. In the previous Mahamanvantara, which was called "Padma" or the Lotus of Gold, there was a humanity with seven root races on the Moon, and it died.

The universe was sleeping within the terrible obscurity before the dawn of the Mahamanvantara.

The eternal Black Light or Absolute Obscurity is converted into Chaos in the beginning or in the aurora of each universe.

C H A O S

Ancient wisdom states that Darkness is in itself Father/Mother, and Light is its Child.

It is evident that the Uncreated Light has an unknown origin, absolutely unknowable to us.

In no way do we exaggerate if we emphasize the idea that the origin of the Uncreated Light is Darkness.

Let us now talk about the borrowed, secondary, Cosmic Light; it is obvious that whatever its origin might be, and whatever its beauty might be, it has in its depth a temporary character of Maya (illusion).

Therefore, the profound ineffable Darkness constitutes the Eternal Womb, within which the origins of Light appear and disappear.

It is said that the Absolute is Darkness. Light emerges from Darkness. The Uncreated Light of the Absolute emerges from the profound Darkness of the Great Night. From this Darkness, that does not have Light, emerges the Uncreated Light. If we are placed in this Darkness, we will see nothing but an abyss and profound Darkness, but for the inhabitants of the Absolute, the Paramarthasattyas, this Darkness is Uncreated Light, which is not created by any God or human being, and where only an inexhaustible happiness and inconceivable joy reigns.

There are tremendous Genii of Evil, such as Belial, Bael, Moloch, etc., who are terrible Masters, and because of knowing that Light emerges from Darkness, they precipitated themselves into the abyss, even when they knew that they were going to devolve. Light emerges from the abyss; this is why we have to descend into the Darkness in order to destroy the "I," Satan, to then snatch away this Light from the Darkness.

The Gods emerge from the abyss by means of fire, and they get lost within the Absolute.

Light and Darkness are two phenomena of the same noumenon, which is unknown, profound, and inconceivable to the reasoning.

The fact of perceiving more or less Light that shines from the Darkness is a matter which depends on our power of spiritual vision. The Absolute is a profound and terrible Darkness for human eyes, and Uncreated Light for the ineffable hierarchy of the Paramarthasattyas.

"What is light for us is darkness for certain insects, and the spiritual eye sees illumination where the normal eye can only see obscurity..."

After the Mahamanvantara, when the Universe is immersed into a Pralaya, when it is dissolved within its primordial element, it necessarily reposes within the profound Darkness of the infinite space.

It is urgent to deeply comprehend the profound mystery of the Chaotic Darkness.

The cosmos emerges from the Chaos, and Light sprouts from Darkness. Let us profoundly pray!

It is written with words of fire in all of the sacred books of the world that the seed-plot of the cosmos is the Chaos.

The Nothingness, the Chaos, is certainly, and without a doubt, the Alpha and the Omega, the beginning and the ending of all the worlds which live and palpitate in the unalterable infinite.

The *Aitareya Brahmana,* a precious and magisterial lesson of the *Rig Veda,* has truly demonstrated until satiation the tremendous identity between the luminous ideas of Brahmans and Pythagoreans, because Brahmans and Pythagoreans are supported by mathematics. In the previously cited Hindustani volume, the Light, the Black Fire, or abstract obscure wisdom, absolute unconditioned and without name, is frequently mentioned.

That abstract Seity, the primitive Zero-Aster of the Parsis, is the life-saturated

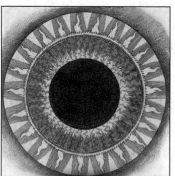

LIGHT SPROUTS FROM DARKNESS

Nothingness, is That... That... That... God Himself. In other words, the Army of the Voice, the Verb, the Great Word, dies when the Great Pralaya, the Cosmic Night arrives, and is reborn terribly divine in the aurora of the divine Mahamanvantara.

The absolutely radical zero in transcendental arithmetic, the abstract space in geometry, the unknowable "Seity" (do not confuse it with Deity, which is different) is not born, nor dies, nor reincarnates.

In the beginning, from this unknowable entirety or radical zero, emanates any sidereal universe, Pythagorean Monad, Gnostic Father/Mother, Hindu Purusha-Prakriti, Egyptian Osiris-Isis, Dual Protocosmos or Kabbalistic Adam Kadmon, the Theos-Chaos of the Theogony of Hesiod, the Chaldean Uranas or fire and water, Semitic Iod-Heve, Parsi Zeru-Ama, Unique One, Buddhist Aunadad-Ad, Ruach Elohim or Divine Spirit of the Lord floating upon the Genesiac waters of the first instant.

In the profound night, only Darkness alone filled the boundless all, for Father, Mother, and Son were once more one, and the Son had not awakened yet for the new wheel and His pilgrimage thereon.

It is written with characters of unmistakable fire in the book of the great life, that at the end of the Mahamanvantara, Osiris (the Father), Isis (the Mother), and Horus (the Divine Spirit) are integrated and fused like three fires in order to make one single flame.

Let us search for Osiris, Isis, and Horus within ourselves, within the unknowable profundities of our own Being.

It is obvious that Osiris, Isis, and Horus constitute in themselves the Monad, the Duad, and the Triad of our Internal Being.

Did you ever hear about Brahma? He is in Himself Father-Mother-Son.

In each new cosmic aurora, the universe resurrects like the Phoenix Bird from within its own ashes.

In the dawn of each Mahamanvantara, the Monad unfolds again into the Duad and into the Triad.

At the daybreak of the new Cosmic Day, after the profound Night, the Son, the Triad, Horus (the Divine Spirit in each one), emanates the Essence, His mystic principles, from Himself into the Wheel of Samsara with the purpose of acquiring a Diamond Soul.

Ah! How great is the joy of Horus when acquiring a Diamond Soul! Then, He is absorbed within His Divine Mother, and She is also fused with the Father, who form a unique Diamond Flame, a God of resplendent interior beauty.

Space is filled with universes, and while some systems of worlds are emerging from the profound Night, others are arriving at their sunset. Here are cradles, and far away there are sepulchers.

When the aurora of the Mahamanvantara is initiated, the heterogony unfolds into the homogeneity, and the Army of the Voice (God) is born again in order to create anew.

The universe shook with terror when the aurora of the new Cosmic Day was announced. Then, a strange and frightful twilight emerged in the consciousness of the Gods and the human beings, and the Uncreated Light began to withdraw from the consciousness of them.

Afterwards, the Gods and the human beings wept like children before the aurora of the Great Cosmic Day... Then, the Causal Logos reminded the Gods and human beings of their Karmic debts, and the pilgrimage of the human being from one world into the other began. Finally, they arrived on Earth, where they are presently living, submitted to the wheel of birth and death until they learn to live governed by the law of love.

The Universe emerged from within the bosom of the Absolute, and the Uncreated Light sank into a nostalgic sunset. Thus, this is how the Gods and human beings descended within the shadows of the universe.

The sacrifice was consummated, and the Kabbalah registered in its Major Arcanum Twelve. If we add the number twelve in itself, it gives us three. One is the masculine principle, the fire. Two is the feminine principle, the water, the semen. Three is the universe, the Son.

The present Cosmic Day is symbolized by a blue pelican which is opening its chest with its beak in order to drink from its own bosom from which all creation sprouted.

Chapter LII

The Ain Soph Aur

Each universe in infinite space possesses its own central sun, and the addition of all of those Spiritual Suns constitutes the **Ain Soph Aur**, the Protocosmos, the Solar Absolute.

The Solar Absolute is formed by multiple, transcendental, and divine Spiritual Suns.

The emanation of our "Omnimerciful and sacred Solar Absolute" is that which H. P. Blavatsky denominates *"the Great Breath, profoundly unknowable to Itself..."*

A great deal has been spoken of the sacred Solar Absolute, and it is obvious that each solar system is governed by one of these Spiritual Suns. Indeed, these are extraordinary Spiritual Suns that sparkle with infinite splendor in space. These are radiant spheres that astronomers will never perceive through their telescopes.

This means that our organization of worlds possesses its own sacred Absolute Sun, as well as the other solar systems of the inalterable infinite.

The Protocosmos, or first cosmos, is infinitely divine, ineffable; no mechanical principle exists within it. It is governed by one unique law.

If you profoundly reflect on the solar Absolute, you will see that beyond it exists the most complete liberty, the most absolute happiness, because everything is governed by that singular law.

Unquestionably, within the sacred solar Absolute, in the central Spiritual Sun of this system in which we live, move, and have our Being, there does not exist any type of mechanization. Therefore, it is

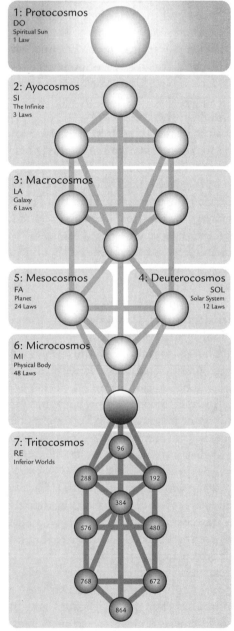

1: Protocosmos
DO
Spiritual Sun
1 Law

2: Ayocosmos
SI
The Infinite
3 Laws

3: Macrocosmos
LA
Galaxy
6 Laws

5: Mesocosmos
FA
Planet
24 Laws

4: Deuterocosmos
SOL
Solar System
12 Laws

6: Microcosmos
MI
Physical Body
48 Laws

7: Tritocosmos
RE
Inferior Worlds

96
288   192
384
576   480
768   672
864

The Tree of Life and the Descending Notes of Creation

obvious that the most complete blessing reigns there.

It is indubitable that in the central Spiritual Sun, governed by the unique law, exists the unutterable happiness of the eternal living God. Unfortunately, while we get further and further from the sacred Absolute Sun, we penetrate each time into more and more complicated worlds, where automatism, mechanization, and pain are introduced.

Obviously, in the second cosmos of three laws, the Ayocosmos (planets, suns, and firmament), joy is incomparable because there is less materialism. In that region, every atom processes only three atoms of the Absolute within its interior nature.

How distinct is the third cosmos, the Macrocosmos (our galaxy, the Milky Way) which is governed by six laws. There, materiality increases because any of its atoms possesses six atoms of the Absolute within its interior.

By penetrating into the fourth cosmos, the Deuterocosmos (our solar system) which is governed by twelve laws, we find more dense matter due to the concrete fact that any of its atoms possesses twelve atoms of the Absolute.

If we carefully examine the fifth cosmos, the Mesocosmos (the planet Earth) governed by twenty-four laws, we will see that any of its atoms possess twenty-four atoms of the Absolute within its interior nature.

Let us study in detail the sixth cosmos, the Microcosmos (the human being), which is governed by forty-eight laws. We will see by means of divine clairvoyance that any atom of the human organism possesses forty-eight atoms of the Absolute.

Let us descend a little more and enter into the kingdom of the most crude materialism, the seventh cosmos, the Tritocosmos (the Infernal Worlds); we will discover that under the crust of the planet where we live, the first infradimensional zone governed by ninety-six laws exists. The density of this region has increased frightfully, because any atom processes ninety-six atoms of the Absolute within its intimate nature.

In the second infernal zone, every atom possesses one hundred and ninety-two atoms of the Absolute. In the third zone, every atom possesses three hundred and eighty-four atoms of the Absolute, etc., etc., etc., and the materialism increases in a very frightful and horrific way.

Obviously, we become independent in a progressive way from the will of the Absolute when we fall into the complicated mechanics of this great Nature, when we become submerged within more and more complicated laws. If we want to reconquer freedom, we must liberate ourselves from too much mechanization, and too many laws, and return unto the Father.

Clearly, we must fight in a vigorous way in order to liberate ourselves from the 48, 24, 12, 6, and 3 laws in order to really return into the sacred Absolute Sun of our solar system.

Chapter LIII

The Ain Soph Paranishpanna

A divine ray exists within the human being. That ray wants to return back into its own star that has always smiled upon it. The star that guides our interior is a super divine atom from the abstract absolute space. The Kabbalistic name of that atom is the sacred Ain Soph.

The Ain Soph is our atomic star. This Star radiates within the absolute abstract space full of glory. Precisely in this order, Kether (the Father), Chokmah (the Son), and Binah (the Holy Spirit) of every human being emanate from this star. The Ain Soph, the star that guides our interior, sent its ray into the world in order to become cognizant of its own happiness.

Happiness without cognizance of happiness is not real happiness.

The ray (the Spirit) had cognizance as a mineral, plant, and animal. When the ray incarnated for the first time within the wild and primitive human body, the ray awoke as a human being and had self-cognizance of its own happiness. Then the ray could have returned into its own star that guides its interior.

Disgracefully, within the profound bosom of the voracious and dense jungle, wild **desire** gave birth to the "I." The instinctive forces of nature trapped the innocent mind of the human being and the false mirage of desire emerged.

Then, the "I" continued reincarnating in order to satisfy its desires. Thus, we remained submitted to the law of evolution and Karma.

Experiences and pain complicated the "I." Evolution is a complicated process of the energy. The "I" became strong with experiences. Now it is too late. Millions of people have been converted into monstrous demons. Only a tremendous revolution can save us from the abyss.

When the human being dissolves the "I," then there is a complete revolution.

Human beings will stop suffering when they are capable of dissolving the "I." Pain is the result of our evil deeds.

Pain is Satan (the psychological "I"), because Satan is the one that makes the evil deeds. The abstract absolute space, the

THE EMERGENCE OF DESIRE AS SYMBOLIZED BY THE KABBALIST MOSES IN THE BOOK OF GENESIS.

universal Spirit of life, is absolute happiness, supreme peace, and abundance.

Those who make mysticism out of pain are masochists. Satan was the creator of pain. Pain is satanic. No one can be liberated with pain. We need to be Alchemists.

The "I" is dissolved with Alchemy. Desire is the root of the "I." Desire is transmuted with Alchemy.

If you want to annihilate desire, you need to transmute. Sexual desire is transformed into willpower and willpower is fire. Miserly desire (greed) is transmuted into altruism. Anger (frustrated desire) is transmuted into sweetness. Envy (frustrated desire) is transmuted into happiness for the good of others. The words of desire are transmuted into words of wisdom, etc.

Analyze all the human defects and you will see that they have their foundation in desire. Transmute desire with Alchemy and desire will be annihilated. Whosoever annihilates desire dissolves the "I." Whosoever dissolves the "I" is saved from the abyss and returns into his own interior Star that has always smiled unto him.

Only with Holy Alchemy we can dissolve the "I." The fundamental base of Alchemy is the Arcanum A.Z.F. The Angels, Archangels, Seraphim, Potencies, Thrones, etc., are the exact outcome of tremendous interior revolutions.

We already passed through an **involution** (the descent of the Spirit into matter). We already suffer horribly in the **evolution** (a complicated process of the energy). Now a complete **revolution** is urgent (the dissolution of the "I"). No one can be happy until reaching his interior star. We return to the super divine atom based only on internal revolutions; little by little, we pass through the Angelic, Archangelic, Seraphimic, Logoic, etc. states until finally the ray will fuse with its star, the Ain Soph that shines with happiness.

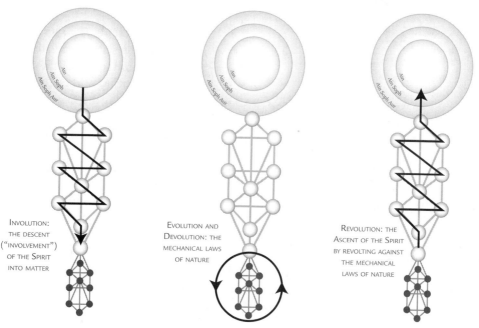

INVOLUTION: THE DESCENT ("INVOLVEMENT") OF THE SPIRIT INTO MATTER

EVOLUTION AND DEVOLUTION: THE MECHANICAL LAWS OF NATURE

REVOLUTION: THE ASCENT OF THE SPIRIT BY REVOLTING AGAINST THE MECHANICAL LAWS OF NATURE

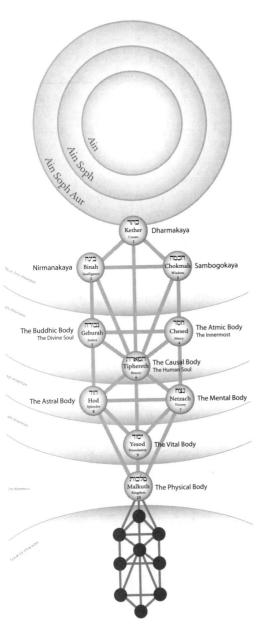

The abyss is terribly painful. The horrible antithesis of the Ain Soph is the abyss, the Klipoth of Kabbalah. The Klipoth are atomic, tenebrous; they belong to the lunar path.

Let us analyze the divine primordial atom from which the ten Sephiroth of the Kabbalah emanate.

If we self-observe we find:

1. The Physical Body

2. The Ethereal or Vital Body

3. The Astral Body or Body of Desires

4. The Animal Mental Body

5. The Essence (normally bottled up within the "I")

Beyond this Essence exists the divine triad that is not incarnated within the human being:

6. The Causal Body, the Human Soul, Manas

7. The Buddhic Body, the Divine Soul

8. The Atmic Body, the Innermost

The fifth and the sixth are related because the fifth is a fraction of the sixth. We have a fraction of the Human Soul incarnated. This is the Essence or Buddhata.

Atman in Himself is the ineffable Being, the one who is beyond time and eternity, without end of days. He does not die, neither reincarnates (the ego is what returns), but Atman is absolutely perfect.

Atman unfolds Himself into the Spiritual Soul. The Spiritual Soul unfolds into the Human Soul who is the Superior Manas; the Human Soul unfolds into the Essence, or Buddhata. In total, these are principles. This Essence is the one that incarnates in its four vehicles. The Essence is dressed with them and remains bottled up within the psychological "I," the ego.

The Mental Body, the body of desires, the Ethereal Body, and the physical body integrate the personality. The Essence remains bottled up within the ego when penetrating these bodies. That which returns is a fraction of the Human Soul.

Beyond the Theosophical triad exists a ray that unites us to the Absolute. This ray within the human being is the resplendent dragon of wisdom, the internal Christ, the Sephirothic Crown; the Kabbalah describes it as follows:

Kether: The Ancient of Days

Chokmah: The Son, the Cosmic Christ

Binah: The Holy Spirit

The Sephirothic Crown is the first triad that emanates from the Ain Soph.

In the final synthesis, each one of us is nothing but an atom of the abstract absolute space, the Ain Soph, which is found secretly related with the pineal gland, the Sahasrara chakra or church of Laodicea.

We must make a specific differentiation between the Ain Soph and the Ain Soph Paranishpanna: in the Ain Soph, interior realization of the Self does not exist, but in the Ain Soph Paranishpanna interior realization of the Self does exist.

Any Mahatma knows very well that before entering into the Absolute, the Solar Bodies must be dissolved. The day in which we will be liberated we will leave, we will abandon all of the vehicles.

For what purpose do we build the Solar Bodies? With which purpose do we descend into the Ninth Sphere if we must abandon the Solar Bodies? With what purpose do we build something that we are not going to use? An atomic seed from

each one of these Christic vehicles remains when they are dissolved. It is clear that in these vehicles four atomic seeds remain. It is indubitable that these atoms correspond to the physical, Astral, Mental, and Causal Bodies.

It is obvious that the four atomic seeds are absorbed within the super divine atom, the Ain Soph Paranishpanna, along with the Essence, spiritual principles, laws, and the three primary forces. Afterwards, the profound night of the Mahapralaya comes.

The Ain Soph without intimate realization of the Self does not possess the four atomic seeds; it is just a simple atom of the absolute abstract space with only the three primary forces, Father, Son, and Holy Spirit, within.

The Paranishpanna atom of a Master that has been liberated is very distinct from the Ain Soph atom that is without realization of the Self. In the aurora of a Mahamanvantara, a Self-realized Master unfolds his bodies by putting their germs into activity. He possesses his Solar Bodies; he can restore them at any moment that he wishes. The fact of having built these bodies gives him autonomous cognizance.

The Ain Soph that possesses the atomic seeds can reincarnate at the hour that It pleases, and It remains dressed with Its Solar Bodies. When the Ain Soph wishes to manifest itself, it emanates those solar atom seeds and appears at any given place in space.

There is a formula that defines all of this:

C. O. N. H.

These are four forces, the four bodies of the initiate, four bodies with which the Seity is dressed when the Seity wants to be manifested.

1. **C - Carbon.** In Alchemy, the letter "C" symbolizes the Conscious Body of Willpower; it is the carbon of occult chemistry.

2. **O - Oxygen.** In Alchemy, the letter "O" symbolizes the true Solar Mental Body which was built in the forge of the Cyclops, the oxygen of sacred chemistry.

3. **N - Nitrogen.** In Alchemy, the letter "N" symbolizes the authentic Solar Astral Body, which is very different from the Body of Desires. It is obvious that the legitimate Sidereal Body is the nitrogen of occult chemistry.

4. **H - Hydrogen.** In Alchemy, the "H" symbolizes the physical body, the three-dimensional vehicle of flesh and bones.

The four atoms are within the Ain Soph Paranishpanna and from there emanate the four bodies with which the Seity dresses Itself. The Seity builds them instantaneously, in other words, at any given moment, when the Seity wishes to work in a world for the good of humanity, and then It appears as a Self-realized, a self-cognizant Master, owner of life and death.

The three primary forces:

The Holy Affirmation: The Father

The Holy Negation: The Son

The Holy Reconciliation: The Holy Spirit

These three primary forces manifest themselves through the three atoms **C.O.N.** (carbon, oxygen, nitrogen). The **H** (Hydrogen) is a force that is independent from the other three. Therefore, it is the physical vehicle which serves as an instrument for the body of will, Mental, and Astral Bodies.

We do not exaggerate if we emphasize the Alchemist's transcendental idea that an Ain Soph Paranishpanna atom possesses within itself the four atom seeds C.O.N.H.

With these four alchemical atoms, the Ain Soph Paranishpanna rebuilds the Mercabah, the chariot (the Solar Bodies), in order to enter into any universe when it is necessary.

We must not forget that Mercabah is the chariot of the centuries, the celestial human being of the Kabbalah.

As a sequence or corollary, we can and we must affirm that those who have not performed the work in the Ninth Sphere (sex) indeed do not possess the chariot, the Mercabah.

It is unquestionable that everything changes in the active field of the Prakriti due to modifications of the Trigunamayashakti, and that we, the human beings, also modify ourselves in a positive or negative way. But, if we do not build the chariot, the Mercabah, the Ain Soph remains without intimate realization of the Self.

Those who have not eliminated the Abhayan Samskara, innate fear, will flee from the Ninth Sphere by telling unto others that the work in the forge of the Cyclops (sex) is worthless.

These are the hypocritical Pharisees who drain the mosquito and swallow up the camel. These are the failed ones who do not enter into the Kingdom, thereby not allowing others to enter. Truly, sex is a stumbling rock and a rock of offense.

Chapter LIV

The Tree of Life

If we observe the Tree of Life as it is written by the Hebrew Kabbalists, we see ten Sephiroth.

The Tree begins with the Ancient of Days, Kether, who is in the most elevated place of the Tree. Chokmah follows as the second Sephirah, in other words, the Second Logos, which is precisely the Cosmic Christ, or Vishnu. Then Binah follows, which is the Third Logos, the Lord Shiva. Kether, Chokmah, and Binah are the Father, Son, and Holy Spirit as they are drawn in the Tree of Life of the Hebraic mysteries; this is how the Rabbis taught it.

Kether, Chokmah, and Binah are the trimurti of perfection; they are the divine triangle: the very beloved Father, the very adored Son, and the very wise Holy Spirit.

There is an abyss found after this divine triangle. After this abyss, a second triangle is formed by Chesed—the fourth Sephirah that corresponds to the Innermost, or when speaking in Sanskrit, Atman the ineffable one—continuing with Geburah, the might of the Law, the fifth Sephirah, Buddhi, the Divine Soul, which is feminine. Then follows Tiphereth, the sixth Sephirah, the Human Soul, which is masculine.

A third triangle comes as an unfoldment and this is represented by Netzach—the mind, the seventh Sephirah—

And out of the ground made the LORD God to grow every tree that is pleasant to the sight, and good for food; the tree of life also in the midst of the garden, and the tree of knowledge of good and evil.
- Genesis 2:9

continuing with Hod, the eighth Sephirah, the Astral Body. Further down is Yesod, the ninth Sephirah, the main foundation of sex, the vital depth of the physical organism, the Vital Body or the ethereal vehicle, the Theosophist lingam sarira.

Finally, at the lowest part of the Tree of Life, we find Malkuth, the tenth Sephirah, the physical world or physical body, the body of flesh and bones.

The first triangle—Kether, Chokmah and Binah—is **Logoic**. The second triangle—Chesed, Geburah, and Tiphereth—is **Ethical**. The third triangle—Netzach, Hod, and Yesod—is **Magical**. Malkuth, the physical world, is a fallen Sephirah.

The first triangle, or **Logoic Triangle**, obviously has its center of gravity in the divine Father, the Ancient of Days, Kether. This is something that anyone can observe. Kether is a mathematical point in the infinite, immense, and unalterable space. This triangle is the triangle of the Father.

If we analyze the second triangle, we find that it is **Ethical**. Why is it called ethical? It is simply because ethics or upright behavior is primed there. There, we know the might of the law; there, we know good and evil, about what is good and evil. This triangle is the World of Pure Spirit, which is Atman, Buddhi, Manas—that is, the Hindu Trimurti. Obviously, the center of gravity in this triangle becomes at a simple glance the Human Soul, that Soul who suffers and who gives that human part to us; the Sephirah Tiphereth coincides with the Causal Body. This triangle is also denominated as the Triangle of the Son. Here we find the Cosmic Christ, Chokmah, who when so endowed manifests himself through the Human Soul, which is Tiphereth in the Hebraic Kabbalah.

The third triangle becomes very interesting because this is the **Magical Triangle** formed by the mind or Netzach, the Astral Body or Hod, and the Ethereal Body or Yesod, which is also the basic sexual principle of Universal Life. Why this is called the Magical Triangle? Undoubtedly, it is because High Magic is exercised in the kingdom of the mind and the kingdom of the Astral and even in the Klipoth or the Infernal Worlds.

There is no doubt that Netzach is where we can find Hermetic Magic, and in Hod we find Natural Magic. Other authors think differently. They believe that Natural Magic is found in Netzach; I have to disagree with them in that matter because when precisely seen, the mind is found to be Mercurial. There are authors that disagree with my concepts. They suppose that the mind is Venusian. I regret to discuss this type of concept because anyone can realize that the mind is Mercurial. Therefore, Hermetic Magic must be identified with Mercury, which is related with the mind. Regarding natural, ceremonial, or ritualistic magic, we find it in the Astral World, in the Astral Body.

Where do we find the central gravity of the Magical Triangle? Obviously, it is found in sex, because it is from here

that birth, death and regeneration come. Everything rotates around sex. In other words, the third triangle has its center of gravity in sex, or Yesod, which is the force of the Third Logos, the sexual potency.

In this way we have found that there are three basic centers of gravity in the whole Tree of Life. In the first triangle, the center of gravity is in the First Logos, Kether, the Elder of the Centuries.

In the second triangle, Chokmah, the Cosmic Christ, the Second Logos, has its center of gravity in the Human Soul, Tiphereth.

In the third triangle Binah, the Holy Spirit, the Third Logos has its center of gravity in Yesod. It is from within the sexual force that life emerges, where the physical body emerges, where all living organisms emerge. Since we are the children of a man and a woman, not even Malkuth could exist without the presence of sex. Therefore, Yesod is the foundation of the Third Logos; Yesod is the center where the sexual force of the Third Logos gravitates.

There are two trees in Eden: the Tree of the Science of Good and Evil and the Tree of Life.

The Tree of the Science of Good and Evil is sex, and this Tree of Knowledge is represented by the sexual organs.

The Tree of Life is the Being, and in our physical body this tree is represented by the spinal column.

Every true cultural doctrine has to study in detail these two trees, because the study of one tree without the study of the other gives incomplete and useless knowledge.

For what purpose do we study the Being if we do not know about sex? Both Trees are from Eden and even share the same roots. These are the two main great columns of the White Lodge: wisdom and love. Wisdom is the Tree of the Science of Good and Evil, and love is the Tree of Life.

The doctrine of the two trees was deeply studied in ancient Egypt. The fatal shadow of the Tree of Life is the psychological "I." The fatal shadow of the Tree of Knowledge is fornication. People usually mistake the shadows for reality.

Whosoever finishes with the processes of the psychological "I" will Self-realize his Being. Whosoever stops fornicating is converted into a Christ.

And the Lord God commanded the man, saying, Of every tree of the garden thou mayest freely eat, But of the tree of the Knowledge of good and evil, thou shall not eat of it, For in the day that thou eatest thereof thou shalt surely die. - Genesis 2:16, 17 *And when the woman saw that the tree was good for food, and that it was pleasant to the eyes, and a tree to be desired to make one wise, she took of the fruit thereof, and did eat, and gave also unto her husband with her; and he did eat.*

- Genesis 3: 6

And the Lord God said, Behold the man is become as one of us, to know good and evil and now, lest he put forth his hand, and take also of the tree of life, and eat, and live for ever...
So he drove out the man and he placed at the east of the Garden of Eden Cherubim, and a flaming sword which turned every way, to keep the way of the tree of life.

- Genesis 3: 22, 2

If the fallen human being could have eaten from the delicious fruits of the Tree of Life, then today we would have fornicating Gods. That would have been the damnation of damnations. That would have been the most terrible sacrifice. That would have been the impossible.

Therefore, the flaming sword of Cosmic Justice is brandished; it is blazing, frightening, and terrible guarding the way towards the Tree of Life.

The Innermost was born from the Sephirothic Crown: Father, Son, and Holy Spirit. The Innermost is enveloped within six inferior vehicles that inter-penetrate one another and form the human being. All of the faculties and powers of the Innermost are the fruits of the Tree of Life. The human being will eat from the fruits of the Tree of Life when he returns to Eden in the same way that he departed. Then, the human being will see God face to face without dying. Lightning will serve as a scepter for him and tempests as carpet for his feet.

Ten surges of life exist that penetrate and co-penetrate within themselves without any type of confusion; these ten eternal emanations are the ten Sephiroth of Kabbalah, the ten branches of the Tree of Life. Now we begin to understand why God put ten fingers on our hands.

The twelve senses of the human being (7 chakras or churches + 5 physical senses = 12) are related with our spinal column. The spinal column is the physical exponent of the Tree of Life. The twelve senses are the twelve fruits of the Tree of Life.

Chapter LV

The Sephiroth

The ten Sephiroth of universal vibration emerge from the Ain Soph, which is the microcosmic star that guides our interior. This star is the real Being of our Being.

Ten Sephiroth are spoken of, but in reality there are twelve; the Ain Soph is the eleventh, and its tenebrous antithesis is in the abyss, which is the twelfth Sephirah.

These are twelve spheres or universal regions which mutually penetrate and co-penetrate without confusion. These twelve spheres gravitate in the central atom of the sign of the infinite. Solar humanity unfolds in these twelve spheres. We have said that the sign of the infinite is in the center of the earth, in the heart of the earth. The Sephiroth are atomic. The ten Sephiroth can be reduced into three tables:

1. A quantum table of the radiant energy that comes from the sun
2. An atomic weight table of the elements of nature
3. A molecular weight table of compounds

This is Jacob's ladder which goes from Earth to heaven. All of the worlds of cosmic consciousness are reduced to the three tables.

The Four Worlds

A Sephirah cannot be understood only in one plane because it is of a quadruple nature. Therefore, the Kabbalists clearly express the fact that there are **Four Worlds**.

Atziluth: the Archetypal World or World of Emanations. It is the Divine World.

Briah: the World of Creation, also called Khorcia or the World of Schema.

Yetzirah: the World of Formation and of the Angels.

Assiah: the World of Action, the World of Matter.

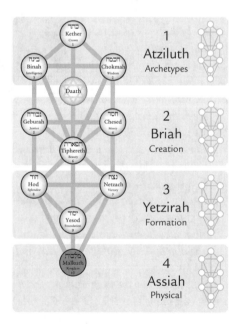

The Three Pillars

Three Sephiroth of *form* are found in the **Pillar of Severity** (Binah, Geburah, and Hod).

Three Sephiroth of *energy* are found in the **Pillar of Mercy** (Chokmah, Chesed, and Netzach).

The **Pillar of Equilibrium** is between these two pillars, where all of the distinct levels of *consciousness* are found (Kether, Tiphereth, Yesod, and Malkuth).

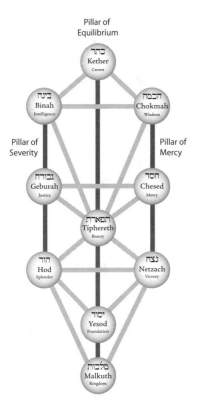

The Ten Sephiroth

The ten known Sephiroth come from *Sephirah*, the Divine Mother, who resides in the heart temple. The mantra of the Divine Mother is **IO** which is the 10 emanations of Prakriti, in other words, the 10 (ten) Sephiroth.

Kether is the Father within us, a breath from the Absolute, profoundly unknowable to Himself. Kether is the Ancient of Days. Each one of us, in our depth, is a blessed Ancient of Days.

Chokmah is the Son, the atomic Christ in us.

Binah is the Mother in us, the Holy Spirit in us.

Kether, Chokmah, and Binah are our Sephirothic Crown.

The very beloved Father, the very adored Son, and the very wise Holy Spirit live within the profundities of our superlative consciousness, waiting for the supreme instant of our realization.

The Holy Spirit is our Divine Mother that dresses with a blue mantle and a white tunic of exquisite splendors.

The Mother holds in her hand a precious lamp. This lamp is the Innermost who burns within the depth of our hearts. The Innermost is contained within a fine and transparent glass of alabaster. This glass is our own superlative consciousness; it is our Buddhi.

The Innermost is the Sephirah Chesed, and Buddhi is the Sephirah Geburah.

The Innermost and Buddhi express themselves through the Human Soul.

The Human Soul is Tiphereth, will-power, beauty.

Therefore, the Innermost, with his two Souls, the Divine and Human, officiates on his throne, which is the cerebrospinal nervous system.

The Innermost is crowned with the Sephirothic Crown. The Innermost abides in his temple. The temple of the Innermost has two columns, Jachin and Boaz. Jachin is the mind and Boaz is the Astral Body. The mind is the Sephirah Netzach and the Astral Body is the Sephirah Hod. These two columns of the temple are sustained upon the Cubic Stone of Yesod. This Cubic Stone also serves as a foundation for the Kingdom, Malkuth.

This Cubic Stone is the Ethereal Body. Malkuth is the physical body.

Therefore, the human being is a complete decade. We have ten fingers on our hands, ten Sephiroth, and Ten Commandments.

When the Elder of Days has Self-realized the ten Sephiroth, he transforms himself into Adam-Kadmon, the Heavenly Man.

Whosoever Self-realizes the ten Sephiroth will shine in the world of the Light with ineffable Christic splendors.

When the Ancient of Days reaches the realization of the ten Sephiroth in himself, these Sephiroth shine in the world of Light as precious gems, as resplendent stones within the body of the Ancient of Days.

> He that hath an ear, let him hear what the Spirit saith unto the churches; To him that overcometh will I give to eat of the tree of life, which is in the midst of the paradise of God. - Revelation 2:7

The ten Sephiroth shine as precious stones in the body of the Ancient of Days. This is how we convert ourselves into the Heavenly Jerusalem.

> And the foundations of the wall of the city were garnished with all manner of precious stones. The first foundation was jasper; the second, sapphire; the third, a chalcedony; and the fourth, emerald;

> The fifth, sardonynx; the sixth, sardius; the seventh, chrysolite; the eighth, beryl; the ninth, a topaz; the tenth, a chrysoprasus; the eleventh, a jacinth; the twelfth, an amethyst. - Revelation 21:19-20

The ten Sephiroth are atomic; the ten Sephiroth are the holy city of Jerusalem that comes to shine within the depth of our heart.

> In the midst of the street of it, and on either side of the river, was there the tree of life, which bare twelve manner of fruits, and yielded her fruit every month and the leaves of the tree were for the healing of the nations. And there shall be no more curse but the throne of God and of the Lamb shall be in it; and his servants shall serve him And they shall see his face; and his name shall be in their foreheads. And there shall be no night there; and they need no candle, neither light of the sun; for the Lord God giveth them light and they shall reign for ever and ever. - Revelation 22:2-5

When a human being incarnates the Sephirothic Crown, then the Elder of Days will shine upon him and he shall reign forever and ever.

Nonetheless, brothers and sisters of my Soul, truly I tell you that no one reaches the Father except through the Son. The Son is the atomic Christ in us; he is Chokmah, the divine Christic wisdom, the Gnosis which shines in the depth of our heart.

We have to inundate all of our vehicles with atoms of a Christic nature. We have to form Christ within ourselves in order to rise towards the Father, for one reaches the Father only through the Son.

It would be worthless for the Christ to be born one thousand times in Bethlehem if he is not born in our hearts as well. We have to form Christ within ourselves in order to enter through the doors into the triumphant and victorious city on Palm Sunday.

Christmas is a cosmic event that must be performed in each one of us. The Nativity (Christmas) is absolutely individual.

It is necessary for the Christ to be born in each one of us. The Nativity of the heart is urgent.

We need to transform the Tree of the Science of Good and Evil into the Immolated Lamb of the Holy City.

> *Him that overcometh will I make a pillar in the temple of my God, and he shall go no more out.* - Revelation 3:12
>
> *Be thou faithful unto death, and I will give thee a crown of life.* - Revelation 2:10
>
> *I am the bread of life, I am the living bread, Whosoever eateth my flesh, and drinketh my blood, hath eternal life; and I will raise him up at the last day, He that eateth my flesh, and drinketh my blood, dwelleth in me, and I in him."* - John 6:48, 51, 54, 56

Indeed, Christ is a Sephirothic Crown (Kether, Chokmah, and Binah) of incommensurable wisdom, whose purest atoms shine within Chokmah, the world of the Ophanim.

This Sephirothic Crown (incommensurable) sent his Buddha, Jesus of Nazareth, who through innumerable reincarnations prepared himself in our terrestrial evolution.

It was in the river Jordan where the Christic crown, the Solar Logos, shone and penetrated within his Buddha, Jesus of Nazareth.

Behold here the mystery of the double human personality, which is one of the greatest mysteries of occultism.

When the human being receives the Sephirothic Crown, then the Ancient of Days illuminates him and guides him towards the waters of pure life.

Nonetheless, brothers and sisters of mine, no one reaches the Father except through the Son, and the Son is in the depth of the Ark of the Alliance waiting for the instant of realization.

The Ark of the Alliance is our sexual organs. Only through perfect chastity can we form the Christ within ourselves and rise towards the Father.

Brothers and sisters of mine, I already gave you, I already granted unto you, the Ark of the New Testament. I already taught you the path of Sexual Magic.

> *And the temple of God was opened in heaven, and there was seen in his temple the ark of his testament and there were lightnings, and voices, and thunderings, and an earthquake, and great hail.*
> - Revelation 11:19

Chapter LVI

Kether

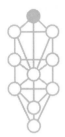

Indeed, each one of us has in the depths of our consciousness a Venerable Elder. This is the First Logos. The Kabbalists denominate Him **Kether**.

The Ancient of Days is androgynous, meaning man and woman at the same time. Kether is the first and last synthesis of our Being. The Elder of Days is the first terribly divine emanation of the abstract absolute space.

The Ancient of Days is original in each human being. He is the Father; therefore, there are as many Fathers in Heaven as there are human beings on Earth.

The Ancient of Days is the occult of the occult, the mercy of mercies, the goodness of goodness, the root of our Being, the "Great Wind."

The hair of the Ancient of Days has thirteen ringlets. If we add thirteen into itself we will have 1 + 3 = 4; one is the masculine principle, fire; two is the feminine principle, water; three is the Son of creation, plus the unity of life equals four. This is the holy Tetragrammaton. This is the name of the Eternal One, יהוה Iod Hei Vav Hei.

The beard of the Ancient of Days has thirteen locks. This beard represents the hurricane, the four winds, the breath, the Word. The four winds are יהוה Iod Hei Vav Hei.

The Thirteenth Arcanum is the Ancient of Days. Only by defeating death can we incarnate the Ancient of Days. The funeral ordeals of the Thirteenth Arcanum

are more frightful and terrible than the abyss.

In order to achieve the realization of the Ancient of Days within ourselves, we must totally accomplish the Thirteenth Arcanum within ourselves.

We need a supreme death and a supreme resurrection in order to have the right of incarnating the Ancient of Days. Only the one who incarnates him has the right of internally wearing the hair and the beard of a venerable Elder.

Only in the presence of the Angels of Death, after becoming victorious in the funeral ordeals, can we incarnate the Ancient of Days. Whosoever incarnates Him becomes another Elder in Eternity.

The mantra **Pander** permits us to reach unto the Ancient of Days. This is possible within profound meditation. In the world of Atziluth there is a marvellous temple where the majestic presence of the Ancient of Days is shown unto us.

The Ancient of Days dwells in the world of Kether. The chief of that world is the Angel Metraton. This Angel was the prophet Enoch. With the help of this Angel we can enter into the world of Kether. The disciple who wants to penetrate into Kether will beg the Angel Metraton during his states of profound meditation and he will be helped.

The Aztec goddess of death has a crown with nine human skulls. The crown is the symbol of the Ancient of Days.

The skull is the microcosmic correspondence of the Ancient of Days in the human being. Indeed, we need a

THE SKULL CROWN OF COATLICUE, THE AZTEC GODDESS OF DEATH

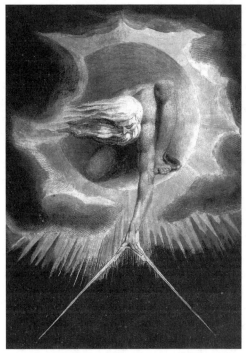

THE ANCIENT OF DAYS BY WILLIAM BLAKE

supreme resurrection in order to attain the realization of the Ancient of Days within ourselves.

In the world of Kether we comprehend that the great Law controls all that is created. From the world of the Elder of the Days, we see the human multitudes as leaves hurled by the wind.

The Great Wind is the terrible law of the Ancient of Days. *"Vox Populi Vox Dei."* A social revolt contemplated from the world of the Ancient of Days is a law in action. Each person, the entire multitudes, look like leaves detached from the trees, hurled by the terrible wind of the Ancient of Days.

People do not know about these things. People are only preoccupied by acquiring money and more money. This is the poor, suffering humanity, who are only miserable leaves hurled by the great wind, miserable leaves hurled by the great Law.

Our authentic Being in his essential root is the Ancient of Days. He is the Father in us. He is our true Being. Our disciples must now concentrate and meditate very deeply on the Ancient of Days. The ecstasy, Samadhi, must be induced during meditation.

May peace reign in all hearts; let us not forget that peace is light. Let us not forget that peace is an Essence emanated from the Absolute. It is light emanated from the Absolute. This light is the light of the Ancient of Days. Christ said, *"Peace I leave with you, my peace I give unto you."* [John 14:27]

Chapter LVII

Chokmah

Come, oh hallowed Word, come, oh sacred name of the Chrestos force, come, oh sublime energy, come, oh divine mercy, come, supreme seity of the most high.
- Gnostic Mass

The Sephirah Chokmah of the Hebraic Kabbalah is the Cosmic Christ, the Christus. He is Vishnu among the Hindus.

The Second Logos, Chokmah, is love, the Agnus Dei, the immolated Lamb; it is the fire that burns since the beginning of the world, in all of creation, for our salvation. Chokmah is fire and underlies the depth of all organic and inorganic matter.

Solar energy is Astral Light. Its essence is the Christonic power which is enclosed in the fertile pollen of the flower, enclosed within the heart of the fruit of the tree, enclosed within the internal secretion glands of the animal and the human being. The principal seat of this essence within the human being is in the coccyx. The Aztecs denominated this sacred power as the feathered serpent Quetzalcoatl that only awakes and ascends up to our pineal gland by means of amorous magic.

Christ is the same wisdom, the Solar Logos, whose physical body is the sun. Christ walks with his sun just in the same way that the human soul walks with its body of flesh and bones. Christ is the light of the sun. The light of the sun is the light of Christ.

The light of the sun is a Christonic substance which causes the plant to be created and the seed to be sprouted. This substance of the Solar Logos remains enclosed within the dark hardness of the grain and permits the plant to incessantly reproduce itself with a glorious, vigorous, and active life.

The energy detached from the Solar Fire is fixed within the heart of the earth, and it is the vibrating nuclear energy of the cells within all living beings. This energy is the Astral Light, the Azoth and the Magnesia of the ancient Alchemists.

The Astral Light co-penetrates into the entire atmosphere; it is the source of all the marvellous powers within the human being, and is the sacred fire of all life.

This world has consciousness thanks to the help of the Second Logos. Likewise, we can also awaken and have consciousness.

Christ is that terribly divine, ineffable and most pure ray which shone like lightning on the face of Moses, there within the solemn mystery of Mount Nebo.

Christ is not the Monad, Christ is not the Theosophical septenary; Christ is not the Jivan-Atman. Christ is the Central Sun. Christ is the ray that unites us to the Absolute.

I believe in the Son, the Cosmic Chrestos, the powerful Astral mediator that joins our physical personality with the supreme immanence of the Solar Father. - Gnostic Ritual

You must known that Christ is not an individual. The Cosmic Christ is impersonal, universal, and is beyond individuality, personality, beyond the "I." Yet, Christ

THE SOLAR LOGOS REPRESENTED BY THE GREEKS AS HELIOS, THE TITAN OF THE SUN, DRIVING HIS CHARIOT THROUGH THE HEAVENS

is a cosmic force that can express Himself through any human being who is properly prepared.

Once, the Christ expressed Himself through the great Master Jeshua ben Pandira, who is known in the physical world as the Master Jesus of Nazareth. The Christ also expressed Himself through many other Masters.

Christ is a latent cosmic substance within each atom of the infinite. Christ is the substance of truth. Christ is truth and life.

A human being is Christified when the Christ substance is assimilated physically, psychologically and spiritually. Then, the human being becomes a Christ; then, the human being is converted into a living Christ. We need to form Christ within ourselves. To incarnate the truth is urgent.

Among the Chinese, Christ is Fu Xi. Among the Mexicans, Christ is Quetzalcoatl, who was the Messiah and the transformer of the Toltecs. Among the Japanese, Christ is Amida, who has the power of opening doors of Gokurak (paradise). Within the Zoroastrian cult, Christ is Ahura-Mazda. The Germanic *Eddas* cite the Kristos, who is the God of their theogony, similar to Jesus of Nazareth, who was born on the day of Nativity, the 25th of December at midnight, the same as the Nordic Christs Odin, Wotan, and Belen.

The Gospel of Krishna, within millenary India, is similar to the Christian Gospel. In the ancient Egypt of the Pharaohs, Christ was Osiris, and whosoever incarnated him was an Osirified one. Hermes Trismegistus is the Egyptian Christ; He incarnated Osiris. Every human being that achieves the assimilation of the Christ substance is converted into a living Christ.

Let us understand that the Solar Logos is not an individual; the Solar Logos is an army, the Verb, the great Word. The Army of the Voice is an eternal, unconditioned and perfect multiple Unity. He is the Creator Logos; He is the first instant.

In the beginning was the Word, and the Word was with God, and the Word was

God. The same was in the beginning with God. All things were made by him; and without him was not any thing made that was made. And the light shineth in the darkness; and the darkness comprehended it not. - John 1:1-5

Christ is the great breath emanated from within the bosom of the absolute abstract eternal space. The absolute abstract eternal space is the Being of the Being that is within all Beings. The Absolute is the Unutterable One, the Limitless Space. Whosoever incarnates the Christ, Christifies his/her Self and enters into the ranks of the Army of the Voice.

And as Moses lifted up the serpent in the wilderness, even so must the Son of Man be lifted up. - John 3:14

In order to rise up to the Father, we must incarnate Christ within ourselves. No one reaches the Father except through the Son. We all are one within the Christ. Within the Lord, there are no existing differences between one human being and another, because we all are one within Him. In the world of the Lord, individuality does not exist, nor does the personality. Within Him, there are no hierarchical differences. Whosoever incarnates Him then becomes Him, Him, Him. *"Variety is unity."*

We must finish with the personality and with the "I" in order for the Being to be born within ourselves. We must finish with individuality.

If in the state of ecstasy a mystic would abandon all of his seven bodies with the intention of investigating the life of Christ, he will then see himself representing the drama of the passion of the Lord; he will see himself performing miracles and marvels in the Holy Land. He will see himself dead and resurrected on the third day. If this mystic would occupy the place

of Christ in these instances, he would be *Him, Him, Him.* This phenomenon is due to the fact that in the world of Christ, individuality and the personality do not exist. Within the Christ only a single Being exists, that expresses himself as many.

When we finish with the "I" and with individuality, only the values of the consciousness remain, which are the attributes of the absolute abstract eternal space.

Only Christ can say, *"I am the way, the truth and the life. I am the light. I am the life. I am the good shepherd. I am the bread. I am the resurrection."* The Being is the one who receives the Being of his Being, the "I Am," who is (in each one of us) a breath of the great breath, our particular Ray, that is *Him, Him, Him.* The "I AM" is the Internal Christ of each human being, our divine "Augoides," the Logos. Whosoever receives the Crown of Life has the right to say, *"I am Him, I am Him, I am Him."*

Christ is symbolized by the phallus in the state of erection, by the scepter of power held high, by the tower, by the sharp stone and by the tunic of glory. He is the divine origin.

Christ is love. The antithesis of love is hatred. Let it be known unto you nations, kindred and tongues, that hatred is converted into fire that burns. Let it be known unto you that the most terrible monster that exists upon the earth is hatred.

Whosoever lies, sins against the Father, who is the Truth; whosoever hates, sins against the Son, who is love; and whosoever fornicates, sins against the Holy Spirit, who is chastity.

Chapter LVIII

Binah

Hail sacred swan! Miraculous Hamsa. Hail Phoenix bird of paradise! Hail immortal Ibis! Dove of the Grail, creative energy of the Third Logos! - Gnostic Ritual

Binah is the Holy Spirit; He is the Third Logos, the Lord Shiva of the Hindus, who manifests himself as sexual potency within everything which is, has been, and will be.

The Holy Spirit is the sexual force we see within the pistils of flowers, which expresses itself through the creative organs of all living species. The Holy Spirit is a marvellous force without which the universe could not exist.

The Kabbalists place the distinct Sephiroth of the Hebraic Kabbalah in the worlds. For example, they say that the Ancient of Days is a point from infinite space, and as a symbol, he is eternal. Chokmah is governed by the zodiac, this is true. They say that Binah is governed by Saturn; here we arrive at a point of disagreement. I do not want to say that the Holy Spirit is not governed by Saturn, that there is not a relationship between them; indeed a relationship exists between them. But this is not all, because without a doubt the world of Jupiter is in a certain way related with Binah; this is because Binah, the Holy Spirit, has powers, a throne, and He washes the waters of life.

Kether, Chokmah, and Binah, who are the Crown of Life and the resplendent Dragon of Wisdom, emanated from the super-divine atom, from the Ain Soph.

When the Cosmic Night arrives, the resplendent Dragon of Wisdom will be absorbed within the Ain Soph... Behold here, the trinity being absorbed within the unity! Behold here the Holy Four, the Tetragrammaton of the Kabbalists!

The trinity—the perfect triad, Father, Son, and Holy Spirit—plus the unity of life, is the Holy Four, the Four Eternal Carpenters, the Four Horns of the Altar, the Four Winds of the Sea, the holy and mysterious Tetragrammaton, whose mantric word is יהוה **Iod, Hei, Vav, Hei**, the remarkable name of the Eternal One.

The Holy Spirit unfolds himself into an ineffable woman; She is the Divine Mother; She is dressed in a white tunic and a blue mantle. The Holy Spirit is Shiva, the divine spouse of Shakti, the Divine Mother Kundalini.

This divine woman is an ineffable virgin. This Divine Mother is symbolized among the Aztecs by a mysterious virgin (see Chapter Ten of *Aztec Christic Magic*). This virgin has in her throat a mysterious mouth; this is because the throat is the uterus where the Word is gestated. The Gods create with the larynx.

In the beginning was the word, and the word was with God, and the word was God. The same was in the beginning with God. All things were made by him, and without him was not anything made, that was made. In him was life, and the life is the light of men. - John 1:1

The Word made the waters of life fertile and caused the universe in its germinal state to splendidly emerge within the dawn.

The Holy Spirit fecundated the Great Mother, then the Christ, the Second Logos was born. The Christ, the Second Logos, is always the Son of the Virgin Mother.

She is always virginal before childbirth, during childbirth, and after childbirth. She is Isis, Mary, Adonia, Insoberta, Rhea, Cybele, etc.

She is the primitive Chaos, the primordial substance, the raw matter of the Great Work.

The Cosmic Christ is the Army of the Great Word, and He is always born in the worlds, and is crucified in each one of them, in order for all the beings to have life, and to have that life in abundance.

The Holy Spirit is the maker of Light. *"And God said, let there be light, and the light was."* The esoteric meaning of this is, *"It was, because He said it."*

OSIRIS, HORUS, ISIS

The Earth has nine stratums, and the laboratorium of the Third Logos is in the ninth one. Indeed, the ninth stratum is in the whole center of this planetary mass; there we find the Holy Eight, the divine symbol of the infinite, within which the brain, heart, and sex of the planetary Genie are represented.

A sacred serpent is coiled within the heart of the Earth, precisely in the Ninth Sphere. This serpent is septuple in its constitution. Each one of its seven igneous aspects corresponds with each one of the seven serpents of the human being.

The creative energy of the Third Logos elaborates the chemical elements of the earth with all of their multifaceted complexity of forms. When this creative energy leaves the center of the earth, then our world will be converted into a cadaver. This is how worlds die.

The serpentine fire of the human being emanates from the serpentine fire of the Earth. The terrible serpent sleeps profoundly within its mysterious nest of rare and hollow spheres, really similar to a true Chinese puzzle. These concentric spheres are subtle and astral. Truly, as the earth has nine concentric spheres and as on the bottom of all of them, the terrible serpent abides, in the same way the human being has nine spheres, because the human being is the Microcosmos of the Macrocosmos.

The human being is a universe in miniature. The infinitely small is analogous to the infinitely great.

Hydrogen, carbon, nitrogen, and oxygen are the four basic elements with which the Third Logos works. The chemical elements are displaced in accordance to their atomic weight. Hydrogen is the lightest, with an atomic weight of 1, and the last one being uranium, with an atomic weight of 238.5, which becomes, as a fact, the heaviest of all the known elements.

Electrons come to constitute a bridge between Spirit and matter. The hydrogen is the most rarefied element that is known;

it is the first manifestation of the serpent. Every element, every nourishment, every organism, is synthesized in a determined type of hydrogen. The sexual energy corresponds to Hydrogen 12 and its musical note is SI.

The electronic solar matter is the sacred fire of Kundalini. We enter onto the path of authentic initiation when we liberate this energy.

The energy of the Third Logos is expressed through the sexual organs and through the creative larynx. These are the two instruments through which the powerful energy of the Third Logos flows.

The sacred serpent awakens when one is working with the Arcanum A.Z.F.; the ascending flux of the creative energy of the Third Logos is a living fire. This Pentecostal fire rises up along the medullar canal, opening centers and awakening miraculous powers.

In ancient Mexico, the Holy Spirit was worshipped with a tunic and mantle of white, black, and red colors, within the Temple of the Serpents called Quetzalcoatl. They would sprinkle snail shell powder on embers of fire; for this purpose they utilized white, black, and red snail shells from the sea. White is the pure Spirit, black symbolizes the descent of the Spirit into matter, and the red is the fire of the Holy Spirit, with which we return into the whiteness of the pure Spirit.

The incense would rise into heaven and the priest would pray for life and the plants would flourish because the Holy Spirit is the sexual fire of the universe. This rite was verified in the temple of Quetzalcoatl, before sunrise, because the Holy Spirit is the maker of light. The priest vocalizied the mantras **In En**.

The prophet Jonah also performed the rite of the Holy Spirit, exactly in the same way as the Aztecs, and he used for this purpose the same vestures and the same incense. He also vocalized the mantra **In En** when he placed the incense into the fire.

This rite must be established in all of the Gnostic sanctuaries. The snail shells are related with the water of the sea, and the water is the habitat of the fire of the Holy Spirit. Therefore, the snail shells from the sea become a perfect smoke offering to the Holy Spirit.

The Mother, or Holy Spirit, grants us power and wisdom. The symbols of the Virgin are the yoni, the chalice, and the tunic of occultation.

Chapter LIX

Chesed

Chesed, in Himself, is the Innermost; according to the Hindus He is Atman. It has been said that Chesed is directly governed by Jupiter and nothing else. This is false, because the Innermost is Martian, a warrior, a fighter. This is not accepted by many Kabbalists, who might even consider it absurd. But, whosoever has a direct experience in Chesed knows very well that Chesed is a warrior. It is the Innermost who has to be in a struggle to the death against darkness, who has to fight very hard for His own intimate realization of the Self; He is always in battle. It is obvious that He has something of Jupiter, because He can grasp the scepter of Kings; I do not deny it, but it is a false statement that He is only and exclusively Jupiterian.

THE PRIMEVAL KING ARTHUR REPRESENTED THE INNERMOST (CHESED).

Atman is our Innermost, our divine Seity, the seventh principle who is in all Beings, but who is not within all human beings.

In order for oneself to be fused with Atman, the following experience is required: to depart in the Astral Body by abandoning the physical body; afterwards, one has to abandon the Astral Body by ordering the following, "Go out of me." In order to perform this, willpower is required. So when doing this, the Astral Body leaves through the vertebral column and we remain in the World of the Mind. Afterwards, one has to abandon the Mental Body by commanding the following, "Body of the Mind, go out of me." This

is performed with an act of willpower, and one remains with the Causal Body that also has to be ordered to go out of us. This also requires a great effort. The body of Conscious Will obeys better, and one orders it to go out and abandon the thirty-three vertebrae, leaving oneself with the Buddhic or Intuitional Body. This body is very obedient and also has to be ordered to go out. Thus, in this way one remains in the world of Chesed, in the world of Atman, the ineffable one.

In the world of Atman, one has the feeling of being a complete Human Being. Here, the intellectual animal is not a Human Being. The initiate feels full of immense plenitude. This is the world of the real Human Being in the most objective sense.

His negative part is the physical world. The world of Atman is a positive state. Here we see a city in its most real form, because if we look at a table, we see it through many viewpoints, from above, from below, from within, from without, and the same occurs when we look at a mountain. Within a kitchen one can see how many atoms cutlery is made with, how many molecules are in the bread or meat that one is about to eat. We not only perceive solids in an integral form, but moreover, we perceive hypersolids, including the exact quantity of atoms, that in their conjunction constitute the totality of any given body.

If the student is not prepared, he is deceived, because he finds himself within a world filled with the crudest reality. This is the world of mathematics. Here, one sees the drama of nature; one is a spectator of nature. The world of mathematics is the world of Atman.

The one that thinks is the mind, not the Innermost. The human mind in its current state of evolution is the animal that we carry within.

The concept of Descartes, "I think therefore I am," is completely false, because the true human being is the Innermost and the Innermost does not think because he knows. Atman does not need to think because Atman is omniscient.

Our Innermost is *yes, yes, yes.* The wisdom of our Innermost is *yes, yes, yes.* The love of our Innermost is *yes, yes, yes.*

When we say, "*I am* hungry, *I am* thirsty," etc., we are affirming something absurd, because the Innermost is not hungry, neither thirsty. The one that is hungry and thirsty is the physical body. Therefore the most correct way to say this is, "My body is hungry, my body is thirsty."

The same happens with the mind when we say "I have a powerful mental force, I have a problem, I have such a conflict, I have such suffering, some thoughts are arising in me," etc. We then are affirming very grave errors, because these things are from the mind and not from the Innermost.

The true Human Being is the Innermost, He does not have problems. The problems are from the mind.

The Innermost must whip the mind with the terrible whip of willpower.

The human being that identifies with the mind falls into the abyss.

The mind is the donkey that we must ride in order to enter into the heavenly Jerusalem.

We must command the mind in this way: "Mind, withdraw this problem from me; Mind, withdraw such desire from me, etc.. I do not allow you to have it. I am your lord and you are my slave until the consummation of all centuries." Woe to the human being that identifies with the mind, because he will lose the Innermost and will culminate in the abyss.

Those that say that everything is mind (thought) commit a very grave error, because the mind (thought) is only one of the bodies of the Innermost.

All of those books that tend to totally identify the human being with the mind are legitimate books of black magic, because the true human being is not the mind.

We must not forget that the most subtle and dangerous demons that exist in the universe abide in the Mental Plane.

The Innermost talks to the mind as follows: "Do not say that your eyes are your eyes, because I see through them. Do not say that your ears are your ears because I hear through them. Do not say that your mouth is your mouth because I utter through it. Your eyes are my eyes, your ears are my ears, and your mouth is my mouth."

Within the Internal Worlds, we can cast the Mental Body out of ourselves in order to talk with it face to face, as if it was a strange person.

Then we will deeply comprehend that the mind is a strange subject that we must learn to drive with the terrible whip of willpower.

The den of desire is within the mind.

The Innermost is a true human being that lives incarnated within the human body and that all of us carry crucified in our heart.

When the human being awakens from his dream of ignorance, then he delivers himself to his own Innermost. Then the Innermost unites himself with the Christ and the human being becomes powerful as the Absolute from where he emanated.

The Innermost is God within the human being. The human being who ignores this great truth is only a shadow, a shadow of his Innermost.

The symbol of the Innermost is the star of five points, the pyramid, the cross of equal arms, the scepter.

Chapter LX
Geburah

 Geburah is severity, the law, Buddhi, the Spiritual Soul, the Valkyrie that was spoken of by that illustrious Spanish writer Mr. Mario Roso de Luna; and Geburah is also the beautiful Helen, etc.

Geburah, Buddhi, has exclusively been considered Martian. This is a mistake, because in the world of the Spiritual Soul, who is feminine, we find the lion of the law that is Solar. Thus, we find the severity of the law in Geburah, but as well we find the nobleness of the lion. Therefore, the Buddhic, Intuitional World is completely Solar.

Geburah is the law of justice. The world of Geburah is based on justice. The Masters of Karma base themselves on the consciousness in order to judge in the tribunal of Karma.

The Masters of Karma are judges of consciousness. Justice is beyond good and evil. When you reach the Light you will know what love is, and when you know what love is, you will know how to love and will comprehend that conscious love is the law. Thus, to perform a good deed is not what counts but to know how to perform it.

The chief of the archons of the law is the Master Anubis, who exercises the law with his forty-two judges. When they officiate, they utilize a sacred mask with the form of the head of a jackal, or feathered wolf, which is an emblem of truth.

Justice is the supreme piety and the supreme impiety of the law.

Within the tribunal of Karma, whosoever has capital in order to pay, comes off well in their negotiations. We must constantly perform good deeds in order for us to have capital for the payment of our debts of this life and past lives.

To evade justice is impossible because the police of Karma are within us, this is the **Kaom**. Wherever love is lacking, the Kaom, the police, the accuser, appears, who conducts us before the tribunal of the law.

To cancel Karma is possible with good deeds. This is how we combat the lion of the law. When an inferior law is transcended by a superior law, then the superior law washes away the inferior law. Karma is not a mechanical law, it can be forgiven. Perform good deeds in order to cancel your debts.

Each one of us has a book where our faults are registered on the day and hour that they are committed.

Karma is forgiven within us when we become totally inoffensive, when we are not capable of performing evil against anyone.

Karma is a medicine that is granted unto us. Buddha said there are three eternal things in life:

1. The Law
2. Nirvana
3. Space

Chapter LXI
Tiphereth

Tiphereth is the groom of the bride; it is the Superior Manas of Eastern Theosophy; it is nothing else but the Human Soul, the Causal Body. It is that Soul who suffers and gives that very human part onto us.

We must distinguish between what the Human Soul is and what Tiphereth is in itself. It is very easy to mistake Tiphereth with the Causal Body. The Causal Body becomes the vehicle of Tiphereth.

Some Kabbalists presume that Tiphereth, the world of the Human Soul, or properly called the world of the Son of Man, is governed by the Sun. Really, this is not so, because it is governed by Venus. This is why Christ is crucified on Holy Friday, and this is something that we must meditate upon.

The wedding of Guinevere, the divine Amazon, the Divine Soul, to the Knight who is the Human Soul, is a marvellous event within which we experience a radical transformation. This is because Buddhi is like a fine and transparent glass of alabaster within which the flame of Prajna (the Being) is burning.

The esoteric Hindu texts constantly mention the famous trimurti Atman-Buddhi-Manas. This trimurti is the Innermost with his two souls, the feminine Spiritual Soul and the masculine Human Soul.

The source and foundation of High Magic is found in the perfect betrothal of Buddhi-Manas within the purely spiritual regions or in the terrestrial world.

The Initiatic Colleges teach with complete clarity that the beautiful Helen is Buddhi, the Spiritual Soul of the sixth Venustic Initiation, the feminine Shakti potential of the internal Being. The beautiful Helen of Troy is the same Helen in the *Faust* of Goethe.

Helen clearly signifies the betrothal of **Nous** (Atman-Buddhi) with **Manas** (the Human Soul), a union through which consciousness and willpower are combined. Therefore, both souls are bestowed with divine powers as a result of such a union.

The essence of Atman, who is the primordial, universal and eternal divine fire, is found within Buddhi, who in complete conjunction with Manas determines "the masculine-feminine."

She and He, Buddhi and Manas, are the twin souls within us (even when the intellectual animal still does not have them incarnated). They are the two adored children of Atman. They are the eternal bride and groom who are always in love.

The eternal Lady, the Spiritual Soul, always demands from her knight, the Human Soul, all types of outrageous sacrifices and prodigies of courage.

Fortunate will be the knight that after the hard battle will celebrate his betrothal with Guinevere, the Queen of the "Jinn Knights"!

The intellectual animal, mistakenly called "man," has incarnated within himself a fraction of the Human Soul. Such a fraction of Soul is denominated "Essence."

THE HUMAN SOUL (TIPHERETH) HAS TO CONQUER THE EGO
IN ORDER TO SAVE THE DIVINE SOUL (GEBURAH)

constitute the ego, has to pass through incessant alchemical transformations in the Ninth Sphere before converting itself into the "Seminal Pearl."

The Seminal Pearl is developed by means of Sexual Magic and the formidable work with the lance of Longinus (with which we convert the animal ego into cosmic dust), in order to be converted into the Auric Embryo.

The marvellous reflex of the sexual energy in a form of a luminous whirlwind, like when a ray of light returns after crashing against a wall, comes to crystallize within ourselves as the Auric Flower. Thus, this establishes within the neophyte a permanent center of consciousness.

The Auric Embryo dressed with the Wedding Garment of the Soul truly experiences a supreme joy in the moment in which it is fused with the Human Soul. From that moment, it can be said that we are Human Beings with Soul, sacred individuals, truly responsible people in the most complete sense of the word.

All of the experiences of life are found contained within the Auric Embryo. That is why it is clear that the Auric Embryo originates deep transformations within the Pneumatic Immortal Principles of the human being. This is how we convert ourselves into Adepts of the White Brotherhood.

The world of Tiphereth is the world of willpower. In that world only the will of the Father is done, done on earth as it is in heaven.

In Japanese Zen, it is simply named "Buddhata," which is the psychic material with which we can and must build the Golden Embryo (see the book *The Mystery of the Golden Blossom.*)

Lamentably, the Essence dreams, lying within that variegated and grotesque conjunction of submerged and tenebrous entities which constitute the ego, the myself, the itself. Nonetheless, such Essence is the Raw Matter needed in order to build Soul. This concept still has not been very well understood by our Gnostic students.

The Chinese Tao clearly teaches that the Essence, which is bottled up within all of these conjunctions of devil-I's which

It is a world which is beyond the mind. It is of an intense electric blue color; many other colors exist, but the fundamental one is blue.

One finds in this World of Natural Causes many Bodhisattvas who work under the direction of their real Being.

Music and sound prime within this world; whosoever reaches the Fifth Initiation of the Fire becomes an adept and has the right to enter into the world of music. Here we find the temple of the Music of the Spheres. One of the Guardians of that temple is a great Master who, when he was alive in the physical world, was called Beethoven. He is a great initiate; his nine symphonies are marvellous.

Everyone who reaches this region has to learn the fundamental notions of music, because music is the Verb. In that sublime region, the Music of the Spheres is heard. It is based on the three compasses of Mahavan and Chotavan, which keep the universe in its rhythm, and its march is perfect, for there cannot be an error in this music.

Within the region of Tiphereth, the Cloth of Veronica is found, which signifies "Christic Willpower," meaning one has to perform the will of the Father.

To obtain conscious will is impossible without working in the Ninth Sphere. Many places exist where people are submitted to tremendous tortures in order to acquire conscious will, but really they only store some energy.

The true fakir has his guru and he does not leave India. The fakirs acquire many powers but nothing else. Some of them raise an arm and they do not lower it ever again. The arm becomes withered. They pursue willpower with such actions, but their willpower does not pass beyond such action. They do not achieve the building of the body of Conscious Will. All of this miraculous stuff deviates people; therefore, the fakirs are deviated.

Once the body of Conscious Will is built, one becomes a Twice-born.

Chapter LXII

Netzach

*The Mental Body is the donkey that
we must ride in order to enter into the
Celestial Jerusalem.* - Samael Aun Weor

*The mind that is a slave of the senses
makes the Soul disabled, just as the boat
that the wind misleads upon the waters.*
- Bhagavad-Gita

Netzach is the Mental World, the cosmic mind, the mind of the human being. There are some authors who suppose that the mind is Venusian; I have to disagree with them, because when properly observed the mind is found to be Mercurial. Anyone can realize that the mind is Mercurial, because Mercury gives wisdom, gives the word, etc.

Until now, the Mental Body of the human race is found in the aurora of evolution. By clairvoyantly observing the physiognomy of the Mental Body of the human being, we corroborate this affirmation.

The face of the Mental Body of almost all human beings has an animal appearance. When we observe the customs and habits of the human species, then we understand why the Mental Body of people has animal physiognomy.

The lunar Mental Body is of a bestial nature. The Solar Mental Body is the antithesis; this is the Christ mind.

The lunar Mental Body that we possess is of a bestial nature, and even animals and plants possess it. The unique difference that exists between the beasts and the incorrectly named humans is that humans have been given intellectualism and the beasts only act instinctively.

The Solar Mental Body is not a vague, abstract body. It is a body of flesh and bones, but imperishable flesh that does not come from Adam; it can pass through a wall. One has to build it in the Ninth Sphere. The Solar Mind is a body of perfection that eats, drinks, assimilates, digests, has its special nourishments, its nutrition, its development.

In the world of the mind there are many temples that must be conquered with the point of the sword. When one is working in the Fourth Initiation of Major Mysteries, one finds himself with many tenebrous entities and one has to fight.

When one acquires the Mental Body, the degree of Buddha is received. The blessed goddess Mother of the world presents the initiate in the Temple of the Mind by saying, "Behold, here my beloved son, behold here a new Buddha." She then puts upon the head of her child the diadem of Shiva and the yellow mantle of the Buddha.

Sanat Kumara, the illustrious founder of the great College of Initiates of the White Lodge, then exclaims, "Thou has liberated thyself from the four bodies of sin, and thou has penetrated into the world of Gods. Thou art a Buddha." When the human being is liberated from the four bodies of sin, he is a Buddha, and the globe of the Imperator with the cross upon it is granted unto him.

Our disciples must change the process of reasoning for the beauty of **comprehension**.

The process of reasoning divorces the mind from the Innermost. A mind which is divorced from the Innermost falls into the abyss of black magic.

Many times the Innermost gives an order and the mind reveals itself with its reasoning. The Innermost speaks by hunches, or thoughts, but the mind reveals by reasoning and comparison.

Reasoning is based on opinions, in the struggle of antithetic concepts, in the process of conceptual election, etc.

Reasoning divides the mind between the struggles of the antitheses. Antithetic concepts convert the mind into a battlefield.

A mind which is divided by the battle of reasoning, by the struggle of antithetic concepts, fractions the understanding and converts the mind into a worthless instrument for the Being, for the Innermost.

When the mind cannot serve as an instrument for the Innermost, then it serves as an instrument for the animal "I," and converts the human being into a blind and torpid being, slave of passions and of the sensorial perceptions of the exterior world.

The most torpid and passionate beings that exist upon the earth are precisely the great intellectual reasoners.

The intellectual loses the sense of a sentence only for the lack of a period or comma.

The intuitive one knows how to read where the Master did not write, and to listen when the Master is not speaking.

The reasoner is a complete slave to the external senses and his soul is as disabled

as *the boat that the wind misleads upon the waters.*

The spiritual reasoners are the unhappiest beings that exist upon this earth. They have the mind completely crammed with theories and more theories, and they suffer horribly when they cannot perform anything of which they have read.

Those poor beings have terrible pride and commonly they end up separated from the Innermost, converting themselves into Tantric personalities of the abyss.

If we take the Mental Body of any pseudo-spiritualist theorizing student, and if we examine it in detail, we will find that it is a true walking library.

If then we examine in detail the coccygeal church of Ephesus or chakra Muladhara, we will find that the Kundalini is completely enclosed there, without giving a sign of even the most slight awakening. If we examine the Shushumna canal of the student we will not find vestiges of the sacred fire there. We will find that the thirty-three chambers of the given student are completely full of darkness.

This internal examination will take us to the conclusion that the given student is lamentably wasting his time.

The student could have a Mental Body converted into a true library, but all of the thirty-three chambers of the spinal column would be completely extinguished and in profound darkness.

Conclusion: this student is an inhabitant of darkness, an inhabitant of the abyss.

The intellectuals are full of pride, arrogance, and sexual passion. The intellect is based on reasoning, and reasoning is Luciferic and demonic. There are some people who believe they can know God through reasoning. We say that only God knows himself.

It is better to practice internal **meditation** than to lose time reasoning. Through meditation, we can talk with God, the Innermost, the Being, the Most High, thus we can learn from the internal Master; thus we can study the divine wisdom at the feet of the Master.

The process of reasoning destroys the delicate membranes of the Mental Body. Thought must flow silently, serenely and integrally, without the struggle of antithesis, without the process of reasoning which divides the mind between opposite concepts.

We have to finish with reasoning and awaken the intuition. Only thus can we learn the true wisdom of God, only thus will the mind be in the hands of the Innermost.

The true positive function of the mind is art, beauty, love, music, the mystical art of love towards divine architecture, towards painting, towards singing, towards sculpture, towards technology placed under the service of the human being, but without selfishness, nor evil, nor hatred, etc.

"Comprehension is of the heart."

The intellect as the negative function of the mind is demoniacal. Everyone that enters into these studies, the first thing that they want is to dominate the mind of others. This is pure and legitimate black magic. No one has the right to violate the free will of others. No one has the right to exercise coaction upon the mind of others because this is black magic. The ones that are guilty of this grave error are all of those mistaken authors that are everywhere. All of those books of hypnotism, magnetism and suggestion are books of black magic.

Whosoever does not know how to respect the free will of others is a black magician; those who perform mental works in order to violently dominate the mind of others convert themselves into perverse demons. These people separate themselves from the Innermost and they crumble into the abyss.

We must liberate the mind from all types of preconcepts, desires, fears, hatred, schools. All of those defects are locks that anchor the mind to the external senses.

One has to change the process of reasoning by the quality of **discernment**. Discernment is the direct perception of the truth without the process of reasoning.

Discernment is comprehension without the need for reasoning. We must change the process of reasoning for the beauty of comprehension.

The mind must be completely transformed into an infant; it must be converted into a child full of beauty.

The symbols of Netzach are the lamp, the belt, and the rose.

Chapter LXIII

Hod

Hod is the Astral World, the Astral Body.

The Astral World is governed by the Moon. This is why astral projections become easier during the crescent moon and a little bit more arduous during the waning moon.

The Astral Plane is really the plane of practical magic. For example, in some of the tribes of the most profound jungles of the Amazon, the Piaches or sorcerer-priests give unto their people a special beverage in order to enter into the Astral Plane at will.

They mix the ashes of a tree called Guarumo with very well ground leaves of Coca; this is administered when the moon is a crescent. Thus this is how astral projection is performed. The Piaches know very well that Hod, the Astral World, is governed by the Moon, but many Kabbalists suppose that it is governed by Mercury and they are mistaken.

The messages that descend from the world of the Pure Spirit become symbolic in the Astral Plane. Those symbols are interpreted based on the law of philosophical analogies, on the law of analogous contraries, on the law of correspondences and on the law of numerology. The book of Daniel and the biblical passages of the Patriarch Joseph, son of Jacob, must be studied in order to learn how to interpret your astral experiences.

The legitimate and authentic Astral Body is the Solar Astral Body. The body of desires, which is of a lunar nature, has been mistakenly called the Astral Body.

All of the creatures of nature are lunar. They possess a lunar Astral Body, which is a cold protoplasmatic body, a bestial remnant of the past.

What we need is to build the authentic body of Hod, the legitimate Astral Body, which is a vehicle of a Solar nature. This must be built in the Ninth Sphere by working in the flaming forge of Vulcan.

The Solar Astral body is a body of flesh and bone that does not come from Adam. It is a body that eats, digests, and assimilates.

There are diverse authors of a pseudo-esotericist and pseudo-occultist type that fall into the error of mistaking the ego with the Astral Body.

Modern metaphysical literature speaks a lot about projections of the Astral Body, although we must have the courage to recognize that fans of occultism are used to projecting themselves with their ego in order to travel in the sublunar regions of nature through time and space.

We can travel through the Milky Way towards the central sun Sirius with the Solar Astral Body. To go beyond the Milky Way is forbidden unto us, because in the other galaxies other types of cosmic laws exist which are unknown to the inhabitants of this galaxy.

There is a great temple in Sirius where the great Masters of this galaxy receive an initiation. The disciples of the God Sirius are Rosicrucian Gnostics; the true Rosi-Cross is in the Superior Worlds. The disciples of the Rosi-Cross have the Holy Grail emblazoned on their hoods. They also

THE PYRAMIDS OF EGYPT

celebrate the drama of the Christ, because it is a Cosmic Drama.

Our disciples must acquire the power of travelling with the Astral Body. This power is acquired by daily vocalizing for an hour the sacred mantra **Egipto**. The vowel "E" (sounded *eh*) makes the thyroid gland vibrate and grants unto the person the power of the occult ear. The "G" (as in *good*) awakens the chakra of the liver, and when this chakra has reached its complete development, the person can enter and depart from the physical body whenever it is wished. The "I" (sounded *eee* as in *tree*), when combined with the letter "P" develops unto the person clairvoyance and the power to leave in the Astral Body through the window of Brahma, which is the pineal gland. The letter "T" beats upon the vowel "O," which is intimately related with the chakra of the heart. Thus, the human being can acquire the power in order to detach from this plexus and depart in the Astral Body.

The correct pronunciation of the mantra **Egipto** is as follows:

Eeeeeeeeegggggiiiiiiiiiiptoooo

Those who have not attained the capacity of departing in the Astral Body with other clues do not have that power. Then they must acquire this power firstly by vocalizing for one hour daily the mantra **Egipto**. This mantra completely develops the chakras related with the projection of the Astral Body. This is how the disciple acquires the power of astral projection. The disciple could then enter and leave the physical body at will.

The Egyptian mantra that is utilized in order to depart in the Astral Body is the following: **Faraon**. This mantra is vocalized in those instances of transition between vigil and dream, having the mind placed on the pyramids of Egypt.

The correct pronunciation of the mantra **Faraon** is as follows:

Faarrraaaaaooooonnnn

This mantra is used in order to depart in the Astral Body, and as we have already stated, it is pronounced during the state of transition between vigil and dream and with the mind concentrated on the pyramids of Egypt. Nonetheless, the disciples that do not have the power of departing with the Astral Body must firstly acquire it by vocalizing daily for one hour, as we have already mentioned, the mantra **Egipto**.

Chapter LXIV

Yesod

He that is wounded in the stones, or hath his privy member cut off, shall not enter unto the congregation of the Lord.

- Deuteronomy 23:1

The woman also with whom man shall lie with seed of copulation, they shall both bathe themselves in water, and be unclean until the even. - Leviticus 15:18

Thus shall ye separate the children of Israel from the uncleanness; that they die not in their uncleanness, when they defile my tabernacle that is among them.

- Leviticus 15:31

 Yesod is the Vital or Ethereal Body. Yesod is the foundation of the Third Logos, the center where the sexual force of the Third Logos gravitates. The sexual forces which are the living foundation of our physiology gravitate in Yesod. The Holy Spirit abides in Yesod.

It is convenient to clarify that if we consider Yesod as a Foundation, it is clear that it is found in the sexual organs. The Vital Body, or the foundation of the biological, physical, and chemical activities, is something else, that in someway is influenced by Yesod. In any case, Yesod is the sexual organs.

Perfumes and sandals are the symbols of Yesod.

The secret of all secrets is found in the mysterious stone **Shem ha-Mephoresh** (שם המפורש) of the Hebrews. This is the Philosophical Stone of the Alchemists. This is Sexual Magic; this is love. Blessed be love.

The Bible tells us that when Jacob awoke from his sleep, he consecrated the stone and he poured oil upon the top of it and blessed it. Really, since that moment, Jacob started the practice of Sexual Magic. Later on he incarnated his internal Master, his real Being. Jacob is the Angel Israel.

The ancient sages worshipped the sun under the symbolic form of a black stone. This is the Heliogabalus Stone.

The Philosophical Stone is science, philosophy, and religion.

The Philosophical Stone is squared as the Celestial Jerusalem of St. John. Upon one of its faces is written the name of Adam, upon the other, the name of Eve, and following, the names of Azoe and INRI upon the other sides.

The Philosophical Stone is very sacred. The Masters are Children of the Stones.

The mysteries of sex enclose the key of all powers. Everything that comes into life is a child of sex. Jesus said unto Peter, *"And I say also unto thee, that thou art Peter and upon this rock I will build my church; and the gates of hell shall not prevail against it."* [Matthew 16:18]

No one can incarnate the Internal Christ without having edified the temple upon the Living Stone (sex).

We must raise the seven columns of the temple of wisdom. Upon each one of the seven columns of the temple the word INRI (Ignis Nature Renovatur Integra) is written with characters of fire.

> *And Jesus sent Peter* (whose Gospel is sex) *and John* (whose Gospel is the Word)*, saying, Go and prepare us the passover, that we may eat.* - Luke 22:8

The secret name of Peter is **Patar** with his three consonants that in high esotericism are radical: P.T.R.

The letter **P** reminds us of the Father who is in secret, the Ancient of Days of the Hebraic Kabbalah, the Father of the Gods, our Fathers or *Phitaras*.

The letter **T** or Tau is the famous crossed letter in sex-yoga. It is the divine hermaphrodite, the man and woman sexually united during intercourse.

The letter **R** is vital in the word INRI, it is the tremendously divine sacred fire, the Egyptian **RA**.

Peter the disciple of Jesus Christ is Aladdin, the marvellous interpreter, who is authorized to lift the stone that shut the sanctuary of the great mysteries.

It is impossible to roll the stone, to lift it, if previously we did not give unto it a cubic form by means of the chisel and the hammer.

Peter, Patar, the Illuminator, is the Master of Sexual Magic, the bountiful Master who always awaits us at the entrance of the difficult path.

Peter died crucified on an inverted cross with the head aiming downwards and the feet aiming upwards, inviting us to descend into the Ninth Sphere in order to work with the water and with the fire, which are the origin of worlds, beasts, human beings, and Gods. Every authentic white initiation starts here.

The doctrine of Peter is the doctrine of sex, the science of Maithuna among the Orientals, the Sexual Magic, the Living Stone, the Boulder. The rock is sex, upon which we must build our interior temple for our intimate Christ, our Lord.

> Peter said, *Wherefore also it is contained in the Scripture, Behold, I lay in Sion a chief corner stone, elect, precious and he that believeth on him shall not be confounded.*
>
> *Unto you therefore which believe he is precious but unto them which be disobedient, the stone which the builders rejected, the same is made the head of the corner, And a stone of stumbling, and a rock of offence.* - Peter 2:6-8
>
> Jesus Christ said, *Therefore whosoever heareth these sayings of mine, and doeth them, I will liken him unto a wise man, which build his house upon a rock* (sex). *And the rain descended, and the floods came, and the winds blew, and beat upon that house; and it fell not; for it was founded upon a rock* (sex).
>
> *And every one that heareth these sayings of mine, and doeth them not, shall be likened unto a foolish man, which built his house upon the sand* (theories of all types, practices of all varieties, but with the complete exclusion of the Maithuna or Sexual Magic).

And the rain descended, and the floods came, and the winds blew, and beat upon that house; and it fell and great was the fall of it (falling into the abyss).
   - Matthew 7:24-27

In the world, there are millions of people who edify upon the sands and they hate Sexual Magic, they do not want to edify upon the rock, upon the stone, they edify upon the sands of their theories, schools, etc. Thus, they believe that they are doing well. These poor people are sincerely mistaken ones with very good intentions. Nonetheless, they will fall into the abyss.

Without the doctrine of Peter, the Second Birth is impossible. We, the Gnostics, study the doctrine of Peter.

Infrasexuals and perverts mortally hate the doctrine of Peter.

Many are the sincerely mistaken ones who believe that they can Self-realize by excluding sex.

Many are the ones that talk against sex, the ones that insult sex, the ones that spit all of their slanderous drivel on the sacred sanctuary of the Third Logos.

Those that hate sex, those that say that sex is gross, filthy, animalistic, bestial, are the insulters, the ones that blaspheme against the Holy Spirit.

Flee fornication (spilling of semen), *every sin that a man doeth is without the body but he that committeth fornication sinneth against his own body.*
   - 1 Corinthians 6:18

Wherefore I say unto you, all manner of sin and blasphemy shall be forgiven unto men but the blasphemy against the Holy Ghost shall not be forgiven unto men... neither in this world, neither in the world to come. - Matthew 12:31-32; see also Mark 3:28-29

For if we sin wilfully after that we have received the knowledge of the truth, there remaineth no more sacrifice for sins.
   - Hebrews 10:26; see also Hebrews 10:27-31

Whosoever pronounces himself against Sexual Magic, whosoever spits their infamy against the sanctuary of the Third Logos, cannot ever reach the Second Birth.

In the Occidental world, many people exist that mortally hate Sexual Magic. Those people justify their absurd hatred with many pretexts. They say that the Maithuna is only for Oriental people, and that we the occidentals are not prepared. Such people affirm that with this doctrine of sex yoga, the unique thing that can result is a harvest of black magicians.

What is interesting about all of this is that such people of a reactionary, conservative, regressive and retarded type do not say a single word against fornication, against adultery, against prostitution, against homosexuality, against masturbation, etc., etc. All of this seems normal to them, and they do not have any inconvenience in miserably squandering the sexual energy.

Sex must be in itself the most elevated creative function. Disgracefully, ignorance reigns with sovereignty and humanity is very distant from comprehending the great mysteries of sex.

If we study the book of heaven, the marvellous zodiac, we can comprehend that the new Aquarian Age is governed by the zodiacal sign of Aquarius, the water-bearer.

The symbol of Aquarius is a woman with two urns full of water trying to intelligently mix the waters of the two urns (see the Fourteenth Arcanum).

This symbol brings us the remembrance of Sexual Alchemy. If in the Age of Pisces the human being was only the slave of the sexual instinct (this is symbolized by the two fish within the waters of life), in Aquarius the human being must learn the transmutation of the sexual forces.

Aquarius is governed by Uranus; Uranas (ur = fire, anas = water). Uranus is the planet which governs sexual functions. It becomes incongruent and absurd that some isolated individuals and certain schools of a pseudo-esoteric type reject the Maithuna. However, they have the pretention of being, they say, initiators of the new era.

Uranus is 100 percent sexual, and in the new era governed by this planet the human being must deeply know the mysteries of sex.

Multitudes of schools of black magic exist, many of them with very venerable traditions that teach Sexual Magic with the spilling of semen. They have very beautiful theories that attract and captivate, and if the student falls in that seductive and delicious deceit, he becomes a black magician.

Those black schools affirm to the four winds that they are white and that is why ignorant ones fall. Moreover, those schools talk of beauty, love, charity, wisdom, etc., etc. Naturally, in those circumstances the ignorant disciple attains the belief with firmness that such institutions are not evil and perverse. Remember good disciple, that the abyss is full of sincerely mistaken ones and people of very good intentions.

To reject the Maithuna signifies, as a fact, the pronunciation against the sign of Aquarius,

which is governed by Uranus, the king of sex.

The ignorant fornicators of reactionary pseudo-occultism totally ignore the secret doctrine of the Savior of the world, the Christian esotericism.

The pseudo-esoteric and pseudo-occultist reactionism ignores that the primitive Gnostic Christian sects were practicing the Maithuna. Sexual Magic was always taught in all of the ancient schools of Occidental mysteries. Maithuna was known among the mysteries of the Templars, among the mysteries of the Aztecs, Mayans, Incas, Chibchas, Zapotecs, Araucans, Toltecs, Mysteries of Eleusis, Mysteries of Rome, Mitra, Cartagus, Tyre, Celtic mysteries, Phoenicians, Egyptians, Druids and in all of the primitive Christian sects, such as the sect of the Essenes that had their convent at the shore of the Dead Sea, and had as one of its most exalted members Jesus, the divine Rabbi of Galilee.

The Maithuna, Sexual Magic, is universal. It is known in the mysteries of north, south, east and west of the world. But it is violently rejected by the reactionary, fornicating and regressive pseudo-occultists.

The fundamental stone of the authentic and legitimate schools of the mysteries is the Maithuna, the Arcanum A.Z.F. or Sexual Magic.

Hebe, the daughter of Zeus and Hera, the wife of Heracles and the cupbearer of the gods. She was able to restore the vitality of youth in the aged and decrepit and is an ancient source for the symbolism of Aquarius. Greek.

Chapter LXV
Malkuth

 **M**alkuth is the physical body, the physical world. It is very important to remember that the Vital Body is nothing but the superior part of the physical body. Those who do not accept this concept think that the physical body is one body, alone, and that the Vital Body is another and very distinct one. Thus, they make an order that is a little bit mistaken.

Malkuth is "the kingdom," whose regent is Changam, the Genie of the Earth.

Every planet gives birth to seven races; our planet Earth already gave birth to five races, so only two more will come. After the seven races, our Earth, transformed by great cataclysms, will convert itself through millions of years into a new moon. The whole devolving and evolving life of the Earth came from the Moon. The Moon died and became a desert when the great life abandoned it.

Seven great races existed on the Moon. The lunar soul, the lunar life, is now devolving and evolving in our present planet Earth. This is how the worlds reincarnate.

The Gods of Nature have worked very hard in order to create self-cognizant Beings. The Gods have made difficult experiments within the laboratorium of Nature. Diverse forms of animals have exited from those test tubes of the great laboratorium; some of those forms have exited only with the purpose of elaborating material for the creation of the human

being, and other forms have exited as a refuse of semi-human beings, while other forms are true human failures.

Indeed, all the living species with the exception of a few of them are living refuse from the human kingdom. All the animals of this kingdom of Malkuth characterize some aspect of the human being. All the animals are truly creatures from the human being.

Nonetheless, it is good to know that the struggle of the Gods in order to create the human being has not finished yet; still, the human being (wrongly called human) has to cast aside from himself a great amount which will be in the zoological gardens of the future.

We must know that the Reality is the Being, the Innermost, the Spirit, but a factor of discord also exists in us; this is the "I," the ego, the *myself*.

It is interesting to comprehend that the "I" is pluralized. The "I" is constituted by many "I's" that fight among themselves, and that dispute for the control of the human personality. These "I's" are **three, seven** and **legion**.

The **three** basic ones are the Demon of Desire, the Demon of the Mind, and the Demon of the Evil Will.

The **seven** are the seven capital sins: anger, greed, lust, envy, pride, laziness, gluttony.

The **legion** is constituted by all of the millions of secondary sins.

The three, the seven, and the legion are small "I's," animal elements created by the mind. These animal elements are the enemies which live within our own house. These animal elements live within the kingdom of our Soul; they nourish themselves with the inferior substances of our lower animal depths.

What is worse is that these animal elements have stolen part of our consciousness. This is demonstrated by the following affirmations: *I am* angry, *I am* greedy, *I* desire, *I am* envious, etc.

The true Being is the Spirit, and the Being still has not entered into the human being because the "I" has invaded the Kingdom of the Soul. Really, neither the Soul nor the Spirit have incarnated within the human being. The human being—the so-called human being—is still but a possibility.

The true human being is still in the process of creation. Many samples of the present human races will be in the zoological gardens of the future. What we have of the animal within ourselves must be cast aside with the purpose of properly attaining the human state.

The "I" is dissolved when we finish with all of our sins. When the "I" is dissolved, then the Soul and the Spirit incarnate in the human being. Thus, we are human beings in the most complete sense of the word.

When physical death arrives, the only thing which continues is the "I," the legion of "I's." The ego, the "I," returns in order to satisfy its desires. Death is the return into conception. This is the wheel of the Tenth Arcanum.

Yama, the God of Death, grasps the wheel of transmigration, upon which all beings rotate incessantly, enslaved by the three poisons symbolized at the axle by three animals that represent: craving (greed or desire), aversion (anger or hatred), and ignorance.

The true human being that has the Soul and the Spirit incarnated lives completely awakened in the Astral Body after the death of the physical body. This person enjoys consciousness and objective perception in the Internal Worlds.

The phantom of those that still have not dissolved the "I" and have not incarnated the Soul and the Spirit lives with the consciousness asleep in the Internal Worlds. They have only subjective consciousness and subjective perception.

The physical world is the valley of bitterness, the kingdom of Malkuth, the kingdom of Samsara. The wheel of Samsara incessantly turns and the ego comes and goes; it disincarnates and returns always suffering, always searching without finding. The Tenth Arcanum, the wheel of retribution, is terrible, and the whole world is a slave of this fatal wheel of the centuries.

Whosoever wants to be liberated from the fatal wheel of Samsara must dissolve the "I" and incarnate the Soul.

This labor is very difficult and those who achieve it are very rare. Really, the kingdom of Malkuth is a terrible filter. The refuse of this filter is what is common and current, which is swallowed by the abyss. The gold, the select, the true Human Being, the Angel, is the conception, and the struggle is indeed difficult.

Nature is implacable and the birth of an Angel-Human Being costs thousands, or better said, millions of victims. *"Many are called and few are chosen."*

> Christ said: *"From one thousand that are looking for me, one finds me; from one thousand that find me, one follows me; from one thousand that follow me, one is mine."*
>
> Krishna said: *"Among a thousand men, maybe one will exert in order to attain perfection, and among the thousands that strive towards perfection, maybe one will truly know me."*

This is the tragedy of the Tenth Arcanum of Kabbalah.

The symbols of the Sephirah Malkuth are: the two altars, the cross of equal arms, the magic circle, the triangle of the magic art. Malkuth is related with the feet and the anus.

Chapter LXVI
The Klipoth

*The inferno is the womb of Heaven.
Beauty is born from rottenness. Lucifer
grants us Light when we defeat him.*

It has already been said that the
Sephiroth are really twelve; the Ain Soph
is the eleventh and its antithesis, its fatal
shadow, is the abyss, which is the twelfth
Sephirah, the Klipoth of Kabbalah.

The Klipoth, which are the Infernal
Worlds, are below Malkuth, the physical
world.

The word Inferno comes from the
Latin word *infernus*, which signifies "inferior region." The submerged mineral
kingdom with its own atomic Infernos
exists within every planet. These atomic
Infernos are always situated within the
interior of any planetary mass and within
the infradimensions of nature, beneath the
three-dimensional zone of Euclid.

Really, the abyss is the Avitchi of the
Hindus, the inferno of ice of the Nordics,
the Chinese inferno with all of its yellow tortures, the Buddhist inferno, the
Mohammedan's inferno, the Egyptian
Amenti, the tenebrous Tartarus, the
Avernus, etc. All of these varieties of tradi-
tional infernos emphatically allegorize the
submerged mineral kingdom.

All of us have heard about spiritual-
ism, about Witches' Sabbaths with witches
and rogues. Some people look at this as if
it is something strange, others like to hear
these tales in order to laugh a little, but the
crude reality is that the medieval Witches'
Sabbath and the famous witches of midnight have more reality than that which we
think. Obviously, these "Calchonas" (this

THE SUFFERINGS OF THE INFERNOS

is the name given unto them in the rigorous academic Spanish language) belong to
the world of Klipoth.

Maria de la Antilla, who was spoken of
in ancient convents, was the governess of
them. The sorceresses of ancient Witches'
Sabbaths denominated her "Holy Mary."
When I was investigating this strange creature in the world of Klipoth, I wondered,
how was she able to share her life with so
many black magicians? How was she able
to be involved within so many Witches'
Sabbaths, since I never saw in her that
which we can call perversity.

The tenebrous of the left-hand path,
the sublunar creatures, rendered worship
unto her, and they did not consider this
female magician as tenebrous, but as a
saint. I wanted to know the truth about
the present sanctity of a creature that was
mixing herself with darkness, that was
involved in so many Witches' Sabbaths and
monasteries of the Middle Ages. Who has
never heard of Maria de la Antilla when
occupied with the studies of the old events
of medieval high and low magic? There are
so many hidden secrets among the dust of
so many libraries.

I have to clarify this, of course; I knew about it and I did clarify this precisely in the world of Tiphereth, where I invoked that entity.

I was heard, and to my astonishment, I found myself with a Self-realized Master. Then I comprehended that this Master had emanated her Bodhisattva and was educating herself in the exercises of magic within the Magical Triangle or third triangle. She was passing through rigorous training, starting with Klipoth, but without performing evil against anyone.

Afterwards, I put myself in direct contact with her Bodhisattva, with Maria de la Antilla. When I invited her to visit the world of Nirvana she accepted my invitation with gladness. When she fused herself with her real Being, the secret Master, then I saw that she was a creature that has attained the perfection of High Magic and that if she was really living in the world of Klipoth, it was in order to finish her education, or her psychological training, by exercising tremendous powers without performing evil.

When one observes this creature, one is pleased with her real Being; one realizes that her real Being is an extraordinary White Magician, because she knows the kingdom of light in depth, the world of Malkuth, or the world of Klipoth.

The third triangle is the triangle of Practical Magic and this is a world that we

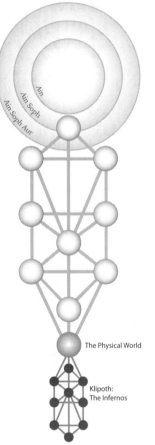

Ain
Ain Soph
Ain Soph Aur

The Physical World

Klipoth: The Infernos

must understand because we have to leave prejudice behind in order to work in the world of Klipoth.

The adverse Sephiroth are the Klipoth; here we find the demons, the souls in penance, the ones that suffer, those that have already finished their cycles of existence and that devolve within time, the fallen Angels, the tenebrous of the lunar path, the black lodge and all of the adepts of the left-hand path, the henchmen of Lucifer and Ariman, the followers of the Bons and Drukpas*, the enemies of the fourth path, the Nicolaitanes, and the Tantric Anagarikas.

Undoubtedly, within the kingdom of Klipoth there also live those that are developing themselves in High Magic.

The Klipoth are the inverted Sephiroth, the Sephiroth in their negative aspect, the inverted virtues. For example, the qualities of Geburah are severity, the law, and when it is inverted it is tyranny, dictatorship. Sometimes a prostitute delivers herself to males because of charity; here we find the principle of an inverted Sephirah. So, charity of Chesed, when inverted, could be complacency with crime.

All Klipoth of Kabbalah are within the Kundabuffer organ, within Malkuth, the physical world, within the interior of the Earth.

* - See the Glossary entry and the next chapter.

Chapter LXVII
Daath, Tantric Knowledge

Some Kabbalists emphasize the idea that Binah, the Holy Spirit, is feminine. Such an affirmation is mistaken. It has been said in *The Divine Comedy* with complete clarity that the Holy Spirit is the husband of the Divine Mother. Therefore, the Holy Spirit unfolds himself into his wife, into the Shakti of the Hindus.

This must be known and understood. Some, when they see that the Third Logos is unfolded into the Divine Mother Kundalini, or Shakti, She that has many names, have believed that the Holy Spirit is feminine, and they have been mistaken. The Holy Spirit is masculine, but when He unfolds Himself into She, then the first ineffable divine couple is formed, the creator Elohim, the Kabir, or great Priest, the Ruach Elohim, that in accordance to Moses, cultivated the waters in the beginning of the world.

The Hebraic Kabbalists speak unto us about the mysterious **Daath** that appears in the Tree of Life, the Sephirah that has no designated divine name, nor Angelic host of any type, and that has neither a mundane sign, planet, nor element.

Daath, the Sephirah of Hebrew mystery, is produced by the esoteric conjunction of Shiva-Shakti, Osiris-Isis, perpetually united in Yesod, the Foundation, the Ninth Sephirah, the Ninth Sphere, sex, but hidden by the mysteries of Daath which has the Tantric knowledge, which is processed with the Sahaja Maithuna, or Sexual Magic, that when correctly utilized permits the intimate realization of the Being.

SHIVA-SHAKTI

It is necessary that all of us profoundly reflect, that we deeply comprehend all of this. He and She are united in the Cubic Stone of Yesod, which is sex. The perfect Tantric knowledge is the outcome of the union of He and She with which we can internally Self-realize ourselves in all the levels of the Being.

Some Kabbalistic authors suppose that Daath, the Sephirah that gives knowledge or sapience, comes from the fusion of the masculine Cosmic Christ, Chokmah, with Binah and assume that Binah is exclusively feminine. Such an affirmation is purely

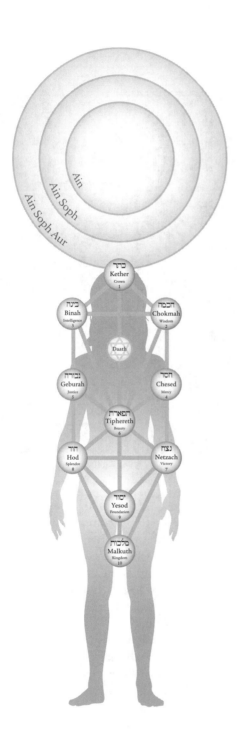

false, because the Holy Spirit is really masculine, and when he unfolds himself into the Divine Mother, the perfect couple is formed.

In the Cubic Stone of Yesod, in the Ninth Sphere, Tantric knowledge, the Tantric initiation comes. The development of the serpent along the dorsal spine is possible by means of the Tantras.

In these studies of Kabbalah, we need to be practical; there are authors who write marvels, but when one looks at them, one realizes that they have not lived what they have written; they did not experience it in themselves, and that is why they are mistaken. I understand that one must write what one has directly experienced by oneself. I have proceeded in this way for my part.

The Cubic Stone of Yesod, situated in the creative organs, is certainly that metallic soul which is the result of sexual transmutations. We can call this metallic soul the Mercury of Secret Philosophy, or, when speaking with simpler language, creative energy. This energy in itself is allegorized or symbolized by the Devil. When we say that we must work with the Devil, this is in order to transform it into Lucifer, the maker of light.

We are clearly referring to the labor in the Great Work. It becomes interesting that precisely here in the Cubic Stone of Yesod is where Shiva and Shakti, Osiris and Isis, are sexually united, and here is precisely where the Tantric knowledge is found. The attainment of the intimate realization of the Being is not possible without it.

In the Eastern world, in Tibet, the monks are radical. For such reason H.P. Blavatsky thought that they were black magicians. All of us have repeated that mistake, and now we see the necessity for rectification.

I am not affirming that the Drukpas are saints, that they are meek sheep. They are black magicians because they teach Black Tantra. However, the Bons, even when they use red caps, are not black as Blavatsky mistakenly supposed. Actually, if one amongst the Bons does not want realization of the Self but only the liberation of himself for a period of time in order to return in the Sixth Root Race, or if he does not want to Self-realize ever but only wants to emancipate himself without realization of the Self, he can achieve it.

First of all, the neophyte is taken into an isolated place, and there, all of the inhuman elements that he possesses are invoked. This is performed with procedures of High Magic in the isolated mountain. Those inhuman elements become visible and tangible and intend to devour the neophyte, but if the neophyte remains serene, there is nothing more to do, he has become triumphant. Then, he has to eliminate the ego, to reduce it to ashes and to work in himself.

This ordeal and some mantras for disincarnation, which are two words, become the maximum efforts for the neophyte in the physical world. It is dreadful to see the Bon priest dressed with his white apron of skulls and dead bones and with a red turban on his head, while holding a dagger with his right hand.

The body of the neophyte falls instantaneously dead in the precise moment when he is pronouncing his two mantras of fatality; then he is submitted to great ordeals in the Internal Worlds. He has to confront the fears of death. He has to tolerate the hurricane of Karma. He has to become victorious in all that the Father-

Tibetan Lama wearing an apron of human bones.
PHOTOGRAPH BY ALEXANDRA DAVID-NEEL.

Mother will submit him to. The goal is to be allowed to enter, or better if we say, to be reborn in a supra-human form within any kingdom of the Devas, maybe in the Kingdom of Those of Great Concentration or in the Kingdom of Those of Long Hair, or in the Kingdom of Maitreya, or in the Kingdom of Supreme Happiness, etc., and it is in that region where he is going to finish with his preparation for the Liberation.

The Divine Mother assists him by eliminating his human elements and finally he achieves the submergence of himself into the bosom of the Great Reality, not as a Self-realized master, but only as an Elemental Buddha. He submerges himself in that state until the Sixth Root Race with the purpose of Self-realizing himself in that root race, or he can remain forever converted into a Buddhic elemental and nothing else, but happy.

Those who intend to liberate themselves, those who really want realization of the Self, those that truly want to be converted into Mahatmas or Hierophants, must be submitted to Tantric discipline, and to work in the Ninth Sphere. All of Tantra, how to awaken the serpent, how to raise it, and how to open the chakras, etc., will be taught unto them.

Therefore, it is discovered that the Bons are radical. One has to either work for the Being or not. One goes with the purpose of realization of the Self or with the purpose of remaining without realization of the Self. This has to be defined. Among the Bons, everything is severe, and for this reason H.P. Blavatsky made judgment on them, considering them to be black magicians. But when one studies the Tantra of the Bons, one realizes that it is white, not black; I repeat, white. They transmute the sperm into energy in order to attain deep realization of the Self.

Yesod is lunar and this we cannot deny. Within Gnostic esotericism, a woman appears, an ineffable divine virgin, dressed with a blue tunic and standing upon a moon. We have to understand this: the moon represents the Sephirah Yesod, which signifies the sexual force. The blue-colored tunic represents night, within which the great mysteries of death and life are developed. The energy of the Third Logos must be worked with only at night. The work in the laboratorium of the Holy Spirit must be performed during the nocturnal hours. The Sahaja Maithuna can only be practiced in the darkness of the night, because during the day the Sun is opposed to any generation.

If one puts a hen with her eggs in the light of the sun in order to incubate them, then these eggs will not attain the incubation, and if some chickens hatch, they will die, because the sun is an enemy of generation.

Whosoever wants to search for the light must ask for it in the profound night, asking the Logos who is behind the Sun that illuminates us.

The crude reality is that because of the disposition of the creative organs, procreation is always achieved in darkness, because when the sperm exits the sexual glands, it does not exit illuminated by the light of the sun, but in darkness. In darkness it opens its way through the fallopian tube in order to encounter the ovum which descends from the ovaries, and within the darkness of the womb, gestation is achieved.

THE VIRGIN OF IMMACULATE CONCEPTION

But if this sperm, instead of exiting the sexual glands protected by the darkness, could exit under the light of the sun, and if the fetus was not in darkness and was uncovered in the womb of the woman in order for the sun to directly enter it, then it is obvious that failure would be a fact.

Therefore, fecundation is performed always in darkness, because of the disposition of the very organs of nature. This is why, in order for one day to attain the intimate realization of the Being, the work must be performed within the obscurity of silence and within the august secret of the Wise. This is what the Virgin of Immaculate Conception, who is standing upon the moon and dressed with a blue tunic, is indicating unto us. The work of the Maithuna is performed within the darkness of night.

We must warn that the practice must never be performed two successive times in the same night. The practice is allowed only one time a day.

When Sexual Magic is practiced two successive times, then violence against nature exists, because the law of the creative magnetic pause is violated.

It is also urgent to know that the spouse must never be obligated by force to practice Maithuna when she is sick or with her menstruation, or when she is pregnant, because these are crimes of violence against nature.

The woman who has given birth to a child can only practice the Maithuna forty days after childbirth.

There also exists the crime of violence against nature when the man or the woman forces their mate to perform the copulation when the organism of the spouse is not found in the suitable conditions for intercourse.

There also exists such a crime when the man or the woman obligate themselves to perform copulation even with the best intentions of realization of the Self and with the pretext of performing Sexual Magic, when in reality the creative organs are not found in the precise amorous moment and in the favorable harmonious conditions which are indispensable for copulation.

Chapter LXVIII

The Initiation of Tiphereth

For as Jonah was three days and three nights in the whale's belly; so shall the Son of Man be three days and three nights in the heart of the earth. - Matthew 12:40

Extraordinary events happen with Tiphereth. Anyone can receive the initiations of Malkuth, Yesod, Hod, Netzach, and then, finally, the fifth initiation, which is related with Tiphereth, in order to become a Master. Someone can receive the fifth initiation of the Human Soul and for this reason become a Master. Nonetheless, this one does not attain the Initiation of Tiphereth.

The Initiation of Tiphereth comes properly after the Fifth Initiation of Fire. The one who receives the fifth initiation does not always have the joy of attaining the Initiation of Tiphereth. This is a very secret initiation and is received by the one who takes the Direct Path.

In the second triangle of the Tree of Life, the Cosmic Christ has Tiphereth as His center of gravity. The Christ manifests Himself in this center.

There are things that deserve to be reflected upon, analyzed, and comprehended. In order for the Second Logos, Vishnu or the Cosmic Christ, to be the savior of a human being, He has to convert himself into the particular intimate Jesus Christ.

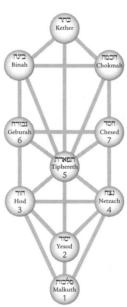

INITIATIONS OF FIRE

Christ in Himself is a cosmic force, and this force can save a human being only if in some way this force is humanized.

Sacrifice for humanity is the law of the Solar Logos, the Cosmic Christ. He has been sacrificing Himself since the dawn of life by crucifying Himself within all the worlds, within every planet that emerges into existence, in order for all the beings to have life and to have this life in abundance.

Christ can reincarnate within us only after we have passed through the five Initiations of Major Mysteries, and only as a very special grace when we have sacrificed ourselves for humanity. In order to understand how this cosmic force is humanized within ourselves, one must learn how to handle the trimurtis.

There are students who exercise a lot of work in order to understand the trimurtis. For example, they are accustomed to think in terms of the First Logos, Second Logos, and Third Logos, or Father, Son, and Holy Spirit. But another, second, trimurti comes after this, in which we speak of Osiris, Isis, and Horus, and here is where students become confused. This is really because the conversion of one trimurti into another trimurti cannot be performed based on pure rationalism. There is a factor which is completely spiritual related with the conversion of

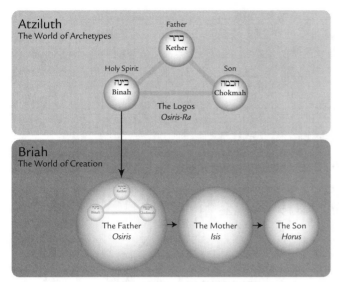

Atziluth
The World of Archetypes

Father
כתר
Kether

Holy Spirit
בינה
Binah

Son
חכמה
Chokmah

The Logos
Osiris-Ra

Briah
The World of Creation

Kether

Binah   Chokmah

The Father
Osiris

The Mother
Isis

The Son
Horus

Trimurtis, because only intuitively can this be learned, captured, grasped.

Kether / Father, Chokmah / Son, and Binah / Holy Spirit are three distinct persons and only one true God. This is how theology teaches this. These three persons, even when they are three, in depth are only one, who is the Father. The Son and the Holy Spirit are within the Father, in the same way as the body, the Soul and the Spirit are within the true Human Being. Thus, within the Ancient of the Centuries, there is also the Son and the Holy Spirit, and they form a unique, integral, unitotal one. In ancient Egypt, that unique unitotal one was called **Osiris** (see chapter seven).

Osiris can unfold himself, and when he does it he unfolds into Isis. Eve always comes from Adam's rib, *as above, so below;* so there is nothing rare in the Solar Eve emerging from Osiris, the Solar Adam; the Solar Eve is the Urania-Venus, the spouse of the Solar Adam. Two always comes from one. This is how the Father who is in secret has his spouse, who is the Divine

Mother Kundalini. Osiris always has Isis as his spouse.

From the perfect union of these two, Osiris-Isis, the child Horus (Aurus) is born. She and He love each other, and as a result of their love, she conceives the Christ or Second Logos, who descends into her virginal and immaculate womb by the action and grace of the Holy Spirit, meaning by the action and grace of her spouse, the Third Logos.

But we have to take into account that even while she is the spouse of the Third Logos, within the Third Logos is the Second Logos and also the First Logos, because in the end, the Logos is the undividable, uni-total, and integral triune. A lot of subtleness is needed in order to understand this, a lot of refinement, synthesism, and intuition.

The conversion of trimurtis, one into another, is something that gives a lot of work to the students, but if you sharpen your intuition a little bit you will understand.

From the divine and holy copulation, Isis is impregnated by a sacred conception. She is a virgin before giving childbirth, within childbirth and after childbirth. Isis is our own particular Divine Mother Kundalini, Ram-Io.

This is how the advent of the child that in Egypt was called Horus occurs, the child that in Hebraic times was called Yeshua, our adorable Savior. Jesus of the Gospels is profoundly significant because Jesus comes from the word **Yeshua**, which in Hebrew signifies *Savior.*

"Blessed be those who comprehend the mystery of their own Divine Mother. She is the root of their own Monad. She carries in her arms our intimate Buddha, the child who is gestated within her immaculate bosom." - Samael Aun Weor from "The Gnostic Magic of the Runes."

Jesus, Yeshua, and Horus are the same; He is the child who always is in the arms of His Mother Isis or Mary. He is the same Christ who has descended from the Second Logos. He is the Cosmic Christ already humanized and already converted into the child of a divine man and a divine woman. He has converted into a Savior-King-Child, but He is a Particular-King-Child, because He is one's own Being. He is the crowned Child of Gold of Alchemy.

He is Jesus Christ, because Christ is the Second Logos, and Jesus because He has converted into a Savior. He has descended from his own sphere and has penetrated into a very pure and virginal womb in order to be converted into a Savior, and to be born by the action and grace of the Holy Spirit.

Actually, He has become the child of the Divine Mother, in actual fact, the child of His own parents. Undoubtedly, we must distinguish between Jesus Christ the great Kabir, who was the man who preached the doctrine of the intimate Christ of each one of us, and who is the individual, particular Jesus Christ of each one of us.

The Cosmic Christ is impersonal and universal and is beyond individuality, personality, and the "I." He is a cosmic force that expresses himself through any human being who is properly prepared. Once he expressed Himself through Jesus of Nazareth and likewise through Hermes Trismegistus, Buddha Gautama Shakyamuni, Quetzalcoatl, etc. He can express Himself through any Avatar. In order to express Himself, He has to descend from the superior spheres and to penetrate into a Virgin's womb, a Virgin called Isis, Mary, Tonantzin, Insoberta, Maya, Cybele, etc., who is the same particular Cosmic Mother, because everyone has their own.

When one reads the Epistles of the Apostle Paul, one can verify for oneself with astonishment that the Apostle Paul very seldom mentions Jesus the great Kabir or the historic Christ. Paul always mentions an intimate Christ.

In order for the intimate Christ or the humanized Yeshua to be born within ourselves, one has to have worked in the forge of the Cyclops and to have built the existential bodies of the Being.

In order for the Savior to be born, the event of Bethlehem has to be repeated; such an event is very profound and at the same time symbolic. The town of Bethlehem which the Gospels refer to is very allegorical. It is said that this small town did not exist in the epoch of Jesus of Nazareth. If we analyze the word **Belen** (which is *Bethlehem* in Chaldean), we have **Bel-En**. Then, we see that **Bel** in Chaldean terminology signifies *"tower of fire."* When is this tower of fire attained? This is attained when one has created the superior existential bodies of the Being, when the sacred fire has reached the superior part of the brain. This is how the Advent of Bethlehem occurs.

Nonetheless, in despite of having the Solar Bodies, the case can be given of an initiate who does not incarnate the child. I want to state with this something very subtle that passes unnoticed for any Kabbalist, because we have Tiphereth united with the Causal Body.

By comparing the Epistle of Paul to Corinthians (1 Corinthians 15) we can clarify this matter. Paul states that the Terrestrial Man and the Heavenly Man exist. Unquestionably, the Terrestrial Man is constituted by the Physical, Ethereal, Astral, and Mental Bodies, and the Body of the Conscious Will. In order for the Advent of the Son of Man to occur, the building of the Terrestrial Man is necessary, because the common and current human being is not a Man yet.

It is only when one has given oneself the luxury of creating the existential bodies of the Being, when one can be called **Man**, even when this one is just Terrestrial. The second man of whom Paul speaks is the Heavenly Man, and he states, *"And as we have borne the image of the earthly, we shall also bear the image of the heavenly."* [1 Corinthians 15:49]

The Advent of the Son of Man occurs when he has to accomplish some specific mission upon the earth, when the initiate has taken the Direct Path for the Final Liberation.

After attaining the Fifth Initiation of Fire, I was called by my Divine Mother Kundalini. She had the child in her arms. I made a certain petition of an esoteric type and she answered unto me, "Ask unto the child." Then, I asked unto the child what I had to ask.

Afterwards, I could receive the Initiation of Tiphereth or the Fifth Initiation of Fire. Then, the Child that I had seen in the arms of its Mother, who was my Divine Mother (because each one of us has their own), penetrated within my organism through the marvellous door of the pineal gland, a gland that was identified by Descartes as "the seat of the soul." In this case, my body became the stable where the Child was born, where the Child entered into the world.

In the beginning, I can tell unto you that the presence of the Child within oneself is not very noticeable, because He is born among the animals of the stables and they are nothing else but the animals of desire, the passions, vices, and defects that keep the consciousness bottled up, in other words the elements that compound the pluralized "I." The "I" is found constituted by animal elements. These nourish themselves with inferior substances of the lower animal depths of the human being. This is where they live and multiply. Each animal element represents a determined defect. They constitute that which is called ego, or the animals of the stables, where the God Child is born in order to save the man.

The child has to suffer greatly because he is not born in a great palace; he is born within a stable. He is born completely weak, very small, between gigantic seas of "I's" that surround the stable.

The God Child grows little by little and through time, He develops himself. How is He growing up? In which way is He growing up? He is growing up by eliminating the "I's," by disintegrating them, reducing them to ashes, to cosmic dust. This is how our particular intimate Yeshua grows up. The labor that this Child has to perform is very hard. He is the Christ, and He is born in our stable in order to save us. Therefore, He has to kill in Himself all of the animals of our stable. He has to fight against the princes of evil in Himself, to fight the children of infidelity in Himself. The temptations through which one is always passing as a human being, as a person that has a body of flesh and bones, are the temptations through which He has to pass as well. These are His temptations because the same body of flesh and bone of each one of us has come to be converted into His own body of flesh and bone. Lo and behold the merit of His sacrifices and of His efforts.

This is how the Son of Man comes into the world and is converted into a man of flesh and bones. He becomes a Man among men, and he is exposed to the suffering of human beings. He has to pass through the same tortures of any man. Our psychological process is converted into the psychological process that He must order and transform. Our preoccupations are His preoccupations. This is the reason why He has been called the Holy Firm, because He cannot be defeated, and finally He triumphs. Then, He covers Himself with glory, and He is worthy of every praise, lordship and majesty.

The kings of intelligence, the three wise kings, the three king magicians, the true Genii, will always recognize the Lord, and they venerate Him, so they will come to worship Him.

In the same way that He is growing, the sufferings for Him become more and greater. Being so perfect, He has to defeat the potencies of darkness in Himself. Being so pure, He has to defeat the impurity in Himself. Having Him pass beyond any possibility of temptation, He has to defeat temptations in himself. The Child will find Himself always within great dangers; Herod, the world, the tenebrous, will always want to slaughter Him. The baptism in the river Jordan of existence will always be indispensable since the waters of life clean, transform, and baptize. The transfiguration occurs when He interprets the law of Moses with total intelligence, by teaching unto the people and unfolding in His works all of the marvellous zeal of Elias.

The intimate Christ will always come towards us walking upon the boisterous waves of the sea of life. The intimate Christ will always establish an order in our mind and He will give back the lost light to our eyes. He will always multiply the bread of the Eucharist for the nourishment and strength of our souls.

The intimate Christ incarnated within the initiate will preach along the roads of this great Jerusalem of the world by delivering the message of the new era unto humanity.

But the scribes, who are the intellectual men of any epoch, those who form the cultural aspect, will say unto him, "This man is crazy." The intellectuals want to resolve everything on the basis of reasoning. Any human being can elaborate within his cerebrum-encephalous a materialistic theory as well as a spiritualistic theory by means of the most severe logical processes, and as much in one theory as in the other, as much in the thesis as in the antithesis, the logic in its depth is really admirable.

His teachings are also rejected by the priests, people of all religions and people of all organizations of a pseudo-esotericist and pseudo-occultist type. Those people who consider themselves very serious always say, "What this man is saying is madness; this man is evil." This is how the Son of Man is rejected in the world.

Every initiate has to live the cosmic drama of crucifixion in himself. The three traitors crucify him, they deliver him; Judas, the demon of desire, sells him for thirty silver coins. Judas exchanges him for women, pleasures, games. Pilate, the demon of the mind, always washes his hands; he always finds justification for all of his errors. Caiaphas, the demon of evil will, always wants to do his own will; he hates the will of the Father. The cosmic drama has to be lived by the initiate in a completely integral and total way.

Christ as the Tree of Life. The sacrifice of Christ sustains life.

We find that he is damned and hanged and that he has to die. In other words, the Terrestrial Man has to die. He submits himself to the will of the Father and goes towards death, which is his posthumous work.

Formidable cosmic events will always be in the consciousness of the initiate, and among lightning, thunder, and great earthquakes of the soul, the Lord will always deliver his spirit to the Father by exclaiming, *"My Father, into thy hands I command my spirit."* Then, his death occurs.

With his death, he disintegrates his psychic aggregates, and after descending the body into the sepulcher, he resurrects after three days. These three days are also allegorical. At the end of these three days, the Son of Man passes through three great purifications; even the last inhuman element that was in his interior dies.

This is why it is said that the Son of Man has died in himself; he has killed death because death can only be killed with death. Then, the Son of Man has to resurrect with the physical body. Then he is a Resurrected Master with the Elixir of Longevity. He is a true King of Nature in accordance to the Order of Melchizedeck. Then we can exclaim as the Apostle Paul exclaims, *"Death is swallowed up in victory. O death, where is thy sting? O grave, where is thy victory?"* [I Corinthians 15:54-55]

Therefore, what is important is that He can redeem Himself; when He resurrects, the soul resurrects in Him. All of our animated and spiritual principles resurrect in Him and one resurrects in Him.

It is necessary to comprehend that He is our authentic interior Savior, our particular intimate Jesus Christ.

Thus, He resurrects in the Father, and the Father resurrects in Him. When Philip, that Master who is an expert of the Jinn State, said unto Jesus, *"Show us the Father,"* the great Kabir answered, *"He that hath seen me hath seen the Father."* [John 14:9]

The three great purifications are found symbolized by the three nails upon the cross. On top of the cross, the word **INRI** appears (Ignis Natura Renovatur Integra): the fire renews nature incessantly. The three nails signify the three purifications by fire and iron. After the three purifications based upon fire and iron, the resurrection from the dead is achieved. The three days are three periods of work within which the Son of Man must perform the Great Work.

Let us take into account that the cross is that with which the undesirable elements must be disintegrated. Fidelity towards the Father is tested with the cross. There are many people that say, "I am faithful to the Father, to the Mother, to the Son of Man." But, when the hour of destiny arrives, which is the hour of hours, they fail with the cross. Where is the cross? This is the crossing of the lingam-yoni. On that cross they fornicate, adulterate, and perform their evilness. Then, we must disintegrate the undesirable elements in order to search for the death of the Terrestrial Man.

It is necessary to know that Jesus the great Kabir, who came into the world two-thousand years ago and preached this doctrine, knew very well that each one carries their particular intimate Jesus Christ within. That is why he said that what he wanted is for each one of us to follow their own particular intimate Jesus Christ, who is the one that matters because He is our Savior. He comes in order to reconcile ourselves with our own Father who is in secret,

Christ resurrects from the dead.

with the Ancient of the Centuries. He is the great reconciliator.

Once He has achieved the triumph, He glorifies Himself and is worthy of any praise and glory, because He has defeated the evil in Himself. He had not defeated evil from without but in Himself. He has immolated Himself as a lamb. That is why it is said of Him that He is the Immolated Lamb. He has immolated Himself in order to save us with his blood, meaning with the fire, because in Alchemy, the blood represents the sacred fire of Kundalini.

It is good to understand all of this. I am explaining unto you what I have lived within myself, what I am experiencing within myself. However, I would not commit the crime of telling unto you that I am the Christ. This would be a blasphemy, a lack of respect to the Savior.

But truly I say unto you that Christ is saving me, as he has saved others. I can be one more of the saved, as I am trying and as I have had experience with it. What I am saying is what I am proving in myself, what I have lived.

Fourth Part

Numerology and Esoteric Mathematics

"Disclose ye the veil that covers the celestial spirits. See ye that each man and each woman are a star, just as mysterious lamps hang from the firmament. God is the flame that stirs in everything, the vivifying geometry of everything. That is why the number is holy, is infinite, is eternal. There where he resides there are no differences; diversity is unity." - Gnostic Ritual

Chapter LIX

Numerological Tablet

This board or plate is very important in order to deeply comprehend the esoteric mysteries. It is a quadrilateral which is divided into nine numbers. There is a vertical and horizontal triple division. The principles of arithmetic and geometry are expressed here.

1	2	3
4	5	6
7	8	9

We find on this tablet **Individual Architecture**, the interior universe, which must be built within each one; it is the construction of our interior intimate universe. Cosmic architecture is related with the seven cosmos of the infinite. Social architecture is related with the construction of our temples, houses, and buildings.

It is necessary to comprehend that this plate is related with the three principles previously mentioned: architecture, geometry, and mathematics. One has to relate with numbers, because the Kabbalah is based upon them.

The square divided into nine parts represents a triple extension, the triplicity of the ternary, or the Ninth Sphere. A lot has been explained about the Ninth Sphere, but it can be demonstrated mathematically. Everything related with the Ninth Sphere or the realization of the Self of the human being can be proven with numbers or esoteric mathematics, which come from remote epochs.

❦

Let us analyze the **first** vertical ternary:

1 = Monad

4 = Cross

7 = Septenary

One is the Monad, the unity, יהוה Iod-Heve or Jehovah, the Father who is in secret. It is the divine triad that is not incarnated within a Master who has not killed the ego. He is Osiris, the same God, the Word. He has his expression in the "4," because the four is the chariot, the Mercabah of Kabbalah, which is formed with the four bodies:

1. Physical Body

2. Authentic Solar Astral Body

3. Authentic Solar Mental Body

4. Authentic Solar Causal Body

This is the chariot of the centuries, which assumes the figure of the Heavenly Man. The Monad expresses Himself through the chariot. The Monad travels in it.

The four also represents the four points of the cross, in which are enclosed the mysteries of lingam-yoni. In the crossing of lingam-yoni is found the clue with which realization of the Self can be achieved. The Monad is Self-realized by means of the cross.

Without the four there is no realization of the Self, otherwise the law of the ternaries that belongs to esoteric mathematics would be violated.

4 = ☥

The mysteries of sex are contained within the four.

Masculine + Feminine = ☥

The self-realization of the Monad is verified in the septenary, the authentic Man. The septenary is complete when the seven principles are obtained: the seven christified bodies with the seven developed chakras and the arisen seven Serpents of Fire.

❦

Let us analyze the **second** vertical ternary:

2 = Divine Mother

5 = Intelligence

8 = Caduceus of Mercury

The two is Heve [הוה], the Divine Mother. It is the unfolded Father. Then, She is Brahma, because She is the feminine aspect of the Father.

י **Iod:** Monad

הוה **Heve:** Divine Mother

יהוה **Iod Heve:** Jehovah

The authentic Jehovah is our Father and our Divine Mother who are in secret.

The cruel Jehovah of the Jews is an anthropomorphization of the true Jehovah, which is within each one of us. Heve, the Divine Mother, expresses herself through intelligence, which is the number five. It is by means of her that the elimination of the ego is achieved, because true intelligence is within her. If the dissolution of the ego is requested, we have to appeal to the Divine Mother, by deeply comprehending our own errors and asking unto her for their elimination.

The Divine Mother manifests herself through the Holy Eight, or Caduceus of Mercury, which represents the dorsal spine, the ascending energy of Kundalini along the Shushumna canal.

The Holy Eight has its root in sex. The Holy Eight is the sign of the infinite. The relation of the numbers 2, 5 and 8 is extraordinary. The Caduceus of Mercury is found in the Ninth Sphere.

All of this wisdom was known among the Pythagorean Mysteries. It is known within Masonry; however, they are no longer being profound in these studies.

❦

Let us analyze the **third** vertical Ternary.

3 = Trinity

6 = Love, man and woman

9 = The Ninth Sphere

The number three corresponds to the Third Logos, the Holy Spirit. The Third Logos is in Himself the creative sexual force which expresses itself in the entire universe.

We labor by means of the number six, which is related with sex. Here we find the man and woman. In the Tarot, a man appears between vice and virtue, between the Virgin and the Harlot. The sexual force must be worked by means of the six, meaning with love. This has expression in the number nine, which is equivalent to the Ninth Sphere. The number nine is the number of the Master.

❦

The three triads or horizontal lines represent the **three worlds**.

Spiritual: Spirit

Psychic: Soul

Physical: Body

In this plate, the principles for the realization of the Self of the human being are contained.

Chapter LXX

The Number One (1)

The number one is the Sun, the Star King who gives us life. It corresponds to the constellation of Aries which governs the head. The musical note Do and the color white also correspond unto it. Its metal is gold and its precious stone is the diamond.

Among the plexuses, where the chakras are situated, the number one is attributed to the cardiac plexus, because if the heart stops functioning, death arrives. This is why this plexus is the number one. The number one is the wisdom of the Father; it is the Crown, because the Ancient of Days is the King, the one who has the power over nature. He is the number one because He has the power, because He is the one who commands.

Wisdom belongs to the Father; one cannot teach the Monad. The wisdom of the Father foresees everything.

We can become merciless if we fail to act with pity, because many times we do not understand the Father. He is the number one on the Kabbalistic Tree.

Original ideas correspond to the number one. It is obvious that they belong to the number one, which is willpower, personal initiative, and enterprising courage. The unity of thought and action must be one with the original will and with constancy, which is a formidable impulse for that which must be done.

Chapter LXXI
The Number Two (2)

The constellation of Taurus corresponds to the number two, which governs the neck where the creative larynx is found, that marvellous uterus where the Word, the Verb is gestated.

Its musical note is Re, its color is violet, its metal is silver, and its precious stone is emerald. The plexus which corresponds to it is the larynx, the thyroid gland, the chakra of the magic ear, clairaudience.

There is a laryngeal mantra in order to awaken this chakra; this is the vowel **E** which must be vocalized with the musical note Re. One has to vocalize this daily. The inhalation must be performed with the note Re, and the exhalation with the same note Re, as follows *Eeeeeeeeehhhhhhhhhhhhhhhh...* Thus, the development of the larynx chakra which grants us the power of hearing the voices of the ultra, the voices of the superior beings, is achieved. One has to develop this larynx chakra because otherwise it is impossible to hear those sounds.

The lymph glands and the stomach correspond to the number two, likewise does the Moon.

The number one unfolds itself into the duad. Number two in the first trimurti is its second aspect, who is the Christ. Do not confuse it with the second trimurti, where the Father unfolds into the Mother, and the Mother into the Child.

The number two of the Kabbalistic tree is the Son, Christ, who is the instructor of the World. This is why Hermes Trismegistus said, "I give you love, in which the summum of wisdom is contained."

The number two has thirty-two paths and fifty doors. The explanation for this is the following:

32 paths = 3 + 2 = 5 (the pentalpha, the human being)

50 doors = 5 + 0 = 5 (the pentalpha, the human being)

Let us add the results:

5 + 5 = 10

10 = 1 + 0 = 1

$$☽ = ☉$$

The masculine and feminine principles are within the 0, which is the foundation of love through sex.

☉ The Divine Mother, the Cosmic Mother

∞ Infinite

★ Pentalpha

5 + 5 = 10

This is reduced as:

☉ = ∞ = ★ = (the human being)

This matter about the fifty doors is very interesting. In one of the Gnostic rituals, it is written that a palace exists:

The floor of that palace is of silver and gold, lapis lazuli and jasper are there, and a variety of aromas of roses and jasmine are inhaled. But in the midst of everything a breeze of death is blown. Let the officiants penetrate or open the gates one by one or all the gates at once. Let them stand on the floor of the palace, it shall not sink. Woe to Thee, oh warrior, oh fighter, if thy servant sinks! But there are remedies and remedies.

Certainly, there is in the Superior Worlds a temple with fifty doors surrounded by the four elements—fire, earth, air and water—and it is guarded by two sphinxes of gold. The student receives instruction in this temple; each one of the rooms of the temple Kabbalistically corresponds to the fifty doors and thirty-two paths (the student sees his past lives).

The fifty doors are within oneself. Everything is within the human being.

Many years ago, at the beginning of a new year, when I consciously astral projected myself, I had to live a certain drama in the theater of the world. Being persecuted, I arrived to the temple of the fifty doors with its two sphinxes of gold guarding the doors. (We already studied the symbol of the face, legs of lion, etc., of the sphinx).

I entered the palace, which was surrounded by water, and I passed through a very beautiful garden, but a breath of death was there. I entered through one of the fifty doors, and there i was welcomed by a group of brothers who were applauding me; afterwards I left that room, and I penetrated into another beautiful garden that likewise had a breath of death. Then I entered through the second door, and those people who were congratulating me were now converted into traitors; they were screaming and slandering me. I kept silent, and I passed through another garden towards the other door; then I found other people who were congratulating me. I passed into another room, and other people appeared. Likewise, I passed all the fifty doors and followed the thirty-two paths, meaning I walked the internal path. Also, I found Masters who were dressed as executioners (they are executioners of the ego); they told me, "Study thee the ritual of life and death, while the Officiant arrives." The Officiant is my real Being.

With this event I have explained unto you the thirty-two paths and the fifty doors. This is the number two. All of this corresponds to the intimate Christ that has to be born in each one of us. He is love.

The number two is love, the suffering Christ, the one who has to live the whole drama.

In the number two there are two columns, Jachin and Boaz. There are associations. One has to learn to associate ideas, thoughts, people, things, relatives. One has to know how to listen to opposite opinions without being angry, to dissolve the "I" of anger, to cultivate harmony, in order for the associations to be harmonious.

The relationship of mother with son, woman with man, man with woman; relations with things, with antithesis, with opinions, are in the number two. One has to learn how to drive ideas and businesses with peace and serenity; this is the number two. One has to learn to handle the number two.

Chapter LXXII
The Number Three (3)

The zodiacal constellation of Gemini and the planet Jupiter correspond to the number three.

The musical note of the number three is Mi. Its color is purple. Its metal is tin. Its plexus is the splenic (spleen) and the hepatic (liver).

Transmutation of the creative energy corresponds to the number three. The splenic chakra is the center of the Ethereal Body. The life of the sun enters into our organism through this center.

During the night, the splenic chakra collects the energies left by the sun during the day. With those energies, the splenic chakra transmutes the white blood cells into red blood cells. During the day, the organic refuse obstructs the nervous canals of the grand sympathetic nervous system. During sleep, the vital energy makes that chakra spin, and this chakra uses the energy of the sun which passes into the spleen in order to transmute the white blood cells into red blood cells. Then the energy passes into the solar plexus and is distributed into the whole nervous system. The thyroid gland cooperates by disinfecting the whole organism. It is clear that when the ego (Lunar Astral) returns into the organism after sleep, it is already repaired, and we feel healthier. When one awakes tired, it is because the organism is sick.

The hepatic chakra serves for astral projection. The Astral Body is connected with the liver. By awakening the chakra of the liver, anybody can enter and exit the physical body at will.

The splenic, hepatic, and solar plexus can be developed with the Egyptian mantra **Fe-Uin-Dagt**. This mantra must be sung in the note Mi, then the three mentioned chakras and the lungs are developed.

The number three is power; it has fifty doors and fifty lights. We already know what the fifty doors signify. These doors must be searched for within oneself.

Fifty doors = 5 + 0 = 5 (the pentalpha, the human being)

Fifty lights = 5 + 0 = 5

Making the addition of 5 + 5 = 10

The number ten is the ten Sephiroth of Kabbalah: $10 + 10 = \bigoplus$, which is the symbol of the Divine Mother; the line in the middle of the circle is nothing but an extended point.

We have found that 10 = ★. We know that within the 10 is ∞, the creative energy. The Holy Spirit grants us the power, the power of sex, where the power of the Holy Spirit abides. Without that force, we do not have the sword, and without the sword we are unarmed.

It is stated that the law of Moses is contained within the number three, because the Holy Spirit is in the number three. The Holy Spirit is the one who illuminates us, the one who teaches us the law.

Wisdom: Father

Love: Son

Power: Holy Spirit

By looking at the practical aspect
of life, we find that the number three is
material and spiritual production. It is the
realization of our longings, aspirations,
and ideas.

If we want to be fruitful, to attain success, we have to handle the number three
with intelligence, because within the number three exists harmony, art, beauty.

Express everything in a beautiful way.

We have to use the number three with
the word or with what we wear if triumph
is what we wish to attain. The number
three permits the realization of our beloved
longings.

In order to attain triumph, we must
place a base for it and create favorable
conditions. If one day we get three as a key
note (it will be shown posteriorly), then we
must do things correctly, with precaution,
with beauty, with harmony, with perfection, and know how to create in order to
get what we long for that day, whether it is
in business, in our job or in anything.

Chapter LXXIII
The Number Four (4)

The number four is the tetrad. It corresponds with the planet Uranus, and it is clear that its constellation is Cancer, because it is the fourth constellation.

It is related to a dark red color, and its metal is platinum.

The musical note is Fa. The fluids correspond to the number four, as well as the hormones.

The number four is magnificence. It has seventy-two doors in order to administer justice, and it is administered through the thirty-five principles of mercy. We become magnificent in proportion to our procedures in accordance with each one of these principles.

Justice is administered in accordance with the thirty-five principles of mercy. Justice without mercy is tyranny.

Justice and mercy are perfectly equilibrated.

> Seventy-two doors = 7 + 2 = 9 (Ninth Sphere)

One cannot be just, not really just, if one has not reached the Second Birth. When one has passed through the Ninth Sphere, one receives the flaming sword, then it can be said that one is just. Whosoever has not worked in the Ninth Sphere has no right to have the sword of justice.

> Thirty-five principles of mercy: 3 + 5 = 8 (justice).

In the Eighth Arcanum, the woman has the sword of justice and a scale in order to weigh the good and evil deeds.

We must triumph over sex; the great archons of the law have triumphed over sex. Justice and mercy are equilibrated within them.

In the number four we find the skill of any branch, order, authority.

The number four is the Emperor of Kabbalah. It signifies stability. It is the base in order to get what we want, for instance in order to form our home, business, travel, employment, etc. To get what is solid, perfect as the Cubic Stone, a solid concrete stone is what is required for us. We must not put a false base, because otherwise everything will collapse on us.

If one day we get the key note four, then we have to have a strong base in order to have success. We have to do things correctly, precisely, solidly, in order not to fail. That day we must do things by reflecting on them in a precise and solid way. Nothing should be done quickly because we will fail.

The economic aspect is within the number four, and we must develop this in a correct way, because this aspect has ascensions and descents in its economy. There must be solid bases each time that ascension is needed. All things must be reflected on in relation to the number four. Let us think that the number four is the base, and that this base must be solid. We have to establish this base for family relations.

Chapter LXXIV

The Number Five (5)

The number five is the pentalpha, the star of five points. The planet Mercury corresponds unto it, as does Leo, the fifth constellation.

The solar plexus corresponds to this number, and, among the metals, Azoth (Mercury). Its musical note is Sol. It is related with bile. Esoterically, it corresponds with the planet Mars.

The number five in Kabbalah is the Hierophant, severity, the law. It is said that it has seventy-two accessible doors, and that each door has thirty-five principles. We are strong in proportion to our obedience of these principles. The number five is the living fire that is infused within us, and it is defused everywhere within us; this is the strength of the fire.

Let us analyze the seventy-two doors:
7 + 2 = 9 (Ninth Sphere)

Thirty-five principles: 3 + 5 = 8 (infinite)

The number nine is the Hermit, the Ninth Sphere, sex. In regard to the number eight, it is justice, which is represented by the sign of the infinite. The fire of Phlegethon and the water of Acheron are the fire and the water, origin of human beings, beasts, and Gods. Every authentic initiation starts here.

The Son of Man comes from the fire and the water, which is what gives us strength.

The number five is in itself the star of five points, the pentalpha, the human being. The authentic Human Being has to be born in the Ninth Sphere. To comprehend this is very important, because this is the "seventy-two doors," the Ninth Sphere where he is born, and it is the Ninth Sphere that gives potency to the Son of Man.

The thirty-five principles are justice, the law. The number five is corroboration.

The initiate, clothed in the robe of renunciation and penance, lifts the scale of equilibrium under a cloud of mystery, in order to balance the fire and water over the stone of sex, while guided by self-knowledge (the book).
Engraving from Tripus aureus by Michael Maier, 1618

The water and the fire are intercrossed in the Ninth Sphere and form the sign of the infinite, which is a horizontal eight.

Conclusion: $\infty = \star$

The great esotericist Ariano Montes, who abides in a monastery of Spain, gives us this formula: *infinite = pentalpha*. This formula also is found in ancient books. The Son of Man is born from the water and the fire in the Ninth Sphere, sex.

From the psychological point of view, the number five is persuasion, investigation, selection, comprehension.

We see that studying is within the number five. We have to know how to profoundly handle this number in a reflective and analytical way, by searching and inquiring about new aspects. One needs to analyze and to investigate. Nothing should be done in an nonreflective way, because things are done in the wrong way when these conditions are not fulfilled.

Therefore, one should not make projections, because then one fails. Those who waste their life by making projections, always fail. We have to see the pros and cons of anything in order for there not to be wrong actions. We must learn to think for ourselves. All of those who live by making projections fail. They fail because they are just making projections.

We must march forward based on facts and with intelligence in order not to make a blunder. From the abyss that exists between thoughts and facts, sometimes a projection is formed, but it does not become concrete.

We must not march with projections, but with facts. We have to march with facts, with intelligence, with wisdom, with comprehension; otherwise, we can have great failures. We must be alert.

The number five is also a symbol of power. We must do things with intelligence; we must be vigilant in order to not err.

Chapter LXXV
The Number Six (6)

The sixth constellation Virgo corresponds to the number six.

Its planet is Venus and its musical note is La.

It is related with the islets of Langerhans, which are in the pancreas. These Langerhans secrete insulin, which is very important for the digestion of sugar.

Its color is blue. Its plexus is the sacrum or coccyx, the chakra Muladhara. The number six is related with all the glands.

The number six has seventy-two doors on each side and seventy-two intermediate ones. The initiate who passes through those seventy-two doors can enter into the world of the crudest realities of life and into the Sidereal World.

The world of crude reality is the Ninth Sphere, because seventy-two doors = 7 + 2 = 9. If we comprehend what the seventy-two doors are, if we know what the Great Arcanum is, then we can enter into the world of the crude reality of life and into the Sidereal World, which is the Astral World.

It is very interesting that the number six has seventy-two doors on each side and seventy-two intermediate ones. We find the explanation in the star of King Solomon. In summary, we see that this star has twelve rays—six masculine and six feminine—which are decomposed in the twelve constellations of the zodiac. In this star are

masculine point

feminine indentation

summarized and synthesized the mysteries of the Arcanum A.Z.F., the mysteries of Alchemy, the mysteries of sex. This star is the symbol of the Logos.

Now that the number six is explained in a transcendental Kabbalistic way, you will understand for yourself how we enter into the world of crude reality through comprehension. That is why people are horrified when the Arcanum A.Z.F. is delivered in a shabby, explicit way. The teachings of the Ninth Sphere must be shown through Kabbalah in order for the people to know the truth.

The seventy-two doors that are placed from side to side are within Jachin and Boaz, and in the center of both columns, where the seventy-two intermediate doors are found, is where the mystery of the two columns is placed, which is the Brute Stone.

One must chisel the Brute Stone until making it perfect. If this Holy Six is placed together three times, then we get 666, which is the number of the Beast. If we add 6 + 6 + 6 = 18, eighteen is very tenebrous, it is Twilight, occult enemies, secret enemies.

The tenebrous ones attack terribly when one is working in the Great Work. The tenebrous do not like this and they look for the way to take the disciple off the path by attacking him terribly.

We find within the number six erotic volitions, ornamental ideas, reciprocity, fertility, amorousness.

Chapter LXXVI
The Number Seven (7)

The number seven is a very strong number. Its planet is Neptune and the constellation of Libra corresponds to it.

Its musical note is Si, bronze is its metal, and its stone is opal.

Its color is magenta (a blue color, almost violet, almost like steel). All the Nadis or nerve canals belong to this number.

The number seven is guarded by two hundred and forty-eight precepts. We will progress in proportion to our comprehension of these two hundred and forty-eight precepts. The Seventh Arcanum is Triumph, and the one who triumphs sees the Astral Light and is practically Self-realized.

If we add 248 into itself, we get 2 + 4 + 8 = 14, and 1 + 4 = 5.

The two hundred and forty-eight precepts are reduced to the Fourteenth Arcanum of Kabbalah, which is Temperance, a woman who mixes the two waters of two urns, meaning mixing the white elixir with the red elixir of life, of Alchemy; in other words, the work with the Sun and with the Moon, the work of transmutation.

The number five is the perfect Self-realized flaming star, but the number seven is the number of victory; it has two hundred and forty-eight precepts of an affirmative type. One has to comprehend the two hundred and forty-eight precepts in order to attain victory over oneself and to achieve seeing the Astral Light.

Here we find the effort of the soul, action, image, answer, or result. The number seven is the arcanum of victory; the two hundred and forty-eight precepts are reduced to the Fifth Arcanum, which is none other than the resplendence, the flaming star, the star of divinity.

The number seven is efficiency, integrity, concentration, clemency, longing for an ascendent life.

The Sun and Moon, through sexual cooperation, work with the fire and the water, aided by Neptune (the man with the trident, at right).
The Sixth Key of Basil Valentine, Engraving from Tripus aureus by Michael Maier, 1618

Chapter LXXVII

The Number Eight (8)

The number eight is the octad. Its planet is Saturn. Its constellation is the eighth, which corresponds to Scorpio.

Its metal is lead, and among the stones is the black onyx. The musical note is Do in the second octave.

The laws of evolution and devolution are contained in the number eight. Those who are attached to evolution violate the laws of the Holy Eight; they violate the laws of mathematics, because each evolution is followed by devolution. These two laws form the Holy Eight.

These two laws of evolution and devolution can not guide us into realization of the Self; we need the path of the consciousness for this. Everything in nature and the universe is mathematics.

The Holy Eight represents the brain, heart, and sex of the planetary Genie. We know already that the fight is terrible: brain against sex, sex against brain, heart against heart.

The Holy Eight has three hundred and sixty-five precepts; we must not violate these precepts.

$$3 + 6 + 5 = 14$$

$$1 + 4 = 5$$

Fourteen signifies Temperance. It is the mixture of the waters; it is the work with the white elixir and the red elixir.

When the fight of heart against heart is established, then the star of five points falls and remains with the two inferior angles aiming upwards.

The number eight is the primordial water, because it is situated in the Ninth Sphere, within the planetary brain.

The waters are transmuted into energy, and when they rise through Ida and Pingala until reaching the brain, they form the Caduceus of Mercury, the Holy Eight.

One has to learn how to distinguish between a *descent* and a *downfall*. No one can ascend without previously descending. This is the Law.

Upon the supreme disobedience of Adam the supreme obedience of Christ was superimposed, but Christ had to descend.

Always when we want to ascend, we must descend, otherwise we remain stagnant. One can leave that stagnation only by descending, but let us distinguish between a downfall and a descent.

The number eight is moderation, the Caduceus, distribution with justice.

Chapter LXXVIII
The Number Nine (9)

The number nine is the enneagon; it is the Ninth Sphere. It is related with Mars in the Ninth Sphere. Here one begins a fight within oneself against everything, against nature, because here in the Ninth Sphere, demons and Gods are made.
One must descend into the depth of the Infernos in order to build the Solar Bodies.

The ninth constellation, Sagittarius, corresponds to the number nine. Its metal is iron, its stone is the carbuncle, its color is red, its musical note is Re in the second octave.

The coronary plexus corresponds to the number nine, as well as the creative organs, the gonads.

The work in the Ninth Sphere has an objective: to create the Solar Bodies. One has to comprehend that even when an individual has built the bodies, immortality has not been achieved as a result.

In order to gain immortality, to have worked in the dissolution of the ego is needed, because otherwise one is converted into a Hanasmuss with a double center of gravity. These are abortions of the Cosmic Mother who enter into the Infernal Worlds till reaching the Second Death.

It is necessary to achieve the elimination of the ego and the three traitors. One realizes what the ego and the three traitors are when one reaches 100% consciousness.

The red demons of Seth must be reduced to cosmic dust. It is necessary to verify absolute death, because if some subjective element remains alive, then the deceased is called to order.

Those who have died in themselves are received in the world of the dead.

To the number nine belongs emotion, wisdom, generosity, geniality.

Finally, we have zero, which is eternity, the Universal Spirit of life.

One has to operate with all of the numbers in Kabbalah.

The number is holy, infinite and eternal.

He that hath an ear, let him hear what the Spirit saith unto the churches; to him that overcometh will I give to eat of the tree of life, which is in the midst of the paradise of God. - Revelation 2: 7

Chapter LXXIX

The Seven Churches of the Apocalypse of Saint John and Their Relation with the Kabbalistic Tree

The first church, called Ephesus or chakra Muladhara, has four marvellous petals which are situated in the coccygeal bone. The coccyx is the base-bone of the dorsal spine (everything related with the seven churches or chakras is found in the books *The Aquarian Message* and *Kundalini Yoga: The Mysteries of Fire*).

The second church of Smyrna or chakra Svadhisthana is situated at the level of the prostate (uterus in the woman); it is the prostatic or uterine chakra. The ancient Persians and Egyptian magicians gave a lot of importance to the prostate. The letter which makes this chakra vibrate is the **M**, it is pronounced with closed lips by increasing and decreasing the tone of the sound. The M is of a singular power; the magicians utilize it.

The third church of Pergamos or chakra Manipura is situated in the solar plexus, the umbilical chakra. It has ten petals; five are active in the Ethereal Body and the other five are latent in the telepathic center. Here we find the Emotional Brain, and when this chakra is developed, telepathy is achieved.

The fourth church of Thyatira or chakra Anahata is situated in the heart, the cardias. It is a lotus flower that has twelve petals which blazingly shine within the Astral Light. It is good to develop this chakra in order to learn how to enter and exit from the physical body at will. Moreover, with this chakra developed, to travel with the body of flesh and bones

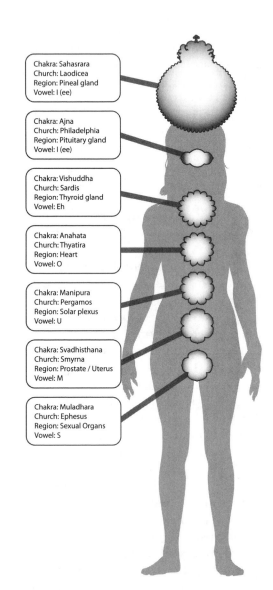

Chakra: Sahasrara
Church: Laodicea
Region: Pineal gland
Vowel: I (ee)

Chakra: Ajna
Church: Philadelphia
Region: Pituitary gland
Vowel: I (ee)

Chakra: Vishuddha
Church: Sardis
Region: Thyroid gland
Vowel: Eh

Chakra: Anahata
Church: Thyatira
Region: Heart
Vowel: O

Chakra: Manipura
Church: Pergamos
Region: Solar plexus
Vowel: U

Chakra: Svadhisthana
Church: Smyrna
Region: Prostate / Uterus
Vowel: M

Chakra: Muladhara
Church: Ephesus
Region: Sexual Organs
Vowel: S

within the fourth dimension while in Jinn state is easy.

The fifth church of Sardis or chakra Vishuddha is situated in the thyroid gland. This is the chakra of the larynx, which grants us clairaudience. It has sixteen petals.

The sixth church of Philadelphia or chakra Ajna is situated between the eyebrows. This is the frontal chakra. It has two petals. Here we find the center of clairvoyance. The aura of people and the Superior Worlds can be seen with it.

The seventh church of Laodicea or chakra Sahasrara is the king of the chakras. This chakra has one thousand petals. It is the center of polyvoyance, the center of intuition, the Diamond Eye.

Each one of the chakras of the Nadi Chitra is awakened while the Kundalini is ascending in the Brahmanadi along the spinal medulla. The igneous serpent is related in Kabbalah with the whole Kabbalistic tree.

What do we need in order to awaken the chakras?

The principal point in the first church of Ephesus is the virtue of **patience**. In order to handle the creative energy, what is required is the patience of Saint Job. Lucifer is a ladder to descend, and Lucifer is a ladder to ascend.

Chastity is the virtue of the second church of Smyrna.

The third chakra is the umbilical chakra or the center of emotions. Then, the special virtue for this is the **control of emotions**, to kill desires, passions, like gluttony, drunkenness, etc. You must be temperate, to not allow emotions to drive you.

The fourth chakra is in the heart; this is the center of love. One has to know how to **love**, to not hate. The foundation of this chakra is love.

The fifth church is Sardis. It is related with the intellect, the mind. One must take care of the **Word**, the Verb; just thought, just word, and just action, upright thought, upright feeling, and upright action. Take care of the mind and of the word. It is just as wrong to speak when one has to be silent as it is to be silent when one has to speak. Sometimes it is a crime to speak, as well as it is sometimes a crime to become silent. There exist criminal silent attitudes.

In the sixth church one needs **serenity** in order to have clairvoyance. In order to see in the Internal Worlds, one has to not allow oneself to be driven by anger, because anger destroys the frontal chakra. Therefore, serenity is required.

Heightened **devotion**, complete **sanctity**, and **willpower** are needed in order for the development of the seventh church.

Virtues and qualities are related with the Kabbalistic tree, with its ten numbers and its correlation with the seven churches.

Chapter LXXX

Kabbalah and the Year One Was Born

We now continue with mathematics. Our entire life develops with mathematics. The law of Karma develops with numbers.

First Example: Eduardo del Portillo. Date of birth, the year 1932.

One adds vertically the year one was born, into the same year, beginning with the last digit.

$$
\begin{array}{r}
1932 \\
1 \\
9 \\
3 \\
+ \quad 2 \\
\hline
1947
\end{array}
$$

1 + 9 + 4 + 7 = **21**
See Arcanum #21

21 = 2 + 1 = **3**
See Arcanum #3

$$
\begin{array}{r}
1947 \\
1 \\
9 \\
4 \\
+ \quad 7 \\
\hline
1968
\end{array}
$$

1 + 9 + 6 + 8 = **24**
See Arcanum #24

24 = 2 + 4 = **6**
The enamoured met his fiancee in 1968.

$$
\begin{array}{r}
1968 \\
1 \\
9 \\
6 \\
+ \quad 8 \\
\hline
1992
\end{array}
$$

1 + 9 + 9 + 2 = **21**
See Arcanum #21

21 = 2 + 1 = **3**
Marks a spiritual and economic triumph that year, do not forget it.

Second Example: Arturo Aguirre. Date of birth, the year 1937.

$$
\begin{array}{r}
1937 \\
1 \\
9 \\
3 \\
+ \quad 7 \\
\hline
1957
\end{array}
$$

1 + 9 + 5 + 7 = **22** = 2 + 2 = **4**
Success in the material plane.

$$
\begin{array}{r}
1957 \\
1 \\
9 \\
5 \\
+ \quad 7 \\
\hline
1979
\end{array}
$$

1 + 9 + 7 + 9 = **26** = 2 + 6 = **8**
Tests and pains; have the patience of Job.

THIRD EXAMPLE: Luis Perez, year 1920.

$$
\begin{array}{r}
1920 \\
1 \\
9 \\
2 \\
+ \quad 0 \\
\hline
1932
\end{array}
$$

$1 + 9 + 3 + 2 = \mathbf{15} = 1 + 5 = \mathbf{6}$

The six did affect the heart, the senti-ments; the six is related with the moral part of ourselves; that year his father died and that was very serious.

$$
\begin{array}{r}
1932 \\
1 \\
9 \\
3 \\
+ \quad 2 \\
\hline
1947
\end{array}
$$

$1 + 9 + 4 + 7 = \mathbf{21} = 2 + 1 = \mathbf{3}$

Material and spiritual production

$$
\begin{array}{r}
1947 \\
1 \\
9 \\
4 \\
+ \quad 7 \\
\hline
1968
\end{array}
$$

$1 + 9 + 6 + 8 = \mathbf{24}$

The Weaver. He became entangled in his own weaving, sufferings from which he has not been able to emerge.

$24 = 2 + 4 = \mathbf{6}$

The Lover

4TH EXAMPLE: Nicolas Naranjo. Date of birth, 1946.

$$
\begin{array}{r}
1946 \\
1 \\
9 \\
4 \\
+ \quad 6 \\
\hline
1966
\end{array}
$$

$1 + 9 + 6 + 6 = \mathbf{22} = 2 + 2 = \mathbf{4}$

Success because he found Gnosis.

$$
\begin{array}{r}
1966 \\
1 \\
9 \\
6 \\
+ \quad 6 \\
\hline
1988
\end{array}
$$

$1 + 9 + 8 + 8 = \mathbf{26} = 2 + 6 = \mathbf{8}$

He will continue working with success.

Chapter LXXXI

Inner Urgency

The Inner Urgency is calculated by Kabbalistically adding the date of birth, the day, month and year.

FIRST EXAMPLE: Victor Manuel Chavez, November 17, 1921

Day: $17 = 1 + 7 = $ **8**
Month: $11 = 1 + 1 = $ **2**
Year: $1921 = 1 + 9 + 2 + 1 = 13 = $
$1 + 3 = $ **4**

$$
\begin{array}{r}
8 \\
2 \\
+ \quad 4 \\
\hline
\mathbf{14} = 1 + 4 = \mathbf{5}
\end{array}
$$

The Fifth Arcanum of the Tarot is rigor, study, science, analysis, investigation, intellect. This Inner Urgency shows him to be a reasoner.

SECOND EXAMPLE: Mr. Rodriguez, 5th of June, 1905

Day: **5**
Month: **6**
Year: $1905 = 1 + 9 + 0 + 5 = 15 = $
$1 + 5 = $ **6**

$$
\begin{array}{r}
5 \\
6 \\
+ \quad 6 \\
\hline
17 = 1 + 7 = \mathbf{8}
\end{array}
$$

The eight makes us patient, passive, energetic, just, upright. There have been sufferings, struggles, studies for him; he has had to pass through many tests.

THIRD EXAMPLE: Eduardo del Portillo, 5th of July, 1932

Day: **5**
Month: **7**
Year: $1932 = 1 + 9 + 3 + 2 = 15 = $
$1 + 5 = $ **6**

$$
\begin{array}{r}
5 \\
7 \\
+ \quad 6 \\
\hline
18 = 1 + 8 = \mathbf{9}
\end{array}
$$

The Ninth Sphere; the Hermit, amidst everyone searches for the Light and will produce great genial works. Developing a great energy has made him a hermit on the path of existence.

Chapter LXXXII
Fundamental Keynote

The Fundamental Keynote is the Inner Urgency added to the Kabbalistic sum of the number of the letters of the complete name.

FIRST EXAMPLE: Victor Manuel Chavez Caballero, Inner Urgency: 5

Victor Manuel Chavez Caballero
6   6   6   9

$6 + 6 + 6 + 9 = 27 = 2 + 7 = 9$

$9 + 5 = 14$

$14 = 1 + 4 = 5$ = Fundamental Keynote

SECOND EXAMPLE: Federico Lauro Arce Heredia, Inner Urgency: 8

Federico Lauro Arce Heredia
8   5   4   7

$8 + 5 + 4 + 7 = 24 = 2 + 4 = 6$

$6 + 8 = 14$

$14 = 1 + 4 = 5$

Fundamental Keynote 5: He always lives thinking, reasoning, analyzing.

THIRD EXAMPLE: Margarita Garcia Sancho Fernandez, Inner Urgency: 5

Margarita Garcia Sancho Fernandez
9   6   6   9

$9 + 6 + 6 + 9 = 30 = 3 + 0 = 3$

$3 + 5 = 8$

Fundamental Keynote 8: Tests and pain, a number of reflection, advice, comprehension, analysis, patience, tests.

Chapter LXXXIII

Keynote of the Day

The Keynote of the day is calculated adding the Fundamental Keynote to the Kabbalistic sum of the date that we have chosen. By means of this system one knows how it will be, so that one can know how to act that day.

FIRST EXAMPLE: Victor Manuel Chavez, Fundamental Keynote: 5. Date: April 30, 1969.

Day: 30 = 3 + 0 = **3**
Month: **4**
Year: 1969 = 1 + 9 + 6 + 9 = 25 = 2 + 5 = **7**

3 + 4 + 7 = 14 = 1 + 4 = **5**

5 + 5 (Fundamental Keynote) = **10**

10 = 1 + 0 = **1**: Keynote of April 30, 1969.
10 is the Wheel of Fortune, change. 1 is initiative, what begins, what starts, originality, effort.

SECOND EXAMPLE: Mr. Guillermo Hickie, Fundamental Keynote: 8. Keynote of May 1, 1969:

Day: **1**
Month: **5**
Year: 1969 = 1 + 9 + 6 + 9 = 25 = 2 + 5 = **7**

1 + 5 + 7 = 13 (Death) = 1 + 3 = 4

4 + 8 (Fundamental Keynote) = **12**
12 = 1 + 2 = **3**: Keynote of May 1, 1969.

3 is what is artistic, the three primary forces, material as well as spiritual production. Production, multiplication, what is lovely, what is creative, harmony, art, beauty.

THIRD EXAMPLE: Mr. Gil, Fundamental Keynote 3. Date: July 27, 1969.

Day: 27 = 2 + 7 = **9**
Month: **7**
Year: 1969 = 1 + 9 + 6 + 9 = 25 = 2 + 5 = **7**

9 + 7 + 7 = 23 = 2 + 3 = **5**

5 + 3 (Fundamental Keynote) = **8**

8 is tests, sorrows; one has to multiply patience, cooperation. One has to know how to wait, reflect, be serious in thought, distinguish between what is more useful and less useful, between what is and what is not. Do not do things rashly, scrutinize the pros and cons with patience. Every one of the numbers of the Kabbalah has to be studied in depth.

Chapter LXXXIV
Event of the Day

One has to know how to choose with exactness the hour of the day or night to carry out successfully any activity. One can choose an hour, a day, a month, a year for his particular activities. Conventionalisms are not considered, for example, one should not use the twenty-first hour, but the ninth hour. *(Note: Do not calculate using the twenty-four hour clock. 9:00 pm would render as 9, not 21.)*

First Example: Victor Manuel Chavez.

> Birthdate: 11/17/1921
> Inner Urgency: 5
> Fundamental Keynote: 5
> Date to investigate: May 14, 1969
> Hour of event: 9 A.M.

Day: 14 = 1 + 4 = **5**
Month: **5**
Year: 1969 = 1 + 9 + 6 + 9 = 25 = 2 + 5 = **7**

5 + 5 + 7 = 17 = 1 + 7 = **8**

8 + 5 (Fundamental Keynote) = 13 = 1 + 3 = **4**: Keynote of 5/14/1969
With 4 one has to know how to complete business matters, details of any activity. The most interesting hour of that day was 9 in the morning.

4 (Keynote of the day) + 9 (time) = 13
13 = 1 + 3 = **4**
At this hour he had to take care of a job-related matter and it went well for him. 4 is the base, it is to know how to complete matters.

Second Example: Mrs. Margarita Sancho Fernandez

> Birth date: November 4, 1943
> Inner Urgency: 5
> Fundamental Key-note: 8
> Date to investigate: June 13, 1969
> Time of event: 11:00 pm

Day: **4**
Month: **6**
Year: 1969 = 1 + 9 + 6 + 9 = 25 = 2 + 5 = **7**

4 + 6 + 7 = 17 = 1 + 7 = **8**

8 + 8 (Fundamental Keynote) = 16
16 = 1 + 6 = **7**: Keynote 6/13/1969
One has to do battle so as to not fall; energy should be directed intelligently. Struggle in order to rise. 16 is the Fulminated Tower.

The event of the day is at 11 at night.

11 = 1 + 2 = **2**

2 + 7 (Keynote of the day) = **9**:
Event of the day. The event of the day is to work with the Ninth Sphere.

With regard to the astrological hours I have to dissent with many Kabbalists, because they believe that the Inner Urgency is governed by certain planets, certain hours, but keep in mind that the order of the calendar is altered, because this was convenient for the priests.

The modern calendar is adulterated. The priests of the Middle Ages altered it with the goal of making Sunday the seventh day. The real calendar is:

#	Present	Authentic	Planet
1	Sunday	Monday	Moon
2	Monday	Wednesday	Mercury
3	Tuesday	Friday	Venus
4	Wednesday	Sunday	Sun
5	Thursday	Tuesday	Mars
6	Firday	Thursday	Jupiter
7	Saturday	Saturday	Saturn

This is the most ancient order because it is the order of the worlds of the solar system.

The Kabbalists get tangled up, and if to that mess is added an adulterated calendar, when they choose an hour and specific day to act, it will not work, it will not yield results because it is adulterated.

Mathematics is very exact.

We should learn to utilize the hours. With this system, the exactness of deeds is proven. This subject of mathematics is very important in Kabbalah.

The true astral clock is found by applying the twenty-two arcana to the hours of the day.

Fifth Part

Predictive Kabbalah

"Hear; for I will speak of excellent things; and the opening of my lips shall be right things. For my mouth shall speak truth; and wickedness is an abomination to my lips. All the words of my mouth are in righteousness; there is nothing twisted or perverse in them. They are all plain to him that understandeth and right to them that find knowledge." - Proverbs 8:6-9

Chapter LXXXV

Preparation

The most elevated kind of clairvoyance that exists in the universe is Supraconsciousness. All of the Avatars or Messengers from the Superior Worlds have been supracognizant clairvoyants. Hermes Trismegistus, Rama, Krishna, Buddha, Jesus Christ, etc., were Supracognizant Beings, messengers from the Superior Worlds, initiators of new eras of historic evolution.

Imagination, **Inspiration,** and **Intuition** are the three obligatory ways of initiation. We are going to examine each one of the three steps seperately.

Let us begin with:

Imagination

For the wise, to imagine is to see. **Imagination** is the translucence of the soul.

What is important is to learn to **concentrate** thought on one thing only.

Whosoever learns to think on only one thing makes marvels and prodigies.

The disciple that wants to reach Imaginative Knowledge must learn to concentrate himself and know how to profoundly meditate.

The best exercise in order to attain imaginative knowledge is the following. While seated in front of a plant, we concentrate on it until forgetting everything which is not related with it. Then by closing the eyes we become drowsy, and we keep in our imagination the form and figure of the plant, its structure, perfume and color.

The disciple will imagine the living cells of the plant. The disciple must provoke drowsiness during these practices. The disciple, while in drowsiness, will profoundly meditate on the internal constitution of the plant. It possesses protoplasm, membrane and nucleus. The protoplasm is a viscous, elastic and transparent substance, similar to the egg white (albuminoid matter). The disciple, while in drowsiness, must reflect upon the four fundamental elements in the protoplasm of the cell of the plant. These four elements are carbon, oxygen, hydrogen and nitrogen. The membrane is a marvellous substance without color, a substance within which the water becomes totally insoluble. This substance is the well-known cellulose.

The disciple, while concentrated, will imagine the nucleus of the cell as a small corpuscle, where the great universal life palpitates. The nuclear filament is within the nucleus, as well as the nuclear juice and the nucleolus which are all covered by the nuclear membrane. The nucleolus is formed by corpuscles infinitely full of shining beauty. These are residual products of the incessant reactions of the plant organism.

The disciple, while well-concentrated, must imagine with complete logical precision all of those mineral substances and organic combinations that are harmoniously unfolding within the cellular protoplasm of the plant. Let us think on the grains of starch and on the portentous chlorophyll, without which it is impossible to reach perfect organic synthesis. The chlorophyll is presented in granulated form (*chloro-leucite*) as a very beautiful yellow color (*santofilia*) that becomes that precious green color of the plant while under the solar rays.

Every plant is a perfect cellular community with incalculable perfections. The student must meditate on the perfection of the plant and in all of its scientific processes that are full of mystic attitudes and are enchanted with beauty.

The mystic is in rapture when remembering all of the phenomena of nutrition, relation and reproduction of each cell of the plant.

Let us see the chalice of the flower. Here are its sexual organs, here is the pollen, the masculine reproductive element. Here is the pistil or gynecium, a very precious feminine organ, with its ovary, stylus and stigma. The ovary is a sack full of marvellous ovums. The stamen can occupy different positions in relation with the pistil, for instance insertion beneath the ovary, insertion around the ovary, or above it.

Fecundation is verified with the function of the feminine germs and masculine gametes. After exiting the anther, the pollen, the masculine gamete, reaches the ovary of the plant where the ovum, the feminine gamete, is waiting anxiously.

The seed is the precious and enchanted ovum that after being fecundated is transformed and grows. Now the student should remember the step on which he is meditating. A sprout will emerge as a delicate bud, imagine it growing slowly, until seeing it with your imagination spreading branches, leaves and flowers. Remember that everything that is born must die. Imagine the plant's process of dying. Its flowers wither its leaves dry and the wind blows them away. Finally, only a few twigs remain.

This process of birth and death is marvellous. By meditating on the whole process of birth and death of a plant, by meditating on its marvellous life, if the concentration is perfect, and the drowsiness achieves a profound level, then the chakras of the Astral Body will spin, develop and unfold.

Meditation must be correct. The mind must be exact. Logical thought and exact concept is needed for the purpose of developing the internal senses absolutely perfectly.

Every incoherence, every lack of logical and moral equilibrium obstructs and damages the evolution and progress of the chakras, disks, or lotus flowers of the Astral Body. The student needs a lot of patience, willpower, tenacity and absolute conscious faith. On any given day, within dreams, while in meditation, a distant picture, a landscape of nature, a feature, etc., emerges. This is a sign that there is progress. The student elevates himself little by little into the Imaginative Knowledge. The student is removing the veil of Isis little by little. On any given day, the plant on which he was meditating disappears. Then, a beautiful child who replaces the plant is seen. That child is the elemental of the plant, the soul of the plant.

Later, during a dream, he awakens his consciousness; then he can say: "I am in the Astral Body." The consciousness awakens little by little. In this way, the moment in which the disciple will acquire continuous consciousness arrives.

When the student enjoys continuous consciousness he no longer dreams; he can no longer dream, because his consciousness is awakened. Then, even when the physical body is sleeping, he moves himself consciously in the Superior Worlds.

Exact meditation awakens the internal senses and performs a complete transformation of the internal bodies.

Whosoever awakens consciousness has reached Imaginative Knowledge. He moves in the world of symbolic images.

The symbols that one saw while he was dreaming are now seen without dreaming; before, he was seeing them with a sleeping consciousness. Now he moves himself among them with a vigilant consciousness, even when his physical body is profoundly asleep. When the student reaches Imaginative Knowledge, he sees the symbols but he does not understand them. He comprehends that all of Nature is a living scripture that he does not know. The student needs to elevate himself into Inspired Knowledge in order to interpret the sacred symbols of great Nature.

Inspiration

Let us now study **Inspiration**. Inspired Knowledge grants us the power of interpreting the symbols of great Nature. The interpretation of symbols is very delicate. Many clairvoyants have become homicidal or have fallen into the crime of public slander because of not knowing how to interpret symbols.

Symbols must be analyzed coldly without superstition, maliciousness, mistrust, pride, vanity, fanaticism, prejudgment, preconceptions, hatred, envy, greed, jealousy, etc. All defects belong to the "I," to the "myself," to the reincarnating ego.

When the "I" interferes by translating and interpreting symbols, then it alters the meaning of the secret scriptures and the clairvoyant falls into a crime which can conduct him to jail.

Interpretation must be tremendously analytical, highly scientific and essentially mystical. One has to learn how to see and how to interpret in the absence of the "I," of the "myself."

It seems very strange to many mystics that we the brothers and sisters of the international Gnostic Movement speak of divine clairvoyance with the penal code in hand. Those that think in this way consider spirituality as something that has nothing to do with our relationship to daily life. These people act wrongly, they are mistaken. They ignore that what each soul is in the Superior Worlds is the exact result of the daily life that everyone of us lives in this valley of tears.

If our words, thoughts, and actions are not just, then the result appears in the Internal Worlds and the law falls upon us.

The law is the law; to be ignorant of the law does not mean the exclusion of its fulfilment. The worst sin is ignorance. To teach unto the one that does not know is a work of mercy. The whole tremendous responsibility of the law falls upon the clairvoyant.

One has to interpret symbols of the great Nature in the absolute absence of the "I." Nonetheless, self-criticism must be multiplied, because when the "I" of the clairvoyant believes he knows a lot, then he feels himself infallible, omniscient, wise and even supposes that he sees and interprets with the absence of the "I." These types of clairvoyants fortify the "I" so much that they end up converting themselves into terribly perverse demons. When a clairvoyant of this type sees his inner God, then he interprets the vision in accordance with his tenebrous criteria, and exclaims: "I am doing well."

We have to know how to interpret basing ourselves on the law of philosophical analogies, on the law of correspondences and on the numerical Kabbalah.

We recommend *The Mystical Kabbalah* by Dion Fortune. This book is marvellous, study it.

One that has hatred, resentment, jealousy, envy, pride, etc., does not achieve elevation of himself to the second step called Inspired Knowledge.

When we elevate ourselves to Inspired Knowledge, we understand and comprehend that the accidental accumulation of objects does not exist. Really, all phenomena of nature and all objects are found intimately and organically joined together, internally dependent upon each other and mutually conditioning each other. Really, no phenomena of nature can be integrally comprehended if we consider it isolated.

Everything is in incessant movement. Everything changes, nothing is quiet. In every object the internal struggle exists. An object is positive and negative at the same time. Quantitative transforms itself into qualitative. Evolution is a process of the complication of energy.

Inspired knowledge permits us to know the inner relationship between everything which is, has been, and will be.

Matter is nothing but condensed energy. The infinite modifications of energy are absolutely unknown, as much as for historic materialism as for dialectic materialism.

Energy is equal to mass by the velocity of the light squared. We the Gnostics separate ourselves from the two antithesis of ignorance, and we integrally study man and nature.

Life is every determined and determinant energy. Life is object and subject at the same time.

The disciple that wants to reach the Inspired Knowledge must concentrate profoundly on music. *The Magic Flute* of Mozart reminds us of an Egyptian initiation. The nine symphonies of Beethoven and many other great classical compositions elevate us to the Superior Worlds.

The disciple, profoundly concentrated in the music, must observe himself within it, as the bee within the honey, which is the product of his whole labor.

When the disciple has already reached Inspired Knowledge, he must then prepare himself for Intuitive Knowledge.

Intuition

The world of **Intuition** is the world of mathematics. The student that wants to elevate himself to the world of Intuition must be a mathematician, or at least must have notions of arithmetic.

Mathematical formulas grant us intuitive knowledge.

The student must concentrate himself on a mathematical formula and profoundly meditate on it. Afterwards, he must empty the mind and make it completely blank, then simply wait for the Inner Being to teach the contained concept which is enclosed in the mathematical formula. For example, before Kepler publicly announced his famous principle that "the square of the period of revolution of a planet varies directly as the distance from the sun cubed," that formula already existed; it was contained in the solar system, even when the wise did not know it.

The student can mentally concentrate himself on that formula. He must empty his mind, become drowsy with his mind completely blank, and wait for his own inner Being to reveal to him all of the marvellous secrets which are contained in the formula of Kepler.

The formula of Newton concerning universal gravity can also serve us in order to exercise ourselves in initiation. This formula is the following. "The force between two objects varies directly with each of the masses and inversely with the square of the distance between them."

If the student practices with tenacity and supreme patience, his own inner Being will teach or instruct him in the Great Work. Then he will study at the feet of the Master and he will elevate himself to Intuitive Knowledge. Imagination, Inspiration, and Intuition are obligatory steps of initiation. Whosoever has raised the three steps of direct knowledge has reached Supraconsciousness.

In the world of Intuition, we find only omniscience; the world of Intuition is the world of the Being; it is the world of the Innermost.

In this world the "I," the "myself," the ego, cannot enter.

The world of Intuition is the universal spirit of life.

The world of Imaginative Knowledge is a world of symbolic images.

Inspiration grants us the power of interpreting symbols.

In the world of Intuition, we see the great cosmic theater and we are the spectators. We assist in the great drama of life. In the world of Intuition, the whole drama, which is represented in cosmic scenes, is reduced to terrible arithmetical operations. This is the amphitheatrum of cosmic science.

From that region of mathematics we see that physical masses exist that are above and below all of the limits of external sensory perceptions. Those masses are invisible. We can perceive them only with clairvoyance.

Matter is condensed energy. When its vibration is very slow, its mass is beneath the limits of external sensorial perceptions. When its vibratory movement is very fast, then the mass is above the limits of external sensory perceptions. With the telescope, we can only see worlds whose degree of vibration is active within the limits of external sensory perception.

Above and below the limits of external sensory perceptions there exist worlds, solar systems, and constellations populated by many types of living beings.

The so-called matter is only energy that condenses into infinite masses.

The senses of external perception only reach a fraction of what is perceivable.

Dialectic materialism and metaphysics are untimely and antiquated.

We the brothers and sisters of the Gnostic Movement go in a distinct way.

It is urgent that scientists study *The Treatise of Occult Science* by Dr. Rudolf Steiner, great Hungarian medic, born in 1861, friend and disciple of Nietzsche and Ernest Hegel, and the founder of the Anthroposophical Society.

It is indispensable that those who are lovers of science investigate in depth the whole portentous oriental wisdom, poured as a river of gold in the immortal pages of *The Secret Doctrine*. This work consists of six volumes and is a monument of the archaic wisdom. The great master H.P.B. is the genius author of this precious treasury of the ancient wisdom.

Those who reach Supraconsciousness convert themselves into true illuminated clairvoyants. No authentic clairvoyant boasts about his faculties.

No legitimate clairvoyant says that he is a clairvoyant.

When a true clairvoyant sees something important, he gives his concepts in a very cultured way and with supreme respect for others. He never says, "I am seeing." He always says. "We understand, we have learned." This is how all of those that have reached the ineffable summits of Supraconsciousness distinguish themselves by their gentility, humbleness and modesty.

You should read *Kundalini Yoga* by Sivananda. Meditate on the blessed White Lodge. Inquire within the Gnostic treasuries. Meditate on the profound symbolism contained in each one of the arcana of the Tarot.

Those who reach the heights of Supraconsciousness enter into the amphitheater of cosmic science.

The triple way of science, philosophy, and revolutionary cosmic mysticism conducts us into the ineffable regions of the great Light.

Gnosis is highly scientific, highly philosophical and transcendentally mystical.

Note: This chapter is a transcription of Chapter 22 of the book *Fundamental Notions of Endocrinology and Criminology*, in order for the disciple to complete his preparation for using the Kabbalah of prediction with complete purity, which is the indispensable requirement. He can also study the seventeenth chapter "Esoteric Discipline of the Mind" from the book *Igneous Rose,* which is the complement of this present chapter. You must profoundly meditate on the number of this chapter (85) and on its Kabbalistic additions. Enquire with the most profound part of your soul, for herein is found the clue to the preparation needed for the Kabbalah of prediction. $85 = 8 + 5 = 13 = 1 + 3 = 4$. 8 = Patience, 5 = Intelligence, 13 = mystical death, 3 = the work with the Divine Mother, 1- = Willpower, 4 = The work with the Cross, with sex.

Chapter LXXXVI

Prediction and Synthesis

Arcanum 1 **The Magician**
Man. Sword, willpower.

Arcanum 2 **The Priestess**
The wife of the Magician. Occult science. Favorable.

Arcanum 3 **The Empress**
The Divine Mother. Material and spiritual production.

Arcanum 4 **The Emperor**
Command, progress, success, mercy.

Arcanum 5 **The Hierarch**
Rigor, the law. Karma, Mars, war.

Arcanum 6 **Indecision**
The Lover. Victory, good luck.

Arcanum 7 **Triumph**
The Chariot of War. Wars, struggles, atonement, pain, bitterness.

Arcanum 8 **Justice**
The Arcanum of Job. Sufferings, tests, pains.

Arcanum 9 **The Hermit**
Initiation. Solitude, sufferings.

Arcanum 10 **Retribution**
The Wheel of Fortune. Good business, changes.

Arcanum 11 **Persuasion**
The tame lion. Favor of the law. Let there be no fear. Mars.

Arcanum 12 **The Apostolate**
Sacrifice. Tests and pains. The Arcanum A.Z.F. takes us out of pain.

Arcanum 13 **Immortality**
Death and resurrection. Transformations, indicates total change.

Arcanum 14 **Temperance**
Marriage, association. Longevity, stability, no change.

Arcanum 15 **Passion**
Typhon Baphomet. Failure in love. Announces dangers.

Arcanum 16 **Fragility**
The Fulminated Tower. Punishment, terrible fall. Avoid this date.

Arcanum 17 **Hope**
The Star of Hope. Signifies to hope and wait.

Arcanum 18 **Twilight**
Occult enemies. Hidden enemies jump out at any moment. Illnesses, no business.

Arcanum 19 **Inspiration**
The radiant Sun. Success, good luck, the Philosophical Stone.

Arcanum 20 **Resurrection**
The resurrection of the dead. Favorable changes, take advantage of them. Put an end to weaknesses.

Arcanum 21 **Transmutation**
The Fool, madness. Total demoralization towards evil. The magic key, the rune Olin. Antithesis, enemies of Hiram Abiff.

Arcanum 22 **The Return**
The truth, the Crown of Life. Triumph. Everything comes out well. Power, strength, good luck.

Chapter LXXXVII

Arcanum 1

THE MAGICIAN

The First Arcanum signifies that which initiates, that which starts, that which is sown, that which begins. Every beginning is difficult. One has to work hard, because one has to sow in order to reap. This arcanum gives aptitude in order to resolve problems. It grants power as much for awakening as for dominating passions in the physical world.

It tends towards the organization of the natural elements and towards the forces in movement. Gives aptitude in order to acquire, dispose, modulate, and apply.

The First Arcanum is the unity, the principle of the Light, the Father, the world as a manifestation, the human being as a complete living unity within himself, the foundation of reason of all actions, the synthesis of all, the initiation into the mysteries and the power to decipher and to be served by them, the volitional power. The First Arcanum gives triumph, but with struggles, due to Karma.

KABBALISTIC SEPHIRAH: Kether

HEBREW LETTER: Aleph א

TRANSCENDENTAL AXIOM: "Be thou in thy deeds as thou art in thy thoughts."

FORECASTING ELEMENT: It promises dominion of material obstacles, new social relations, happy initiatives, the concourse of loyal friends who aid the development of projects, and jealous friends who obstruct it.

Chapter LXXXVIII

Arcanum 2

THE HIGH PRIESTESS

By means of the Second Arcanum, the matrix where all the images take form is made, is modelled. The Second Arcanum is the thesis that plans the antithesis. It is the fountain which accumulates the waters from the water-source. It is the dual manifestation of the unity. By unfolding itself, the unity gives origin to the productive and receptive femininity in all of nature.

KABBALISTIC SEPHIRAH: Chokmah

HEBREW LETTER: Beth ב

TRANSCENDENTAL AXIOM: "Winds and waves always go in favor of the one who knows how to sail."

FORECASTING ELEMENT: Attractions and repulsions, loss and profit, ascensions and descents; favorable inspirations to the initiative and the secret opposition from secondary ones who try to stop that initiative going towards a good goal.

Chapter LXXXIX

Arcanum 3

THE EMPRESS

It is stated that the Third Arcanum is the mold maker. It is clear that within creation, within nature, everything is modelled by means of the Verb. The Third Arcanum signifies success. It is material and spiritual production.

KABBALISTIC SEPHIRAH: Binah

HEBREW LETTER: Gimel ג

TRANSCENDENTAL AXIOM: "Thy loom is weaving cloth for thou to use and cloth that thou shalt not use."

FORECASTING ELEMENT: Multiplication of material goods, prosperity in business, abundance, wealth, success; obstacles which must be defeated, and satisfaction in proportion to efforts made while we are defeating them.

Chapter XC

Arcanum 4

THE EMPEROR

Within the Fourth Arcanum, the four concordances exist. These are affirmation, negation, discussion, and seduction.

KABBALISTIC SEPHIRAH: Chesed

HEBREW LETTER: Daleth ד

TRANSCENDENTAL AXIOM: "Give blessings unto the labor of thy hands, and place thy heart into thy thoughts."

FORECASTING ELEMENT: Guarantees material gains, having the basis for higher enterprises, favorable results on spent efforts and troubled conditions in order to achieve them; friends are simultaneously a help and obstacle. Fate is proper and adverse at the same time.

Chapter XCI

Arcanum 5

THE HIERARCH

The Fifth Arcanum is indication, demonstration, teaching, Karmic law, philosophy, science, art. It is the law, severity.

KABBALISTIC SEPHIRAH: Geburah

HEBREW LETTER: Hei ה

TRANSCENDENTAL AXIOM: "I have heard of thee by the hearing of the ear, but now mine eye seeth thee, and my heart feeleth thee."

FORECASTING ELEMENT: Freedom and restrictions, new experiences, acquisition of advantageous teachings, love and love affairs, journeys of frustrated prosperity. Propitious friends and friends who are of a sinister augury; beings and things that come and go, those who come in order to leave, those who go in order to return.

Chapter XCII

Arcanum 6

INDECISION

The Sixth Arcanum is the Lover, enchainment, equilibrium, struggle between love and desire. Amorous union of man and woman, linking. It is the supreme affirmation of the internal Christ, and the supreme negation of the demon.

With the Sixth Arcanum, one is found in the attitude of having to choose between one way or another way.

The struggle between the two ternaries, the mysteries of lingam-yoni are within the Sixth Arcanum.

KABBALISTIC SEPHIRAH: Tiphereth

HEBREW LETTER: Vav ו

TRANSCENDENTAL AXIOM: "Thou art giving me labor, oh Lord, and fortitude with it."

FORECASTING ELEMENT: Privilege and obligations in the relations of sexes. Antagonism of forces. Separations and divorces. Possession of that which is pursued and ardent desires which are fulfilled, where some of them satisfy and others disappoint.

Chapter XCIII

Arcanum 7

The Seventh Arcanum is struggle, battle, difficulties. The warrior must learn how to use the staff and the sword, thus he will attain the great victory. Our motto is Thelema (willpower).

KABBALISTIC SEPHIRAH: Netzach

HEBREW LETTER: Zayin ז

TRANSCENDENTAL AXIOM: "When science shall enter into thy heart and wisdom shall be sweet unto thy soul, then ask and it shall be granted unto thee."

FORECASTING ELEMENT: Guarantees magnetic power, well-aimed intellection (union of intellect and intuition); justice and reparations, honor and dishonour, achievement of that which is pursued with determination, satisfactions and disappointments.

Chapter XCIV

Arcanum 8

The Eighth Arcanum signifies strong ordeals; it is rectitude, justice, equilibrium. One must seek for performing good deeds at any cost, because the Masters of medicine, when in regards to someone who is sick and is dying, always intend to save that person because this is the law. They accomplish the duty of performing good deeds.

The initiatic ordeals are enclosed within the Eighth Arcanum.

KABBALISTIC SEPHIRAH: Hod

HEBREW LETTER: Chet ח

TRANSCENDENTAL AXIOM: "Thou shalt edify an altar within thy heart, but thou shalt not make an altar of thy heart."

FORECASTING ELEMENT: Guarantees retributions, punishments and rewards, gratitudes and ungratefulness, compensations for given services.

Chapter XCV

Arcanum 9

THE HERMIT

The Ninth Arcanum is the prudent and wise Hermit. It is solitude. There exists great pain within the Ninth Sphere.

Supreme pain exists within the Ninth Sphere, as Dante states in *The Divine Comedy*. We have to learn how to understand, we have to learn how to suffer, how to be resigned. Those who are not, fail.

Kabbalistic Sephirah: Yesod

Hebrew Letter: Teth ט

Transcendental Axiom: "Rise unto the mount and contemplate the Promised Land. But, thou shalt not go over thither."

Forecasting Element: It guarantees science in order for the making of discoveries; a method for when making them; caution when being served by them; advantageous associations and conceited associations; friends who help and who obstruct; light of reason and light of intuition, the first light for the immediate and the second light for that which will be.

Chapter XCVI

Arcanum 10

RETRIBUTION

The Tenth Arcanum is really transcendental from the esoteric point of view. The circle with the point in the center is a complete phallic symbol. The point, when it is prolonged, is converted into a line, the lingam. If the line is placed to the left of the circle, it is the number 10. All of the secrets of lingam-yoni are found within this number, as well as the laws of irradiation and absorption. To reach the intimate realization of the Being without having worked with the Sahaja Maithuna is impossible.

The Tenth Arcanum is the wheel of Samsara, the cosmogonic wheel of Ezekiel. We find in this wheel the struggle of antitheses. The whole secret of the Tree of Knowledge is enclosed within this wheel. The Tenth Arcanum is the wheel of the centuries. It is the tragic wheel which is the law of ancient return, it is logical that this law is intimately joined with the law of recurrence, meaning that everything comes to occur as it occurred, plus its good or evil consequences. The same dramas are repeated. This is called Karma.

Kabbalistic Sephirah: Malkuth

Hebrew Letter: Iod י

> **Note:** When we make a petition, many times the Angels answer unto us by showing us the clock. The disciple must fix his sight

on the hour of the clock. This is the clock of destiny. The answer is within the hour. In esoteric allegory, one is always answered by the clock. We have to learn how to understand the clock.

TIMETABLE: First Hour of Apollonius: "Transcendental study of occultism."

TRANSCENDENTAL AXIOM: "The knowledge that thou buyest with thine experience is expensive and the knowledge that thou lacks and thou need to buy is even more expensive."

FORECASTING ELEMENT: Guarantees good and bad fortune, elevation and descents, legitimate possessions and doubtful possessions; recommendations of past contingencies and circumstances which are repeated in a distinct way.

Chapter XCVII

Arcanum 11

PERSUASION

The Eleventh Arcanum is the work with the fire, with the force of love.

Persuasion, in itself, is a force of a subtle spiritual order. Occult wisdom states: "Vivify the flame of the Spirit with the force of love."

Persuasion has more power than violence.

HEBREW LETTER: Kaf כ

TIMETABLE: Second Hour of Apollonius: "The abysses of the fire and the astral virtues form a circle through (around) the dragons and the fire (studies of the occult forces)."

TRANSCENDENTAL AXIOM: "Joyful in hope, suffered in tribulation, be thou constant in thy prayer."

FORECASTING ELEMENT: Guarantees control of the direction which is followed that leads towards the dominion of the elements; vitality, rejuvenation, acquisition, and loss of friends because of family matters; pains, obstacles, jealousy, treason and resignation in order to bear the disappointments.

Chapter XCVIII

Arcanum 12

The Twelfth Arcanum implies sacrifices, sufferings; it is the card of the Apostolate.

The Twelfth Arcanum brings many sufferings, many struggles.

It has a beautiful synthesis, because 1 + 2 = 3, which signifies material and spiritual production. This arcanum is powerful in the spiritual and in the social aspect. This arcanum promises struggles in the economical and in the social aspect.

HEBREW LETTER: Lamed ל

TIMETABLE: Third Hour of Apollonius: "The serpents, the dogs and the fire (Sexual Magic, work with the Kundalini)."

TRANSCENDENTAL AXIOM: "Even though the sun makes thou fatigued during the day and the moon makes thou grievous during the night, thou shalt not take thy feet unto the slippery, neither thou shall sleep when thou art on guard."

FORECASTING ELEMENT: Guarantees contrarieties, anguish, downfalls; material loss in some conditions of life and profit in others; presentiments which enliven and presentiments which discourage.

Chapter XCIX

Arcanum 13

The Thirteenth Arcanum is death, but also can signify something new, it can be wealth; it can be misery. It is a number with a great synthesis.

The Thirteenth Arcanum contains the Gospel of Judas. Judas represents the death of the "I." The Gospel of Judas is the gospel of death; it is the gospel of the dissolution of the ego. Judas symbolizes the ego, which must be decapitated.

HEBREW LETTER: Mem מ

TIMETABLE: Fourth Hour of Apollonius: "The neophyte will wander at night among the sepulchers, will experience the horror of visions, and will be submitted to magic and goethia (this means that the disciple will see that he is being attacked by millions of black magicians within the Astral Plane. Those tenebrous magicians attempt to drive the disciple away from the luminous path)."

TRANSCENDENTAL AXIOM: "Night has passed and a new day has arrived, then thou shall be dressed with weapons of light."

FORECASTING ELEMENT: Guarantees disappointments, disillusions, death of affections, refusals for that which is solicited, collapse, pure enjoyments and gladness for the soul, improvements with painful enjoyment, help of friends; renewal of conditions, the good ones for the worse and the bad ones for the better.

Chapter C

Arcanum 14

The Fourteenth Arcanum is chastity, transmutations, the waters. One has to work hard by chiselling the stone, without which the sexual transmutation cannot be achieved.

HEBREW LETTER: Nun ב

TIMETABLE: Fifth Hour of Apollonius: "The superior waters of heaven (during this time the disciple learns to be pure and chaste because he comprehends the value of his seminal liquor)."

TRANSCENDENTAL AXIOM: "Thou shalt not be as straw before the wind; neither shalt thou be as the wind before the straw."

FORECASTING ELEMENT: Predicts enmities, reciprocal affections, obligations, combinations, chemical combinations, and combining of interests; afflicted loves, devoted loves, betrayed loves; things that remain and things that depart, the first are in order to leave, the second are in order to return.

Chapter CI

Arcanum 15

The Fifteenth Arcanum is the pluralized "I," which esoterically is called Satan.

The Fifteenth Arcanum represents passion, which is based in the Luciferic fire. It is necessary to know that the principal defect is sexual passion, lust.

In the Kabbalistic synthesis of the Fifteenth Arcanum, we have, 1 + 5 = 6, the 6 in itself is sex. This signifies that in sex is the major force that can liberate the human being, but also the major force that can enslave him.

The Fifteenth Arcanum signifies the work with the demon. It is the process of the dissolution of the "I." Eden is sex; the internal beast, the psychological "I" obstructs our way towards Eden; it is at the door of sex, in order to invite us to the ejaculation of the seminal liquor, or in order to deviate us from that door by showing us schools, theories, sects, etc.

HEBREW LETTER: Samech ם

TIMETABLE: Sixth Hour of Apollonius: "Here it is necessary to remain quiet, still, due to fear (this signifies the terrible ordeal of the Guardian of the Threshold, before whom a lot of courage is needed in order to overcome him)."

TRANSCENDENTAL AXIOM: "They made me the keeper of the vineyards; but mine own vineyard have I not kept."

Forecasting Element: It predicts controversies, passions, fatalities; prosperity through legality and fatality; noxious affections for the one who feels them, and for the one who is affected by them; vehement anxiety and violent situations.

Chapter CII

Arcanum 16

FRAGILITY

The departure from Eden coincides with the Sixteenth Arcanum. Eden or Paradise must be understood as being sex. We departed through the doors of sex, and only through those doors will we return.

The Sixteenth Arcanum is very dangerous. It is necessary to awaken the consciousness in order to not walk blindly. The blind ones can fall into the abyss.

The initiate who spills the glass of Hermes inevitably falls. The struggle between the brain, heart, and sex is terrible. If sex dominates the brain, then the star of five points, the pentagram is inverted, and the human being with his head aiming downwards and his two legs aiming upwards is precipitated towards the bottom of the abyss. The initiate is fulminated by the Sixteenth Arcanum. Whosoever allows himself to fall, then falls with the Sixteenth Arcanum, which is the Fulminated Tower. These are the ones who have failed with the Great Work of the Father.

Hebrew Letter: Ayin ע

Timetable: Seventh Hour of Apollonius: "Fire comforts inanimate beings, and if any priest, a sufficiently purified man, steals the fire and then projects it, if he mixes this fire with sacred oil and consecrates it, then he will achieve the healing of all sicknesses by simply applying it to the afflicted areas (here the initiate sees that his material wealth is threatened and his business fails)."

TRANSCENDENTAL AXIOM: "Light at dawn, light of midday, light of nightfall, what is important is that it is light."

FORECASTING ELEMENT: Predicts unexpected accidents, tempests, commotions, deaths; benefits because of concepts from good and bad circumstances; reciprocity in love and hatred, in indifference and in zeal, in treason and in loyalty.

Chapter CIII

Arcanum 17

HOPE

The star of eight points always represents Venus, the star of dawn. We find the Venustic Initiation within the Seventeenth Arcanum.

The symbol of Venus shows us that the circle of the Spirit must be upon the cross of sex, meaning, sex must be under the control of the Spirit. When the symbol is inverted it represents that the Spirit is dominated by sex.

HEBREW LETTER: Peh פ

TIMETABLE: Eighth Hour of Apollonius: "The astral virtues of the elements, of the seeds of every genre."

TRANSCENDENTAL AXIOM: "Some men require signs in order to believe, others require wisdom in order to act, but the hopeful heart bears everything within its hopes."

FORECASTING ELEMENT: It predicts Intuition, support, illumination, births, brief afflictions and brief satisfactions, displeasures and reconciliations, privations; abandonments and benefits.

Chapter CIV
Arcanum 18

The Kabbalistic synthesis of the Arcanum Eighteen is 1 + 8 = 9, the Ninth Sphere, sex. If we add 9 + 9 = 18, there is a balance found in it. One 9 is the positive aspect and the other 9 is the negative aspect, but the 18 in itself becomes negative, fatal. Eighteen is the secret enemies from the arcanum of Twilight, because one has to fight a lot in the work of the Ninth Sphere. We have to learn how to sublimate the sexual energy, where the clue or key of all empires abides.

We find in the Eighteenth Arcanum the dangers of initiation, the occult and secret enemies who intend to damage the initiation in the subterranean fight within the domains of the Ninth Sphere.

In the Eighteenth Arcanum we have to pass through bloody battles against the tenebrous, the Black Lodge, the abyss, temptation, the demons... that do not want the initiate to escape from their claws. This is the path of the razor's edge. This is the path that is full of dangers from within and without, as it is stated by the Master Sivananda.

In the Internal Worlds, the tenebrous of the Eighteenth Arcanum violently assault the student.

Within the terrible Eighteenth Arcanum we find the witchcraft of Thessalia. Here in this arcanum, we find the Canidio recipes,

erotic magical ceremonies, rites in order to be loved by someone, dangerous potions, etc. We must warn the Gnostic students that the most dangerous potion which the tenebrous utilize in order to withdraw the student from the path of the razor's edge is the intellect.

Hebrew Letter: Tzadi ✿

Timetable: Ninth Hour of Apollonius: "Here nothing is finished yet. The initiate increases his perception until he surpasses the limits of the solar system, beyond the zodiac. He arrives at the threshold of the infinite. He reaches the limits of the intelligible world. The Divine Light is revealed unto him and with all of this, new fears and dangers also appear (it is the study of the Minor Mysteries, the nine arcades on which the student must ascend)."

Transcendental Axiom: "May thy charity be an inexhaustible granary, and thy patience no less inexhaustible than thy charity."

Forecasting Element: It predicts instability, inconstancy, ambush, confusion, changes, uncertain situations, long deliberations, unexpected impediments, tardy results, apparent triumphs and failings.

Chapter CV

Arcanum 19

In the Kabbalah of prediction, the Nineteenth Arcanum predicts total victory, whether by personal effort or with the help of others.

The Nineteenth Arcanum is the arcanum of victory or success. This victory is related with all the aspects of life: economical, social, political, moral, etc.

The Kabbalistic synthesis of the Nineteenth Arcanum is 1 + 9 = 10. The number ten is a profoundly sexual number; here the circle and the line are found, which are the mysteries of lingam-yoni. It is only possible to reach the realization of the Self through the transmutation of the sexual energy.

Within the Nineteenth Arcanum a great alliance is established between two souls. Man and woman must kill desire in order to reach the great alliance, in order to perform the Great Work.

HEBREW LETTER: Kuf ק

TIMETABLE: Tenth Hour of Apollonius: "The doors of heaven open and man comes out of his lethargy (this is the number ten of the second great Initiation of Major Mysteries, that allows the initiate to travel in the Ethereal Body. This is the wisdom of John the Baptist)."

TRANSCENDENTAL AXIOM: "Take the shield of thy faith and advance with a determined step, no matter if the wind is in thy favor or all the winds are against thy favor."

FORECASTING ELEMENT: It predicts the increment of power, success in determination, joy in the acts that are performed, benefits for the concept of personal efforts and efforts of others, inheritances, clarity in that which is desired and fire that consumes the desired.

Chapter CVI

Arcanum 20

RESURRECTION

The Twentieth Arcanum is the resurrection of the dead. Really, the resurrection of the soul is only possible through cosmic initiation. Human beings are dead and can only resurrect through initiation.

HEBREW LETTER: Resh ר

TIMETABLE: Eleventh Hour of Apollonius: "The Angels, Cherubim, and Seraphim fly with the sound of whirring wings; there is rejoicing in heaven; the earth and the sun which surge from Adam awaken (this process belongs to the great Initiations of Major Mysteries, where only the terror of the Law reigns)."

TRANSCENDENTAL AXIOM: "Flower in the apple tree, fruit in the vineyard sown with prudence."

FORECASTING ELEMENT: It predicts harmonious choices, fortunate initiatives, labor, profit. Compensations because of good and because of bad. Loyal friends that annul the action of traitorous friends. Jealousy for the good that is enjoyed. Afflictions because of loss.

Chapter CVII

Arcanum 21

TRANSMUTATION

The Twenty-first Arcanum can be represented with the inverted pentagonal star which represents black magic. The Twenty-first Arcanum is calamity, insensateness, the Fool of the Tarot. Whosoever works in realization of the Self is liable to do foolishness. One has to work with the **three factors** of the revolution of the consciousness.

1. To be born
2. To die
3. To sacrifice for others.

Transmutation indicates that one has to transmute. The brain must control sex. When the brain loses control over sex, when sex attains dominion over the brain, then the star of five points, the human being, descends head-first into the abyss. This is the inverted pentagram, symbol of black magic.

The danger in this arcanum is indicated with precision by the crocodile.

HEBREW LETTER: Shin ש

TIMETABLE: Twelfth Hour of Apollonius: "The towers of fire disturb (this is the triumphant entrance of the Master into the limitless bliss of Nirvana, or better, the Master's renunciation of the bliss of Nirvana for the love of humanity, where then he is converted into a Bodhisattva of compassion)."

TRANSCENDENTAL AXIOM: "My soul does not enter into His secret, neither my ship into His port."

FORECASTING ELEMENT: It predicts exclusion from something that is enjoyed, frustration when trying to achieve what is wanted. Ruin in relation to that which we boast of. It is danger of isolation, perfidious gifts, deceitful promises, disillusions; the end of some things and the beginning of others.

Chapter CVIII
Arcanum 22

THE RETURN

The Twenty-second Arcanum is the Crown of Life, the return to Light, the incarnation of the Truth within us.

The Kabbalistic synthesis of the Twenty-second Arcanum is, 2 + 2 = 4: man, woman, fire, and water. It is יהוה Iod Hei Vav Hei: man, woman, phallus, uterus. Behold here the holy and mysterious Tetragrammaton, the Holy Four.

HEBREW LETTER: Tav ת

TIMETABLE: "A thirteenth hour exists; this is the hour of liberation."

TRANSCENDENTAL AXIOM: "The sun ariseth and the sun goeth down and it hasteth to its place where it was born."

FORECASTING ELEMENT: Predicts longevity, inheritances, notability, delight of honest enjoyments, rivals that dispute the affections, friends that care for us, obstacles and aptitude in order to defeat them, uncertain situations and contingencies that clarify them.

Consulting the Tarot

1. Light the candles on the altar or use three candles.

2. Set up a pentagram.

3. Separate the twenty-two major arcana from the minor.

4. Make the sign of the cross and seal yourself with the Microcosmic Star [see page 284]. Invoke the Father and ask for illumination from the Holy Spirit.

5. Shuffle the twenty-two major arcana with the face of the cards downwards. Pull out one major arcanum and set it aside without looking at it.

6. Shuffle the fifty-six minor arcana and pull out one card; shuffle them again and pull out another minor arcanum. There will be a total of three cards on the altar.

7. Add the major arcanum to the sum of the two digits of each of the minor. If the result is greater than twenty-two, again add up the digits; the resulting total is the card of prediction, the result. This is clarified with the prediction of the two minor arcana.

EXAMPLE ONE:

The tame lion	**11**
Prodigy	26 = 2 + 6 = **8**
Preeminence	42 = 4 + 2 = **6**

11 + 8 + 6 = 25 = 2 + 5 = **7**
Answer: Triumph

EXAMPLE TWO:

Retribution	**10**
Exchange	30 = 3 + 0 = **3**
Revelation	59 = 5 + 9 = 14
	14 = 1 + 4 = **5**

10 + 3 + 5 = **18** (Answer)

It is necessary to know the twenty-two arcana. After knowing them one will use the practical part of prediction intelligently in cases of much importance.

It is necessary to know the significance of prediction. The cards are placed from the astral and mathematical point of view, one asks for help from the Holy Spirit; one uses the number, mathematics. All laws are made up by numbers, weight, and measurement.

Many persons use the Tarot in an empirical manner and that is why they act wrongly. The last item taught in Kabbalistic prediction is that in order for us to use numbers wisely, we have to study and comprehend the significance of each card.

Appendices

Conjurations

Conjuration of the Four

Caput mortum, imperet tibi dominus per vivum et devotum serpentem!

Cherub, imperet tibi Dominus per Adam Iod-Havah!

Aquila errans, imperet tibi Dominus per alas tauri!

Serpens, imperet tibi Dominus Tetragrammaton, per Angelum et Leonem!

Michael, Gabriel, Raphael, Anael!

Fluat udor per Spiritum Elohim

Manet in terra per Adam Iod-Chavah!

Fiat firmamentum per Iod-Havah -Sabaoth!

Fiat judicium per ignem in virtute Michael!

Angel of the blind eyes, obey, or pass away with this holy water!

Work winged bull, or revert to the earth, unless thou wilt that I should pierce thee with this sword!

Chained eagle, obey my sign, or fly before this breathing!

Writhing serpent, crawl at my feet, or be tortured by the sacred fire and give way before the perfumes that I burn in it!

Water, return to water!

Fire, burn!

Air, circulate!

Earth, revert to earth!

By virtue of the Pentagram, which is the morning star, and by the name of the Tetragram, which is written in the center of the cross of Light!

Amen. Amen. Amen.

Conjuration of the Seven of Solomon the Sage

In the name of Michael, may Jehovah command thee and drive thee hence, Chavajoth!

In the name of Gabriel, may Adonai command thee, and drive thee hence, Bael!

In the name of Raphael, begone before Elial, Samgabiel!

By Samael Sabaoth, and in the name of Elohim Gibor, get thee hence, Andrameleck!

By Zachariel et Sachiel-Meleck, be obedient unto Elvah, Sanagabril!

By the divine and human name of Shaddai, and by the sign of the Pentagram which I hold in my right hand, in the name of the angel Anael, by the power of Adam and Eve, who are Iod-Chavah, begone Lilith! Let us rest in Peace, Nahemah!

By the holy Elohim and by the names of the Genii Cashiel, Sehaltiel, Aphiel and Zarahiel, at the command of Orifiel, depart from us Moloch! We deny thee our children to devour!

Amen. Amen. Amen.

Invocation of Solomon

Powers of the kingdom, be ye under my left foot and in my right hand!

Glory and eternity, take me by the two shoulders, and direct me in the paths of victory!

Mercy and justice, be ye the equilibrium and splendor of my life!

Intelligence and wisdom, crown me!

Spirits of Malkuth, lead me betwixt the two pillars upon which rests the whole edifice of the temple!

Angels of Netzach and Hod, establish me upon the cubic stone of Yesod!

Oh Gedulah-el! Oh Geburah-el! Oh Tiphereth!

Binahel, be thou my love!

Ruach Chokmah-el, be thou my light!

Be that which thou art and thou shalt be, Oh Ketheriel!

Ishim, assist me in the name of Shaddai!

Cherubim, be my strength in the name of Adonai!

Beni-Elohim, be my brethren in the name of the Son, and by the powers of Sabaoth!

Elohim, do battle for me in the name of Tetragrammaton!

Malachim, protect me in the name of Iod-Havah!

Seraphim, cleanse my love in the name of Eloah!

Hasmalim, enlighten me with the splendors of Elohim and Shechinah!

Aralim, act!

Ophanim, revolve and shine!

Chaioth-Ha-Kadosh cry, speak, roar, bellow!

Kadosh, Kadosh, Kadosh!

Shaddai, Adonai, Iod-Havah, Eheieh asher Eheieh!

Hallelu-Jah, Hallelu-Jah, Hallelu-Jah.

Amen. Amen. Amen.

The Emerald Tablet of Hermes Trismegistus

The Secret Works of Chiram
One in Essence, but Three in Aspect

It is true, no lie, certain, and to be
depended upon, the Superior agrees with
the Inferior, and the Inferior with the
Superior, to effect that one truly wonderful
work. As all things owe their existence
to the Will of the Only One, so all things
owe their origin to the One Only Thing,
the most hidden, by the arrangement of
the only God. The Father of that one only
thing is the Sun, its Mother is the Moon;
the Wind carries it in its belly, but its nurse
is a spiritous Earth. That One Only Thing
(after God) is the Father of all things in the
Universe. Its power is perfect after it has
been united to a spiritous Earth. Seperate
that spiritous Earth from the dense or
crude by means of a gentle heat with much
attention. In Great Measure it ascends
from the Earth up to Heaven and descends
again, newborn, on the Earth, and the
Superior and the Inferior are increased
in Power. By this wilt thou partake of
the Honours of the whole world. And
darkness will fly from thee. This is the
Strength of all Powers. With this thou
wilt be able to overcome all things, and
to transmute all what is fine and what is
coarse. In this manner the world was created; the arrangements to follow this road
are hidden. For this reason I am called
Chiram Telat Mechasot, One in essence,
but Three in aspect. In this trinity is hidden the wisdom of the whole world. It is
ended now, what I have said concerning
the effects of the Sun.

Hebrew Letters and Numbers

Letter	Name	Sound	Ordinal Value	Absolute Value	Reduced Value	Literal Meaning	Symbolic Meaning	Meaning (Eliphas Levi)
א	aleph	a	1	1	1	ox, bull	strength, leader, first	Father
ב	beth	b/v	2	2	2	tent, house	household, in, into	Mother
ג	gimel	g	3	3	3	camel	pride, lift up	Nature
ד	daleth	d	4	4	4	door	pathway, to enter	Authority
ה	hei	h	5	5	5	window, fence	"the," to reveal	Religion
ו	vav	u	6	6	6	nail	"and," add, secure, hook	Liberty
ז	zayin	z	7	7	7	weapon	cut, to cut off	Propriety
ח	cheth	ch	8	8	8	fence, hedge, chamber	private, to separate	Distribution
ט	teth	t	9	9	9	to twist; a snake	to surround	Prudence
י	yod	i	10	10	1	closed hand	deed, work, to make	Order
ךכ	kaph	j	11	20	2	arm, wing, open hand	to cover, allow, strength	Force
ל	lamed	l	12	30	3	cattle goad, a staff	prod, go toward, tongue	Sacrifice
םמ	mem	m	13	40	4	water	massive, overpower, chaos	Death
ןנ	nun	n	14	50	5	moving fish	activity, life	Reversibility
ס	samech	x	15	60	6	a prop	support, turn	Universal Being
ע	ayin	o	16	70	7	eye	see, know, experience	Balance
ףפ	peh	p/f	17	80	8	mouth	speak, open, word	Immortality
ץצ	tzadi	c	18	90	9	fish-hook	harvest, desire	Shadow and Reflection
ק	kuf/qoph	q	19	100	1	back of the head	behind, the last, least	Light
ר	resh	r	20	200	2	head	person, head, highest	Recognition
ש	shin	s/sh	21	300	3	teeth	consume, destroy	Astral Light
ת	tav	t	22	400	4	sign, cross	convenant, seal	Synthesis

In cases where there are two letters, the second is called 'final' [sophit] and is used when the letter appears at the end of a word.

The Microcosmic Star

The arms are raised upwards until the palms of the hands touch each other above the head. Thereafter, extend the arms laterally so that they remain in a horizontal position, forming a cross with the rest of the body. Finally, cross the forearms (the right over the left) on your chest, touching it with the palms while the fingertips reach the front of your shoulders.

The Nuctemeron of Apollonius of Tyana
Excerpted from "Transcendental Magic" by Eliphas Levi

The Greek text was first published after an ancient manuscript by Gilbert Gautrinus, in De Vita et Moyris, *Lib. 111, p. 206, and was reproduced subsequently by Laurentius Moshemius in his* Sacred and Historico-Critical Observations, *Amsterdam, 1721. It is now translated und interpreted for the first time by Eliphas Levi.*

*N*uctemeron signifies the "day of the night" or "the night illumined by day." It is analogous to the "Light Issuing from Darkness," which is the title of a well-known Hermetic work. It may be translated also "The Light of Occultism." This monument of transcendent Assyrian Magic is sufficiently curious to make it superfluous to enlarge on its importance. We have not merely evoked Apollonius, we have possibly resuscitated him.

The Nuctemeron

The First Hour
In unity, the demons chant the praises of God: they lose their malice and fury.

The Second Hour
By the Duad, the Zodiacal fish chant the praises of God; the fiery serpents entwine about the caduceus and the thunder becomes harmonious.

The Third Hour
The serpents of the Hermetic caduceus entwine three times; Cerberus opens his triple jaw, and fire chants the praises of God with the three tongues of the lightning.

The Fourth Hour
At the fourth hour the soul revisits the tombs; the magical lamps are lighted at the four corners of the circle: it is the time of enchantments and illusions.

The Fifth Hour
The voice of the great waters celebrates the God of the heavenly spheres.

APOLLONIUS OF TYANA

Apollonius was born in Cappadocia around the beginning of the first century. He was a student and teacher of Pythagorean Mysteries. He travelled throughout the known world, studying in the Initiatic schools of India, Babylon, Chaldea, Ephesus, Antioch, and more. He preached to the people of Athens a doctrine of the purest and noblest ethics, and the phenomena and prophecies he produced were numerous and well attested. A contemporary wrote, "How is it that the talismans of Apollonius have power, for they prevent, as we see, the fury of the waves and the violence of the winds, and the attacks of the wild beasts, and whilst our Lord's miracles are preserved by tradition alone, those of Apollonius are most numerous and actually manifested in present facts!"

The Sixth Hour

The spirit abides immovable; it beholds the infernal monsters swarm down upon it, and does not fear.

The Seventh Hour

A fire, which imparts life to all animated beings, is directed by the will of pure men. The initiate stretches forth his hand, and pains are assuaged.

The Eighth Hour

The stars utter speech to one another; the soul of the suns corresponds with the exhalation of the flowers; chains of harmony create unison between all natural things.

The Ninth Hour

Initiations, the number which must not be divulged.

The Tenth Hour

The key of the astronomical cycle of the circular movement of human life.

The Eleventh Hour

The wings of the genii move with a mysterious and deep murmur; they fly from sphere to sphere, and bear the messages of God from world to world.

The Twelfth Hour

The works of the light eternal are fulfilled by fire.

Explanation

These twelve symbolical hours, analogous to the signs of the magical Zodiac and to the allegorical labors of Heracles, represent the succession in works of initiation. It is necessary, therefore:

(1) To overcome evil passions, and, according to the expression of the wise Hierophant, compel the demons themselves to praise God.

(2) To study the balanced forces of Nature and learn how harmony results from the analogy of contraries; to know also the Great Magical Agent and the twofold polarization of the universal light.

(3) To be initiated in the triadic principle of all Theogonies and all religious symbols.

(4) To overcome all phantoms of imagination and triumph over all illusions.

(5) To understand after what manner universal harmony is produced in the center of the four elementary forces.

(6) To become inaccessible to fear.

(7) To practice the direction of the magnetic light.

(8) To foresee effects by the calculus of the balance of causes.

(9) To understand the hierarchy of instruction, to respect the mysteries of dogma and to keep silence in presence of the profane.

(10) To make a profound study of astronomy.

(11) To become initiated by analogy into the laws of universal life and intelligence.

(12) To effect great works of Nature by direction of the light.

The Nuctemeron According to the Hebrews

Extracted from the ancient Talmud termed Mishna by the Jews. By Eliphas Levi

The Nuctemeron of Apollonius, borrowed from Greek Theurgy, completed and explained by the Assyrian hierarchy of genii, corresponds perfectly to the philosophy of numbers as we find it expounded in the most curious pages of the Talmud. Thus, the Pythagoreans go back farther than Pythagoras; thus, Genesis is a magnificent allegory, which, under the form of a narrative, conceals the secrets not only of the creation achieved of old, but of permanent and universal creation, the eternal generation of beings. We read as follows in the Talmud: *"God hath stretched out the heaven like a tabernacle; He hath spread the world like a table richly dight; and He hath created man as if He invited a guest."* Listen now to the words of the King Schlomoh: *"The divine Chokmah, Wisdom, the Bride of God, hath built a house unto herself, and hath dressed two Pillars. She hath immolated her victims, she hath mingled her wine, she hath spread the table and hath commissioned her servitors."* This Wisdom, who builds her house according to a regular and numerical architecture, is that exact science which rules in the works of God. It is His compass and His square. The Seven Pillars are the seven typical and primordial days. The victims are natural forces which are propagated by undergoing a species of death. Mingled wine is the universal fluid, the table is the world with the waters full of fishes. The servants of Chokmah are the souls of Adam and of Havah (Eve). The earth of which Adam was formed was taken from the entire mass of the world. His head is Israel, his body the empire of Babylon, and his limbs are the other nations of the earth. (The aspirations of the initiates of Moses towards a universal oriental kingdom stand here revealed.) Now, there are twelve hours in the day of man's creation.

First Hour

God combines the scattered fragments of earth; He kneads them together and forms one mass, which it is His will to animate.

Explanation: Man is the synthesis of the created world; in him creative unity begins again; he is made in the image and likeness of God.

Second Hour

God designs the form of the human body; He separates it into two sections, so that the organs may be double, for all force and all life result from two, and it is thus the Elohim made all things.

Explanation: Everything lives by movement, everything is maintained by equilibrium, and harmony results from the analogy of contraries. This law is the form of forms, the first manifestation of the activity and fecundity of God.

Third Hour

The limbs of man, obeying the law of life, come forth of themselves and are completed by the generative organ, which is composed of one and two, emblem of the triadic number.

Explanation: The triad issues spontaneously from the Duad; the movement which produces two also produces three; three is the key of numbers, for it is the first numeral synthesis; in geometry it is the triangle, the first complete and enclosed figure, generatrix of an infinity of triangles, whether like or unlike.

Fourth Hour

God breathes upon the face of man and imparts to him a soul.

Explanation: The tetrad, which in geometry produces cross and square, is the perfect number; now, it is in perfection of form that the intelligent soul manifests; according to which revelation of the Mishna, the child is not animated in the mother's womb till after the formation of all its members.

Fifth Hour

Man stands erect; he is weaned from earth; he walks and goes where he will.

EXPLANATION: The number five is that of the soul, typified by the quintessence which results from the equilibrium of the four elements; in the Tarot this number is represented by the High-Priest or spiritual autocrat, type of human will, that High-Priestess who alone decides our eternal destinies.

Sixth Hour

The animals pass before Adam, and he gives their proper name to each.

EXPLANATION: Man by toil subdues the earth and overcomes the animals; by the manifestation of his liberty he expresses his word or speech in the environment which obeys him: herein primordial creation is completed. God formed man on the sixth day, but at the sixth hour of the day man fulfils the work of God and to some extent recreates himself, by enthroning himself as king of Nature, which he subjects by his speech.

Seventh Hour

God gives Adam a companion brought forth out of the man's own substance.

EXPLANATION: When God had created man in His own image, He rested on the seventh day, for He had given unto Himself a fruitful bride who would unceasingly work for Him. Nature is the bride of God, and God reposes on her. Man, becoming creator in his turn by means of the word, gives himself a companion like unto himself, on whose love he may lean henceforth. Woman is the work of man; he makes her beautiful by his love; and he makes her also a mother. Woman is true human nature, daughter and mother of man, grand-daughter and mother dear of God.

Eighth Hour

Adam and Eve enter the nuptial bed; they are two when they lie down, and when they arise they are four.

EXPLANATION: The tetrad joined to the tetrad represents form balancing form, creation issuing from creation, the eternal equipoise of life; seven being the number of God's rest, the unity which follows it signifies man, who toils and co-operates with Nature in the work of creation.

Ninth Hour

God imposes His law on man.

EXPLANATION: Nine is the number of initiation, because, being composed of three times three, it represents the divine idea and the absolute philosophy of numbers, for which reason Apollonius says that the mysteries of the number nine are not to be revealed.

Tenth Hour

At the tenth hour Adam falls into sin.

EXPLANATION: According to the Kabbalists ten is the number of matter, of which the special sign is zero. In the tree of the Sephiroth ten represents Malkuth, or exterior and material substance. The sin of Adam is therefore materialism, and the fruit which he plucks from the tree represents flesh isolated from spirit, zero separated from unity, the schism of the number ten, resulting on the one side in a despoiled unity and on the other in nothingness and death.

Eleventh Hour

At the eleventh hour the sinner is condemned to labor and to expiate his sin by suffering.

EXPLANATION: In the Tarot, eleven represents force, which is acquired through trials. God inflicts penalties on man as a means of salvation, because he must strive and endure, that he may conquer intelligence and life.

Twelfth Hour

Man and woman undergo their sentence; the expiation begins, and the Liberator is promised.

EXPLANATION: Such is the completion of moral birth; man is fulfilled, for he is dedicated to the sacrifice which regenerates; the exile of Adam is like that of Oedipus; like Oedipus he becomes the father of two enemies, but the daughter of Oedipus is the pious and virginal Antigone, while Mary issues from the race of Adam.

Sephirotic Symbols

1. Kether
Kabbalistic Name: Hayoth Ha Kadosh
Christian Name: Seraphim
Attributes: "Supreme Crown"
Body: The Father

2. Chokmah
Kabbalistic Name: Ophanim
Christian Name: Cherubim
Attributes: "Wisdom"
Body: The Son

3. Binah
Kabbalistic Name: Aralim
Christian Name: Thrones & Dominions
Attributes: "Intelligence"
Body: Holy Spirit

4. Chesed
Kabbalistic Name: Hasmalim
Christian Name: Dominions & Powers
Attributes: "Love"
Body: The Innermost, The Atmic Body.

5. Geburah
Kabbalistic Name: Seraphim
Christian Name: Powers & Virtues
Attributes: "Justice"
Body: The Divine Soul, The Buddhic Body.

6. Tiphereth
Kabbalistic Name: Malachim
Christian Name: Virtues & Principalities
Attributes: "Beauty"
Body: The Human Soul, The Causal Body

7. Netzach
Kabbalistic Name: Beni-Elohim
Christian Name: Archangels
Attributes: "Victory"
Body: The Mental Body

8. Hod
Kabbalistic Name: Elohim
Christian Name: Angels
Attributes: "Splendor"
Body: The Astral Body

9. Yesod
Kabbalistic Name: Cherubim
Christian Name: Immortals
Attributes: "Foundation"
Body: The Vital Body

10. Malkuth
Kabbalistic Name: Ischim
Christian Name: initiates
Attributes: "The Kingdom"
Body: The Physical Body

The Predictive Tarot

23: The Farmer

THE FARMER

The farmer is in the act of cultivating the earth and his consciousness. It symbolizes the human virtue of its own realization.

MODULATING ATTRIBUTE: It is associated with the action of the planet Mercury. It represents elemental intelligence in regard to the labor of knowing and thus taking advantage of the fruits of experience.

TRANSCENDENTAL AXIOM: "My mill is grinding; flour for me and flour for my neighbor."

As an element of prediction it promises powerful friends, the necessity of their help and their ability to accomplish it if there is faith in their friendship. It signifies elevation by means of those friends and one's own willpower.

24: The Weaver

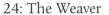

THE WEAVER

The weaver is in the action of cultivating domestic virtues. It symbolizes a diligent woman, keeper of home and honor.

MODULATING ATTRIBUTE: It is associated with the action of the planet Venus. It represents elemental intelligence related to the labor of applying the fruits of what we learned.

TRANSCENDENTAL AXIOM: "My loom is weaving net after net; a cloth for my honor and cloth to honor."

As an element of prediction it promises organized economy, chastity in maternity, feminine protection and a good accomplishment of obligations.

25: The Argonaut

THE ARGONAUT

The argonaut is in the action of sailing in search of the unknown. It symbolizes the human virtue of one's own inspiration.

MODULATING ATTRIBUTE: It is associated to the planet Neptune. It represents the willed man who confronts the dangers of the unknown.

TRANSCENDENTAL AXIOM: "My boat is sailing, insistently; sailing at night, sailing at dawn."

As an element of prediction it promises absences, emigrations, abandonment, changes, domestic complaints, something that is acquired and much that is lost.

26: The Prodigy

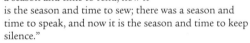

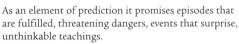

THE PRODIGY

The prodigy is in the action of being fulfilled. It symbolizes the human virtue that creates the astonishing and that searches for the marvelous.

MODULATING ATTRIBUTE: It is associated to the planet Saturn. It represents the action of time as justice and power of manifestation.

TRANSCENDENTAL AXIOM: "There was a season and time to rend, now it is the season and time to sew; there was a season and time to speak, and now it is the season and time to keep silence."

As an element of prediction it promises episodes that are fulfilled, threatening dangers, events that surprise, unthinkable teachings.

27: The Unexpected

The unexpected is in the action of becoming manifested. It symbolizes the human virtue of subconscious processes.

MODULATING ATTRIBUTE: It is associated to the planet Mars. It represents the inner life as a determining cause for the exterior one.

TRANSCENDENTAL AXIOM: "Not too much honey to sweeten, neither vainglory to prosper."

As an element of prediction it promises conditioned triumphs, surprises, conjurations, treasons, findings, discoveries, some of them tardy.

28: Uncertainty

Uncertainty is in the action of deliberation. It symbolizes the human virtue of one's own determination.

MODULATING ATTRIBUTE: It is associated to the planet Pluto. It represents judgment as a determining cause for actions.

TRANSCENDENTAL AXIOM: "Do not seek in thy neighbor what is within thee; neither thou seek in thee what is within thy neighbor."

As an element of prediction it promises delays, obstacles, contrarieties, mysteries to be solved and science to solve them.

29: Domesticity

Domesticity is in the action of agreement. It symbolizes the human virtue of domination by means of persuasion.

MODULATING ATTRIBUTE: It is associated to the Moon. It represents Nature's peace, equilibrium of elements, pastoral joy.

TRANSCENDENTAL AXIOM: "Let your eyes become youthful eyes, and let thy word become an elder's prudence."

As an element of prediction it promises remorse, indecision, perplexities, timidity, pastoral life, advantageous affairs, enterprises that bring struggles but with satisfactory outcomes.

30: Exchange

Exchange is in the action of reciprocal conviviality. It symbolizes the human virtue of life in society.

MODULATING ATTRIBUTE: It is associated to the planet Jupiter. It represents individual expansion by means of commercial conviviality.

TRANSCENDENTAL AXIOM: "Reap thy land with care; but do not harvest your goods with avarice."

As an element of prediction it promises social life, intercommunications, commerce, traffic, variety, discussion, although many times without solution.

31: Impediments

Impediments as incentives in order to develop one's own efficiency. It symbolizes the human virtue of reaction against opposition.

MODULATING ATTRIBUTE: It is associated to the planet Uranus. It represents the principle of purification as an element of progress.

TRANSCENDENTAL AXIOM: "Do not pass judgment without mercy; neither pass mercy without judgment."

As an element of prediction it promises expectations, promises, domestic devices, restrictions, dealing with minor ranks in quality and position not always beneficial for both parties.

32: Magnificence

Magnificence is in the action of material communion. It symbolizes the human virtue of evidencing one's own value.

MODULATING ATTRIBUTE: It is associated to the planet Mercury. It represents the principle of ostentation as a cause of discussion.

TRANSCENDENTAL AXIOM: "Exhaust the resources of thine intelligence, but do not exhaust those of thine heart."

As an element of prediction it promises dangers because of choleric excess or loquacity, ostentation of material elements, litigations, luxury as a cause of triumph or failure, oppositions or cooperations between people of equal hierarchy.

33: Alliance

Alliance is in the action of communion between equals. It symbolizes the human virtue of affinity by means of identity.

MODULATING ATTRIBUTE: It is associated to the planet Venus. It represents the principle of one's own realization by means of association.

TRANSCENDENTAL AXIOM: "Rejoice with the love of thy youth and rejoice even more with the love of thine maturity."

As an element of prediction it promises upright dealings, lasting alliances, increasing of prosperity, progress, happy contingencies.

34: Innovation

Innovation as an element of evolution. It symbolizes the human virtue of guided effort.

MODULATING ATTRIBUTE: It is associated to the planet Neptune. It represents the principle of one's own inspiration as a guidance for activities.

TRANSCENDENTAL AXIOM: "The length of days is in thy right hand and in thy left works and honor."

As an element of prediction it promises inventions, new enterprises, temptations, temerity, findings, some fortunate and others amazing.

35: Grief

Grief is in the action of moral affliction. It symbolizes the human virtue of tribulation in its purificatory laboring.

MODULATING ATTRIBUTE: It is associated to the planet Saturn. It represents the principle of knowledge of one's own insufficiency.

TRANSCENDENTAL AXIOM: "From behind the here and now is coming what was before; and what was before is that which will be here and now."

As an element of prediction it promises alarms, consternations, melancholies, sadness, obstacles, unexpeced events.

36: Initiation

Initiation is in the action of revivification. It symbolizes the human virtue of progressive actualization of powers.

MODULATING ATTRIBUTE: It is associated to the planet Mars. It represents the principle of unfolding one's own virtues.

TRANSCENDENTAL AXIOM: "It is pleasant to play music, pleasant to sing, and pleasant to listen."

As an element of prediction it promises births, new beginnings, premises, fore-coming fortune, success in businesses, dissipations, declinations.

37: Art and Science

Art and science as factors of individual evolution. It symbolizes the human virtue of one's own discipline as an element of progress.

MODULATING ATTRIBUTE: It is associated to the Sun. It represents the principle of creation by means of applied knowledge.

TRANSCENDENTAL AXIOM: "Behold the Promised Land before mine eyes; help me, oh foot, to arrive there."

As an element of prediction it promises sincere friendship, magnificent aids, probity, equity, ingenious resources, compulsions, perversions, popularity, but not entirely edifying.

38: Duplicity

Duplicity is in the action of sagacity. It symbolizes the human virtue of knowledge voluntarily induced.

MODULATING ATTRIBUTE: It is associated to the Moon. It represents the principle of the antonymous as an element of comparison and selection.

TRANSCENDENTAL AXIOM: "Virtuous woman, not all of those who see thy works can see thy virtues."

As an element of prediction it promises the influence of women in one's own affairs, wisdom and torpidity when resolving them, virtue and scandal, honesty and vice, chastity and corruption.

39: Testimony

Testimony as an irrecusable evidence. It symbolizes the human virtue of verification for proof.

TESTIMONY

MODULATING ATTRIBUTE: It is associated to the planet Jupiter. It represents the principle of demonstration as an element of conviction.

TRANSCENDENTAL AXIOM: "Place thy intentions as witnesses before thyself; however, place thy works as witnesses before thy neighbor."

As an element of prediction it promises conformity, approximations, comparison, banquets, travelling, delayed matrimonies, presumed or real adultery, unforeseen or foreseen arrivals.

40: Presentiment

Presentiment as an instinctual knowledge. It symbolizes the human virtue of anticipated knowledge about that which will occur.

PRESENTIMENT

MODULATING ATTRIBUTE: It is associated to the planet Uranus. It represents the principle of prescience as a natural faculty.

TRANSCENDENTAL AXIOM: "Thou must never be as a man with open eyes to covetousness, nor as a woman with open ears to flattery."

As an element of prediction it promises a very well-retributive work, application, reflection, attraction, sympathy, seduction, threat of ruin, mortifying affections.

41: Uneasiness

Uneasiness as an action of inquietude of one's mood. It symbolizes the human virtue of the constant search for the best.

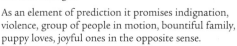

UNEASINESS

MODULATING ATTRIBUTE: It is associated to the planet Mercury. It represents the principle of citizen life.

TRANSCENDENTAL AXIOM: "The bows of the mighty ones were broken, and the bows of the weak were fitted with strength."

As an element of prediction it promises indignation, violence, group of people in motion, bountiful family, puppy loves, joyful ones in the opposite sense.

42: Preeminence

Preeminence as an acknowledgment of superiority. It symbolizes the human virtue of acceptation of hierarchical order.

PREEMINENCE

MODULATING ATTRIBUTE: It is associated to the planet Venus. It represents the principle of power and voluntary obedience.

TRANSCENDENTAL AXIOM: "If utmost in dignity and power, be then utmost in thy merits."

As an element of prediction it promises advantages, triumph, pomposity, superiority, sincerity, surprising loves.

43: Hallucination

Hallucination as an action of rejoicing one's own mood. It symbolizes the human virtue of the expression of contentment.

HALLUCINATION

MODULATING ATTRIBUTE: It is associated to the planet Neptune. It represents the creative principle of induced ideas.

TRANSCENDENTAL AXIOM: "The joy of my heart beautifies my face."

As an element of prediction it promises satisfactions, contentment, decency, modesty, enjoyments, parties, pleasant preparations, violent passions, forbidden loves, divorce, prosperous businesses.

44: Thought

Thought as a creative element. It symbolizes the human virtue which gives sensible form to that which it has intelligible.

THOUGHT

MODULATING ATTRIBUTE: It is associated to the planet Saturn. It represents the creative principle of self-edification.

TRANSCENDENTAL AXIOM: "Excel distrust with wisdom, and enjoy with hope that which is thine."

As an element of prediction it promises projects, deliberation, resolutions, determinations, mutual understanding, fulfilment after arduous struggles of that which is desired by means of a person of the opposite sex.

45: Regeneration

Regeneration as a reiterative action. It symbolizes the human virtue of remembering the past and preventing the future.

MODULATING ATTRIBUTE: It is associated to the planet Mars. It represents the principle of memorization and visualization.

TRANSCENDENTAL AXIOM: "Everything is beautiful in its time and everything is flavorful in its ripeness."

As an element of prediction it promises spiritual resurrection, physical rejuvenation, reconsideration of that which was and some first-fruits of that which will be, vigor, decrepitude, something from infancy and from elderhood, influence of relatives in loving matters, breakage and abandonment.

46: Patrimony

The patrimony as an action of continuity. It symbolizes the human virtue of possession by inheritance.

MODULATING ATTRIBUTE: It is associated to the Sun. It represents the principle of natural prosecution.

TRANSCENDENTAL AXIOM: "The contented one with a little bit opens the doors of plethora."

As an element of prediction it promises friendship bequest, inheritances by own rights, donations, testaments, traditions, forefathers, family, conjugal affinity; for a man: danger because of a woman; for a woman: danger of seduction.

47: Conjecture

Conjecture as an action of knowledge. It symbolizes the human virtue of knowing by means of one's own inspiration.

MODULATING ATTRIBUTE: It is associated to the Moon. It represents the principle of deduction as an element of illumination.

TRANSCENDENTAL AXIOM: "To be resplendent in the light and the heat in the fire is now thy mission and from now on."

As an element of prediction it promises new lights, new teachings, spiritual afflictions, mature hopes, forecoming joys or sufferings, support of relatives; virtuous and lasting loves.

48: Consummation

The consummation as an action of plenitude. It symbolizes the human virtue of one's own conviction.

MODULATING ATTRIBUTE: It is associated to the planet Jupiter. It represents the principle of determination of conduct.

TRANSCENDENTAL AXIOM: "Drink the drops of thy cistern or the flowing of thy well."

As an element of prediction it promises achievements, science, victory, conclusions, resolutions, impossible loves, that which is already irremediable.

49: Versatility

Versatility as an action of reciprocity. It symbolizes the human virtue of correspondence in equivalents.

MODULATING ATTRIBUTE: It is associated to the planet Uranus. It represents the principle of permutation as element of prosperity.

TRANSCENDENTAL AXIOM: "Sweet is work to the one who labors with contentment, and sweet is rest to the one who deserves it."

As an element of prediction it promises removal, changes, new affections, rivalry in loves and undertakings, vicissitudes, but some for good.

50: Affinity

Affinity as an efficient cause of the awakening of emotions. It symbolizes the human virtue of personal attractiveness.

MODULATING ATTRIBUTE: It is associated to the planet Mercury. It represents the principle of natural incentive as a modulating power of action.

TRANSCENDENTAL AXIOM: "Woman, thou art an ember in the fire; and thou, man, the wind that intensifies it."

As an element of prediction it promises illusions, passions, appetites, desires, love, hallucinations, recklessness, dangers that are ignored.

51: Counselling

Counselling as an action of a prudent advice. It symbolizes the human virtue of reverence to knowledge and responsibility on what one knows.

MODULATING ATTRIBUTE: It is associated to the planet Venus. It represents the principle of respect to established order.

TRANSCENDENTAL AXIOM: "The word uttered as advice by a wise person is like silver, and like gold for the one who listens to his advice and follows it."

As an element of prediction it promises judgement, judicial matters, relations with people of authority, dangerous enemies among those people; fortune in the field of weapons or the magistracy, danger of perfidies.

52: Premeditation

Premeditation as a calculated action. It symbolizes the human virtue of preconceiving the desired results.

MODULATING ATTRIBUTE: It is associated to the planet Neptune. It represents the principle of evaluation of factors.

TRANSCENDENTAL AXIOM: "Place thine heart in all thy words, but do not place all the words within thine heart."

As an element of prediction it promises artifices, faking manners, malice, dissimulation, astuteness, sterility, indigence, feminine hatreds and fights as an outcome of such hatreds.

53: Resentment

Resentment as an action of a wounded mood. It symbolizes the human virtue of one's own defense.

MODULATING ATTRIBUTE: It is associated to the planet Saturn. It represents the principle of reprisal.

TRANSCENDENTAL AXIOM: "Do not thou swing a revengeful sword, neither thou fear the fault-finding sword."

As an element of prediction it promises range, imprudence, ineptitude, attacks, defences, criticisms, calumnies, danger by the fire, fights against people of status.

54: Examination

Examination as a deliberation of one's own mood upon conclusion. It symbolizes the human virtue of proceeding with justice.

MODULATING ATTRIBUTE: It is associated to the planet Mars. It represents the principle of free debate.

TRANSCENDENTAL AXIOM: "Search around thy vine and harvest the fallen grains; but do not research for resentments, nor thou collect offences either."

As an element of prediction it promises speculations, enquiries, imputations, treasons; occult enemies; defamation.

55: Contrition

Contrition as an action of repentance. It symbolizes the human virtue of recognizing one's own error.

MODULATING ATTRIBUTE: It is associated to the planet Pluto. It represents the principle of voluntary repair.

TRANSCENDENTAL AXIOM: "Never sow an assortment of seeds in thine orchard, neither harvest them within thine heart."

As an element of prediction it promises lamentations, spiritual afflictions, unpleasantness, unsatisfied profit, acquisition of material wealth by means of moral suffering.

56: Pilgrimage

Pilgrimage as an action of interior purification. It symbolizes the human virtue of affliction.

MODULATING ATTRIBUTE: It is associated to the Moon. It represents the principle of one's own redemption.

TRANSCENDENTAL AXIOM: "Hearten and comfort the afflicted one and keep thyself enthused within thine own tribulations."

As an element of prediction it promises celibacy, timidity to vanquish, matters related with sanctuaries or with people who attend them, sufferings, mysterious dangers, enmity amongst people of status.

57: Rivalry

Rivalry as a proof of competition between opponents. It symbolizes the human virtue of one's own esteem.

MODULATING ATTRIBUTE: It is associated to the planet Jupiter. It represents the principle of skill.

TRANSCENDENTAL AXIOM: "For a just man falleth seven times, and if indeed he is just, seven times he riseth up again."

As an element of prediction it promises delicate circumstances, critical moments, oppositions, conjunction of events, criticism, debates, the fatal thing, and the fulfillment of destiny.

58: Requalification

Requalification as an action of reconsideration of facts. It symbolizes the human virtue of evaluation of opposites.

MODULATING ATTRIBUTE: It is associated to the planet Uranus. It represents the principle of conjecturing by exam.

TRANSCENDENTAL AXIOM: "If thy neighbor leaves thee confused, consult the case with thine own heart."

As an element of prediction it promises warning of dangers, observations right on time, reproaches, pretensions without merit, lost positions, unsuccessful hopes, desire to do, courage to suffer.

59: Revelation

Revelation as an action of unveiling the occult. It symbolizes the human virtue of making intelligible that which was unintelligible.

MODULATING ATTRIBUTE: It is associated to the planet Mercury. It represents the principle of manifestation.

TRANSCENDENTAL AXIOM: "As the metals are tested in the fire, likewise the value of a man is tested in the mouth of those who praise or censure him."

As an element of prediction it promises declarations, authorizations, messages, messengers, contradictory news, voyages, adversity, loquacity, violation of secrets.

60: Evolution

Evolution as a process of transformation. It symbolizes the human virtue of the successive awakening of the consciousness.

MODULATING ATTRIBUTE: It is associated to the planet Venus. It represents the principle of metamorphosis.

TRANSCENDENTAL AXIOM: "The one who sows and the one who waters the sown are the same for the seed."

As an element of prediction it promises detriments, setback of fortune, diminishing, affections that die, beings which are buried, danger of ruin because of fixation of ideas, adverse changes, painful events.

61: Solitude

Solitude as an action of concentration of one's own mood. It symbolizes the human virtue of interior contemplation.

MODULATING ATTRIBUTE: It is associated to the planet Neptune. It represents the principle of isolation.

TRANSCENDENTAL AXIOM: "Pay what thou owe; pay tax to the tax collector, pay treasure to the treasurer, and pay honors to the one who honors."

As an element of prediction it promises reserve, precaution, retirement, inability, vigilance, economy, good behavior, voluntary or unavoidable retirement from social life.

62: Proscription

Proscription as an action of dispersion. It symbolizes the human virtue of counteracting and pushing away the harmful.

MODULATING ATTRIBUTE: It is associated to the planet Saturn. It represents the principle of incompatibility.

TRANSCENDENTAL AXIOM: "The one who watches over his tongue watches over his soul as well."

As an element of prediction it promises oppositions, ruptures, divisions, antagonisms, reclusions, absences, aversions, controversies, embarrassing enterprises.

63: Communion

Communion as an action of partnership. It symbolizes the human virtue of sharing.

MODULATING ATTRIBUTE: It is associated to the planet Mars. It represents the principle of unity within diversity.

TRANSCENDENTAL AXIOM: "Give a seed to the one who wants to sow and does not have it, and advice to the one who wants to succeed and does not know how."

As an element of prediction it promises affections, tenderness, intimacy, affinity, correspondences, mutual protection against third parties, fights for common ideals.

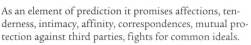

64: Vehemence

Vehemence as an exalted expression of one's own mood. It symbolizes the human virtue of a fervent longing.

MODULATING ATTRIBUTE: It is associated to the Sun. It represents the principle of inner fire.

TRANSCENDENTAL AXIOM: "Mighty is wisdom, and almighty the longing that moves it."

As an element of prediction it promises extreme passions, transpositional mood; range, animosity, enterprises that requires fights; conquests because of vigor, success in matters of love.

65: Learning

Learning as a teaching and warning. It symbolizes the human virtue of knowledge through experience.

MODULATING ATTRIBUTE: It is associated to the Moon. It represents the principle of one's own discipline.

TRANSCENDENTAL AXIOM: "Day or night the one who increaseth knowledge for his own good also increaseth his sorrow."

As an element of prediction it promises internal and external teachings, defects and virtues, ascensions and descents, protection granted by a person major in age and in status; more joy for the coming future than the joy which the present is supposedly presenting.

66: Perplexity

Perplexity as an action of indecision when preferring. It symbolizes the human virtue of selection.

MODULATING ATTRIBUTE: It is associated to the planet Jupiter. It represents the principle of appraisal within decisions.

TRANSCENDENTAL AXIOM: "Whosoever removeth stones shall be hurt therewith, and he that cleaveth wood shall be endangered thereby."

As an element of prediction it promises vacillations, matters in suspense, conditional protection, ascensions and descents, wealth by the support of influential ladies, security in some things and insecurity in others, yet hope in everything.

67: Friendship

Friendship as an action of devotion in affection. It symbolizes the human virtue of veneration.

Modulating Attribute: It is associated to the planet Uranus. It represents the principle of pure love.

Transcendental Axiom: "A quick hand for giving and a fast foot for fulfilling, with both of you I am on the hill or in the valley."

As an element of prediction it promises profit by means of accomplished duties, placidness of spirit, unexpected arrivals, triumph over obstacles, support from friendship, devoted affections.

68: Speculation

Speculation as an appraisal action for values. It symbolizes the human virtue of reasoning.

Modulating Attribute: It is associated to the planet Mercury. It represents the principle of directed diligence.

Transcendental Axiom: "May thine eyes see without fear and thine hands with love."

As an element of prediction it promises intelligent laboring; beneficial learning; abundance of material goods; generosity, liberality; favorable news on monetary matters; right calculation for undertakings.

69: Chance

Chance as a law known by the instinct. It symbolizes the human virtue of transcendental knowledge.

Modulating Attribute: It is associated to the planet Venus. It represents the principle of the primary faculties as guidance in the way of life.

Transcendental Axiom: "There is a fruit in any labor and there is a labor in any fruit."

As an element of prediction it promises retributions, compensations, satisfactory changes; opportunity to ascend, success in real estate properties, thoughtless accomplishment of wishes; fortuitous attractions.

70: Cooperation

Cooperation as an action of collaboration in effort. It symbolizes the human virtue of knowing how to complement oneself.

Modulating Attribute: It is associated to the planet Neptune. It represents the principle of reciprocity.

Transcendental Axiom: "There is no man without science, neither science without man."

As an element of prediction it promises sincere affections, fulfilled promises, the vanishing of hopes without foundation; prosperity by means of death or by means of mysterious causes, progress by application of arts or sciences.

71: Avarice

Avarice as an action of a selfish calculation. It symbolizes the human virtue of the longing for power.

Modulating Attribute: It is associated to the planet Saturn. It represents the principle of prevention.

Transcendental Axiom: "Greedy is greed, it satiates itself with miseries and with abundance of worries."

As an element of prediction it promises usury, egotistical plans that bring remorse, great hopes and small results, danger of robbery, difficulties in preserving the place that is occupied or the acquired status.

72: Purification

Purification as a depurative action. It symbolizes the human virtue of self-overcoming.

Modulating Attribute: It is associated to the planet Mars. It represents the principle of one's own liberation.

Transcendental Axiom: "Hear the doctrine of thy father and forsake not the law of thy mother."

As an element of prediction it promises ingenuousness, vexation of spirit, light that illuminates and heats, fortune by means of a laborious effort, fortunate acquisitions, satisfactory news.

73: Love and Desire

Love and desire as natural stimulations. It symbolizes the human virtue of possessing the elements that provide delight.

MODULATING ATTRIBUTE: It is associated to the Sun. It represents the principle of natural science.

TRANSCENDENTAL AXIOM: "Shuttle of my loom, weaving the cloth that shall become my coat."

LOVE AND DESIRE

As an element of prediction it promises illusions; ardent passion; attractions, ambitions, hope in something that depends on the will of persons of the opposite sex; unexpected goods and danger of losing them because the interference of false friends.

74: Offering

The offering as a propitiatory action. It symbolizes the human virtue of rendering cult to what is superior.

MODULATING ATTRIBUTE: It is associated to the Moon. It represents the principle of reverent love.

TRANSCENDENTAL AXIOM: "Like an offering of the flour's flower on the best of thy plates must be thy giving to the afflicted heart."

OFFERING

As an element of prediction it promises devotion, adoration, fervor, loving passion, harmony and discord, inspirational thoughts, acts of prodigy, variable initiatives, more dissipating than edifying achievements.

75: Generosity

Generosity as a magnanimous action. It symbolizes the human virtue of liberty.

MODULATING ATTRIBUTE: It is associated to the planet Jupiter. It represents the principle of abnegation.

TRANSCENDENTAL AXIOM: "Pleasing fruit to the taste, so sweet when receiving them as well as when giving them."

GENEROSITY

As an element of prediction it promises alms, satisfactory definitions in the end, rewards, inheritance without death; acquisition of wealth; stable fortune.

76: The Dispenser

The dispenser in the action of distributing grace. It symbolizes the human virtue of mercy.

MODULATING ATTRIBUTE: It is associated to the planet Uranus. It represents the principle of human providence.

TRANSCENDENTAL AXIOM: "Join us, foreigner, and eat thereof from our bread and our sauce."

THE DISPENSER

As an element of prediction it promises noble considerations, importance, celebrity, generosity, birth, fortune by means of intelligently directed enterprises; abundant laboring and genius in order to make it useful.

77: Disorientation

Disorientation as an action of requalification. It symbolizes the human virtue of acknowledge and reflection.

MODULATING ATTRIBUTE: It is associated to the planet Mercury. It represents the principle of association of ideas.

TRANSCENDENTAL AXIOM: "Paths are requested for a diligent foot and tools for a laborious hand."

DISORIENTATION

As an element of prediction it promises embarrassing situations, confusion of ideas, perplexity upon decisions, unexpected obstacles, probabilities of good and bad fortune, depending on one's own inspiration towards one or the other.

78: Renaissance

Renaissance as an action of initiation. It symbolizes the human virtue of attaining successive pre-eminences.

MODULATING ATTRIBUTE: It is associated to the planet Venus. It represents the principle of natural evolution.

TRANSCENDENTAL AXIOM: "Sun of midday, moon of midnight, thank goodness for good or bad fortune."

RENAISSANCE

As an element of prediction it promises ecstasies, pure joy, satisfactions, moral and material contentment; honors and luck.

Glossary

Abel: Son of Adam and Eve. Abel or Habel (spelled Hei, Beth, Lamed) means vanity, vapor, or breath.

Abhayan Samskara: (Sanskrit) Abhayan comes from a "without," bhaya "fear" and means 1. Fearless. 2. One who does not produce fear in others. Samskara means "impression, "consequence," "mental formation."

Absolute: Abstract space; that which is without attributes or limitations. Also known as sunyata, void, emptiness, Parabrahman, Adi-buddha, and many other names. The Absolute has three aspects: the Ain, the Ain Soph, and the Ain Soph Aur.

"The Absolute is the Being of all Beings. The Absolute is that which Is, which always has Been, and which always will Be. The Absolute is expressed as Absolute Abstract Movement and Repose. The Absolute is the cause of Spirit and of Matter, but It is neither Spirit nor Matter. The Absolute is beyond the mind; the mind cannot understand It. Therefore, we have to intuitively understand Its nature." - Samael Aun Weor, *Tarot and Kabbalah*

"In the Absolute we go beyond karma and the gods, beyond the law. The mind and the individual consciousness are only good for mortifying our lives. In the Absolute we do not have an individual mind or individual consciousness; there, we are the unconditioned, free and absolutely happy Being. The Absolute is life free in its movement, without conditions, limitless, without the mortifying fear of the law, life beyond spirit and matter, beyond karma and suffering, beyond thought, word and action, beyond silence and sound, beyond forms." - Samael Aun Weor, *The Major Mysteries*

Acheron: (Greek) One of the rivers of Hades in Greek Mythology.

Adam: (Hebrew) "The first."

Adam Kadmon: (Hebrew) A Kabbalistic term with levels of meaning, including: (1) the Archetypal Man; (2) humanity; (3) the Heavenly Man, not fallen into sin.

Adept: (Latin) Adeptus. "He who has obtained." In occultism, one who has reached the stage of initiation and become a Master in the science of esotericism.

Age of Aquarius: On February 4, 1962, when the Age of Aquarius arrived, humanity entered into a very new situation. With the new celestial influence we saw the arrival of a huge shift in society: mass rebellion against the old ways, sexual experimentation, and giant social earthquakes shaking up all the old traditions. We also saw the arrival in the West of a strong spiritual longing, and deep thirst for true, authentic spiritual experience. These two elements: 1) rebellion to tradition and 2) thirst for spiritual knowledge are a direct effect of the influence of Aquarius, the most revolutionary sign of the zodiac. Aquarius is the Water Carrier, whose occult significance is Knowledge, the bringer of Knowledge. With the new age came a sudden revealing of all the hidden knowledge. The doors to the mysteries were thrown open so that humanity can save itself from itself. Of course, the Black Lodge, ever-eager to mislead humanity, has produced so much false spirituality and so many false schools that it is very difficult to find the real and genuine Path.

Alchemy: Al (as a connotation of the Arabic word Allah: al-, the + ilah, God) means "The God." Also Al (Hebrew) for "highest" or El "God." Chem or Khem is from kimia (Greek) which means "to fuse or cast a metal." Also from Khem, the ancient name of Egypt. The synthesis is Al-Kimia: "to fuse with the highest" or "to fuse with God."

Amenti: (Egyptian) Esoterically and literally, the dwelling of the God Amen. A reference to the Underworld.

Arcanum: (Latin. plural: arcana). A secret, a mystery. The root of the term "ark" as in the Ark of Noah and the Ark of the Covenent.

Arcanum A.Z.F.: The practice of sexual transmutation as couple (male-female), a technique known in Tantra and Alchemy. Arcanum refers to a hidden truth or law. A.Z.F. stands for A (agua, water), Z (azufre, sulfur), F (fuego, fire), and is thus: water + fire = consciousness. . Also, A (azoth = chemical element that refers to fire). A & Z are the first and last letters of the alphabet thus referring to the Alpha & Omega (beginning & end).

Archon: (Greek) Literally, "prince" or "ruler." Esoterically, primordial planetary spirits.

Army of the Great Word/Voice: A reference to Elohim Sabbaoth (Hebrew), the army or host of gods and goddesses.

Aspid: An aspid is a viper (Vipera aspis).

Astral: This term is dervied from "pertaining to or proceeding from the stars," but in the esoteric knowledge it refers to the emotional aspect of the fifth dimension, which in Hebrew is called Hod.

Astral Body: What is commonly called the Astral Body is not the true Astral Body, it is rather the Lunar Protoplasmatic Body, also known as the Kama Rupa (Sanskrit, "body of desires") or "dream body" (Tibetan rmi-lam-gyi lus). The true Astral Body is Solar (being superior to Lunar Nature) and must be created, as the Master Jesus indicated in the Gospel of John 3:5-6, "Except a man be born of water and of the Spirit, he cannot enter into the kingdom of God. That which is born of the flesh is flesh; and that which is born of the Spirit is spirit." The Solar Astral Body is created as a result of the Third Initiation of Major Mysteries (Serpents of Fire), and is perfected in the Third Serpent of Light. In Tibetan Buddhism, the Solar Astral Body is known as the illusory body (sgyu-lus). This body is related to the emotional center and to the sephirah Hod.

"Really, only those who have worked with the Maithuna (White Tantra) for many years can possess the Astral Body." - Samael Aun Weor, *The Elimination of Satan's Tail*

Atala: (Sanskrit) One of the regions of the Hindu Lokas (realms).

Atman-Buddhi-Manas: (Sanskrit) The three aspects of our Innermost Monad.

Atman: (Sanskrit, literally "self") An ancient and important word that is grossly misinterpreted in much of Hinduism and Buddhism. Many have misunderstood this word as referring to a permanently existing self or soul, yet the true meaning is otherwise.

"Brahman, Self, Purusha, Chaitanya, Consciousness, God, Atman, Immortality, Freedom, Perfection, Bliss, Bhuma or the unconditioned are synonymous terms." - Swami Sivananda

Thus, Atman as "self" refers to a state of being "unconditioned," which is related to the Absolute, the Ain Soph, or the Shunyata (Emptiness). Thus, Atman refers to the Innermost, the Spirit, the Son of God, who longs to return to that which is beyond words.

"Atman, in Himself, is the ineffable Being, the one who is beyond time and eternity, without end of days. He does not die, neither reincarnates (the ego is what returns), but Atman is absolutely perfect." - Samael Aun Weor

In general use, the term Atman can also refer to the spirit or sephirah Chesed.

"The Being Himself is Atman, the Ineffable. If we commit the error of giving the Being the qualifications of superior "I," alter ego, subliminal "I," or divine ego, etc., we commit blasphemy, because That which is Divine, the Reality, can never fall into the heresy of separability. Superior and inferior are two sections of the same thing. Superior "I" or inferior "I" are two sections of the same pluralized ego (Satan). The Being is the Being, and the reason for the Being to be is to be the same Being. The Being transcends the personality, the "I," and individuality." Samael Aun Weor

"Bliss is the essential nature of man. The central fact of man's being is his inherent divinity. Man's essential nature is divine, the awareness of which he has lost because of his animal propensities and the veil of ignorance. Man, in his ignorance, identifies himself with the body, mind, Prana and the senses. Transcending these, he becomes one with Brahman or the Absolute who is pure bliss. Brahman or the Absolute is the fullest reality, the completest consciousness. That beyond which there is nothing, that which is the innermost Self of all is Atman or Brahman. The Atman is the common Consciousness in all beings. A thief, a prostitute, a scavenger, a king, a rogue, a saint, a dog, a cat, a rat-all have the same common Atman. There is apparent, fictitious difference in bodies and minds only. There are differences in colours and opinions. But, the Atman is the same in all. If you are very rich, you can have a steamer, a train, an airship of your own for your own selfish interests. But, you cannot have an Atman of your own. The Atman is common to all. It is not an individual's sole registered property. The Atman is the one amidst the many. It is constant amidst the forms which come and go. It is the pure, absolute, essential Consciousness of all the conscious beings. The source of all life, the source of all knowledge is the Atman, thy innermost Self. This Atman or Supreme Soul is transcendent, inexpressible, uninferable, unthinkable, indescribable, the ever-peaceful, all-blissful. There is no difference between the Atman and bliss. The Atman is bliss itself. God, perfection, peace, immortality, bliss are one. The goal of life is to attain perfection, immortality or God. The nearer one approaches the Truth, the happier one becomes. For, the essential nature of Truth is positive, absolute bliss. There is no bliss in the finite. Bliss is only in the Infinite. Eternal bliss can be had only from the eternal Self. To know the Self is to enjoy eternal bliss and everlasting peace. Self-realisation bestows eternal existence, absolute knowledge, and perennial bliss. None can be saved without Self-realisation. The quest for the Absolute should be undertaken even sacrificing the dearest object, even life, even courting all pain. Study philosophical books as much as you like, deliver lectures and lectures throughout your global tour, remain in a Himalayan cave for one hundred years, practise Pranayama for fifty years, you cannot attain emancipation without the realisation of the oneness of the Self." - Swami Sivananda

Athanor: A digesting furnace, formerly used by alchemists.

Avatar: From the Sanskrit avatarah, meaning descent (of a deity from heaven), avatar: ava, down + tarati, he crosses. An incarnation of the cosmic, universal Christ (Vishnu, Chokmah). Samael Aun Weor used the term "avatar" to mean "messenger."

"The reincarnated Christ expresses himself through every authentic Avatar. " - Samael Aun Weor, *The Pistis Sophia Unveiled*

"...the Omni-merciful, the infinitude that sustains all, the very, very sacred Absolute Sun, periodically sends Avatars, Saviors, to this valley of tears. These sacred individuals, these messengers, these Saviors, are living incarnations of the Omni-merciful. Nevertheless, this lunar race, this perverse race of Adam, mortally hates such helpers. [...] The blessed Krishna, the blessed Buddha, the blessed Lama, the blessed Mohammed, the loving, essential Ashiata Shiemash, Moses, Quetzalcoatl (and many others) were all Avatars. The doctrine of all Avatars has its roots in the three basic factors of the revolution of the consciousness: to be born, to die, and to sacrifice the self for humanity." - Samael Aun Weor, *The Doomed Aryan Race*

Blavatsky, Helena Petrovna: Founder of the Theosophical Society and author of The Secret Doctrine.

Bobbin-Kandelnosts: Refers to the values or energetic potential carried in the individual. An obscure term, but known in the teachings of Gurdjieff.

Bons: (or Bhons) The oldest religion in Tibet. It was largely overshadowed (some say persecuted) by the arrival of Buddhism. Samael Aun Weor had accepted the statements of earlier investigators which described the Bon religion as essentially black (corrupted by ego and desire); but upon further investigation he discovered that they are not necessarily black, just extreme in some practices.

Book of the Dead: (Egyptian) An ancient ritualistic and occult work attributed to Thoth-Hermes, found in the coffins of ancient mummies.

Buddha: Literally, "awakened one." One of the Three Jewels (Tri-ratna). Commonly used to refer simply to the Buddha Shakyamuni (the "founder" of Buddhism), the term Buddha is actually a title. There are a vast number of Buddhas, each at different levels of attainment. At the ultimate level, a Buddha is a being who has become totally free of suffering. The Inner Being (Chesed) first becomes a Buddha when the Human Soul completes the work of the

Fourth Initiation of Fire (related to Netzach, the mental body).

Buddhata: Also "buddhadatu" (Sanskrit), which means "essence of the Buddha," referring to the Buddha Nature or seed. This is the embryo of soul, also known as the Essence or Tathagata-garbha. This is the small spark of consciousness which descends from the Human Soul into the Four Bodies of Sin (mental, astral, vital, physical) in order to grow through experience in this painful world.

Cain, or Kahyin: (Hebrew) Son of Adam and Eve. The name Kahyin literally means, "to possess." Cain, like all esoteric symbols, carries different meanings.

Causa Causorum: (Latin) "Cause of causes"

Centers, Seven: The human being has seven centers of psychological activity. The first five are the Intellectual, Emotional, Motor, Instinctive, and Sexual Centers. However, through inner development one learns how to utilize the Superior Emotional and Superior Intellectual Centers. Most people do not use these two at all.

Chakra: (Sanskrit) Literally, "wheel." The chakras are subtle centers of energetic transformation. There are hundreds of chakras in our hidden physiology, but seven primary ones related to the awakening of consciousness.

"The chakras are points of connection through which the divine energy circulates from one to another vehicle of the human being." - Samael Aun Weor, *Aztec Christic Magic*

Christ: Derived from the Greek Christos, "the Anointed One," and Krestos, whose esoteric meaning is "fire." The word Christ is a title, not a personal name.

"Indeed, Christ is a Sephirothic Crown (Kether, Chokmah and Binah) of incommensurable wisdom, whose purest atoms shine within Chokmah, the world of the Ophanim. Christ is not the Monad, Christ is not the Theosophical Septenary; Christ is not the Jivan-Atman. Christ is the Central Sun. Christ is the ray that unites us to the Absolute." - Samael Aun Weor, *Tarot and Kabbalah*

"The Gnostic Church adores the Saviour of the World, Jesus. The Gnostic Church knows that Jesus incarnated Christ, and that is why they adore him. Christ is not a human nor a divine individual. Christ is a title given to all fully self-realised Masters. Christ is the Army of the Voice. Christ is the Verb. The Verb is far beyond the body, the soul and the Spirit. Everyone who is able to incarnate the Verb receives in fact the title of Christ. Christ is the Verb itself. It is necessary for everyone of us to incarnate the Verb (Word). When the Verb becomes flesh in us we speak with the verb of light. In actuality, several Masters have incarnated the Christ. In secret India, the Christ Yogi Babaji has lived for millions of years; Babaji is immortal. The Great Master of Wisdom Kout Humi also incarnated the Christ. Sanat Kumara, the founder of the great College of Initiates of the White Lodge, is another living Christ. In the past, many incarnated the Christ. In the present, some have incarnated the Christ. In the future many will incarnate the Christ. John the Baptist also incarnated the Christ. John the Baptist is a living Christ. The difference between Jesus and the other Masters that also incarnated the Christ has to do with Hierarchy. Jesus is the highest Solar Initiate of the Cosmos..." - Samael Aun Weor, *The Perfect Matrimony*

Consciousness: "Wherever there is life, there exists the consciousness. Consciousness is inherent to life as humidity is inherent to water." - Samael Aun Weor, *Fundamental Notions of Endocrinology and Criminology*

From various dictionaries: 1. The state of being conscious; knowledge of one's own existence, condition, sensations, mental operations, acts, etc. 2. Immediate knowledge or perception of the presence of any object, state, or sensation. 3. An alert cognitive state in which you are aware of yourself and your situation. In Universal Gnosticism, the range of potential consciousness is allegorized in the Ladder of Jacob, upon which the angels ascend and descend. Thus there are higher and lower levels of consciousness, from the level of demons at the bottom, to highly realized angels in the heights.

"It is vital to understand and develop the conviction that consciousness has the potential to increase to an infinite degree." - The 14th Dalai Lama.

"Light and consciousness are two phenomena of the same thing; to a lesser degree of consciousness, corresponds a lesser degree of light; to a greater degree of consciousness, a greater degree of light." - Samael Aun Weor, *The Esoteric Treatise of Hermetic Astrology*

Cteis: The Cteis was a circular and concave pedestal, or receptacle, on which the Phallus, or column [obelisk] rested. The union of these two, as the generative and producing principles of nature, in one compound figure, was the most usual mode of representation. Here we find the origin of the point within a circle, a symbol which was first adopted by the old sun worshipers. The Compass arranged above the Square symbolizes the (male) Sun, impregnating the passive (female) Earth with its life-producing rays. The true meanings, then are two-fold: the earthly (human) representations are of the man and his phallus, and the woman with her receptive cteis (vagina). The male female divinities were commonly symbolized by the generative parts of man and woman... The Phallus and Cteis (vagina), emblems of generation and production, and which, as such, appeared in the mysteries. The Indian Lingam was the union of both, as were the Boat and Mast, and the Point within the Circle. The Cteis was symbolized as the moon. The female personification of the productive principle. It generally accompanied the Phallus... and as a symbol of the prolific powers of nature, and was extensively venerated by the nations of antiquity.

Daimon or Daemon: (Greek) Not to be confused with the Christian term 'demon.' The Daemon of Socrates is the inner instructor, the Divine Spirit who guides the soul to perfection. In the original Hermetic works the name has a meaning identical with that of "god," "angel," or "genius." The name was given by ancient people to all kinds of spirits, whether good or bad.

Demiurge: (Greek for "worker" or "craftsman") The Demiurgos or Artificer; the supernal power that built the universe. Freemasons derive from this word their phrase "Supreme Architect." Also the name given by Plato in a passage in the Timaeus to the creator God.

"Esotericism admits the existence of a Logos, or a collective Creator of the universe, a Demi-urge architect. It is unquestionable that such a Demiurge is not a personal deity as many mistakenly suppose, but rather a host of Dhyan Chohans, Angels, Archangels, and other forces." - Samael Aun Weor, *The Three Mountains*

"It is impossible to symbolize or allegorize the Unknowable One. Nevertheless, the Manifested One, the Knowable Elohim, can be allegorized or symbolized. The Manifested Elohim is constituted by the Demiurge Creator of the Universe. [...] The great invisible Forefather is Aelohim, the Unknowable Divinity. The great Triple-Powered God is the Demiurge Creator of the Universe: Multiple Perfect Unity. The Creator Logos is the Holy Triamatzikamno. The Verb, the Great Word. The three spaces of the First Mystery are the regions of the Demiurge Creator." - Samael Aun Weor, *The Pistis Sophia Unveiled*

"The Demiurge Architect of the Universe is not a human or divine individual; rather, it is Multiple Perfect Unity, the Platonic Logos." - Samael Aun Weor, *Gnostic Anthropology*

Devolution: (Latin) From devolvere: backwards evolution, degeneration. The natural mechanical inclination for all matter and energy in nature to return towards their state of inert uniformity. Related to the Arcanum Ten: Retribution, the Wheel of Samsara. Devolution is the inverse process of evolution. As evolution is the complication of matter or energy, devolution is the slow process of nature to simplify matter or energy by applying forces to it. Through devolution, protoplasmic matter and energy descend, degrade, and increase in density within the infradimensions of nature to finally reach the center of the earth where they attain their ultimate state of inert uniformity. Devolution transfers the psyche, moral values, consciousness, or psychological responsibilities to inferior degradable organisms (Klipoth) through the surrendering of our psychological values to animal behaviors, especially sexual degeneration.

Divine Mother: "Among the Aztecs, she was known as Tonantzin, among the Greeks as chaste Diana. In Egypt she was Isis, the Divine Mother, whose veil no mortal has lifted. There is no doubt at all that esoteric Christianity has never forsaken the worship of the Divine Mother Kundalini. Obviously she is Marah, or better said, RAM-IO, MARY. What orthodox religions did not specify, at least with regard to the exoteric or public circle, is the aspect of Isis in her individual human form. Clearly, it was taught only in secret to the Initiates that this Divine Mother exists individually within each human being. It cannot be emphasized enough that Mother-God, Rhea, Cybele, Adonia, or whatever we wish to call her, is a variant of our own individual Being in the here and now. Stated explicitly, each of us has our own particular, individual Divine Mother." - Samael Aun Weor, *The Great Rebellion*

"Devi Kundalini, the Consecrated Queen of Shiva, our personal Divine Cosmic Individual Mother, assumes five transcendental mystic aspects in every creature, which we must enumerate:

1. The unmanifested Prakriti

2. The chaste Diana, Isis, Tonantzin, Maria or better said Ram-Io

3. The terrible Hecate, Persephone, Coatlicue, queen of the infernos and death; terror of love and law

4. The special individual Mother Nature, creator and architect of our physical organism

5. The Elemental Enchantress to whom we owe every vital impulse, every instinct." - Samael Aun Weor, *The Mystery of the Golden Blossom*

Drukpa: (Also known variously as Druk-pa, Dugpa, Brugpa, Dag dugpa or Dad dugpa) The term Drukpa comes from from Dzong-kha and Tibetan འབྲུག་ཡུལ ('brug yul), which means "country of Bhutan," and is composed of Druk, "dragon," and pa, "person." In Asia, the word refers to the people of Bhutan, a country between India and Tibet. Drukpa can also refer to a large sect of Buddhism which broke from the Kagyug-pa "the Ones of the Oral Tradition." They considered themselves as the heirs of the indian Gurus: their teaching, which goes back to Vajradhara, was conveyed through Dakini, from Naropa to Marpa and then to the ascetic and mystic poet Milarepa. Later on, Milarepa's disciples founded new monasteries, and new threads appeared, among

which are the Karmapa and the Drukpa. All those schools form the Kagyug-pa order, in spite of episodic internal quarrels and extreme differences in practice. The Drukpa sect is recognized by their ceremonial large red hats, but it should be known that they are not the only "Red Hat" group (the Nyingmas, founded by Padmasambhava, also use red hats). The Drukpas have established a particular worship of the Dorje (Vajra, or thunderbolt, a symbol of the phallus). Samael Aun Weor wrote repeatedly in many books that the "Drukpas" practice and teach Black Tantra, by means of the expelling of the sexual energy. If we analyze the word, it is clear that he is referring to "Black Dragons," or people who practice Black Tantra. He was not referring to all the people of Bhutan, or all members of the Buddhist Drukpa sect. Such a broad condemnation would be as ridiculous as the one made by those who condemn all Jews for the crucifixion of Jesus.

Ego: The multiplicity of contradictory psychological elements that we have inside are in their sum the "ego." Each one is also called "an ego" or an "I." Every ego is a psychological defect which produces suffering. The ego is three (related to our Three Brains or three centers of psychological processing), seven (capital sins), and legion (in their infinite variations).

"The ego is the root of ignorance and pain." - Samael Aun Weor, *The Esoteric Treatise of Hermetic Astrology*

"The Being and the ego are incompatible. The Being and the ego are like water and oil. They can never be mixed... The annihilation of the psychic aggregates (egos) can be made possible only by radically comprehending our errors through meditation and by the evident Self-reflection of the Being." - Samael Aun Weor, *The Pistis Sophia Unveiled*

Ens Seminis: (Latin) Literally, "the entity of semen." A term used by Paracelsus.

Ens Virtutis: (Latin) Literally, "army; host; mighty works (pl.); strength/power; courage/bravery; worth/manliness/virtue/character/excellence. Paracelsus stated that the ens virtutis must be extracted from the ens seminis, thus saying that all virtue and excellence is developed from the force within the sexual waters.

Evolution: "It is not possible for the true Human Being (the Self-realized Being) to appear through the mechanics of evolution. We know very well that evolution and its twin sister devolution are nothing else but two laws which constitute the mechanical axis of all Nature. One evolves to a certain perfectly defined point, and then the devolving process follows. Every ascent is followed by a descent and vice-versa." - Samael Aun Weor, *Revolutionary Psychology*. "Evolution is a process of complication of energy." - Samael Aun Weor, *The Perfect Matrimony*

Fohat: (Theosophical/Tibetan) A term used by H.P. Blavatsky to represent the active (male) potency of the Shakti (female sexual power) in nature, the essence of cosmic electricity, vital force. As explained in *The Secret Doctrine*, "He (Fohat) is, metaphysically, the objectivised thought of the gods; the "Word made flesh" on a lower scale, and the messenger of Cosmic and human ideations: the active force in Universal Life.... In India, Fohat is connected with Vishnu and Surya in the early character of the (first) God; for Vishnu is not a high god in the Rig Veda. The name Vishnu is from the root vish, "to pervade," and Fohat is called the "Pervader" and the Manufacturer, because he shapes the atoms from crude material..." The term fohat has recently been linked with the Tibetan verb phro-wa and the noun spros-pa. These two terms are listed in Jäschke's Tibetan-English Dictionary (1881) as, for phro-wa, "to proceed, issue, emanate from, to spread, in most cases from rays of light..." while for spros-pa he gives "business, employment, activity."

Fornication: Originally, the term fornication was derived from the Indo-European word *gwher*, whose meanings relate to heat and burning (the full explanation can be found online at http://sacred-sex.org/terminology/fornication). Fornication means to make the heat (solar fire) of the seed (sexual power) leave the body through voluntary orgasm. Any voluntary orgasm is fornication, whether between a married man and woman, or an unmarried man and woman, or through masturbation, or in any other case; this is explained by Moses: "A man from whom there is a discharge of semen, shall immerse all his flesh in water, and he shall remain unclean until evening. And any garment or any leather [object] which has semen on it, shall be immersed in water, and shall remain unclean until evening. A woman with whom a man cohabits, whereby there was [a discharge of] semen, they shall immerse in water, and they shall remain unclean until evening." - Leviticus 15:16-18

To fornicate is to spill the sexual energy through the orgasm. Those who "deny themselves" restrain the sexual energy, and "walk in the midst of the fire" without being burned. Those who restrain the sexual energy, who renounce the orgasm, remember God in themselves, and do not defile themselves with animal passion, "for the temple of God is holy, which temple ye are."

"Whosoever is born of God doth not commit sin; for his seed remaineth in him: and he cannot sin, because he is born of God." - 1 John 3:9

This is why neophytes always took a vow of sexual abstention, so that they could prepare themselves for marriage, in which they would have sexual relations but not release the sexual energy through the orgasm. This is why Paul advised:

"...they that have wives be as though they had none..." - I Corinthians 7:29

"A fornicator is an individual who has intensely accustomed his genital organs to copulate (with orgasm). Yet, if the same individual changes his custom of copulation to the custom of no copulation, then he transforms himself into a chaste person. We have as an example the astonishing case of Mary Magdalene, who was a famous prostitute. Mary Magdalene became the famous Saint Mary Magdalene, the repented prostitute. Mary Magdalene became the chaste disciple of Christ." - Samael Aun Weor, *The Revolution of Beelzebub*

Genius Lucis: (Latin) Genius is Latin for "guardian deity or spirit that watches over each person; spirit, incarnation" from root of gignere "beget, produce." Lucis is Latin for "light."

Gnosis: (Greek) Knowledge.

1. The word Gnosis refers to the knowledge we acquire through our own experience, as opposed to knowledge that we are told or believe in. Gnosis - by whatever name in history or culture - is conscious, experiential knowledge, not

merely intellectual or conceptual knowledge, belief, or theory. This term is synonymous with the Hebrew "daath" and the Sanskrit "jna."

2. The tradition that embodies the core wisdom or knowledge of humanity.

"Gnosis is the flame from which all religions sprouted, because in its depth Gnosis is religion. The word "religion" comes from the Latin word "religare," which implies "to link the Soul to God"; so Gnosis is the very pure flame from where all religions sprout, because Gnosis is Knowledge, Gnosis is Wisdom." - Samael Aun Weor, *The Esoteric Path*

"The secret science of the Sufis and of the Whirling Dervishes is within Gnosis. The secret doctrine of Buddhism and of Taoism is within Gnosis. The sacred magic of the Nordics is within Gnosis. The wisdom of Hermes, Buddha, Confucius, Mohammed and Quetzalcoatl, etc., etc., is within Gnosis. Gnosis is the Doctrine of Christ." - Samael Aun Weor, *The Revolution of Beelzebub*

Gunas: (Sanskrit) Literally, "fundamental quality." "Prakriti is composed of the three Gunas or forces, namely, Sattva, Rajas and Tamas. Sattva is harmony or light or wisdom or equilibrium or goodness. Rajas is passion or motion or activity. Tamas is inertia or inaction or darkness. During Cosmic Pralaya these three Gunas exist in a state of equilibrium. During Srishti or projection a vibration arises and the three qualities are manifested in the physical universe." - Swami Sivananda, *Kundalini Yoga*

"Sattva, Rajas and Tamas (harmony, emotion and inertness) were in a perfect, nirvanic equilibrium before the dawning of the dawn of the Mahamanvantara. The fire put the cosmic scale in motion. Sattva, Rajas and Tamas were unbalanced; therefore, the Mahamanvantara dawned. The yogi must liberate himself from Sattva, Rajas and Tamas to gain the right to enter into the Absolute. Sattva, Rajas and Tamas will be in perfect equilibrium again at the end of the Mahamanvantara; thus, the universe will sleep again within the profound bosom of the Absolute, within the supreme Parabrahman, the In-nominated." - Samael Aun Weor, The Mysteries of the Fire

Heliogabalus Stone: A reference to the Cubic Stone of Yesod. Historically, a large black stone, a meteorite, that some describe from its image on coins and in sculpture as shaped like a beehive; others as phallic. This stone first appears in history atop its altar in the temple of Emesa on coins minted in the reign of Caracalla. It was taken by Varius Avitus Bassianus, Roman emperor (218-222), during his own reign, to Rome, and placed in a huge temple dedicated to it on the Palatine hill. Each summer, of the three he spent there, he led the stone in ceremonial procession, attended by musicians and dancers, to another palace in a garden at the outer edge of Rome. At the end of summer he would take it back to the Palatine. This is recorded in his coinage, as well as in the written sources. Varius was appointed priest of the sun-god Elagabal, whose name he adopted. Heliogabalus lived in Rome as an oriental despot and, giving himself up to detestable sensual pleasures, degraded the imperial office to the lowest point by most shameful vices, which had their origin in certain rites of oriental naturalistic religion.

Heptaparaparshinokh: The law of seven; the law of organization. This law is visible in the seven notes of the western musical scale, the seven chakras, the seven bodies of the soul, the Seven Spirits before the Throne, etc.

Hermanubis: (Greek) The revealer of mysteries of the lower world, not of hell or hades, but of our Earth (the lowest world in the chain of worlds), and also of the sexual mysteries. He was always represented with a cross in his hand, one of the earliest symbols of generation or procreation.

Hiram Abiff: A biblical personage; a skillful builder and architect whom King Solomon procured from Tyre for the purpose of supervising the construction of the Temple. According to the Masonic story, Hiram Abiff was murdered by three traitors who were subsequently found by twenty-seven Master Masons.

Hydrogen: (From *hydro-* water, *gen-* generate, genes, genesis, etc.) The hydrogen is the simplest element on the periodic table and in Gnosticism it is recognized as the element that is the building block of all forms of matter. Hydrogen is a packet of solar light. The solar light (the light that comes from the sun) is the reflection of the Okidanok, the Cosmic Christ, which creates and sustains every world. This element is the fecundated water, generated water (hydro). The water is the source of all life. Everything that we eat, breathe and all of the impressions that we receive are in the form of various structures of hydrogen. Samael Aun Weor often will place a note (Do, Re, Mi...) and a number related with the vibration and atomic weight (level of complexity) with a particular hydrogen. For example, Samael Aun Weor constantly refers to the Hydrogen Si-12. "Si" is the highest note in the octave and it is the result of the notes that come before it. This particular hydrogen is always related to the forces of Yesod, which is the synthesis and coagulation of all food, air and impressions that we have previously received. Food begins at Do-768, air begins at Do-384, and impressions begin at Do-48.

Initiation: The process whereby the Innermost (the Inner Father) receives recognition, empowerment and greater responsibilities in the Internal Worlds, and little by little approaches His goal: complete Self-realization, or in other words, the return into the Absolute. Initiation NEVER applies to the "I" or our terrestrial personality.

"Nine Initiations of Minor Mysteries and seven great Initiations of Major Mysteries exist. The Innermost is the one who receives all of these Initiations. The Testament of Wisdom says: "Before the dawning of the false aurora upon the earth, the ones who survived the hurricane and the tempest were praising the Innermost, and the heralds of the aurora appeared unto them." The psychological "I" does not receives Initiations. The human personality does not receive anything. Nonetheless, the "I" of some Initiates becomes filled with pride when saying 'I am a Master, I have such Initiations.' Thus, this is how the "I" believes itself to be an Initiate and keeps reincarnating in order to "perfect itself", but, the "I" never ever perfects itself. The "I" only reincarnates in order to satisfy desires. That is all." - Samael Aun Weor, *The Aquarian Message*

Innermost: "Our real Being is of a universal nature. Our real Being is neither a kind of superior nor inferior "I." Our real Being is impersonal,

universal, divine. He transcends every concept of "I," me, myself, ego, etc., etc." - Samael Aun Weor, *The Perfect Matrimony*

Also known as Atman, the Spirit, Chesed, our own individual interior divine Father.

"The Innermost is the ardent flame of Horeb. In accordance with Moses, the Innermost is the Ruach Elohim (the Spirit of God) who sowed the waters in the beginning of the world. He is the Sun King, our Divine Monad, the Alter-Ego of Cicerone." - Samael Aun Weor, *The Revolution of Beelzebub*

Internal Worlds: The many dimensions beyond the physical world. These dimensions are both subjective and objective. To know the objective internal worlds (the Astral Plane, or Nirvana, or the Klipoth) one must first know one's own personal, subjective internal worlds, because the two are intimately associated.

"Whosoever truly wants to know the internal worlds of the planet Earth or of the solar system or of the galaxy in which we live, must previously know his intimate world, his individual, internal life, his own internal worlds. Man, know thyself, and thou wilt know the Universe and its Gods. The more we explore this internal world called "myself," the more we will comprehend that we simultaneously live in two worlds, in two realities, in two confines: the external and the internal. In the same way that it is indispensable for one to learn how to walk in the external world so as not to fall down into a precipice, or not get lost in the streets of the city, or to select one's friends, or not associate with the perverse ones, or not eat poison, etc.; likewise, through the psychological work upon oneself we learn how to walk in the internal world, which is explorable only through Self-observation." - Samael Aun Weor, *Revolutionary Psychology*

Through the work in Self-observation, we develop the capacity to awaken where previously we were asleep: including in the objective internal worlds.

Jinn State: The condition that results from moving the physical body into the fourth dimension. "A body while in the "Jinn" state can float in the air (Laghima) or be submerged within the waters (Prakamya), or pass through fire without being burned, or be reduced to the size of an atom (Anima), or be enlarged to the point of touching the sun or the moon with the hand (Mahima). A body submerged within the supra-sensible worlds is submitted to the laws of those worlds. Then, this body is plastic and elastic, so it can change form, decrease its weight (Laghima), or increase its weight (Garima) willingly... When Jesus was walking upon the waters of the Sea of Galilee, he had his body in the state of "Jinn." Peter was able to liberate himself from the chains and to leave the prison, thanks to the assistance of an Angel who helped him place his body in the state of "Jinn."'" - Samael Aun Weor, *The Aquarian Message*

Kabbalah: (Hebrew) Alternatively spelled Cabala, Qabalah (etc., ad nauseum) from the Hebrew KBLH or QBL, "to receive." An ancient esoteric teaching hidden from the uninitiated, whose branches and many forms have reached throughout the world. The true Kabbalah is the science and language of the Superior Worlds and is thus objective, complete and without flaw; it is said that "all enlightened beings agree," and their natural agreement is a function of the awakened consciousness. The Kabbalah is the language of that consciousness, thus disagreement regarding it's meaning and interpretation is always due to subjective elements in the psyche.

Kabir: The word "Kabir" is equally well-known in India and in the Middle East, although in each case the word means different things (in many areas it is used as a proper name). From Arabic it means "great" or "the Most High." It is usually attached to the name of a great teacher, as "Sri" is in India. Esoterically, it refers to the Divine Calf, the child of the Divine Mother (who is symbolized by a cow in India, Greece, etc.) The word is related to the ancient and mysterious Cabeiri of the Greek mysteries.

Kabir is also the name of an Indian religious leader who pioneered a religious movement that combined elements of Islam and Hinduism and is considered the precursor of Sikhism.

Karma: (Sanskrit, literally "deed"; derived from kri, "to do...") The law of cause and effect.

"Be not deceived; God is not mocked: for whatsoever a man soweth, that shall he also reap." - Galatians 6:7

Keys of Saint Peter: From *The Pistis Sophia Unveiled:* "The intimate Christ always instructs Peter. The intimate Christ reveals the mysteries to Peter. The intimate Christ has the power in order to perfect Peter in all his splendour. The Lord gives all the mysteries of all the regions of the Father and all the regions of the First Mystery to the interior Peter within each one of us. Consequently, the secret Peter of each one of us is interesting. He, who Peter admits on earth, shall be admitted into the Light of the height, and he who Peter expels on earth, shall be expelled from the Kingdom of the Father in Heaven. It is clear that Peter is the Hierophant of sex within ourselves. Therefore, he has the power to open or to close the doors of Heaven in ourselves, and within ourselves. Verily, verily, I say unto you that Peter has the keys of the Kingdom. The secret power that opens or closes the doors of Eden is in sex. The sexual energy, when correctly orientated, opens the doors of Paradise. The creative energy, when incorrectly orientated, closes the doors of Paradise. Sulphur and Mercury are the two keys of the Kingdom. These two keys, one of Gold and the other of Silver, form a Cross in the hands of Peter."

From Dantes *The Divine Comedy,* Purgatory, canto IX: "Then with his sword he traced upon my brow the scars of seven P's. "Once entered here, be sure you cleanse away these wounds," he said. Ashes, or earth when it is dug up dry - this was the colour of the robes he wore; he reached beneath them and drew out two keys. One key was silver and the other gold; first he applied the white one, then the yellow - with that the gate responded to my wish. "Whenever either one of these two keys fails to turn properly inside the lock," the angel said, "the road ahead stays closed. One is more precious, but the other needs wisdom and skill before it will unlock, for it is that one which unties the knot. I hold these keys from Peter, who advised: 'Admit too many, rather than too few, if they but cast themselves before your feet.'" Then, pushing back the portal's holy door, "Enter," he said to us, "but first be warned: to look back means to go back out again."

Klipoth: (Hebrew) "The World of Shells."

Kout Humi: A Master of the White Lodge, often referred to as K.H.

Kundalini: "Kundalini, the serpent power or mystic fire, is the primordial energy or Sakti that lies dormant or sleeping in the Muladhara Chakra, the centre of the body. It is called the serpentine or annular power on account of serpentine form. It is an electric fiery occult power, the great pristine force which underlies all organic and inorganic matter. Kundalini is the cosmic power in individual bodies. It is not a material force like electricity, magnetism, centripetal or centrifugal force. It is a spiritual potential Sakti or cosmic power. In reality it has no form. [...] O Divine Mother Kundalini, the Divine Cosmic Energy that is hidden in men! Thou art Kali, Durga, Adisakti, Rajarajeswari, Tripurasundari, Maha-Lakshmi, Maha-Sarasvati! Thou hast put on all these names and forms. Thou hast manifested as Prana, electricity, force, magnetism, cohesion, gravitation in this universe. This whole universe rests in Thy bosom. Crores of salutations unto thee. O Mother of this world! Lead me on to open the Sushumna Nadi and take Thee along the Chakras to Sahasrara Chakra and to merge myself in Thee and Thy consort, Lord Siva. Kundalini Yoga is that Yoga which treats of Kundalini Sakti, the six centres of spiritual energy (Shat Chakras), the arousing of the sleeping Kundalini Sakti and its union with Lord Siva in Sahasrara Chakra, at the crown of the head. This is an exact science. This is also known as Laya Yoga. The six centres are pierced (Chakra Bheda) by the passing of Kundalini Sakti to the top of the head. 'Kundala' means 'coiled'. Her form is like a coiled serpent. Hence the name Kundalini." - Swami Sivananda, *Kundalini Yoga*

Kunrath, Heinrich: A well-known Kabbalist, Alchemist, Christian and mystic, he was born in Leipzig in 1560 and died in Dresden in 1605. He was a celebrity during his life, and produced many remarkable works.

Leadbeater, C.W.: A writer of Theosophical Occultism famous for such books as The Elementals and The Chakras. He said, "It is one of the commonest of mistakes to consider that the limit of our power of perception is also the limit of all there is to see."

Logos: (Greek) means Verb or Word. In Greek and Hebrew metaphysics, the unifying principle of the world. The Logos is the manifested deity of every nation and people; the outward expression or the effect of the cause which is ever concealed. (Speech is the "logos" of thought). The Logos has three aspects, known universally as the Trinity or Trimurti. The First Logos is the Father, Brahma. The Second Logos is the Son, Vishnu. The Third Logos is the Holy Spirit, Shiva. One who incarnates the Logos becomes a Logos.

"The Logos is not an individual. The Logos is an army of ineffable beings." - Samael Aun Weor, *Endocrinology & Criminology*

Magic: The word magic is derived from the ancient word "mag" that means priest. Real magic is the work of a priest. A real magician is a priest.

"Magic, according to Novalis, is the art of influencing the inner world consciously." - Samael Aun Weor, *The Mystery of the Golden Blossom*

"When magic is explained as it really is, it seems to make no sense to fanatical people. They prefer to follow their world of illusions." - Samael Aun Weor, *The Revolution of Beelzebub*

Magnes: (Latin) Canon, principle or prima materia.

Magnus: (Latin) "Great." See "Misterium Magnum."

Mahamanvantara: (Sanskrit) "The Great Day." A period of universal activity, as opposed to a Mahapralaya, a cosmic night or period of rest.

"Truthfully, the quantities of years assigned to a Cosmic Day are symbolic. The Cosmic Night arrives when the ingathering of the perfect souls is complete, which means, when the Cosmic Day is absolutely perfected." - Samael Aun Weor, *The Pistis Sophia Unveiled*

"I was absorbed within the Absolute at the end of that Lunar Mahamanvantara, which endured 311,040,000,000,000 years, or, in other words, an age of Brahma." - Samael Aun Weor, *The Revolution of Beelzebub*

Maithuna: Sanskrit, "sacramental intercourse."

Mantra: (Sanskrit, literally "mind protection") A sacred word or sound. The use of sacred words and sounds is universal throughout all religions and mystical traditions, because the root of all creation is in the Great Breath or the Word, the Logos. "In the beginning was the Word…"

Master: Like many terms related to spirituality, this one is grossly misunderstood. Samael Aun Weor wrote while describing the Germanic Edda, "In this Genesis of creation we discover Sexual Alchemy. The Fire fecundated the cold waters of chaos. The masculine principle Alfadur fecundated the feminine principle Niffleheim, dominated by Surtur (the Darkness), to bring forth life. That is how Ymir is born, the father of the giants, the Internal God of every human being, the Master." Therefore, the Master is the Innermost, Atman, the Father.

"The only one who is truly great is the Spirit, the Innermost. We, the intellectual animals, are leaves that the wind tosses about… No student of occultism is a Master. True Masters are only those who have reached the Fifth Initiation of Major Mysteries. Before the Fifth Initiation nobody is a Master." - Samael Aun Weor, *The Perfect Matrimony*

Matripadma: (Sanskrit) The mother-lotus; the womb of nature.

Meditation: "When the esotericist submerges himself into meditation, what he seeks is information." - Samael Aun Weor

"It is urgent to know how to meditate in order to comprehend any psychic aggregate, or in other words, any psychological defect. It is indispensable to know how to work with all our heart and with all our soul, if we want the elimination to occur." - Samael Aun Weor, *The Pistis Sophia Unveiled*

"1. The Gnostic must first attain the ability to stop the course of his thoughts, the capacity to not think. Indeed, only the one who achieves that capacity will hear the Voice of the Silence.

"2. When the Gnostic disciple attains the capacity to not think, then he must learn to concentrate his thoughts on only one thing.

"3. The third step is correct meditation. This brings the first flashes of the new consciousness into the mind.

"4. The fourth step is contemplation, ecstasy or Samadhi. This is the state of Turiya (perfect clairvoyance). - Samael Aun Weor, *The Perfect Matrimony*

Mercabah: (Hebrew) Literally, "chariot." Refers to the Soul the Initiate must build.

Misterium Magnum: (Latin) "The Great Mystery"

Monad: (Latin) From monas, "unity; a unit, monad." The Monad is the Being, the Innermost, our own inner Spirit.

"We must distinguish between Monads and Souls. A Monad, in other words, a Spirit, is; a Soul is acquired. Distinguish between the Monad of a world and the Soul of a world; between the Monad of a human and the Soul of a human; between the Monad of an ant and the Soul of an ant. The human organism, in final synthesis, is constituted by billions and trillions of infinitesimal Monads. There are several types and orders of primary elements of all existence, of every organism, in the manner of germs of all the phenomena of nature; we can call the latter Monads, employing the term of Leibnitz, in the absence of a more descriptive term to indicate the simplicity of the simplest existence. An atom, as a vehicle of action, corresponds to each of these genii or Monads. The Monads attract each other, combine, transform themselves, giving form to every organism, world, microorganism, etc. Hierarchies exist among the Monads; the Inferior Monads must obey the Superior ones that is the Law. Inferior Monads belong to the Superior ones. All the trillions of Monads that animate the human organism have to obey the owner, the chief, the Principal Monad. The regulating Monad, the Primordial Monad permits the activity of all of its subordinates inside the human organism, until the time indicated by the Law of Karma." - Samael Aun Weor, *The Esoteric Treatise of Hermetic Astrology*

"(The number) one is the Monad, the Unity, Iod-Heve or Jehovah, the Father who is in secret. It is the Divine Triad that is not incarnated within a Master who has not killed the ego. He is Osiris, the same God, the Word." - Samael Aun Weor, *Tarot and Kabbalah*

"When spoken of, the Monad is referred to as Osiris. He is the one who has to Self-realize Himself... Our own particular Monad needs us and we need it. Once, while speaking with my Monad, my Monad told me, 'I am self-realizing Thee; what I am doing, I am doing for Thee.' Otherwise, why are we living? The Monad wants to Self-realize and that is why we are here. This is our objective." - Samael Aun Weor, *Tarot and Kabbalah*

"The Monads or Vital Genii are not exclusive to the physical organism; within the atoms of the Internal Bodies there are found imprisoned many orders and categories of living Monads. The existence of any physical or supersensible, Angelic or Diabolical, Solar or Lunar body, has billions and trillions of Monads as their foundation." - Samael Aun Weor, *The Esoteric Treatise of Hermetic Astrology*

Morya: An initiate of the last century and author of the famous *Dayspring of Youth* and *The Lord God of Truth Within*.

Negative Disclosure: (Egyptian) A prayer or testament found in the Egyptian Book of the Dead in which the Initiate describes in detail all of the sins he has NOT committed. See Chapter 48 of Cosmic Teachings of a Lama by Samael Aun Weor.

Nephesh: (Hebrew; alternatively, nefesh) In Kabbalah, one of the three souls of the human being. The animal soul.

"And the LORD God formed man [of] the dust of the ground, and breathed into his nostrils the breath [neshamah] of life; and man became a living soul [nephesh]." - Genesis 2:7

Neshamah: (Hebrew, literally "breath") In Kabbalah, one of the three souls of the human being, called the Spiritual Soul.

"The Neshamah of Adam (man) is a lamp of Jehovah..." - Proverbs 20:27

Neurasthenia: A category of mental disorder that is no longer in use. It described a condition with symptoms such as irritability, fatigue, weakness, anxiety, and localized pains without any apparant physical causes. It was thought to result from exhaustion of the nervous system.

Nirvana: (Sanskrit, "extinction"; Tibetan: nyangde, literally "the state beyond sorrow") In general use, refers to the permanent cessation of suffering and its causes, and therefore refers to a state of consciousness rather than a place. Yet, the term can also apply to heavenly realms, whose vibration is directed related to the cessation of suffering. In other words, if your mindstream has liberated itself from the causes of suffering, it will naturally vibrate at the level of Nirvana (heaven).

"When the Soul fuses with the Inner Master, then it becomes free from Nature and enters into the supreme happiness of absolute existence. This state of happiness is called Nirvana. Nirvana can be attained through millions of births and deaths, but it can also be attained by means of a shorter path; this is the path of "initiation." The Initiate can reach Nirvana in one single life if he so wants it." - Samael Aun Weor, *The Zodiacal Course*

Objective: [See: Subjective]

Ophites: (Greek) A Gnostic fraternity in Egypt and one of the earliest sects of Gnosticism; known as the Brotherhood of the Serpent. It flourished early in the second century and while holding some of the principles of Valentinus had its own occult rites and symbology. A living serpent representing the Krestos-principle (not Jesus the man) was displayed in their mysteries and reverenced as a symbol of wisdom, Sophia.

Pancatattva Ritual: (Sanskrit) Panca: "five." Tattwa: "essence; principle." A Tantric ritual in which the five elements are transmuted. The five M's are Maithuna (Sexual Magic), Madya ("Wine"), Mamsa (Meat), Matsya (Fish), Mudra (Grain). See *The Mystery of the Golden Blossom* by Samael Aun Weor.

Paramarthasattya: (Sanskrit) Para, "absolute, supreme." Parama, "that which knows, or the consciousness." Artha, "that which is known." Sattya, "existence, Truth." In synthesis, "The supreme knowledge of all that exists: TRUTH." A being of very high development; an inhabitant of the Absolute.

Personality: (Latin personae: mask) There are two fundamental types of personality:

1. Solar: the personality of the inner Being. This type is only revealed through the liberation of the mind from samsara.

2. Lunar: the terrestrial, perishable personality. We create a new lunar personality in the first seven years of each new physical body, in accordance with three influences: genotype, phenotype and paratype. Genotype is the influence of the genes, or in other words, karma, our inheritance from past actions. Phenotype is the education we receive from our family, friends, teachers, etc. Paratype is related to the circumstances of life.

"The personality is time. The personality lives in its own time and does not reincarnate. After death, the personality also goes to the grave. For the personality there is no tomorrow. The personality lives in the cemetery, wanders about the cemetery or goes down into its grave. It is neither the Astral Body nor the ethereal double. It is not the Soul. It is time. It is energetic and it disintegrates very slowly. The personality can never reincarnate. It does not ever reincarnate. There is no tomorrow for the human personality." - Samael Aun Weor, *The Perfect Matrimony*

"Our personality has to become more and more passive..." - Samael Aun Weor, from the lecture "Knowing How to Listen"

"The human personality is only a marionette controlled by invisible strings... Evidently, each one of these I's puts in our minds what we must think, in our mouths what we must say, and in our hearts what we must feel, etc. Under such conditions the human personality is no more than a robot governed by different people, each disputing its superiority and aspiring to supreme control of the major centers of the organic machine... First of all, it is necessary, urgent and imperative that the Magnetic Center, which is abnormally established in our false personality, be transferred to the Essence. In this way, the complete human can initiate his journey from the personality up to the stars, ascending in a progressive, didactic way, step by step up the Mountain of the Being. As long as the Magnetic Center continues to be established in our illusory personality we will live in the most abominable psychological dens of iniquity, although appearing to be splendid citizens in everyday life... These values which serve as a basis for the Law of Recurrence are always found within our human personality."- Samael Aun Weor, *The Great Rebellion*

"The personality must not be confused with the "I." In fact, the personality is formed during the first seven years of childhood. The "I" is something different. It is the error which is perpetuated from century to century; it fortifies itself each time, more and more through the mechanics of recurrence. The personality is energetic. It is born during infancy through habits, customs, ideas, etc., and it is fortified with the experiences of life. Therefore, both the personality as well as the "I" must be disintegrated. These psychological teachings are more revolutionary than those of Gurdjieff and Ouspensky. The "I" utilizes the personality as an instrument of action. Thus, personalism is a mixture of ego and personality. Personality worship was invented by the "I." In fact, personalism engenders egoism, hatred, violence, etc. All of this is rejected by A-himsa. Personality totally ruins esoteric organizations. Personality produces anarchy and confusion. Personalism can totally destroy any organization... The personality is multiple and has many hidden depths. The karma of previous existences is deposited into the personality. It is karma in the process of fulfillment or crystallization. The impressions which are not digested become new psychic aggregates, and what is more serious, they become new personalities. The personality is not homogenous but rather heterogeneous and plural. One must select impressions in the same manner that one chooses the things of life. If one forgets oneself at a given instant, in a new event, new "I's" are formed, and if they are very strong they become new personalities within the personality. Therein lies the cause of many traumas, complexes and psychological conflicts. An impression which one does not digest may form into a personality within the personality, and if one does not accept it, it becomes a source of frightening conflicts. Not all the personalities (which one carries within the personality) are accepted; the latter giving origin to many traumas, complexes, phobias, etc. Before all else, it is necessary to comprehend the multiplicity of the personality. The personality is multiple in itself.

Therefore, there could be someone who may have disintegrated the psychic aggregates, but if he does not disintegrate the personality, he will not be able to attain authentic enlightenment and the joy of living." - Samael Aun Weor, *The Revolution of the Dialectic*

"The personality is energetic. The personality takes form during the first seven years of childhood and is strengthened with time and experiences... The Mental Body, the Body of Desires, the Ethereal Body, and the Physical Body integrate the personality... We must finish with the personality and with the "I" in order for the Being to be born within ourselves." - Samael Aun Weor, *Tarot and Kabbalah*

Philosophical Stone: An Alchemical symbol of the Intimate Christ dressed with bodies of Gold. When acquired, this stone gives powers over nature. It is lost when thrown in water (through fornication). When the stone is dissolved in (sexual) water, then the metallic Spirit is melted, and interior Magnes escapes. It is said when this happens, one dissolves the stone in water on Saturday (Saturn = death). The Philosophical Stone is passes through phases of development: black, red & white. It is also the Cubic stone of Yesod (Parsifal Unveiled), the stone that Jacob anointed with oil and "a Stone of stumbling, a rock of offense."

Nicolas Valois: "It is a Stone of great virtue, and is called a Stone and is not a stone."

Phlegethon: (Greek) One of the rivers of Hades in Greek Mythology.

Pleroma: (Greek) "Fullness," an ancient Gnostic term adopted to signify the divine world or Universal Soul. Space, developed and divided into a series of aeons. The abode of the invisible Gods.

Prajapatis: (Sanskrit) Progenitors; the givers of life to all on this earth.

Prakriti: (Sanskrit) Nature, or the womb of nature.

Red Demons of Seth: (Egyptian) Our own psychological defects as symbolized in the Egyptian Book of the Dead.

Ruach: Also ruwach (Hebrew, "spirit, wind, or breath")

"And the Ruach (Spirit) of Elohiym (God) moved upon the face of the waters." - Genesis 1:2

In Kabbalah, Ruach also refers to one the three souls of the human being. Ruach is called the Thinking Soul.

"Who knoweth the Ruach of the sons of man that is going up on high, and the Ruach of the beast that is going down below to the earth?" - Ecclesiastes 3:21

Sahaja Maithuna: (Sanskrit) Sahaja, "natural." Maithuna, "sacramental intercourse"

Sahu: (Egyptian) The Egyptian Sahu is the same as the Greek To Soma Heliakon, the Hebrew Merkabah; it is the Physical, Astral, Mental and Causal Solar Bodies as a whole.

Samsara: (Sanskrit; Tibetan khorwa) Cyclic, conditioned existence whose defining characteristic is suffering. It is contrasted with nirvana.

Samadhi: (Sanskrit) Literally means "union" or "combination" and its Tibetan equivilent means "adhering to that which is profound and definitive," or ting nge dzin, meaning "To hold unwaveringly, so there is no movement." Related terms include satori, ecstasy, manteia, etc. Samadhi is a state of consciousness. In the west, the term is used to describe an ecstatic state of consciousness in which the Essence escapes the painful limitations of the mind (the "I") and therefore experiences what is real: the Being, the Great Reality. There are many levels of Samadhi. In the sutras and tantras the term Samadhi has a much broader application whose precise interpretation depends upon which school and teaching is using it.

"Ecstasy is not a nebulous state, but a transcendental state of wonderment, which is associated with perfect mental clarity." - Samael Aun Weor, *The Elimination of Satan's Tail*

Sanctum Regnum: Latin for "The Holy Kingdom."

Satan: (Hebrew, opposer, or adversary) Is the fallen Lucifer, who is born within the psyche of every human being by means of the sexual impulse that culminates in the orgasm or sexual spasm of the fornicators. Satan, the fallen Lucifer directs the lustful animal currents towards the atomic infernos of the human being, thus it becomes the profoundly evil adversary of our Innermost (God) and human values within our own psyche. This is why it is often identified with the leader of the fallen angels or fallen human values (parts) of our consciousness trapped within the animal mind (legions of egos, defects, vices of the mind) in other words, Satan is the Devil or "evil" adversary of God "Good" that every body carries within their own psychological interior.

Seal of Solomon: (✿) Also known in India as the sign of Vishnu and used as a talisman against evil.

Second Death: The complete dissolution of the ego in the infernal regions of nature, which in the end (after unimaginable quantities of suffering) purifies the Essence of all sin (karma) so that it may try again to reach complete development.

"He that overcometh (the sexual passion) shall inherit all things; and I will be his God (I will incarnate myself within him), and he shall be my son (because he is a Christified one), But the fearful (the tenebrous, cowards, unbelievers), and unbelieving, and the abominable, and murderers, and whoremongers, and sorcerers, and idolaters, and all liars, shall have their part in the lake which burneth with fire and brimstone: which is the second death. (Revelation 21) This lake which burns with fire and brimstone is the lake of carnal passion. This lake is related with the lower animal depths of the human being and its atomic region is the abyss. The tenebrous slowly disintegrate themselves within the abyss until they die. This is the second death." - Samael Aun Weor, *The Aquarian Message*

Seity: Commonly defined as "that which is particular to oneself." In occultism, Seity is "the profound and joyous Space that is the ineffable mystic root of the seven Cosmos. It is the mysterious origin of all of that which we know as Spirit, matter, universes, suns, worlds, etc."

Self-observation: An exercise of attention, in which one learns to become an indifferent observer of one's own psychological process. True Self-observation is an active work of directed attention, without the interference of thought.

"We need attention intentionally directed towards the interior of our own selves. This is not a passive attention. Indeed, dynamic attention proceeds from the side of the observer, while thoughts and emotions belong to the side which is observed." - Samael Aun Weor, *Revolutionary Psychology*

Self-realization: The achievement of perfect knowledge. This phrase is better stated as, "The realization of the Innermost Self," or "The realization of the true nature of self." At the ultimate level, this is the experiential, conscious knowledge of the Absolute, which is synonymous with Emptiness, Shunyata, or Non-being.

Self-remembering: A state of active consciousness, controlled by will, that begins with awareness of being here and now. This state has many levels (see: Consciousness). True Self-remembering occurs without thought or mental processing: it is a state of conscious perception and includes the remembrance of the inner Being.

Semen: The sexual energy of any creature or entity. In Gnosis, "semen" is a term used for the sexual energy of both masculine and feminine bodies. English semen originally meant 'seed of male animals' in the 14th century, and it was not applied to human males until the 18th century. It came from Latin semen, "seed of plants," from serere `to sow.' The Latin goes back to the Indo-European root *se-, source of seed, disseminate, season, seminar, and seminal. The word seminary (used for religious schools) is derived from semen and originally meant 'seedbed.'

That the semen is the source of all virtue is known from the word "seminal," derived from the Latin "semen," and which is defined as "highly original and influencing the development of future events: a seminal artist; seminal ideas."

In the esoteric tradition of pure sexuality, the word semen refers to the sexual energy of the organism, whether male or female. This is because male and female both carry the "seed" within: in order to create, the two "seeds" must be combined.

Sephirah: (Hebrew) plural: Sephiroth. literally, "jewel."

1. An emanation of Deity.

"The Ten Sephiroth of universal vibration emerge from the Ain Soph, which is the Microcosmic Star that guides our interior. This Star is the Real Being of our Being. Ten Sephiroth are spoken of, but in reality there are Twelve; the Ain Soph is the eleventh, and its tenebrous antithesis is in the abyss, which is the twelfth Sephirah. These are twelve spheres or universal regions which mutually penetrate and co-penetrate without confusion." - Samael Aun Weor, *Tarot and Kabbalah*

2. A name of the Divine Mother.

Septenary: seven-fold.

Sexual Magic: The word magic is dervied from the ancient word magos "one of the members of the learned and priestly class," from O.Pers. magush, possibly from PIE *magh- "to be able, to have power." [Quoted from Online Etymology Dictionary].

"All of us possess some electrical and magnetic forces within, and, just like a magnet, we exert a force of attraction and repulsion... Between lovers that magnetic force is particularly powerful and its action has a far-reaching effect. - Samael Aun Weor, *The Mystery of the Golden Blossom*

Sexual magic refers to an ancient science that has been known and protected by the purest, most spiritually advanced human beings, whose purpose and goal is the harnessing and perfection of our sexual forces. A more accurate translation of sexual magic would be "sexual priesthood."

In ancient times, the priest was always accompanied by a priestess, for they represent the divine forces at the base of all creation: the masculine and feminine, the Yab-Yum, Ying-Yang, Father-Mother: the Elohim.

Unfortunately, the term "sexual magic" has been grossly misinterpreted by mistaken persons such as Aleister Crowley, who advocated a host of degenerated practices, all of which belong solely to the lowest and most perverse mentality. The Gnostic teachings presented here reject all such philosophies, theories, and practices, for they lead only to the enslavement of the consciousness, the worship of lust and desire, and the decay of humanity.

True, upright, heavenly sexual magic is the natural harnessing of our latent forces, making them active and harmonious with nature and the divine.

"People are filled with horror when they hear about sexual magic; however, they are not filled with horror when they give themselves to all kinds of sexual perversion and to all kinds of carnal passion." - Samael Aun Weor, *The Perfect Matrimony*

Hashem Hamephorash: (Hebrew) The "separated name," or the "name of extension, or "the blessed name." Specifically, a name of God that has 72 aspects and is hidden in the original Hebrew of Exodus 14:19-21. It is said that there are two versions: one positive, corresponding to White Magic, and one negative, corresponding to Black Magic. It is also the Cubic stone of Yesod, the stone that Jacob anointed with oil and "a Stone of stumbling, a rock of offense." Nicolas Valois: "It is a Stone of great virtue, and is called a Stone and is not a stone." It is the Serpentine Fire of the Holy Spirit.

Sidereal World: The Astral World.

Solar Bodies: The physical, vital, astral, mental, and causal bodies that are created through the beginning stages of Alchemy/Tantra and that provide a basis for existence in their corresponding levels of nature, just as the physical body does in the physical world. These bodies or vehicles are superior due to being created out of Solar (Christic) Energy, as opposed to the inferior, lunar bodies we receive from nature. Also known as the Wedding Garment (Christianity), the Merkabah (Kabbalah), To Soma Heliakon (Greek), and Sahu (Egyptian).

"All the Masters of the White Lodge, the Angels, Archangels, Thrones, Seraphim, Virtues, etc., etc., etc. are garbed with the Solar Bodies. Only those who have Solar Bodies have the Being incarnated. Only someone who possesses the Being is an authentic Human Being." - Samael Aun Weor, *The Esoteric Treatise of Hermetic Astrology*

Solve et Coagula: (Latin) An alchemical phrase that literally means "Dissolve and coagulate."

Subjective: "What do modern psychologists understand as 'objective?' They understand it to be that which is external to the mind: the physical, the tangible, the material.

"Yet, they are totally mistaken, because when analysing the term "subjective," we see that it signifies "sub, under," that which is below the range of our perceptions. What is below our perceptions? Is it not perhaps the Infernal Worlds? Is it not perhaps subjective that which is in the physical or beneath the physical? So, what is truly subjective is what is below the limits of our perceptions.

"Psychologists do not know how to use the former terms correctly.

"Objective: the light, the resplendence; it is that which contains the Truth, clarity, lucidity.

"Subjective: the darkness, the tenebrous. The subjective elements of perception are the outcome of seeing, hearing, touching, smelling and tasting. All of these are perceptions of what we see in the third dimension. For example, in one cube we see only length, width and height. We do not see the fourth dimension because we are bottled up within the ego. The subjective elements of perception are constituted by the ego with all of its "I's."" - Samael Aun Weor, *Tarot and Kabbalah*

Summa Matter: (Latin) "The ultimate expression of matter; the highest form of matter."

Tantra: Sanskrit for "continuum" or "unbroken stream." This refers first (1) to the continuum of vital energy that sustains all existence, and second (2) to the class of knowledge and practices that harnesses that vital energy, thereby transforming the practitioner. There are many schools of Tantrism, but they can be classified in three types: White, Grey and Black. Tantra has long been known in the West as Alchemy.

"In the view of Tantra, the body's vital energies are the vehicles of the mind. When the vital energies are pure and subtle, one's state of mind will be accordingly affected. By transforming these bodily energies we transform the state of consciousness." - The 14th Dalai Lama

Tarot: "Through the Gypsies the Tarot cards may be traced back to the religious symbolism of the ancient Egyptians. [...] Court de Gébelin believed the word Tarot itself to be derived from two Egyptian words, Tar, meaning "road," and

Ro, meaning "royal." Thus the Tarot constitutes the royal road to wisdom. (See Le Monde Primitif.) [...] The Tarot is undoubtedly a vital element in Rosicrucian symbolism, possibly the very book of universal knowledge which the members of the order claimed to possess. The Rota Mundi is a term frequently occurring in the early manifestoes of the Fraternity of the Rose Cross. The word Rota by a rearrangement of its letters becomes Taro, the ancient name of these mysterious cards. [...] The Pythagorean numerologist will also find an important relationship to exist between the numbers on the cards and the designs accompanying the numbers. The Qabbalist will be immediately impressed by the significant sequence of the cards, and the alchemist will discover certain emblems meaningless save to one versed in the divine chemistry of transmutation and regeneration.' As the Greeks placed the letters of their alphabet--with their corresponding numbers--upon the various parts of the body of their humanly represented Logos, so the Tarot cards have an analogy not only in the parts and members of the universe but also in the divisions of the human body.. They are in fact the key to the magical constitution of man. [...] The Tarot cards must be considered (1) as separate and complete hieroglyphs, each representing a distinct principle, law, power, or element in Nature; (2) in relation to each other as the effect of one agent operating upon another; and (3) as vowels and consonants of a philosophic alphabet. The laws governing all phenomena are represented by the symbols upon the Tarot cards, whose numerical values are equal to the numerical equivalents of the phenomena. As every structure consists of certain elemental parts, so the Tarot cards represent the components of the structure of philosophy. Irrespective of the science or philosophy with which the student is working, the Tarot cards can be identified with the essential constituents of his subject, each card thus being related to a specific part according to mathematical and philosophical laws. "An imprisoned person," writes Eliphas Levi, "with no other book than the Tarot, if he knew how to use it, could in a few years acquire universal knowledge, and would be able to speak on all subjects with unequalled learning and inexhaustible eloquence." - Manly P. Hall, *The Secret Teachings of All Ages* (1928)

Tartarus: (Greek, tartaros) A section of Hades (hell) reserved for the worst offenders.

Tattva: (Sanskrit) "truth, fundamental principle." A reference to the essential nature of a given thing. Tattvas are the elemental forces of nature. There are numerous systems presenting varying tattvas as fundamental principles of nature. Gnosticism utilizes a primary system of five: akash (which is the elemental force of the ether), tejas (fire), vayu (air), apas (water), and prittvi (earth). Two higher tattvas are also important: adi and samadhi.

Thelema: (Greek) Willpower.

Thermuthis: (Egyptian) from Renenutet, Renenet, Ernutet, Thermuthis, Thermouthis, Termuthis. "She Who Rears" was a cobra goddess of nursing or rearing children, fertility and protector of the Pharaoh. Known as the "Nourishing Snake," she not only was a goddess who was sometimes shown nursing a child, but she offered her protection to the Pharaoh in the Land of the Dead. In later times she was thought to be the goddess who presided over the eighth month of the Egyptian calendar, known by Greek times as Parmutit.

To Soma Heliakon: (Greek) Literally, "The Golden Body of the Solar Man."

Triamatzikamno: The Law of Three, the Trinity, which creates. In any form of creation, there are always three forces.

Trigunamayashakti: (Sanskrit) A very profound term composed of tri (three) guna (qualities, see gunas), maya (the Divine Mother), and shakti (the energy of the Divine Mother).

Trimurti: (Sanskrit) Literally, "three faces" or "triple form."

Typhon Baphomet: (Egyptian) An aspect or shadow of Osiris. Typhon is not an "evil principle" or "Satan," but is rather the lower cosmic principle of the divine body of Osiris, being the shadow of Him. In the Book of the Dead, he is described as being one who "steals reason from the soul."

White Fraternity, Lodge, or Brotherhood: That ancient collection of pure souls who maintain the highest and most sacred of sciences: White Magic or White Tantra. It is called White due to its purity and cleanliness. This "Brotherhood" or "Lodge" includes human beings of the highest order from every race, culture, creed and religion, and of both sexes.

Valentine, Basil: An alchemical legend whose actual identity has yet to be discovered, yet is is presumed that he lived in the fifteenth century and was likely to have been a Benedictine monk. According to tradition, his name is derived from the Greek basileus, the King, and valens, powerful, thus meaning the Powerful King, the Philosopher's Stone. His legacy is immortalized in his Twelve Keys, a series of highly symbolic drawings.

Vulcan: The Latin or Roman name for the Greek God Hephaistos, known by the Egyptians as Ptah. A God of fire with a deep and ancient mythology, commonly remembered as the blacksmith who forges weapons for Gods and heroes.

Quotes from Paracelsus: "The office of Vulcan is the separation of the good from the bad. So the Art of Vulcan, which is Alchemy, is like unto death, by which the eternal and the temporal are divided one from another. So also this art might be called the death of things." - De Morbis Metallicis, Lib. I., Tract III., c. 1. "Vulcan is an astral and not a corporal fabricator." - De Caduco Matricis, Par. VI. "The artist working in metals and other minerals transforms them into other colours, and in so doing his operation is like that of the heaven itself. For as the artist excocts by means of Vulcan, or the igneous element, so heaven performs the work of coction through the Sun. The Sun, therefore, is the Vulcan of heaven accomplishing coction in the earth." - De Icteritiis. "Vulcan is the fabricator and architect of all things, nor is his habitation in heaven only, that is, in the firmament, but equally in all the other elements." - Lib. Meteorum, c. 4. "Where the three prime principles are wanting, there also the igneous essence is absent. The Igneous Vulcan is nothing else but Sulphur, Sal Nitrum, and Mercury." - Ibid., c.5.

Index

To learn more about Gnosis, visit gnosticteachings.org

Glorian Publishing is a non-profit publisher dedicated to spreading the sacred universal doctrine to suffering humanity. All of our works are made possible by the kindness and generosity of sponsors. If you would like to make a tax-deductible donation, you may send it to the address below, or visit our website for other alternatives. If you would like to sponsor the publication of a book, please contact us at 877-726-2359 or help@gnosticteachings.org.

Glorian Publishing
PO Box 110225 Brooklyn NY 11211 USA
Phone: 877-726-2359

VISIT US ONLINE AT:

glorian.info
gnosticbooks.org
gnosticteachings.org
gnosticradio.org